CAMBRIDGE STUDIES IN MODERN POLITICAL ECONOMIES

Editors
SUZANNE BERGER, ALBERT HIRSCHMAN, AND CHARLES MAIER

In search of stability: explorations in historical political economy

In search of stability
Explorations in historical political economy

CHARLES S. MAIER

Harvard University

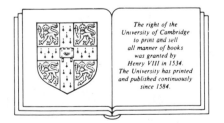

The right of the
University of Cambridge
to print and sell
all manner of books
was granted by
Henry VIII in 1534.
The University has printed
and published continuously
since 1584.

CAMBRIDGE UNIVERSITY PRESS
Cambridge
New York   New Rochelle   Melbourne   Sydney

Published by the Press Syndicate of the University of Cambridge
The Pitt Building, Trumpington Street, Cambridge CB2 1RP
32 East 57th Street, New York, NY 10022, USA
10 Stamford Road, Oakleigh, Melbourne 3166, Australia

First published 1987

Printed in the United States of America

Library of Congress Cataloging-in-Publication Data
Maier, Charles S.
In search of stability.
(Cambridge studies in modern political economies)
1. Europe – Economic conditions – 20th century.
2. Europe – Economic policy.   3. Fascism – Europe – History
– 20th century.   4. Representative government and
representation – Europe – History – 20th century.   I. Title.
II. Series.
HC240.M17   1987   338.94   87–6383

British Library Cataloguing in Publication Data
Maier, Charles
In search of stability: explorations
in historical political economy. –
(Cambridge studies in modern political
economies).
1. Economic history – 20th century
I. Title
330.9'04   HC55

ISBN 0 521 23001 2

To Dorothy Connor, Franklin Ford, James Joll, Ernest May,
Arno Mayer

Teachers of history, friends

Contents

Acknowledgments

I am grateful to the following publishers for permission to reprint articles that appeared originally as cited below. In some cases, as explained in the individual chapters that follow, I have made changes in the text or the documentation.

To the *Journal of Contemporary History* and Sage Publications for permission to reprint "Between Taylorism and Technocracy: European Ideologies and the Vision of Industrial Productivity in the 1920s," from vol. 5, no. 2, © 1970; to Croom Helm and Barnes and Noble Books for permission to reprint an amended version of "The Factory as Society: Ideologies of Industrial Management in the Twentieth Century," from R. J. Bullen, H. Pogge von Strandmann, and A. B. Polonsky, eds., *Ideas into Politics: Aspects of European History 1880–1950* (London, 1984); to the University of Notre Dame Press for permission to adapt and expand a version of "The Economics of Fascism and Nazism: Premises and Performance," from Alejandro Foxley, Michael S. McPherson, and Guillermo O'Donnell, eds., *Development, Democracy, and the Art of Trespassing: Essays in Honor of Albert O. Hirschman* (Notre Dame, Ind., © 1986); to *International Organization* and the University of Wisconsin Press for permission to reprint "The Politics of Productivity: Foundations of American International Economic Policy after World War II," from Peter Katzenstein, ed., *Between Power and Plenty: Foreign Economic Policies of Advanced Industrial States*, articles collected from the Autumn 1977 issue of *International Organization* © 1978 (Madison, Wis., 1978); to the *American Historical Review* for permission to reprint "The Two Postwar Eras and the Conditions for Stability in Twentieth-Century Western Europe," from vol. 86, no. 2 (April 1981); to Basil Blackwell and Harvard University Press for permission to reprint "The Politics of Inflation in the Twentieth Century," from Fred Hirsch and John H. Goldthorpe, eds., *The Political Economy of Inflation*

(London and Cambridge, Mass., 1978); and to Cambridge University Press for permission to reprint " 'Fictitious Bonds . . . of Wealth and Law': On the Theory and Practice of Interest Representation," from Suzanne Berger, ed., *Organizing Interests in Western Europe: Pluralism, Corporatism and the Transformation of Politics* (Cambridge, 1981).

This book originated as a collection of diverse pieces, and the preliminary, shorter version of one has already been published in honor of Albert O. Hirschman. But the overall task of revision and addition has claimed enough labor that I feel the volume can be justifiably dedicated as a whole. I offer it to some of the good teachers of history I have had since high school. They have liked their work, they have encouraged questions, and they have invited colleagueship.

Introduction:
Political economy and history

With patience historians may resolve a few of the issues that arouse their curiosity. Eventually they tire of many they cannot settle. Finally they keep returning to still others that cannot easily be solved but do not lose their intellectual or moral fascination: the persistent questions that get under the scholar's skin. From one angle or another, over a period of fifteen years, the pieces collected here have addressed one of these besetting issues, namely, how are the inequalities inherent in modern economic organization defused or overcome as a source of explosive social conflict? This inquiry includes several interlocking questions:

What mixture of constraint and ideological legitimation, what forms of representation, what promises of material reward support political and social stability?
Under what circumstances is stability threatened; under what circumstances is it recovered?
How does the alignment of power among nation-states influence the tensions and rivalries within national societies?

These common issues provide one reason for publishing this diverse collection of essays in a single volume. A further incentive is that several of the pieces appeared in journals or conference proceedings that political scientists and economists were more likely to encounter than fellow historians. I like to think that, although they are essentially *historical*, that is, more intent on explaining specific past outcomes than generalizing about political or economic development as recurrent possibilities, some of the essays do cross disciplinary frontiers. Though not really economic history, some are informed by economic issues; though not really political science, some try to provide typologies of political groups and behavior. Perhaps they can best be described as efforts at intellectual poaching. Precisely because they cross disciplinary lines, they raise some initial questions concerning method.

Methodological issues

I have called these essays "explorations in historical political economy." "Political economy" in contemporary social science usage no longer refers simply to economic analysis, as it did from the seventeenth through the mid–nineteenth century.[1] The concept now tends to refer to one of two related but opposed approaches, each relying on a characteristic methodology and each often associated with a characteristic political stance, one on the right, the other on the left.

For one group of theorists, political economy is the analysis of political choices according to criteria of economic maximization. When first applied, this theory sometimes suggested that public goods would be prevailingly undersupplied. The benefits, such as health care or good schools or clean air, were so much more diffuse than the assigned costs that they would have few advocates. In the past couple of decades, however, many of the proponents of this theory have come to emphasize the inverse problem. As theorists of "public choice," some have argued that politicians prefer to oversupply public goods because the benefits are highly visible while the costs remain hidden. Similarly, according to their diagnoses, voters are seduced by illusory economic expansion, leaders select policies solely to perpetuate their tenure in

---

1 From its first usage by Antoine Montchrétien de Watteville, *Traicté de l'oeconomie politique* (1614) through Dugold Steuart, *Inquiry into the Principles of Political Oeconomy* (1757), Pietro Verri, *Meditazioni sull' economia politica* (1771), Nassau Senior, *An Outline of the Principles of Political Economy* (1836), and John Stuart Mill, *Principles of Political Eocnomy* (1848), thereafter to be abandoned as a term for economic analysis, certainly by the publication of Alfred Marshall's *Principles of Economics* (1890). See Edwin R. A. Seligman, "Economics," in *International Encyclopaedia of the Social Sciences*, 2d ed. (New York: Macmillan, 1931), 5:344–5; and Joseph A. Schumpeter, *History of Economic Analysis* (London: Allen & Unwin, 1967), 21–2, 38–9, 177–8, 484–6. Thomas Schelling has more recently defined political economy as "economics in a context of policy, where the policy is more than economics but the 'more' cannot be separated from the economics." See *Choice and Consequence* (Cambridge, Mass.: Harvard University Press, 1984), vii. Schelling's methodology involves untangling the conflicting objectives that are often knotted together in human situations. Rather than appeal to "priceless" values, honest policy should start by asking what price the relevant public is actually ready to pay for professed goods. The essays collected here might be said to use "political economy" in a reverse sense: as economics in a context of politics, where the economics is less than the politics but the "less" cannot be separated from the political.

office, bureaucrats work to expand their programs, state intervention in the economy has perverse results, and collective associations can be created only to achieve private payoffs.[2]

Political economy can be applied in the opposite sense, however: not to account for politics according to criteria of alleged economic rationality, but to analyze economic choices in terms of political forces. Those who advocate this approach, which is the one called upon in these essays, ask what power relations underlie economic outcomes. How do classes or interests use political and ideological resources to bring about contested economic policies – the decision, for example, to continue or to halt inflation? How do they shape alternative paths of development – the incentives, for instance, to move toward more capital intensive or centralized production?[3] Certainly the distributional conflicts inherent in nineteenth-century development suggested such an intellectual agenda. "Political Economy you think is an enquiry into the nature and causes of wealth," Ricardo wrote Malthus in 1820. "I think it should rather be called an enquiry into the laws which determine the division of the produce of industry amongst the classes

---

2 See, for instance, Anthony Downs, *An Economic Theory of Democracy* (New York: Harper Bros., 1957); Mancur Olson, *The Logic of Collective Action: Public Goods and the Theory of Groups* (Cambridge, Mass.: Harvard University Press, 1965); and James M. Buchanan and Gordon Tullock, *The Calculus of Consent* (Ann Arbor: University of Michigan Press, 1962). Such deductive methods have the merit of rescuing collective action from the imputation of irrationality, but their criteria of rationality are often far too narrow. For trenchant critiques see Brian Barry, *Sociologists, Economists and Democracy* (University of Chicago Press, 1978); and Barry, "Does Democracy Cause Inflation? Political Ideas of Some Economists," in Leon Lindberg and Charles S. Maier, eds., *The Politics of Inflation and Economic Stagnation* (Washington, D.C.: Brookings Institution, 1985), 280–317. "Rational choice" criteria for decisions, moreover, have formal limits, as demonstrated by Kenneth Arrow's "A Difficulty in the Concept of Social Welfare" and "The Principle of Rationality in Collective Decisions," in *Collected Papers of Kenneth J. Arrow*, 6 vols. (Cambridge, Mass.: Harvard University Press, 1983, 1:1–29, 45–58, and they may have disabling psychological or anthropological objections. For the starting point of one alternative logic, which does not presuppose that more of a good is always better than less, see Albert Hirschman, *Shifting Involvements* (Princeton, N.J.: Princeton University Press, 1982). For recent applications of political economy modeling of electoral and policy outcomes see Paul Whitely, ed., *Models of Political Economy* (Beverly Hills, Calif.: Sage, 1980).
3 This formulation implies that conflict among interests and classes can be described more usefully as a political than as an economic phenomenon. Of course, the groups may ultimately be sociologically anchored in economic divisions. Nonetheless, they are usually observed by the historian as political contenders, drawing upon resources of collective public or private power. For a useful guide to theories of class, see Anthony Giddens, *The Class Structure of the Advanced Societies* (New York: Harper & Row, 1973).

who concur in its formation."[4] These laws, however, respond to distributions of political power, not just the logic of economic maximization.

This second approach to political economy, therefore, cannot take economic theory merely as a quasi-mathematical elaboration of deductive premises. It interrogates economic doctrines to disclose their sociological and political premises. For instance, neo-Keynesian and monetarist economics diverge in part because neo-Keynesians envisage an underlying society of collective actors, whereas the economic agents that monetarists posit remain individuals, rational about economic maximization but often foolish about political promises.[5]

This approach to political economy, moreover, is often associated with critics on the left. Marxists have offered some of the most powerful contributions, indeed often implying – in line with the master's most famous title, *Capital: A Critique of Political Economy* – that political economy should refer exclusively to their own intellectual enterprise.[6] This is not the case, however. Political economy applications need not entail what might be considered the Marxist minimum: the conviction that class conflict is the motor force of general historical development and that capitalism tends toward increasingly profound crises and must someday, by its own inner logic, generate a new form

4   David Ricardo to Thomas Malthus, October 9, 1820, in Piero Sraffa, ed., *The Works and Correspondence of David Ricardo*, 11 vols. (Cambridge University Press), 8:278. Similarly, Carlyle in 1829: "What changes, too, this addition of [mechanical] power is introducing into the Social System; how wealth has more and more increased, and at the same time gathered itself more and more into masses, strangely altering the old relations, and increasing the distance between the rich and the poor, will be a question for Political Economists, and a much more complex and important one than any they have yet engaged with." From "Signs of the Times," in G. B. Tennyson, ed., *A Carlyle Reader* (Cambridge University Press, 1984), 35. The idea that income distribution to capital and labor is not ultimately determined by their marginal products or a given technique and endowment of capital, but that the return to capital follows from prior distributions of social power, characterizes the thinking of contemporary "post-Keynesian" economists in the tradition of Joan Robinson and Piero Sraffa.

5   For a fuller development see the conclusion to Lindberg and Maier, eds., *Politics of Inflation*, 569–85. The idea that modes of production result more from political choices than from technological impetus is represented best in the work of Michael Piore and Charles Sabel, *The Second Industrial Divide* (New York: Basic Books, 1984), although the demonstration is circumstantial.

6   Two examples of neo-Marxist applications are James O'Connor, *The Fiscal Crisis of the State* (New York: St. Martin's, 1973); and David Abraham, *The Collapse of the Weimar Republic: Political Economy and Crisis* (Princeton, N.J.: Princeton University Press, 1981).

of collectivist social and economic organization.[7] In the essays included here, class and interest-group divisions do form the starting point for analyzing political development. No claim is advanced, however, that economically based social divisions govern politics in general or culture and values. Crises, moreover, certainly arise, but they can be overcome as well as become more profound. Dialectical or self-generated transformations do characterize the historical process, as do continuing "contradictions," but they need not lead to different social systems. What, in fact, constitutes a social system remains more an issue of agreed-upon definition than one based on objective criteria.[8] The question of whether, say, the Swedish social system under the late Olaf Palme, the German social system under Adolf Hitler, and the American social system under Herbert Hoover all belong to the genus "capitalism" must be recognized more as a semantic issue than as a historical one.

Political economy approaches characteristically seek to probe the connections between categories of social interaction that nineteenth-century liberals analytically separated, namely, state and market. From the mercantilists on, Anglo-American economic thinkers worked to establish economics as an autonomous discipline, taking as its field of study the world of production and exchange of goods and services. The exchanges were supposedly governed by individual equivalents of utility expressed in a common denominator through a price system, not by political or private power drawing on force and constraint.

---

7   For a brief exposé of the range of Marxist historical approaches (labeled, following Habermas, positivist, hermeneutic, and critical), see J. Dennis Willigan, "Marxist Methodologies of History," in *Historical Methods*, 17, no. 4 (Fall 1984): 219–28. Cf. Gregor McLennan, *Marxism and the Methodology of History* (London: NLB: Verso, 1981); and Alfred Schmidt, *History and Structure: An Essay on Hegelian-Marxist and Structuralist Theories of History*, Jeffrey Herf, trans. (Cambridge, Mass.: MIT Press, 1981).

8   "System" refers here to a feedback network of complex interactions in which the final outcome of a particular change in any one variable is not readily deduced. I would propose that social and political "systems" differ from nonhuman systems precisely because they always generate destabilizing changes endogenously. They must do so, if only because their creation involves establishing "borders" that separate privileged insiders from marginalized outsiders, and the frontier itself will be under perennial contention. (This does not mean that the system must break down, but it will require periodic and often painful readjustment.) For a discussion of methodological problems that arise in dealing with systems as such and of the relevant sociological literature, see John Sharpless, "Collectivity, Hierarchy, and Context: The Theoretical Framework for the Aggregation Problem," *Historical Methods*, 17, no. 3 (Summer 1984): 132–40.

6   Introduction

These latter recourses belonged to the political sphere and its most inclusive agency, the state. At the margin of the market, where competition disappeared and monopoly prevailed, power might be mobilized, but this was deemed a limiting case.[9] The analytic advances made possible by establishing the autonomy of the economic realm justified the simplifying formulations. Critics have pointed out that market behavior, resting on comparison and maximization of utility, has hardly comprised the only framework for exchange. They have also emphasized that establishing a functioning market required a prior legal and political framework; conversely, individual or collective economic actors who were successful in the market could thereby exert decisive political influence. These critiques of supposed market autonomy have been central to modern political economy. At the same time, however, political economy approaches have endeavored to retain the analytic power that modeling the state and market as distinct arenas originally allowed.[10]

Political economy, in sum, regards economic ideas and behavior not as frameworks for analysis, but as beliefs and actions that must themselves be explained. They are contingent and problematic; that is, they might have been different and they must be explained within particular political and social contexts. Historical political economy applies this approach to the study of the past.

What historical political economy shares with economic analysis is a reliance on "revealed preference" to help explain social choice. Whereas most history writing relies on a hermeneutic assumption, namely, that to explain action is to recreate the intentions of the actors, historical political economy presupposes that societies *in some sense* wanted what turned out to be. It bases its analysis on the premise that outcomes followed intentions and that the historian can talk meaningfully about "social choice" in terms of what happened. For instance, to take the theme of Chapter 5, in a society that undergoes

9 For the creation of the "economic" sphere, see Joyce Appleby, *Economic Thought and Ideology in Seventeenth-Century England* (Princeton, N.J.: Princeton University Press, 1978); Louis Dumont, *From Mandeville to Marx* (University of Chicago Press, 1977).

10 For one of the major challenges, still influential, see Karl Polanyi, *The Great Transformation* (Boston: Beacon, 1957). Polanyi and successors in economic anthropology have sought to show that market transactions provided only one basis of exchange, along with kinship, reciprocity, demonstrative gift giving, and so forth. For a demonstration that individual utility is socially constructed, see Arrow, "Values and Collective Decision Making," in *Collected Papers*, 1:59–77; and for a critique of corporate bias see Charles E. Lindblom, *Politics and Markets: The World's Political-Economic Systems* (New York: Basic Books, 1977).

wild inflation we can presume that in some way the society *chose* inflation or at least preferred to risk that outcome rather than pursue the policies that would have precluded it.

It might be objected that this is a perilous notion. People may elect to take incremental risks but rarely choose final consequences that cannot easily be imagined. Those who cheered the fall of the Bastille did not envisage the Terror. The 43 percent of the German electorate who cast ballots for Hitler in March 1933 were hardly liberal democrats, but they did not necessarily vote for the Second World War or the murder of more than 5 million Jews. Does not the idea that outcomes imply intent become dangerously close to the concepts of "objective guilt" that were invoked in the Stalinist purge trials of the late 1930s? Or does it not lead to the historiographical absurdity that every outcome was desired, or even perhaps deserved?[11]

It is more accurate to state that "revealed preference" is used as an analytic hypothesis, not an explanation of what actually occurred. To say that a society chose inflation[12] or unemployment or fascism is to say, first of all, that some groups in the society who were willing to countenance that outcome prevailed over those who resisted it. How they prevailed, whether by majoritarian rules or rigged politics or coercion, need not be specified. Second, it is to argue not that these social groups necessarily wanted a particular historical or human disaster, but that they were more willing to risk the next step toward such an outcome than to face the consequences of resisting it. If the final outcome is an evil one, what the penalties for their wager should be is a very difficult issue, but not the one these essays confront. It is the question underlying political justice. The perspective here is that of the detective, not the district attorney. By treating an economic or political outcome as the expression of a collective preference, the historian asks what set of interests such a preference might have served, hence what alignments and divisions characterize a particular society under stress. *Cui bono?* is not the only question a historian should pose, but it is a useful one to start with. It helps to impute structures of power and to perceive the stakes for even widely shared ideologies, such as those – to take the case raised in Chapters 1 and 3 – of economic growth and productivity.

11 See the problems raised by Amartya K. Sen, "Rational Fools: A Critique of the Behavioral Foundations of Economic Theory," in H. Harris, ed., *Scientific Models and Man* (New York: Oxford University Press, 1978).
12 See Jon Burton, "The Demand for Inflation in Liberal-Democratic Societies," in Whitely, ed., *Models of Political Economy*, 221–48; and Robert J. Gordon, "The Supply and Demand for Inflation," *Journal of Law and Economics*, 18, no. 3 (1975): 807–36.

This is not to argue for the simplistic view that ideologies merely mask a set of concrete interests that have to be unveiled or demystified. More than a generation of sophisticated historiography and methodological reflection has taught us that such an approach obscures as much as it illuminates. First, it cannot eliminate the "interests" of the researcher, even if these, to use Habermas's concept, are critical and "emancipatory."[13] Second, collective beliefs are generated at many levels of social interaction and in cultural contexts that must be analyzed with anthropological and semiotic tools as well as those of political economy. They may correspond, as a Freudian view would indicate, to a civilization's general requirement for labor or for erotic renunciation.[14] If so, they serve more than an internal distributive purpose. Finally, systems of ideas can persuade those who hold them to restructure the power relations from which they arise, subjecting the historian of ideas to an analogue of the uncertainty principle.[15]

Despite these methodological problems, however, some relation between ideology and interests persists, even if ideologies also reflect diffuse systems of culture and values. Analysis of this relationship is all the more challenging because structurally opposed groups in a society usually accept a common code for distributive justice despite their differing interests. In Gramscian language, ideologies are often hegemonic; they command consensus across class lines, and alternatives seem unthinkable. Differential rewards do not preclude common loyalties, even collective enthusiasm.[16]

13 Jürgen Habermas, *Knowledge and Human Interests,* Jeremy Shapiro, trans. (Boston: Beacon, 1971), 308–17. For the difficulties with the position, Thomas McCarthy, *The Critical Theory of Jürgen Habermas* (Cambridge, Mass.: MIT Press, 1981), 75–125.

14 See also Pierre Bourdieu, *Outline of a Theory of Practice,* Richard Nice, trans. (Cambridge University Press, 1977), 195–6: "The endless reconversion of economic capital into symbolic capital, at the cost of a wastage of social energy which is the condition for the permanence of domination, cannot succeed without the complicity of the whole group: the work of denial which is the source of social alchememy is, like magic, a collective undertaking. As Mauss puts it, the whole society pays itself in the false coin of its dream."

15 This, of course, is the implication of the work of Jacques Derrida, Michel Foucault, and a historian such as François Furet, *Interpreting the French Revolution* (Cambridge University Press, 1981), esp. pp. 43–51; but for a useful challenge, see Perry Anderson, *In the Tracks of Historical Materialism* (London: Verso, 1983), 32–55.

16 For an alternative insight into the sources of social cohesion, consider Georg Simmel's inquiry of 1908, "How Is Society Possible?" This is more fundamental than the question of how stability is possible in light of differential rewards. As a neo-Kantian, Simmel sought the a priori of society, not of any particular historical situation, in the fact that people stood inside and outside its network at the same time. Preserving the scope of individuation remained dialectically necessary for

Ideological responses and twentieth-century crises

The issue of how reigning concepts of political economy serve social integration brings into focus the particular historical transition discussed in these essays. Chapters 1 and 3 examine some industrial utopias of liberal society, namely, recurrent appeals to production and growth as justifications for managerial hierarchies or public policies that supposedly benefit all social classes equitably and provide scientifically optimal guidelines for economic alternatives. Such was the case with Taylorism and later with "productivity." Chapter 2, of which only an abbreviated version has previously been printed, asks about the economic concepts inherent in Italian fascism and German national socialism and the institutional role they played in the respective regimes. To counterpose American concepts of Taylorism and productivity to fascist economic premises is *not* to argue that liberal democracy and fascism should be construed as merely alternative political frameworks for a capitalist social order. Political and legal frameworks, in my view, remain of overriding importance – never to be construed as merely functional supports for given property relations.

Nonetheless, ideologies of industrial productivity, as they were propagated in liberal society, did share a non-zero-sum character with fascist concepts. That is, they presupposed that conflicts of interest were ultimately misunderstandings, that apparently incompatible economic interests could be harmonized according to criteria of efficiency, that there existed "one best way" to organize production such that a society should not have to undergo continual conflict. Economic organization should not remain an arena for contending preferences, but become a matter of technological or social engineering. Non-utopian liberal economics, in contrast, has stressed the necessity of trade-offs, has provided criteria for the allocation of goods (according to marginal products) in the recognition that they are limited. The procedural rules that guarantee political debate and establish some

---

social existence, as did play and nonrational sociability (*Geselligkeit*). Contrast Simmel's continual tension between what is socially purposeful and what is individual or is merged into sociability as an unconstrained "play" with the phased succession of "structure" and "anti-structure" proposed by Victor Turner, which is taken up in the Conclusion. See Georg Simmel, *On Individuality and Social Forms*, Donald N. Levine, ed. (University of Chicago Press, 1971), 6–22, 127–40. For Turner the moments of antistructure make long-term structure possible, whereas Simmel's perspective suggests that a continuing tension between hierarchical differentiation and egalitarian, individualist vision may be the prerequisite of political society.

scope for the market and business enterprise take priority, according to liberals, over any substantive distributive outcome.[17]

Laissez-faire liberals thus claimed that there would always be painful choices. There was no firm reason to justify particular distributive results, only to guarantee liberty, initiative, and civic rights such as the suffrage. Productivist utopias went on to suggest that even in a liberal regime no one had to lose; all could win. Fascism and nazism claimed more ruthlessly that only those who deserved to lose would in fact succumb, whereas some of the badly abused former losers might henceforth win. Hard-pressed peasants and artisans, even the working classes, would no longer face economic exploitation. They would gain security and new dignity through inclusion in corporatist and estatist organizations. Only political parasites (liberal parliamentary elites or Marxist political party bosses) or national and racial enemies would end up being losers.

Why should these differing non-zero-sum concepts have become so persuasive in the first half of the twentieth century? Their appeal testifies to the crisis that Western liberal societies underwent between, say, about 1905 and 1950. Admittedly, the word "crisis" is overused by historians; still, for an epoch involving two world wars, massive economic depression, and the rise of totalitarian states, crisis seems all too appropriate a characterization and certainly as justified a term as the "crisis" of the seventeenth century, that earlier fifty-year span also marked by economic difficulty, political conflict, major war (and philosophical and scientific genius). The final essay in Part I suggests that the twentieth-century crisis can be usefully construed as twofold. On the one hand, it involved a crisis of political representation engendered by parallel developments within each European national

17 This rigorous position, of course, has been modified by reformist liberals who have demanded welfare minimums. Two major variants that have sought to ameliorate laissez-faire rigor include the British social democratic defense of the welfare state – best exemplified by the writings of T. H. Marshall as collected in *Class, Citizenship, and Social Development* (New York: Doubleday 1965), and Richard M. Titmuss, *Essays on "the Welfare State"* (Boston: Beacon, 1969) – and the Rawlsian social liberal effort to define a contractual order with an initial position, from which differential gains for some could be justified only in "compensating benefits for everyone, and in particular for the least advantaged members of society." See John Rawls, *A Theory of Justice* (Cambridge, Mass.: Harvard University Press, 1971), 14–15, and 274–84 for the necessary transfer and distribution branches to ensure the result. Both positions allow for more social intervention than the laissez-faire liberal (or neoconservative) view that only equality of opportunity be provided. The historian cannot help resolve these alternatives except to note that continued inequality of outcomes often makes many members of a society doubt that equality of opportunity really pertains.

society. On the other hand, it included an international competition augmented by imperialist rivalries – that is, by the increasing tensions of international competition in an era when economic or military expansion into less developed areas of Europe and non-European territories became easy and beckoning.

The crisis of representation afflicting the European regimes (and to a degree the United States) had at least three components. The mixed regimes of upper-class bureaucracies and middle-class parliamentary delegations that governed most European societies found it difficult to cope with several momentous developments. The first consisted of the long-term pressure on agrarian producers, and therefore on landed elites or independent farmers, that was generated by the vast expansion of grain production and the tightening of money and credit in the late nineteenth century. The second arose out of continuing ethnic conflicts – the claims of linguistic cultures deprived of their own states – which proved more difficult to resolve once minorities won parliamentary representation and could paralyze legislatures. (These claims also revealed the fragility of the Turkish and Austrian imperial structures in southeastern Europe, exposing this region, especially, to international competition.) The third epochal change, and the one that most dramatically preoccupied political spokesmen, arose from the vigorous organizational thrust of the working classes as they rallied to doctrines of collective political and industrial action. In brief, the liberal victories of the nineteenth century had opened up parliamentary representation to new political activists, only to find this enlarged government by "opinion" burdened with claims it had not been intended to mediate.[18] In the resulting turbulence of class and ethnic conflict before World War I, prescriptions for non-zero-sum resolutions, for industrial utopias and social engineering, could prove especially appealing. So, too, in a Europe further undermined by the First World War, could authoritarian remedies designed to overcome the conflicts inherent in liberalism. But fascism was defeated in turn; the Second World War refurbished the reputation of the United States economy, and Western liberals perceived a Soviet-supported communist movement to be the overriding political challenge. Under these conditions the appeal to growth and productivity reemerged as potent enough to rally a noncommunist international coalition around American leadership.

18 See Charles S. Maier, "Political Crisis and Partial Modernization: The Outcomes in Germany, Austria, Hungary, and Italy after World War I," in Charles Bertrand, ed., *Revolutionary Situations in Europe, 1917–1922: Germany, Italy, Austria-Hungary* (Montreal: Interuniversity Center for European Studies, 1977).

The essays in Part I of this volume were not written as a singly conceived work; nonetheless, they focus on successive aspects of the ideological alternatives – productivist and fascist – to what was construed as explosive political and economic conflict. The two pieces grouped in Chapter 1, "Society as factory," examine the appeals first of Taylorism and Fordism and then of successive management doctrines, not as narrowly conceived prescriptions for running factories, but as social utopias. Chapter 2, "The economics of fascism and nazism," asks to what extent fascist regimes really proposed economic alternatives to liberal capitalism and how the operating premises of the regimes may have influenced economic performance. Chapter 3, "The politics of productivity," then examines how important an influence concepts of productivity still exerted in the United States and in Europe at midcentury and how the discourse of production could integrate the major effort of the United States at international leadership. In effect, the ideological themes generated before and after World War I at the level of civil society – that is, by engineers, corporate spokesmen, and trade associations – were now propagated as a theme of American foreign policy, just as the private overseas investment of the 1920s was replaced after 1945 by congressionally approved foreign aid. Finally, as a conclusion to Part I, Chapter 4 analyzes the two postwar eras as a unitary epoch, seeking to explain how the twentieth-century crisis was overcome and stability achieved, within states and between them.

The long-term organization of interests

The era of world wars and Western European dictatorships now lies forty years behind us. If the crisis of the "first" twentieth century can be understood as a crisis of representation and imperial rivalries, how ought the historian to conceive of the generations since? The argument proposed here is that, at least until the late 1960s, a reorganization of interest representation accommodated political tensions more easily than could the overburdened parliamentary institutions of the preceding half-century. The essays in Part II seek to analyze the evolving structures of representation over the long term, and especially what political scientists have termed their neocorporatist components, that is, the mediation of interests in advanced capitalism. What has been at stake in the evolution of interest representation throughout the century has been a shifting equilibrium between parliamentary and interest-group mediation. If the political difficulties of the first half of the century can usefully be construed as consequences of a crisis of representation, then the analytic task must be to show how that crisis was superseded. Whereas Chapter 4, "The two postwar eras," attempts to demonstrate how stability was constructed at a particular historical moment, Chapter 6, " 'Fictitious bonds . . . of wealth and law,' " seeks to explain the long-term evolution of alternative modes of representation in liberal industrial societies.

The degree of stability achieved after World War II seemed remarkable by the early 1960s but was thrown into question by the political and social upheavals of 1968 and after, as well as by the economic difficulties that have followed since the 1970s. The sustained inflation of the 1970s did not bring down liberal regimes in Europe (although it did so periodically in Latin America), but it did shake the ruling coalitions, discrediting the social democratic Left where it governed (in Britain, Sweden, West Germany, and the United States) and conservatives where they were in power (in France, Spain, and Italy). Chapter 5, "The politics of inflation," conceived originally for a conference in 1974, was an effort to ask whether such a powerful and widespread cycle of inflation – then already well underway and to continue for another seven or eight years – did not reflect more than the contingency of higher oil prices. The inquiry proved difficult, because regression analysis can indeed decompose the economic components of inflation into contingent components, ranging from oil prices to real-wage demands to misconceived monetary policies – one partial cause piled on another.[19] Nonetheless, this essay argues that inflationary outcomes in the twentieth century have been systematically related to characteristic political alignments. Particular coalitions of interests have been likely to attempt policies that have led to particular inflationary outcomes, and these results in turn have reinforced or broken up the relevant class alignments.

Such an analysis does not conflict with economists' more conventional measurement of inflationary components. Instead, it offers an alternative explanatory framework that we must test, first, to see whether it is contradicted by particular cases and, if not, whether it proposes a plausible causal sequence. I would argue that a more exhaustive test of explanatory adequacy can rarely, if ever, be provided when phenomena from one range of social phenomena (say, economic

19 For an introduction to the massive literature on the causes of the great inflation of the 1970s, begin with the two Brookings Institution collections: Lawrence Krause and Walter Salant, eds., *Worldwide Inflation: Theory and Recent Experience* (Washington, D.C., 1976), and *The Politics of Inflation and Economic Stagnation*, cited in note 2. Cf. the Organization for Economic Cooperation and Development, *Towards Full Employment and Price Stability* (Paris: OECD, 1977), the so-called McCracken report, for the view that only "an unusual bunching of unfortunate circumstances" (p. 14) was at stake.

or political groupings) are adduced to "explain" outcomes in another range of experience, for example, price movements. We suffer from too many causes, not too few. Causality in the social sciences remains "multidimensional." That is, parallel explanations can often be constructed in several different dimensions – economic, political, sometimes psychological, cultural, or intellectual – any one of which claims to be adequate in its own right.[20] Some of these dimensions can include quantifiable observations, whether economic or survey data. But this does not invalidate the role of nonquantifiable or only crudely quantifiable factors.[21] The point of "The politics of inflation" was to demonstrate that historical political economy could offer a powerful dimension of explanation, one that might account for the continuing dynamic of economic fluctuations.

This introduction must close, however, on a note of uncertainty. The approach incorporated in these essays may help us to understand the resources for stabilization in twentieth-century historical development to date. But will it remain useful for understanding trends now emerging? The analysis depends on the capacity to discern coherent class or interest-group structures. Even in Chapter 5, where it is suggested that classes regroup under the impetus of sustained inflation, the interpretation presupposes that objective interests can be

20   The historian must steer between two opposed difficulties in this operation. Political scientists and economists often appeal to "parsimony" or Ockham's razor to discredit multicausal explanation: If a bunch of discreet causes account for a result (if there is a high R^2 from a regression), why adduce some additional type of explanation? The objection seems ill-conceived to me. The social scientist is not multiplying causes in any one explanatory dimension, an operation that might indeed violate canons of parsimony. He or she is bringing to bear equally parsimonious causal chains from another range of explanation. The levels of explanation are alternatives, not additive. The models of galaxies provided by radio telescopes are not thrown out on grounds of parsimony if we also have visual images. In the sense of always having multiple causal levels, history can be usefully defined as an overdetermined system. However, liberal historiography, with its insistence on multicausality, often fails to distinguish between simply adding incommensurable explanatory factors and consistently following through different dimensions of causation (economic, ideological, political). To insist on multicausality should require only that we admit the legitimacy of different dimensions of explanation, not that we mix their components inconsistently.

21   We are proposing what J. Rogers Hollingsworth and Robert Hanneman refer to as a "simulation model" (deterministic and nonstochastic) when they argue, "All that verification means, regardless of model type, is that the process embodied in the model could have generated the data. There is never a guarantee that a particular model is the correct one for a set of data." See "Modelling and Simulation in Historical Inquiry," in *Historical Methods*, 7, no. 3 (Summer 1984): 150–63 (quotation, p. 155).

defined and can rally collective actors. But this minimal degree of class cohesion may no longer correspond to contemporary European or American development (just as it may not have pertained before the age of industrialism). On the one hand, ad hoc movements crystallizing around new issues – feminism, the environment, disarmament – have absorbed much of the organizing energy, if not of the working-class directly, certainly of those intellectuals who once played such an important role in the socialist and communist camps.[22] On the other hand, the occupational categories of contemporary Western society have tended to dissolve as productive units have dispersed and services have displaced traditional manufacturing industries. The great socialist parties and trade-union confederations of Europe were products of the era of "smokestack industries," of centralized production and assembly lines. Today these enterprises count for less as employers than do public-sector agencies, universities, hospitals, insurance companies, food outlets, airlines, electronics subcontractors, and the like. Insofar as there is a new proletariat, it emerges not out of cohesive blue-collar labor, but from the urban unemployed, including women, from youth, and from migrants. The class structure of Europe today is more akin to the flux of "outcast London" a century back than to the stolid community of Wigan Pier fifty years ago. Breaking with the spatial metaphor that has prevailed since at least the French Revolution, we should perhaps visualize class structure less in terms of a pyramid of social strata than as an array of concentric circles.[23] Prosperous classes who enjoy steady employment and status-generating work remain close to the center, surrounded by increasingly peripheral or marginal elements shuffling jobs or on welfare.

In such a transition, the agencies that represent collective interests become more fragmentary. Parties become unmoored from traditional constituencies as these constituencies themselves disaggregate. Issue-oriented coalitions exert a powerful but ephemeral impact according to the rhythm of public protests. Trade unions lose members or else become labor contractors and pension managers for diverse occupational groups. Thus the *structures* of representation disintegrate or must be reorganized.

---

22 On this theme see Claus Offe, "Changing the Boundaries of Institutional Politics: New Social Movements," in Charles S. Maier, ed., *Changing Boundaries of the Political* (Cambridge University Press, 1987).
23 On this see Stanislaw Ossovski, *Class Structure in the Social Consciousness*, Sheila Patterson, trans. (London: Routledge & Kegan Paul, 1963).

Just as significant, the *stakes* of representation also change. Politics is less who *gets* what, how, and when. It is more who *says* what, where, and when: It is a contest for the authoritative values that orient society. Hence the control of mass media, the status and message of organized religion, the shaping of markets and consumption, the correct *interpretation* of protest or poverty at home or revolution abroad become crucial political concerns. These concerns are not new, but the high tide of liberalism and social democracy tended to displace them from the center stage of politics for a century or more. Now they have reclaimed politics at a time when the control of mass opinion counts for more than it did when they were last so important. Television and survey data allow perpetual plebiscites. Politics might be said to tend toward a Bonapartism of public discourse, except that grassroots discontents and initiatives, which played a large role in shaking the earlier structures of parties and interest groups, have kept open impulses for diversity and local organization. No matter how one evaluates the new trends, however, significant change has intervened since the 1960s. The international triumph of social democratic and reformist trends in that decade closed an era. It was the last period in which issues of economic growth, high employment, and income redistribution seemed paramount yet still to be successfully confronted through the parties, coalitions, and interest groups of the welfare state.

Is historical political economy merely an artifact of that earlier era, a historiographical reflection of neocorporatism and the brief success of social democracy? Can this analytical approach retain its utility in interpreting the new agents of cultural politics? If so, how will it recast the categories of interest groups, classes, and production? Can the method be deemed fruitful at the very moment when coming to terms with subjectivity and explaining the generation of values have become a major task for the social sciences, whether anthropology, sociology, or even economics? Or does our endeavor amount to merely having epitomized, so to speak, the historical culture of the Keynesian welfare state – with the limits of our approach finally discernible in the dusk of the era we sought to illuminate? I would like to think that this is not the case, that the historian of political economy can perhaps still build a bridge between two irrevocably separate inquiries: on the one side, the deductive economic analysis that traces the behavioral implications of "value" as a given; on the other, the hermeneutic reconstruction that asks how "values" are themselves generated in the institutions where individuals and society intersect. But these are questions of method that a historian of the late twentieth century, writing perhaps after the year 2000, will be better able to answer.

Part I

Ideology and economics from World War I to midcentury

1

Society as factory

This chapter incorporates an article from 1970 and the major part of a 1984 essay on related themes. "Between Taylorism and Technocracy. European Ideologies and the Vision of Industrial Productivity in the 1920s" was written for a prize competition in memory of Klaus Epstein sponsored by the *Journal of Contemporary History*, where it appeared in vol. 5, no. 2 (April 1970), 27–61. Since its original publication, scientific management and industrial rationalization have continued to attract scholarly interest in Europe and the United States. The essay was also published in French in *Recherches*, no. 32–3 (September 1978: *Le soldat du travail*), 95–136, D. Dumoy, trans.; reportedly in an obscure Italian review, *Quaderni del Progetto*, which never contacted the author; and in an abridged German version as "Zwischen Taylorismus und Technokratie: Gesellschaftspolitik im Zeichen industrieller Rationalität in den zwanziger Jahren in Europa," in Michael Stürmer, ed., *Belagerte Civitas, Die Weimarer Republik* (Cologne: Neue Wissenschaftliche Bibliothek, 1980), 188–213.

Whereas the 1970 essay stressed the political implications of Taylorism and Fordist concepts, scholarship in the intervening years has focused on the actual implantation and practice of scientific management. Recent research would lead me to amend some of my detailed points, and especially to credit a wider French enthusiasm for scientific management than my article suggested. Taylorism, the original essay proposed, derived much of its appeal from its implicit political promise to overcome class conflict. But as recent writers have emphasized, in the wake of repeated revolutions, nineteenth-century French liberals sought to preclude political upheaval by strengthening social networks: emphasizing "solidarity," sanctioning professional associations and even unions, encouraging benevolent societies, cooperatives, and insurance pools. (See Jacques Donzelot, *L'invention du social: Essai sur le declin des passions politiques* [Paris: Fayard, 1984], and the argument in

Pierre Rosanvallon, *Le moment Guizot* [Paris: Gallimard, 1985].) Scientific management not only enjoyed technological chic. It could benefit from this search for stability through the reinforcement of social cadres (a theme to be taken up in the conclusion to this book). Despite changes in emphasis I would make today, I believe that the 1970 arguments remain sufficiently valid – the distinction between Taylorism and Fordism has been taken up by subsequent researchers – to justify republishing the original version. And rather than attempt to bring individual notes up to date, I include here an omnibus citation of important contributions that have appeared since original publication.

The second essay of this chapter comprises part of a festschrift contribution written to honor a former teacher, James Joll: "The Factory as Society: Ideologies of Industrial Management in the Twentieth Century," in R. J. Bullen, H. Pogge von Strandmann, and A. B. Polonsky, eds., *Ideas into Politics: Aspects of European History 1880–1950* (London: Croom Helm, 1984). It was intended to be more speculative and less explicitly comparative, relying primarily on some classic sources for the discourse of management. For publication here, I have abbreviated the first section and renumbered the footnotes.

Neither essay, it must be emphasized, is concerned with actual managerial practices or the organization of factories. Theories of management are to the practice of business as theories of architecture are to buildings. Few buildings follow the canons of design announced by leading architects, even if they incorporate individual elements. Still, architectural manifestoes are crucial for orienting the profession to what might be their solution if clients, money, and site constraints allowed. So, too, few industrial plants incorporate the doctrines of management experts as coherent ensembles. Few factories were organized as Taylorite institutions, even in the United States. Nonetheless, Taylorism or scientific management dominated the discourse of industrial relations through the 1920s, and it is the discourse of management that is scrutinized here.

The recent literature pursues several themes: Harry Braverman's *Labor and Monopoly Capitalism: On the Degradation of Work in the Twentieth Century* (New York: Monthly Review Press, 1974) condemns Taylorism as a major effort to undermine workers' skills and autonomy. In turn Braverman's work has been criticized by Michael Burawoy, *The Politics of Production* (London: Verso, 1985), who argues that Braverman has overgeneralized one form of capitalist management. See also Judith A. Merkle, *Management and Ideology* (Berkeley and Los Angeles: University of California Press, 1980). The debate on Taylorism that emerged from the industrial sociology school of Georges Friedman was carried on in a special issue of *Sociologie du Travail*, 16, no. 4 (Oc-

tober–December 1974): *Conditions de travail: Le Taylorisme en question.*
A recent discussion by Bernard Doray, *Le Taylorisme: Une Folie ration-
nelle* (Paris: Dunod, 1981), includes familiar themes but interesting
documentation from the newsletters of automobile manufacturers. The
major historical work on the implantation of Taylorism in France has
been done by Aimée Moutet: "Les origines du système du Taylor en
France 1907–1914," *Le Mouvement Social,* no. 93 (October–December
1975): 15–51; "Patrons de progrès ou patrons de combat? La politique
de rationalisation de l'industrie française au lendemain de la première
guerre mondiale," *Recherches,* no. 32–3 (September 1978): 449–92; "La
première guerre mondiale et le Taylorisme," in Maurice de Montmollin
and Olivier Pastré, eds., *Le Taylorisme: Actes du colloque international
sur le Taylorisme organisé par l'Université de Paris – XIII, 2–4 mai 1983*
(Paris: Editions La Découverte, 1984), 67–81; and "Ingénieurs et rationalisation en France, de la guerre à la crise 1914–1929," in *Ingénieurs
et Société,* Le Creusot, Colloque des 23–25 octobre 1980. On the French
situation see also Olivier Christin, "Les enjeux de la rationalisation
industrielle (1901–1929)," Master's thesis, 1982; the work of Yves Le-
quin, "Aux origines des débats sur la rationalisation en France," presented at the Colloque international sur le Taylorisme, 2–4 mai 1983,
but not included in the printed version; Patrick Fridenson, *Histoire
des usines Renault* (Paris: Seuil, 1974), vol. 1; "L'idéologie des grands
constructeurs dans l'entre-deux-guerres," *Le Mouvement Social,* no. 81
(October–December 1972); also "France–Etats-Unis: Genèse de l'usine
nouvelle," *Recherches,* no. 32–3 (September 1978); and most recently,
"Automobile Workers in France and Their Work, 1914–83," in Steven
L. Kaplan and Cynthia J. Koepp, eds., *Work in France* (Ithaca, N.Y.:
Cornell University Press, 1986), 514–47. On the business side, Martin
Fine, "L'Association Française pour le Progrès Social (1927–1929), *Le
Mouvement Social,* no. 93 (October–December 1975): 15–49. For a survey
of recent literature and problems in a contemporary perspective: Robert
Boyer, "L'introduction du Taylorisme en France a la lumière de re-
cherches recentes" (Paris: Cepremap, Xerox publication, 1983). For
Germany see Heidrun Homburg, "Anfänge des Taylorsystems in
Deutschland vor dem Ersten Weltkrieg," *Geschichte und Gesellschaft,* 4
(1978): 170–95; "Scientific Management and Personnel Policy in the
Modern German Enterprise 1918–1939: The Case of Siemens," pub-
lished in part in de Montmollin and Pastré, eds., *Le Taylorisme,* 99–
113, and in Howard F. Gospel and Craig R. Littler, eds., *Managerial
Strategies and Industrial Relations in Historical and Comparative Study*
(London: Heinemann, 1983), 137–56, a volume that contains several
essays bearing on the theme by Gospel, Littler, Lewchuk, and Lazonik.
See also Jean Querzola, "Sulle origini del taylorismo: Perché negli

Stati Uniti?" in Mariuccia Salvati, ed., Annali of the Fondazione Basso, ISSOCO, vol. 6: *Cultura operaia e disciplina industriale* (Rome, 1982): 141–58; Giulio Sapelli, "Appunti per una storia dell'organizzazione scientifica del lavoro in Italia," *Quaderni di Sociologia*, 25, no. 2–3 (1976): 166–70; and Sapelli, *Organizzazione lavoro e innovazione industriale nell'Italia tra le due guerre* (Turin: Rosenberg & Sellier, 1978). For what he has called technocorporatism in the United States, see the contributions by Ellis Hawley, especially "Herbert Hoover, the Commerce Secretariat, and the Vision of an 'Associative State,' 1921–1928," *Journal of American History*, 61 (1974): 116–40.

BETWEEN TAYLORISM AND TECHNOCRACY: EUROPEAN
IDEOLOGIES AND THE VISION OF INDUSTRIAL PRODUCTIVITY
IN THE 1920S

As Antonio Gramsci recognized in his prison reflections from the end of the 1920s, the impact of United States technology offered a valuable key for understanding the present European development: 'The European reaction to Americanism . . . must be examined attentively. Analysis of it will provide more than one element necessary for understanding the present situation of a series of states of the old continent and the political events of the post-war period.'[1]

By Americanism Gramsci meant a whole complex of approaches to industrial production and labour relationships. 'Fordism' embodied one aspect, 'Taylorism' another; yet as a German commentator pointed out in 1927, these appeared merely as the most typical contribution to America's prodigious economic achievement as a whole.[2] By the 1920s, scientific management – which extended the original approaches of Taylorism into all areas of labour productivity, technological efficiency, and even corporate organization – evoked enthusiasm among European emulators as 'a characteristic feature of American civilization'.[3]

As Gramsci sensed, this vogue of so-called Americanism testified to important transformations within Europe; it reflected most directly

1 Antonio Gramsci, *Note sul Machiavelli, sulla politica, e sullo stato moderno* (Turin: Einaudi, 1949), 312.
2 F. von Gottl-Ottlilienfeld, *Fordismus? Paraphrasen über das Verhältnis von Wirtschaft und technischer Vernunft bei Henry Ford und Frederick W. Taylor* (Jena: G. Fischer, 1924), 6.
3 League of Nations, International Labour Office, *International Economic Conference Geneva, May 4, 1927, Documentation: Scientific Management in Europe* (Geneva, 1926), 7–8. This report is an abbreviated version of Paul Devinat, *Scientific Management in Europe*, ILO, Studies and Reports, Series B, No. 17 (Geneva, 1927).

the powerful demand for technocratic expertise that had been especially encouraged by the first world war. But the war aside, European society could easily press into service doctrines of technological efficiency: structural changes in the twentieth-century economy awoke a concern for 'rationalization'; artistic and architectural innovation revealed a fascination with the social possibilities of mechanization. Taylorism and Fordism provide a good starting point for analysing what was at stake. They evoked a European resonance less for their strictly technical features than for their social and political implications. The engineer, who was central to the new industrial gospel, appeared not so much a master of machines as a potential manipulator of all industrial relationships. The cultural and political appeal, rather than actual factory applications, forms in fact the focus of this essay. Because of the ideological implications, a survey of scientific management, and the related concern for economic and social planning, open new perspectives on the period between the first world war and the Great Depression.

Whereas in America the commitment to technological efficiency and productivity pervaded almost the entire culture, in Europe it appeared more selectively. The central question is what determined that pattern of receptivity – at least that receptivity as measured by public discussion and government sponsorship. It is noteworthy that the ideological breakdown between the enthusiasts and the indifferent or hostile, did not follow any simple left-to-right alignment. Generally during the early post-war years technocratic or engineering models of social management appealed to the newer, more syncretic, and sometimes more extreme currents of European politics. Italian national syndicalists and fascists, German 'revolutionary conservatives' and 'conservative socialists', as well as the so-called left liberals who sought to mediate between bourgeois and social democracy, and finally the Soviet leaders, proved most receptive. Later in the decade, as the American vision of productivity was divested of its more utopian implications, it came to serve a useful function for business conservatives. Between the original enthusiasm for Taylorite teachings and the later *éclat* of Fordism lay an important evolution in the ideological thrust of Americanist doctrines. In general, however, all the variants enjoyed most appeal where representative government was deemed to be working badly. Ironically enough, American productivity contributed to the critical attitude towards parliamentary liberalism.

What the Americanist vision seemed to promise through its brash teachings of productivity, expertise, and optimalization was an escape from having to accept class confrontation and social division. Albeit for very different reasons, all the enthusiasts of scientific management and technological overhaul were seeking to deny the necessary existence of the pre-war model of ideological conflict and to validate a new image of class relationships.

The promise of engineering in America

Before 1914 Taylorism had already been picked up in Europe as one of the most provocative aspects of America's formidable economic expansion, although even in the United States it was rarely applied in full. Still, its career and intellectual elaboration reveal the dynamic inherent in the idea of technology as social arbiter. Following its influence from this point of view makes clear the stakes that any recourse to the technician or 'producer' would entail, in Europe as well as America.

Throughout the first decade of the new century Frederick W. Taylor (1856–1915) popularized a process of labour discipline and workshop organization based upon supposedly scientific studies of human efficiency and incentive systems. Preoccupied with the problem of 'soldiering' or labour slowdowns, Taylor timed basic work actions, developed programmed task instruction cards for employees, recommended factory planning departments, and devised wage scales based on piece work, such that the productive worker shared in the expansion of output, but would fall below a subsistence wage and be forced to quit were he to prove inefficient. Taylor's system was propagated by his zealous disciples and similar versions were advanced by eager competitors, while it became fixed in the public eye through a series of controversies concerning its benefits and its alleged inhumanity.[4]

Certainly there had been notions of rationalized management practice before. What was novel about Taylorism was the application of the supposedly machine-oriented discipline of engineering to labour relations. How, in fact, had engineering intruded into this sphere?

---

4   See Samuel Haber, *Efficiency and Uplift, Scientific Management in the Progressive Era, 1890–1920* (Chicago: University of Chicago Press, 1964); M. J. Nadworny, *Scientific Management and the Unions, 1900–1932* (Cambridge, Mass: Harvard University Press, 1955), esp. 1–42; F. W. Taylor, *Scientific Management, Comprising Shop Management, The Principles of Scientific Management, Testimony before the Special House Committee* (New York: Harper Bros., 1947); C. B. Thompson, ed., *Scientific Management. A Collection of the More Significant Articles Describing the Taylor System of Management* (Cambridge, Mass., Harvard University Press, 1914). On Taylor himself: F. B. Copley, *Frederick Winslow Taylor* (New York: Taylor Society, 1923). For the controversies over application: H. G. J. Aitken, *Taylorism at Watertown Arsenal* (Cambridge, Mass.: Harvard University Press, 1960).

The American Society of Mechanical Engineers, founded in 1880, represented a profession significantly different in origin from European counterparts such as the *polytechniciens* of France. In France and Germany engineering schools had originally been sponsored by royal, revolutionary, or Bonapartist regimes concerned with national wealth and power. In England and America the mechanical engineering profession came of age with the surge of industrialization, and its early practitioners emerged not from the technical institute but from the factory itself. By the late nineteenth century a heightened professionalism was drawing many of America's engineers from the old, ethnically and socially established middle classes – men who perhaps did not wish to give themselves up entirely to business pursuits, who insisted on the credentials of expertise as well as the sanctification of money, and who retained a marked distrust of labour's collective ambitions. For the professionally committed, engineering suggested a self-image of impartial technical arbitration, a dedication to scientific standards and objectivity above the clash of interests in the factory.[5]

As the application of science to the world of economic constraints, engineering logically had to work with the concept of efficiency: the ratio of output to input and benefits to cost. Optimality – although the term was not used in early Taylorism itself – became the implicit key notion behind the application of engineering to industrial relations. Worker and employer had no scope for quarrelling about wages or hours or conditions of labour when both parties were yoked to the arbitration of science. 'What we need', wrote Henry L. Gantt, one of Taylor's most engaging followers, 'is not more laws, but more facts, and the whole question will solve itself'.[6]

In practice, not surprisingly, the supposedly impartial findings of science tended to confirm the approach of management, not labour. Collective bargaining had little place in a world of technological imperatives and piece-work wages. Management alone, Taylor insisted, could call upon the directing intelligence and alone set the norms of

5 Haber, *Efficiency and Uplift*, 9–17; Monte Calvert, *The Mechanical Engineer in America, 1830–1910* (Baltimore: Johns Hopkins University Press, 1967); on English and European training: W. H. G. Armytage, *A Social History of Engineering* (London: L. Faber, 1961), esp. 108 ff., 149–52, 185 ff.; J. P. Callot, *Histoire de l'Ecole Polytechnique* (Paris: Presses Modernes, 1958); for a note on French origins, Georges Sorel, *Les illusions du progrès* (3rd ed., Paris: Marcel Rivière, 1921), 357–8. Cf. also H. Klages and G. Hartleder, 'Gesellschaft und soziales Selbstverständnis des Ingenieurs', *Schmollers Jahrbuch*, 1965.
6 Cited in L. P. Alford, *Henry Laurence Gantt: Leader in Industry* (New York: American Society of Mechanical Engineers, 1934), 262.

efficient production.[7] Nonetheless, in theory there could be no arbitrary decisions. And if Taylor himself usually emphasized the need to eliminate worker 'soldiering', reformist Taylorites were later to stress how conservative entrepreneurial practice must change. The important thing was that both findings still carried a commitment to transcend conflicts of interest. To borrow the language developed for game theory, Taylorism promised an escape from zero-sum conflict, in which the gain of one party could be extracted only from the equal sacrifice of the other.

In addition to the optimal allocation of given production and income, the expansion of output through improved workshop organization was also to benefit both sides. Increased production would be shared with labour as well as with investors, so that there need be no bitter scrapping over any given level of return. Efficiency, optimality, enhanced productivity and expanded output thus formed a coherent system. It both demanded and promised much. As Taylor told the House of Representatives, the essence of scientific management was not merely piece work, task cards, or time studies, but 'a complete mental revolution on both sides', such that old contentions were eradicated:

The great revolution that takes place in the mental attitude of the two parties under scientific management is that both sides take their eyes off of the division of the surplus as the all-important matter, and together turn their attention toward increasing the size of the surplus until this surplus becomes so large . . . that there is ample room for a large increase in wages for the workman and an equally large increase in profits for the manufacturer.[8]

In short, what Taylorism offered – certainly within the plant, and ultimately, according to its author, in all spheres of government and social life[9] – was the elimination of scarcity and constraint. It therefore implied a revolution in the nature of authority: the heralded utopian change from power over men to the administration of things. Such an evolution logically removed the basis for class formation as conceived by sociology.[10] Ostensibly Taylor's factory could become the

---

7   Taylor, *Testimony before the Special House Committee*, 235; cf. also Nadworny, *Scientific Management and the Unions*, 9. The implicit assumptions in favour of the employer are also discussed in Reinhard Bendix, *Work and Authority in Industry* (New York: Harper & Row, 1963), 276–87. Taylor, moreover, did not believe pay should rise in exactly the same proportion as output; smaller increments would force the worker to remain ambitious. See *Shop Management*, 29.

8   Taylor, *Testimony*, 27–30.

9   Taylor, *Scientific Management*, 8.

10 See Ralf Dahrendorf, *Class and Class Conflict in Industrial Society* (Stanford: Stanford University Press, 1959), 157–205. A theoretical framework for a view more in line with Taylorite implications is provided by Talcott Parsons, 'Social Classes and Class Conflict in the Light of Recent Sociological Theory', in *Essays in Sociological Theory* (New York: Free Press, 1964).

nucleic building block of a post-bourgeois world, or at least a secure managerial one.

For Americans of the Progressive era this sort of doctrine had great appeal. Social efficiency in the years before the first world war became a shibboleth for reform as well as for productivity. It showed the interests of employers and employees to coincide, in the words of Taylor and then of the Gilbreths – Taylor's rivals who relied on motion-picture analysis of basic work-movements anagramatically christened Therbligs – with 'the one best way to do work'.[11] A publicist of related views, Harrington Emerson, organized the Efficiency Society, while in December 1916 Henry Gantt helped to found the short-lived 'New Machine', an association seeking to acquire political power and exercise it according to the criteria of industrial efficiency. Inspiration for this effort was found in the works of Thorstein Veblen and the now obscure Charles A. Ferguson, who combined evangelism with an elitist proto-syndicalism.[12]

Given an overall national commitment to democracy, its redefinition to square with criteria of optimality and efficiency seemed imperative, and this the Progressive era writers undertook. Democracy, wrote Ferguson, 'is not the rule of the majority but of the wilful servants of all', and he advocated the devolution of power to self-administering economic associations.[13] 'Democracy is a method, a scientific technique of evolving the will of the people', claimed Mary P. Follett, a future theorist of scientific management influenced by English neo-Hegelianism and Guild Socialism.[14] Minimal, but scientific government by experts, complex schemes for the self-regulation of industry, with production, not profit as the criterion, reflected a similar quest for a new concept of authority that would transform the economic interests now smothering the public welfare into the very bearers of the com-

---

11 Haber, *Efficiency and Uplift*, 41. Cf. F. B. Gilbreth, *Motion Study: A Method for Increasing the Efficiency of the Workman* (New York: Van Nostrand, 1911). For a general discussion of efficiency as a national theme see Daniel Bell, 'Work and its Discontents: the Cult of Efficiency in America', in *The End of Ideology* (Glencoe, Ill.: Free Press, 1960).

12 Haber, *Efficiency and Uplift*, 44–9; Alford, *Gantt*, 264 ff.; for Emerson's rotarian prose see *The Twelve Principles of Efficiency* (New York: Engineering Magazine Co., 1913); for Ferguson, *The Great News* (New York: M. Kennerley, 1915).

13 Ferguson, *The Great News*, 59, 73–5; for the Progressives and scientific management: Haber, *Efficiency and Uplift*, 75 ff.

14 Mary P. Follett, *The New State: Group Organization, the Solution of Popular Government* [1918] (3rd ed., London: Longmans, Green, 1934), 180. Miss Follett spotlighted the tension – to be found in later planning concepts – between the public interest and the policies of the quasi-syndical bodies to whom the English pluralists wished to give authority (258–319); for an illuminating discussion of ambiguities tending the other way, see Charles Forcey, *The Crossroads of Liberalism* (New York: 1967), 37 ff.

munity's advance into abundance. 'There is no legitimate power but the power to deliver goods', stated Ferguson,[15] while Gantt wrote that 'The era of force must give way to the era of knowledge'. The engineers would be summoned to impose optimality upon society as they did in the factory: 'The new democracy does not consist in the privilege of doing as one pleases, whether it is right or wrong, but in each man's doing his part in the best way that can be devised from scientific knowledge and experience.'[16]

This functional model naturally became more topical when a War Industries Board offered a prototype of the new industrial co-ordination. Unprecedented material requirements also pressed home the need for efficient use of national resources. Hence the war made the problem of industrial relations both more urgent and more tractable, according to Morris Llewellyn Cooke, another reformist engineer, for it had convinced all parties of the necessity of increasing production.[17]

It was logical, too, that the war and its aftermath should help to crystallize two explicit alternatives for the role of the engineer: Veblen's isolated revolutionary prescription, and Herbert Hoover's ameliorist activism. By the early 1920s Veblen was addressing himself directly to the engineers in an effort to reshape modern capitalist society. Throughout his works he had envisaged an enduring social conflict between the industrious and the exploiters. The 'pecuniary' occupations justified their frankly parasitic role by the conventions of private ownership, while those conditioned by technological rationality – engineers and workers – were most liable to question the nexus of private property (or absentee ownership).[18] By the end of the first world war, Veblen was concentrating on the engineer as strategically pre-eminent, for through him the genuinely productive forces at last had a hand upon the nerve centres of modern society. The engineers could act, were they so disposed, to end the conventions of absentee ownership on behalf of all those engaged in non-exploitative labour. Veblen probably misunderstood the temper of the engineers; certainly he inverted the social role of engineering as its actual practitioners conceived it.[19] In their 1921 investigation of waste in industry, for

15 Ferguson, *The Great News*, 103.
16 Alford, *Gantt*, 253, 196.
17 M. L. Cooke, 'Forward', *Modern Manufacturing, A Partnership of Idealism and Common Sense. Annals of the American Academy of Political and Social Science*, September 1919, vi.
18 Thorstein Veblen, *The Theory of Business Enterprise* [1904] (New York: New American Library, n.d.), esp. 144–76.
19 Edwin Layton, 'Veblen and the Engineers', *American Quarterly*, Spring 1962; Calvert, *The Mechanical Engineer in America*, 263–76; Veblen, *The Engineers and the Price System* [1914–21] (New York: Harcourt, Brace & World, 1963), 93–108.

example, the Hoover committee, sponsored by the Federated American Engineering Societies, pointed to the engineer not as a syndicalist revolutionary, but as a rationalizer of a basically successful system:

His lifelong training in quantitative thought, his intimate experience with industrial life, leading to an objective and detached point of view, his strategic position as a party of the third part with reference to many of the conflicting economic groups, and above all his practical emphasis on construction and production, place upon him the duty to make his point of view effective.[20]

Certainly the attributes of the engineer were the potentially technocratic ones, but Hoover's view of his task was more circumscribed than Veblen's. For Veblen the business system had virtually to manufacture waste to preserve hierarchy, and commitment to optimality or abundance was impossible within American capitalism. For Hoover the engineer helped to eliminate the frictions of a basically superior economic order.[21] It was not surprising that Veblen's conception found little response until the depression, while Hoover's helped to set the tone of the 1920s. Together, they showed the malleability of the stress on productivity: as the next decade in Europe revealed, the technological vision could serve the ends of transformation or of the status quo.

The ambivalence of the right-radical response

The imagery of the technological vision was as potent as its utopian ideology; if the machine was to alter society it must transform the environment. Viewed retrospectively, the response of art and architecture revealed in what milieux the imaginative concepts of technology proved influential, as they did in Germany and Austria, Italy, and later in Russia and France. The formation of the German Werkbund in 1907, for example, brought together the left-liberal and national-social political leader Friedrich Naumann, representatives of forward-looking industries such as German General Electric (AEG), and architectural innovators, including Hermann Muthesius, Peter

---

20 Committee on Elimination of Waste in Industry of the Federated American Engineering Societies, *Waste in Industry* (New York, 1921), 33. Later popularization of the waste theme is found in Stuart Chase, *The Tragedy of Waste* (New York: Macmillan, 1925). For the transition from engineering to planning at the end of the decade, see Charles A. Beard, ed., *Toward Civilization* (New York: Longmans, Green, 1930).

21 On general economic views, see Hoover to Woodrow Wilson, 28 March 1919, in A. J. Mayer, *Politics and Diplomacy of Peacemaking* (New York: Knopf, 1967), esp. 25; and Herbert Hoover, *American Individualism* (Garden City, NY: Doubleday, 1922).

Behrens, and Walter Gropius. Its establishment, however, did not mean that the claims of modernity were carrying the day in central Europe. Instead it suggested that a self-conscious technological inspiration might very well arise where society revealed deep fissures and strong reactionary impulses. The vision behind the Werkbund represented in fact an effort to overcome the fracturing materialism of Wilhelmine society. Gropius himself praised the stark American factories and grain elevators as models for the new style and claimed that a good factory aesthetic was important from a social point of view, for it permitted a more joyful cooperative effort.[22]

Contributing to a related tendency, but one with a different political outcome, were the Italian Futurists, whose work drew on the machine as a fount of eroticism, violence, and death. Severini's and Balla's paintings as well as Marinetti's notorious *Manifesto* prefigured a crucial development in the engineering vision: the right-radical union of technology and irrationalism. Revealingly, liberal France and England seemed at the time to produce less work of specific technological inspiration but by the early 1920s, as the American industrial model attracted ever more attention, it stimulated an artistic response there too. Le Corbusier praised Ford and Taylor in his treatises and sought to bring France's sadly fallen architects up to the level of 'healthy and virile, active and useful, balanced and happy engineers'. The house, then the city, was to be transformed from monument to tool. The new aesthetic required a new technocracy: Le Corbusier's town-planning evangelism of the early twenties demanded a linear regularity imposed by a far-seeing authority – a 'technical work' on behalf neither of communism nor of capitalism.[23] Not that communism lacked similar inspiration: in Moscow an abstract formalism that celebrated the union of technological possibilities with social revolution flourished for a

22 For general discussion, Nikolaus Pevsner, *Pioneers of Modern Design* (Baltimore, Penguin, 1965), 31–9, 179 ff.; Reyner Banham, *Theory and Design in the First Machine Age* (London: Architectural Press, 1960), 68–87; Walter Gropius, 'Die Entwicklung moderner Industriebaukunst'. *Jahrbuch des deutschen Werkbundes* (Jena, 1913), 17–22. Cf. also Hermann Muthesius, 'Das Formproblem im Ingenieurbau' in the same issue; W. H. Jordy, 'The Aftermath of the Bauhaus in America: Gropius, Mies, and Breuer', *Perspectives in American History*, II (1968), esp. 489–91.

23 For Futurism and Le Corbusier, Baham, *Theory and Design*, 99–137, 220–63; cf. James Joll, 'F. T. Marinetti: Futurism and Fascism', in *Intellectuals in Politics* (London: Weidenfeld & Nicolson, 1960), esp. 169–70 for Mussolini's delight in the mechanical, and T. Marinetti, *La democrazia futurista* (Milan: Facchi, 1919), for a technocratic projection. See Le Corbusier, *Vers une architecture* (2nd ed. Paris: G. Crès, 1924), 6 ff. for the engineer, and 234 on the needs of the 'service class', and *The City of Tomorrow* (London: Architectural Press, 1947), transl. of *L'urbanisme* 1929 ed., 308–09.

few exciting years, reflecting some of the same impulses that led to Lenin's flirtation with Taylorism and the Russian enthusiasm for scientific management and American engineering.[24]

Conversely, those places where the cultural avant-garde showed little response displayed less interest in the new doctrines in general. In England, before the war, schemes of scientific management awoke scant interest among engineers and managers. Not merely did this reflect an industrial leadership set in its ways; an underlying satisfaction with decentralized production, with the premises of a liberal regime in a country where the middle-classes felt little anxiety about the social order, postponed real interest until the economic difficulties of the 1920s and 1930s.[25] Initially France, too, seemed little moved by American technological messianism. There the response to scientific management also remained scattered until the later 1920s, when, serving more conservative ends, American-inspired visions of productivity and modernization were able to arouse businessmen and politicians.[26]

Certainly impulses towards 'Americanism' were present earlier; the necessities of war production encouraged interest in the innovations of France's ally; in early 1918 Clemenceau asked that attention be paid

24 Banham, *Theory and Design*, 193ff.; Camilla Gray, *The Great Experiment: Russian Art 1863–1922* (New York: Abrams, 1962), 181–97, 215–27; cf. also K. G. Pontus-Hultén, *The Machine as seen at the End of the Mechanical Age* (New York: Museum of Modern Art, 1968), 107 ff., 128 ff. On Russian enthusiasm for scientific management, Devinat, *Scientific Management in Europe*, 86 ff.

25 A. L. Levine, *Industrial Retardation in Britain, 1880–1914* (London: Weidenfeld & Nicolson, 1967), 60–8; Cf. the judgment of a leading advocate that scientific management was long delayed in England as a general movement despite occasional Taylorite applications – a lag attributed to empirical modes of thought and a dislike of large-scale organization which lasted beyond the first world war. L. Urwick, *The Development of Scientific Management in Great Britain* (London: British Management Council, 1938), 75–80.

26 For a brief account of the progress of scientific management in France and other European nations, see Devinat, *Scientific Management in Europe*, 233–45, and the preface by Albert Thomas, which describes initial French working-class resistance. See above all the works of Henri Le Chatelier, metallurgist at the Sorbonne, editor of a Comité des Forges-sponsored journal, and translator of Taylor, including *Le Taylorisme* (2nd ed. Paris: Dunod, 1934). For the related approach of Henry Fayol and his *doctrine administrative* see Fayol, *Industrial and General Administration* (Engl. transl. London: Pitman, 1930), with an extensive bibliography, and J. Billard, *Organisation et direction dans les affaires privées et les services publics. Un essai de doctrine, le Fayolisme* (Paris: Thèse; Paris: Jouve, 1924); for a contrast between Taylorism and Fayolism: François Bourricaud, 'France', in A. M. Rose, ed., *The Institutions of Advanced Societies* (Minneapolis: Minnesota University Press, 1958), 490–1. For the major French socialist critique of Taylorism as practised in America see André Philip, *Le problème ouvrier aux Etats-Unis* (Paris: F. Alcan, 1927), 39–87.

to Taylorism in war-plants and suggested the establishment of Tay-lorite planning departments.[27] Even more promising was the ideological tendency in French politics that anticipated the quest for the engineer as social manager. Saint-Simonianism embodied a proto-technocratic ideology that rejected traditional class divisions in favour of the unity of all 'productive' and 'industrious' elements, bourgeois, peasant, and proletarian, against the useless aristocrats and rentiers.[28] Veblen's contemporary categories were strikingly reminiscent of the Saint-Simonian scheme; and, of course, American condemnations of idleness and waste might have been taken directly from the French utopian's writings. Saint-Simonianism had projected a disinterested social optimalization from above, a functional administrative structure, and a commitment to the aggregate wealth and welfare of society – all themes that appeared in American writings.

But in France after the first world war only a handful of confessed Saint-Simonians existed to publish the obscure *Le Producteur*.[29] To be sure, the idea of 'production' aroused many observers, including, for instance, the popular Mayor of Lyon, Edouard Herriot, who in 1919 called attention to Taylorism and appealed for bureaucratic, economic, and educational modernization in a technologically inspired 'fourth republic'. The new regime was to abandon the pre-war party cliques, local patronage, and *café-comptoir comités* that formed the warp and woof of French politics.[30] But Herriot's rhetorical ebullience did not imply practical commitment, nor were his own Radical Socialists likely to follow his advice on technological overhaul and abandon the small-town network of interests that was their own power base. Likewise, when Etienne Clémentel, Clemenceau's Minister of Commerce, sought to present an organization model for French industrial self-adminis-tration in a Fédération des Syndicats, he encountered suspicion and apathy from businessmen who desired primarily to shake off wartime supervision and return to their old and less daring habits.[31]

That these strict Saint-Simonian themes found only a faint echo was understandable, for their origins linked them with the logic of strong executive authority, and they had enjoyed their greatest influ-ence under the Second Empire. As long as the parliamentary regime functioned satisfactorily, the process of political selection kept the

---

27 Cited in Copley, *Taylor*, I, xxi.
28 For summaries of the ideology see Frank Manuel, *The New World of Henri Saint-Simon* (Cambridge, Mass.: Harvard University Press, 1956), and Manuel, *The Prophets of Paris* (Cambridge, Mass.: Harvard University Press, 1962), 105–48.
29 For this group see Marc Bourbonnais, *Le néo saint-simonisme dans la vie sociale d'au-jourd'hui* (Paris: Presses Universitaires de France, 1923).
30 Edouard Herriot, *Créer* (2 vols.: Paris: Payot, 1919), esp. I, 448–68, II, 335.
31 For Clémentel's efforts, *La Journée Industrielle*, 8–9 March, 16, 25–8 April 1919.

would-be technocrats from positions of influence. Nonetheless, the war could not leave the parliamentary status quo absolutely immune. The legacy of the 1917 crisis, the impatience with earlier Radical-Socialist domination, the pervasive feeling that total war must yield profound if vague transformations – all contributed to the anti-parliamentary overtones that emerged in the Bloc National elections of November 1919. For the first time since the 1890s, not merely a clerical or reactionary, but a genuine right-radical tone was evident[32]: here and there among Bloc National candidates themselves, occasionally in the scattered efforts of Action Française, finally in the ephemeral new movement led by Lysis (Ernest Letailleur). Lysis complained that France lacked 'l'idée d'une technique nationale', and was stifled by backward oligarchies and parliamentary stockjobbers. He called for the representation of professional groups, distinguished 'productive' capitalism from its parasitic version, and advocated a new socialism that postulated class unity instead of class conflict.[33] His followers fared badly in the elections, because the Bloc National can didates responded well enough to the discontents he manipulated, not because his programme was rejected outright. For a significant political organization to exploit Lysis' ideological themes, France had to wait until the mid-1920s with its parliamentary paralysis and an angered bourgeoisie.

Elsewhere right-radical spokesmen for a 'productivist' ideology had more impact. Nevertheless, a central ambivalence towards technology itself marked their thinking, much as it did Futurist art. If right-radical spokesmen wished to assail the liberal capitalist order, or at least the liberal parliamentary order, their anti-intellectualism undermined a reliance upon the engineer, the manager, or other specialized expert as a potential leader. Before the war this had been foreshadowed in the problematic writings of Georges Sorel. Like Veblen, with whom he forms an instructive contrast, Sorel retained the old dichotomy between useful production and financial exploitation. By training an engineer, Sorel saw the virtuous man as maker, but he treasured a pre-industrial *morale des producteurs* that only the small workshop could preserve. Whereas Veblen's glorification of workmanship was un-ambiguously pacific, Sorel's ideal included a vigorously militant component that in modern conditions could be restored only through

32 André Siegfried, *Tableau des partis en France* (Paris: Grasset, 1930), 131–2.
33 Lysis, *Vers la démocratie nouvelle* (Paris: Payot, 1919), 37 ff., 117 ff., 277; for the Bloc National programmes see *Programmes, professions de foi et engagements électoraux de 1919* (Paris: Chambre des Deputes, 1920).

commitment to a myth of imminent revolutionary struggle. The enlightenment-bred rationalism that helped to advance the machine age also denatured man, while for Veblen technology in no way diminished humanity.[34]

The Italian episode of early fascist technocracy reflects the stresses inherent in Sorel's theories within a real institutional context. In Italy the themes of new industrial leadership and anti-parliamentarism were tightly interwoven. Pre-war Italian nationalist writers had assailed liberal and social democracy on behalf of a right-radical syndicalism.[35] In 1917 the President of the Comitato Nazionale Scientifico Tecnico, G. Belluzzo, later fascist economics minister, called for an eventual transformation of the state, to be preceded by industrial rationalization and concentration.[36] By August 1918, Mussolini had changed the subtitle of his own newspaper from *Socialist Daily* to *Daily for Soldiers and Producers*. Indicatively, he condemned the socialist-party 'parasites of blood', and 'parasites of labour', adding that 'to defend the producers means to let the bourgeoisie complete its historical function.'[37] This theme was still pursued after the war: 'No political revolution, no extremism, no expropriation and not even a class struggle, if the chiefs of the enterprises are intelligent. Intensive, harmonious collaboration of industrialists and workers in production.'[38]

34   Georges Sorel, *Réflexions sur la violence* (11th ed., Paris: Marcel Rivière, 1950), 109–20, 377 ff.; *Les illusions du progrès* (Paris: Marcel Rivière, 1947); cf. also I. L. Horowitz, *Radicalism and the Revolt against Reason; The Social Theories of Georges Sorel* (Carbondale, Ill.: Southern Illinois University Press, 1968), esp. 127–63; Michael Freund, *Georges Sorel, Der revolutionaere Konservatismus* (Frankfurt am Main: Klostermann, 1932).

35   See among other works, Enrico Corradini, *La marcia dei produttori* (Rome: L'Italiana, 1916) and *Discorsi politici (1902–1923)* (Florence: Vallechi, 1923); P. M. Arcari, *L'elaborazione della dottrina politica nazionalista (1870–1914)* (3 vols., Florence: Marzocco, 1934–1939); and the very useful Paolo Ungari, *Alfredo Rocco e l'ideologia giuridica del fascismo* (Brescia: Morcelliana, 1963).

36   G. Belluzzo, *La organizzazione scientifica delle industrie mecchaniche in Italia* (Milan, 1917), 3–4; cited in Paola Fiorentina, 'Ristrutturazione capitalistica e sfruttamento operaio in Italia negli anni '20', *Rivista Storica del Socialismo*, January–April 1967, 135–6. For an Italian discussion of the progress of Taylorism and scientific management in this period, see Angelo Mariotti, 'L'organizzazione del lavoro', *Rivista Italiana di Sociologia*, 1918.

37   Benito Mussolini, 'Novita', *Il Popolo d'Italia*, 1 August 1918, included in *Opera Omnia di Benito Mussolini*, XI (Florence: La Fenice, 1953); cf. also Renzo De Felice, *Mussolini il rivoluzionario* (Turin: Einaudi, 1965), 405–6; Roberto Vivarelli, *Il dopoguerra in Italia e l'avvento del fascismo (1918–1922)*, I (Napoli: Istituto Italiano per gli Studi Storici, 1967), 234–5, 271–7.

38   'Il sindicalismo nazionale. Per rinascere!' *Popolo d'Italia*, 17 November 1918; cited De Felice, *Mussolini*, 493–4; *Opera Omnia*, XII, 11–14. For the influence of Lysis on Mussolini see De Felice, 410. While De Felice sees Mussolini's 'productivism' as a new reformism seeking to undercut the socialists, Vivarelli emphasizes the link with rightwing nationalism from the outset.

Mussolini's *produttovismo* depended less on the engineer, or technology, than on the expert in general. One of the young exponents of fascist technocracy was to capture the prevailing imagery later, when he claimed: 'The fascist state is more than a state, it is a dynamo' – a rhetorical flourish reflecting the Futurist influence in the early movement.[39] Once in power, the fascists sought to establish committees of experts from all fields. The party statutes of autumn 1921 required local *fasci* to prepare lists of cooperative specialists in the public services and economic life. In theory, these *gruppi di competenza* were to furnish the Fascist Party with a general staff ready to take over the state; more practically, to win potential sympathizers by making the movement seem less narrowly ideological. Nonetheless, the cadres were conceived almost entirely in terms of restoring state and bureaucratic authority, oriented towards ministries, not factories. Those instituted in 1923, moreover, were presided over by leading government figures, which meant they could scarcely escape political supervision.[40]

The tentative character of the effort and its lack of real anchorage as a technocracy were demonstrated by the fate of the groups during the party disputes of 1923–4. Massimo Rocca, former journalist and champion of the *gruppi di competenza*, was also the exponent of fascist 'revisionism'. This represented a policy of normalization, a downgrading of the revolutionary claims of fascism, consequently of its local violence, its militia, *ras* and squadrist leadership such as that exercised by Roberto Farinacci of Cremona.[41] It was prepared to sacrifice ideological purity for the sake of collaboration with the liberal elites. This was a line Mussolini found useful to encourage during the initial year or so of his rule, especially as he looked forward to an electoral campaign that would consolidate his position in parlia-

39 Camillo Pellizzi, *Problemi e realtà del fascismo* (Florence, 1924), 165.
40 Alberto Aquarone, 'Aspirazioni tecnocratiche del primo fascismo', *Nord e Sud*, April 1964; Camillo Pelizzi *Una rivoluzione mancata* (Milan: Langanesi, 1949), esp. ch. I; Massimo Rocca, *Come il fascismo divenne una dittatura* (Milan: Librarie Italiane, 1952), 132 ff.
41 Massimo Rocca, 'Il fascismo e l'Italia', *Critica Fascista*, 15 September 1924, reprinted in Rocca, *Idee sul fascismo* (Florence: La Voce, 1924), esp. 64; also Rocca, 'Diciotto Brumaio,' *Critica Fascista*, 24 September 1923, now in Rocca, *Il primo fascismo* (Rome: G. Volpe, 1964), 99. For Rocca's memoirs: *Come il fascismo divenne una dittatura*, esp. 145 ff. For Farinacci's views see his article 'La seconda ondata', *Cremona Nuova*, 29 May 1923, cited in De Felice, *Mussolini il fascista, I. La conquista del potere (1921–1925)* (Turin: Einaudi, 1966), 413–15; also his letter to Mussolini of 4 August 1923, complaining about the preference given to non-fascist, even allegedly anti-fascist technical appointments. See *Segretaria particolare del Duce*, National Archives film, T 586 Roll 448, 062223–24. For a general discussion of the tendencies within the party, Giacomo Lumbroso, *La crisi del fascismo* (Florence: Vallecchi, 1925).

ment. Enjoying an electoral law that promised him two thirds of the seats, Mussolini chose a tactic of collaboration to woo the parliamentary notables of the liberal groups for his own slate, while simultaneously working to shatter their old party structures. With the electoral victory of April 1924, however, collaboration with non-fascists was less necessary, and the impatient stalwarts of a radical fascist policy could be appeased. Rocca, whom the fascist intransigents had sought to expel from the party in the fall of 1923, now came under renewed fire and was dropped. Moreover, in the late 1924 crises following the assassination of Matteotti, the spokesmen for integral party dictatorship prevailed over the voices for moderation and normalization, and in the process non-party technocratic aspirations succumbed.[42]

In fact, from the outset of 1924, the *gruppi di competenza* were being reshaped into less independent *consigli tecnici*, intended explicitly to serve only as bodies that would support the new rulers. In similar manner the syndicalist organizations of Edmondo Rossoni were being circumscribed in such a way that any independent labour-oriented objectives would be clearly subordinated to state and party requirements. The regime's growing commitment to state corporations instead of the former syndicates portended a general braking of any genuine radical experimentation. Fascist technocracy was to wane alongside this emasculation of any independent economic or administrative centres of expertise.[43]

In any case, the very concept of technocratic cadres suffered from a basic ideological equivocation. By appealing to production and technology, fascism, like Saint-Simonianism, wished to assert the role of a new ruling group originating outside the traditionally conceived classes. Fascist, or more precisely national-fascist ideology, resembled Taylorism in a key particular. It promised a 'non-zero-sum' world in which classes no longer prospered only at each other's expense, in contrast to the implications of the traditional spectrum of European ideologies, which were all zero-sum or redistributive. Their prescriptions entailed transferring portions of a given quantity of power, status, and wealth from one social group to another – or preventing such transfer. Marxism involved only the most radical redistributive objective. The appeal of Saint-Simonianism, or of the American engi-

42 For the political developments, see the works by Rocca cited in the preceding note; also *Mussolini il fascista*, 518–730; Luigi Salvatorelli and Giovanni Mira, *Storia d'Italia nel periodo fascista* (Turin: einaudi, 1957), 269–332; Adrian Lyttelton, 'Fascism in Italy: The Second Wave', *Journal of Contemporary History*, 1966, republished as *International Fascism, 1920–1945* (New York: Harper Torchbook, 1966), 75–100.

43 Aquarone, 'Aspirazioni tecnocratiche del primo fascismo', *loc. cit.*, 125–28; *L'organizzazione dello stato totalitario* (Turin: Einaudi 1965), 113–18.

neering vision, consisted precisely in its claim to avoid such painful transfers. Expanding productivity meant that no repartition of a fixed quantum of national wealth was required. Postulating a new social category of producers, or more narrowly, an elite of scientific managers who arbitrated conflict, meant that the hostile confrontation between the traditional classes was superseded.

While making similar claims, fascist ideology differed in some key respects. The model of social engineering indicated that internal disputes about power could be sublimated into technical questions of optimalization. Fascism added the concept that class disputes must dissolve before overriding clashes among nation-states: Italy as a whole was a proletariat among European powers. Secondly, if Saint-Simonianism stressed the contribution of a vanguard of entrepreneurs, and Taylorism spotlighted the engineers, fascism drew upon other potential leaders. Arising out of a fervent interventionist commitment, it posited the *combattenti* as a directing elite by virtue of their trials at the front. It did not reject the claims of technology and productivity to coordinate hitherto opposed interests, but these could not be the only claims to leadership; 'blood', and exposure in the trenches also counted.

This effort to combine technology with vitalist sources of energy contributed powerfully to the appeal of the right-radical ideology. German right-radicalism or so-called revolutionary conservatism often revealed the same problematic synthesis – a dual hostility to liberalism and to a materialism that the Left also condemned. The Werkbund, for example, attracted future right-radical spokesmen as well as democratic ones; and its early architects looked back to the inspiration of the *Rembrandtdeutscher*, Langbehn, who demanded a break with the stuffy and syncretic styles of the 1880s.[44] Oswald Spengler, who was considered one of the elders of Weimar's revolutionary conservative movement, symptomatically fused machine imagery and hostility to liberalism. 'The centre of this artificial and complicated realm of the Machine', he wrote, 'is the organizer and manager'. But with the manager was 'the *engineer*, the priest of the machine, the man who knows it . . . the machine's master and destiny'.[45] Nonetheless, Spengler saw the powers of money – 'our inner England' he called them elsewhere: 'capitalism and parliamentary liberalism'[46] – enslaving

44 Banham, *Theory and Design*, 72.
45 Oswald Spengler, *The Decline of the West* (Charles F. Atkinson, trans. New York: Knopf, 1932), II, 504–5.
46 Oswald Spengler, 'Prussianism and Socialism', *Selected Essays* (Engl. transl., Chicago, 1964), 87.

the forces of technology to be defeated, in their turn, only by 'blood' and a new Caesarist collectivism, or perhaps a Prussian socialism of labour and subordination to the state.[47] In Spengler's conception, therefore, technology could never replace power. Technocracy, strictly speaking, was impossible, even though the engineer was the indispensable auxiliary of rule in the machine age.

Thus from Sorel to Mussolini and the German conservative revolutionaries, the technological vision was incorporated in an uneasy relationship with a commitment to nonrational values. For its adherent there was a compelling psychological validity in the image of the engineer at the service of an aggressive national allegiance: the hard master of machine civilization sweeping away nineteenth-century sentimentality and petit-bourgeois democracy. The ideological effort to banish social conflict could invoke national power and a new authoritarianism as well as national welfare and slide-rule optimality. Hence it was consistent that America should be seen in a Janus-like perspective: the empire of technical rationality on the one hand, whose new cities so impressed and horrified men like Spengler (and Le Corbusier);[48] the embodiment, on the other hand, of a hypocritical Wilsonian democratic pathos – detested by nationalists in Italy and Germany as masking Anglo-Saxon financial imperialism. In that contradictory estimate was reflected the radical Right's own inner division between technological reason and the utilitarian rationality of liberalism.

The ambiguities of planning

Approaching the national syndicalism of the Right was a growing interest in planning among men of the Left. Walther Rathenau of AEG and his collaborator, the Prussian aristocrat and engineer Wichard von Moellendorf, elaborated their experience of organizing wartime production and raw-material allocation into a conception of *Planwirtschaft* to be preserved after hostilities ended. Socialist Party members such as Rudolf Wissell, who served as Economics Minister in 1919, and Max Cohen, who advocated a corporatist upper house, as well as Georg Bernhard, editor of the liberal *Vossische Zeitung*, close to the new Democratic Party and a proponent of a National Economic Council, likewise sought to structure the economy by combining elements of the leftist *Räte* (councils) idea with organic concepts of the state

47 Spengler, *Decline of the West*, II, 506; *Selected Essays*, 129–31.
48 Spengler, *Decline of the West*, II, 100–1, on the soullessness of checkerboard planning; Le Corbusier, *The City of Tomorrow*, 63, 76.

and community. What they all envisaged, in general, was a pyramid of industrial planning organs that would include representatives of the entrepreneurs, labour, and the state. With the power to set prices, allocate raw material and market shares, and generally determine economic policy, the new institutions were to embody the vision of class collaboration in the public interest. Even when the advocates of these schemes belonged, like Wissell, to the Social Democratic Party (SPD), they emphasized not proletarian hegemony, but maximum production for the *Gesamtheit* of German society.

But there were as many ambiguities in the Left's conception of planning as in the Right's attitude towards technocracy. It was assumed that by seating together the delegates of industry, labour, and consumers or the state, all decisions reached would be bound to ensure the public interest at large; furthermore, that political constraint could be banished from the economic sphere. Here, of course, was the same industrial utopianism that scientific management and wartime organization had suggested in America. In Germany, however, the attempt actually to institutionalize the vision in early Weimar led to difficulties that were not fully evident in the United States until the experiment with the National Recovery Administration.[49]

The institutional models for *Planwirtschaft* were borrowed primarily from Germany's wartime organization, including the war corporations of mixed state and private ownership that Rathenau had seen as a stage between capitalism and state socialism. The war also created the material preconditions for the collaboration of management and labour that was so central to the planning schemes. The ravenous appetite of the war effort for production at any price – more precisely, the demands of generals and industrialists for often irrational production at inordinate cost – facilitated the bargaining: the entrepreneurs could enjoy extraordinary profits, while trade union leaders won new influence over conditions of labour. Inflationary war finance obviated older conflicts over wages, as industry and labour together appropriated resources from the relatively fixed-income sectors of the economy.[50] Given wartime demand, a commitment to production

49 Cf. Ellis W. Hawley, *The New Deal and the Problem of Monopoly* (Princeton: Princeton University Press, 1966), 35–46, for the tensions within planning conceptions.
50 For Rathenau's views on war companies see the memo cited in Gerald Feldman, *Army, Industry, and Labor in Germany* (Princeton: Princeton University Press, 1966), 49. I have drawn upon this book in general for the description of the war's effects. Interestingly enough, the historian of the German wartime organization of raw material production, superintended by Rathenau and Moellendorf, also went on to discuss Taylorism: Otto Goebel, *Taylorismus in der Verwaltung* (Hanover: Helwingsche Verlagsbuchhandlung, 1927).

could indeed foster cooperation – but the community paid as well as benefited.

Rathenau and Moellendorff did not approve of the economic megalomania of the Hindenburg Plan, but they did wish to consolidate the new collaboration. Besides tackling the same administrative tasks together, they also shared similar spiritual predispositions. The great dynamos of German General Electric, and the austere image of Prussian discipline and tradition, captured their imagination equally. For Rathenau, who could never refrain from philosophizing, the modern era was characterized by the new machine order: 'It is a consolidation of the world into an unconscious association of constraint, into an uninterrupted community of production and economy'. But the way to master this technological destiny was not through any rancorous Marxism, but through a new moral consciousness and, as he suggested first, the 'depersonalization' of property by transforming private enterprises into foundations and giving title to employees, universities, or administrative authorities. In his subsequent discussion of the new economy Rathenau envisaged cartels, with state participation, to coordinate planning and eliminate the destructive aspects of competition: a public syndicalism of the producers analogous to the ideas of association contemplated in the United States as well.[51]

Moellendorff entertained similar ideals, although he occasionally dissented on details. The coming era, he believed, must be either socialist or anarchic; the engineer, moreover, would be central in making the choice. In his view of the engineer Moellendorf had before the war borrowed heavily from Taylorism, which he found Germanic in its intuitive daring. It imposed the criterion of competence as the ordering principle of the economic world, and it demonstrated that the resources of human labour were not a fixed limit upon production. Taylorism was the paradigm of what made America vital; it infused the economic system with the collective élan of those model, primitive German communities described by Tacitus.[52] 'If we really come to grasp Taylor fully we will choke off the evils of our economy from

---

51 Walther Rathenau, *Von kommenden Dingen,* [1916] *Gesammelte Schriften,* III (Berlin: S. Fischer, 1918), 35, 64 ff., 139–40, 158–9; cf. *Die neue Wirtschaft* [1917], *Gesammelte Schriften,* V (Berlin: S. Fischer, 1918), esp. 203 ff., 231 ff. for the state cartel concept: 'These structures are differentiated from the old guild system . . . no sanction for association of individual interests, no interest group of sovereign individual and small firms, but a community of production in which all members are organically interwoven' (235). On the constructive role of the state, 249–50; for the new order's role in advancing welfare, but not imposing a forced equality, 255. For Rathenau's critique of orthodox Social-Democratic solutions, see *Der neue Staat* (Berlin: S. Fischer, 1922), 38, 61 ff.
52 Wichard von Moellendorff, *Konservativer Sozialismus* (Hamburg: Hanseatische Verlagsanstalt, 1932), 34–46.

above and below: the confusion of the incompetent, the constraints of interest on the industrious, the arbitrariness of the shortsighted, the supremacy of the successful, the pity of the timid'. Moellendorff's vision was not without its authoritarian side: Taylorism functioned in his eyes as a 'militarism of production', training workers to drop their complaints about the inevitable division between management and labour.[53] Like Taylor's hierarchical but conflict-free economy, Moellendorff's embodied a stern collectivism. Although he remained to assist Wissell in the capacity of under-secretary at the Economics Ministry he always disliked the debates over the meaning of 'socialization', to which he preferred the concept of *Gemeinwirtschaft*, roughly an economic commonwealth.[54]

Was it surprising that the Social-Democratic leaders, once they had time to reflect on the memoranda being prepared in Wissell's ministry, were far from happy? They confronted a central dilemma: the responsibility of parliamentary leadership without the power to reshape the economy after they had renounced a *Räte* regime and quick expropriation measures. Once they had opted for a parliamentary democracy, would not the results of a self-administered *Gemeinwirtschaft* really depend upon the power that each side could bring to bear within the organs of political and economic administration? The SPD was understandably confused as to whether planning ideas would advance or hinder socialism. The debates over Taylorism within the party were indicative in this respect. In March 1919, Otto Bauer argued that 'in a democratic and rationally socialized state', Taylorism would serve to increase productivity and thus help the country to acquit the reparation debt more quickly. Two years later Kurt Lewin argued that Taylorism – by which he really meant industrial psychology as a whole – could serve a socialist regime by allocating people to professions not on the basis of a class-biased training, but according to competence.[55] Taylorism, in short, could legitimately assist socialism in power. But was socialism in power?

The occasional discussion of Taylorism in its narrow sense raised the very issues which marked the more momentous controversies over

53   Ibid., 49–51, 56.
54   Ibid., 118–24. From *Der Aufbau der Gemeinwirtschaft; Denkschrift des Reichswirtschafts-ministeriums vom 7. Mai 1919* (Jena, 1919).
55   Bauer decree of 19 March 1919 and comment in Gustav Pietsch, 'Das Taylorsystem', *Neue Zeit*, 19 September 1919; Kurt Lewin, *Die Sozialisierung des Taylorsystems* (Berlin: Verlag Gesellschaft, und Erziehung, 1921). Naturally, when labour spokesmen looked at the implications for conditions of work, and not the increment to production, they were less happy; Pietsch's complaint – that man is made into a mere cog in the machine – was a typical criticism. By the mid 1920s, however, German and French labour were more willing to accept Taylorite proposals, so long as they did not imply mere speed-up. See Devinat, *Scientific Management, passim.*

the economic agencies of the new regime. The more radical Independent Socialists, often the labour rank and file, desired as great a scope as possible for the factory councils that were composed of worker representatives. Trade union leaders looked with distrust upon the efforts to anchor these *Betriebsräte* in the new constitution, but in the wake of the huge strikes of spring 1919 had to acquiesce in this demand. Union leaders, and the quasi-corporatist socialists of the *Sozialistische Monatshefte*, including Max Cohen, preferred so-called parity-based economic governing bodies – i.e. composed equally of workers and employers – along the lines of the Arbeitsgemeinschaft that union leaders and industrialists had worked out of their own accord. At the second congress of *Räte* delegates in April 1919, and then at the SPD congress at Weimar in June, Cohen advocated a Labour Chamber as upper house of the new parliament. The Labour Chamber would emanate from production councils, in which professional men, entrepreneurs, and labour representatives would co-operate to safeguard production and ward off rash nationalization projects. Here was a scheme close in intent to the Rathenau–Moellendorff–Wissell ideas, and indeed Cohen shared their assumptions. Socialism in his eyes meant little more than an easier path to enhanced productivity, and it required a continuing partnership with the entrepreneurs, if not as capitalists, then as industrial experts.[56] In short, his plans really abandoned any significant redistribution of power to the working class, concentrating instead on seeking a harmony that would eliminate the need for socialism or workers control.

Actually, the SPD was so used to arguing in terms of a general democratic commitment to the community as a whole that the socialism it did press for had little institutional bite – witness the ineffective Reich Coal Council established in the spring of 1919. Moderate socialists did not really desire a victory of the proletariat at the cost of production, a course that seemed suicidal given the position of the Allies. To consolidate parliamentary democracy, furthermore, was thought the surest way to uplift the working class. Nevertheless, did not Cohen's plans mean the emasculation of any gains in the economic sphere? Enough pitfalls seemed to loom ahead for the SPD to reject

---

56 For the Cohen arguments: *Protokoll über die Verhandlungen des Parteitages der SPD abgehalten in Weimar am 15/16. Juni 1919* (Berlin, 1919), 422–8. Cohen was debating against Hugo Sinzheimer, who brilliantly defended the *Räte*, concurred in the idea of a planned economy with priority for the 'needs of the whole community', but wanted no incorporation of *Räte*-based delegates in parliament, lest a chamber of councils degenerate into a mere representation of interest groups. Ibid., 413–16. On the general problem of the *Räte* and the conflicting pressures in early 1919 see Peter von Oertzen, *Betriebsräte in der Novemberrevolution* (Düsseldorf: Droste, 1963). For the link between *Räte* and planned-economy notions, cf. Rudolf Wissell, 'Zur Räte Idee', *Neue Zeit*, 30 May 1919, 195 ff.

the general conceptions of *Planwirtschaft*, first within the cabinet in July 1919, then finally at the Kassel congress in late 1920. As Karl Landauer admitted, according to organizational criteria, industrial rationalization and planning might appear a step towards socialism. Misleadingly so, however; for without working-class power such planning institutions would only rationalize capitalism.[57]

Here in fact lay the seductiveness of planning for many of the socialists to begin with. From Hilferding's 1910 analysis of finance-capital on, the era of capitalist cartellization and concentration was interpreted as a transformation of the bourgeois economy which might temporarily postpone its collapse but would ultimately render at least the economic transition to socialism all the easier. Even Lenin had accepted this view, and thereafter was also able to endorse a stage of state capitalism that amounted to trustification under proletarian auspices. To Russian observers, in fact, the German war economy, with its nascent planning, actually embodied the economic aspect of the transformation. In his first months of power, Lenin openly endorsed Taylorism as a means to reinforce Soviet power. His economic advisers, Milyutin and Larin, drew explicitly on the notions of Rathenau and Moellendorff; and continuing into the twenties, industrial trusts under Bolshevik command served as a flexible framework within which to reorganize a shattered economy.[58] What was crucial, however, was that Lenin

---

57 For rejection of Wissell's proposals on *Planwirtschaft* see the cabinet meeting of 8 July, 'Alte Reichskanzlei, Kabinett-Protokolle', National Archives German Foreign Ministry Films 1349/742683–731; also the National Assembly session of 28 July: *Verhandlungen der verfassungsgebenden deutschen Nationalversammlung*, Bd. 328, 1848 ff. For Karl Landauer's comment see 'Planwirtschaft. Ein Nachwort zum Parteitage', *Neue Zeit*, 10 December 1920, 249–56. For a recent socialist view making the same point see Wolfgang Abendroth, 'Die Alternative der Planung: Planung zur Erhaltung des Spätkapitalismus oder Planung in Richtung auf eine klassenlose Gesellschaft', in *Antagonistische Gesellschaft und politische Demokratie* (Neuwied: Luchterhand, 1967).

58 V. I. Lenin, 'The Taylor system, the last word of capitalism in this respect, like all capitalist progress, is a combination of the subtle brutality of bourgeois exploitation and a number of its greatest scientific achievements in the field of analysing mechanical motions during work, the elimination of superfluous and awkward motions, the working out of correct methods of work, the introduction of the best system of accounting and control, etc. The Soviet Republic must at all costs adopt all that is valuable in the achievements of science and technology in this field. The possibility of building Socialism will be determined precisely by our success in combining the Soviet government and the Soviet organization of administration with the modern achievements of capitalism. We must organize in Russia the study and teaching of the Taylor system and systematically try it out and adapt it to our purposes.' 'The Immediate Tasks of the Soviet Government', *Izvestia*, 28 April 1918; translated in V. I. Lenin, *Selected Works* (2 vols., Moscow: International Publishing House, 1947), II, 327. For the economic policies of Lenin and his advisers, and the question of trusts and planning, see E. H. Carr, *The Bolshevik Revolution* (3 vols. London: Macmillan, 1950–3), II, 86–95 on state-capitalism, 109–15 on productivity and Taylorism.

had seized effective power before instituting steps towards planning; he had settled the central *kto-kogo* (who-whom) question, and this the German Social Democrats had not done. Taylorism and planning could indeed serve Soviet rule, but were no substitute for it; communism, as Lenin said, might be Soviet power plus electrification – but not electrification alone.[59] Finally, if in the West Taylorism was incorporated into ideologies that denied the necessary existence of class conflict, in Russia it could be accepted precisely because that conflict had been decided and a new era of relationships had opened.

What happened when the Left embraced the utopias of productivity before securing power was demonstrated by the sequel to planning in Germany. Cohen's idea for a Chamber of Labour and Production Council finally was incorporated in the Constitution in a compromise form. A Reich Economic Council, *Reichswirtschaftsrat*, which would group employee, employer, and public representatives and would advise the parliament on legislative proposals, was to crown a pyramid of economic advisory organs. It found its strongest champions among those bourgeois democrats, such as Georg Bernhard, who wished to keep labour in a partnership of moderation. Nevertheless, Bernhard was not entirely happy. He had endorsed Cohen's original plans for the same reason the Left had rejected them – as a step beyond the idea of nationalization towards achieving a 'real equalization of the producers – entrepreneurial producers and labour producers'.[60] What had emerged, however, was a compromise that the SPD had permitted in order to appease the discontents of those working-class elements who wanted an autonomous role for the *Räte*. Rather than submerge all the workers councils into parity committees, the plans for a hierarchy of economic organs amalgamated *Räte* delegates and industry's representatives only at the institutional summit of the projected system:

Nothing more of any Building of Production is to be discovered here. All ideas seeking to create a new professional ethos in the worker and to summon him to co-operation in productive labour to construct our national economic life have been rejected. In place of a productive socialism the fulfilment of an old union propaganda demand has intervened. In place of a reconciliation

59 Ibid., II, 360–75, on the origins of planning and its relationship to the dominant class.
60 Georg Bernhard, *Wirtschaftsparlamente von den Revolutionsräten zum Reichswirtschaftsrat* (Vienna: Rikola, 1923), 42. For an English discussion of the Economic Council: Herman Finer, *Representative Government and a Parliament of Industry. A Study of the German Federal Economic Council* (London: Fabian Society, Allen Unwin, 1923).

of the antagonisms between employer and employee on behalf of a common fruitful cooperation in the service of the enterprise, the old wall between workers and entrepreneurs has been thickened.[61]

In fact, Bernhard had no need to worry. The subordinate economic councils never came into existence; hence the *Räte* influence never reached the Reichswirtschaftsrat directly, and – as its records in Potsdam reveal – the latter rarely progressed beyond stalemate and paralysis.[62]

The final pathetic testimony to the frustrations of the German Left in their invocation of productivity was provided by the renewal of the coal nationalization controversy in mid-1920. Labour reiterated its demand for public control, but was outmanoeuvred largely by the very institutional vagueness their acceptance of production as a goal entailed. Rathenau's scheme for self-administration became the main proposal for discussion, but where in the suggested structure of self-administration would authority rest? And who would guard the guardians? Even Hugo Stinnes and his collaborator Paul Silverberg managed to exploit the flexibility of self-administration schemes by presenting a grandiose programme that would have given public authority to their own enterprises – all in the name of productivity and the common good![63]

The Stinnes plans of 1920 revealed the dangerous institutional ambiguity that all the productivist ideas for transcending class conflict incorporated. Stinnes' insistence upon the necessity of increasing output, which actually meshed with his own interests, represented the logical end-point of the moderates' ideal of productivity. What had in fact occurred was that the original stress on engineering by a

---

61 Bernhard, *Wirtschaftsparlament*, 46.
62 The Reichswirtschaftsrat functioned actively from 1921 through 1923 and was thereafter restricted in role. Though not a policy-making body, it provided a forum for argument and testimony, usually splitting over reports favourable to industry and those welcome to labour; and could therefore usefully delay proposals that internally-divided ministries wished to cool off. For its records: Deutsches Zentralarchiv, Potsdam, Aktenbestand 04.01; cf. C. D. H. Hauschild, *Der vorläufige Reichswirtschaftsrat 1920–1926* (Berlin: Mittler, 1926).
63 The original article drew here on my unpublished Ph.D. dissertation, 'The Strategies of Bourgeois Defense, 1918–1924: A Study of Conservative Politics and Economics in France, Germany, and Italy' (Harvard University, 1966). The account there was subsequently published in revised form in *Recasting Bourgeois Europe* (Princeton: Princeton University Press, 1975), 194–225. Major sources include *Verhandlungen der Sozialisierungs-Kommission für den Bergbau im Jahre 1920* (2 vols., Berlin, 1920); Bundesarchiv Koblenz, Paul Silverberg Nachlass; Bundesarchiv Koblenz, Reichskanzlei papers, 'Verhandlungen des Unterausschusses der Sozialisierungsfrage', R 43 I/2114.

Moellendorf had subtly evolved into an emphasis primarily upon corporate reorganization. Like the scientific-management enthusiasts in America, Stinnes, and even Rathenau – for despite their celebrated clashes they shared many key attitudes – wanted private networks of producers to form the nuclei of public authority. To be sure, Rathenau intended a more truly public commitment than Stinnes did; but institutionally his schemes did not guarantee this to any greater degree, for they depended upon little more than a moral commitment to community. Moreover, what was now the substance of these organs for planning and production was no longer technical expertise, but financial manipulation. The two aspects of enterprise that Veblen, for one, had always separated, now became fused in business conceptions in Weimar Germany – and with the exploitative results Veblen had feared. In the last analysis, however, this development was not confined to Germany alone: it was to remain a central ambiguity in all conceptions of technocracy or planning that devolved authority upon private interests. Whether in fascist Italy or liberal Weimar, those who by invoking industrial utopias sought to deny the relevance of power, subordinated themselves to those who really had power, political or economic. But perhaps that was what they actually desired.

Fordism and the rationalization of capitalism

With the period of 'stabilization' in Europe came significant changes in the ideological implications of industrial productivity. Here only the salient transformations can be indicated. From mid-decade it was the German-elaborated concept of 'rationalization' that dominated discussions of scientific management. Rationalization focused upon enhancing productivity and technical efficiency, but above all it was associated in Germany with extensive corporation activity – the formation of new cartel-like arrangements upon the ruins of such fragile vertical configurations of the inflation period as the Stinnes empire. German spokesmen, however, still credited the United States with originating the underlying ideas; and American businessmen, such as Edward Filene of Boston and his Twentieth Century Fund, continued to sponsor international studies and congresses to advance scientific management.[64] But the favoured images of advanced tech-

64   See Devinat, *Scientific Management in Europe*, esp. preface and 63 ff. National organizations of importance included the Reichskuratorium für Wirtschaftlichkeit, the Masaryk Labour Academy in Prague, the Institut Solvay in Brussels, dedicated to the 'productivist', Saint-Simonian views of its founder, the Russian 'Time Leagues' and the All-Russian Scientific Management Conference, and the Italian Ente

niques that America presented to the world were changing. The teachings of Taylorism, in its strict sense, were viewed more critically, while Fordism became the vogue. A German commentator explained the change as a widening of scope: while Taylorism concerned only the management of labour, Ford's doctrines stressed reorganization of the entire productive process.[65] In part this was a rationalization, for Taylorism, too, had earlier been interpreted in the widest sense. But now for practical reasons European apostles of scientific management and rationalization chose to confine Taylorism to its original concern with labour efficiency, thus limiting its utopian implications at the same time. Conversely, the contributions of Ford – the moving assembly line, standardization, and the enlargement of a mass market by low prices and high wages – were seized upon to prove the social potential open to capitalism and large-scale industry, as they existed. Paradoxically, Ford's images of abundance best served the bourgeois-conservative, often Malthusian ends of European business and industry in the later 1920s. Fordism, in sum, offered a technological élan for the beneficiaries of the economic system that Taylorism could not safely provide.

The change arose in large part from the general economic situation of the later 1920s. Currency stabilization and revaluation, accompanied by sharp, if brief, deflationary pressures, characterized much of the

---

Nazionale per l'Organizzazione Scientifica (ENIOS). The best overall survey for rationalization in its European home is Robert Brady, *The Rationalization Movement in German Industry* (Berkeley: University of California Press, 1933). Congresses were held at Prague in 1924, Brussels 1925, and Rome 1927; an International Management Institute was formed in Geneva in January 1927.

65 G. Briefs, 'Rationalisierung der Arbeit', in: Industrie- und Handelskammer zu Berlin, *Die Bedeutung der Rationalisierung für das deutsche Wirtschaftsleben* (Berlin: Stilke, 1928), 41: 'Only one name need be cited here, that of Ford, who developed American rationalization of labour beyond its Taylorite excess and built it into the larger rhythm of the flowing production process. . . . If in Taylor the unveiled profit idea is dominant, with Ford it reigns only within the limits of the idea of social service.' Cf. Ernest Mercier: 'what the average European understands by "Taylorism" tends towards a rigid doctrine that industrial practice has abandoned in many cases to adopt a more supple solution'; he added that the last word in scientific organization was symbolized by *travail à la chaine*, i.e. Ford's assembly line. See 'Les conséquences sociales de la rationalisation en France', in *L'aspect social de la rationalisation*, Redressment Français (Paris, 1927). On the other hand, one commentator was willing to put both men in perspective: 'No matter how important the influence of a Ford or a Taylor, what is it compared to that of a Luther or Rousseau?' A. Verdurand, 'L'homme d'affaires et la France', *Revue de France*, 31 December 1927, 618. For the doctrine that inspired all this, as touched up by subordinates, see Henry Ford, *My Philosophy of Industry* (1921). For a survey of German responses to Fordism see Peter Berg, *Deutschland und Amerika 1918–29* (Lubeck: Matthiesen, 1963), 96–132.

period. Although national incomes rose, the increases were associated with severe sectoral or class dislocation: American agriculture and the European coal and steel industry were burdened with excess capacity. More ominously, the fear that the market would be saturated acted as a major spur to rationalization in Europe, with its emphasis upon cutting factor costs, including that of labour. A French spokesman for rationalization pointed to the 'notable diminution of the internal market', and the threat of rigorous foreign competition for customers at home and abroad. A German advocate wrote that the benefit of scientific management to labour must always be smaller in Germany than in the United States, for if America could produce primarily for her own domestic market, German goods had to be competitive abroad and consequently wages had to remain low.[66] The coal and steel men of the continent were engaged in long and wearying negotiations to stabilize market quotas without price competition.[67] All this tended to reorient the thrust of scientific-management ideas. No longer an economic policy that promised a radical reorganization of society with gains for all, the emphasis on engineering and scientific management took on what we have termed a redistributionist or zero-sum role. Despite protestations to the contrary, rationalization entailed an effort, first to subordinate small producers to large-scale industry, second to reduce the percentage claims of labour upon output as a whole. Fordism justified these policies as a commitment to abundance. In American practice often conservative, Taylorism's stress on the technocrat had a disquieting potential for subversion; Fordism refurbished the entrepreneur directly.

The new conservative role for scientific management doctrines was certainly evident in Germany and Italy. The enthusiasm for rationalization in the Weimar Republic accompanied the four-year political domination of the conservative and bourgeois parties, not the governments with SPD participation. It was prefaced by a stabilization crisis which brought a contraction of credit that not only spurred industrial concentration but encouraged harsh measures against the trade union gains of 1918.[68] In Italy, during an era of strait-jacketing

---

66   Auguste Detoeuf, *La réorganisation industrielle* (Paris: Redressement Français, 1927); Bruno Birnbaum, *Organisation der Rationalisierung Amerika-Deutschland* (Berlin: Hobbing, 1927), 70–1.
67   Valuable documentation on these parleys is provided by the National Archives, German Foreign Ministry films: L 177, Handakten Min. Dir. Ritter. See, now, Maier, *Recasting Bourgeois Europe*, 516–45.
68   See Ludwig Preller, *Sozialpolitik in der Weimarer Republik* (Stuttgart: F. Mittelbach, 1949), 294–316; Hans-Hermann Hartwich, *Arbeitsmarkt, Verbände und Staat, 1918–1933* (Berlin: de Gruyter, 1967), *passim*; for the employers' viewpoint: Hermann Buecher, *Finanz-und Wirtschaftsentwicklung Deutschlands in den Jahren 1921 bis 1925* (Berlin: Heymann, 1925), 41–53.

of labour, manufacturers organized one of the most active cadres for scientific management in Europe – ENIOS – and played host to a congress of like-minded associations in Rome in September 1927. In practical terms, it aimed at the subordination of the many small producers to the large firms and the ascendancy of *Confindustria* policies within the councils of state.

Italian rationalization took place within a context analogous to the German; it accompanied a government shift to protectionism and a deflationary reconversion to the gold standard. In such a transition, with its own liquidity crisis, concentration of industries and pressure on wages was a logical response; nor were the fascist labour organizations likely to resist. *L'organizzazione del Lavoro*, therefore, tended to add up to a search for methods of cost-cutting by which the major metallurgical and electrical industries might survive advantageously under changed conditions.[69]

This general redirection of emphasis characterized France and Britain too in the later 1920s. With the contradictory policies of a divided Left between 1924 and 1926, discontent with the French parliamentary regime became more pronounced. The American image of technological expertise contrasted with the spectacle of floundering policies at home; furthermore, it reinforced the drive for consolidation and overhaul on the part of spokesmen for the new large-scale mechanized industries. The most typical product of the growing vogue for Americanism was probably Ernest Mercier's *Redressement Français*. This association, founded during the last protracted agonies of the Cartel des Gauches, represented an effort to form a directing elite of economic experts supposedly above party politics, a cadre for institutional and industrial modernization.[70]

The Redressement recapitulated the themes inherent in the quest for productivity. America again loomed as a model of class collaboration and, thanks to Secretary of Commerce Hoover, of efforts at standardization and elimination of waste.[71] Even if there were no 'definitive solution to the social question', Mercier noted, the United

---

69 Rosario Romeo, *Breve storia della grande industria in Italia* (Bologna: Cappelli, 1963), 153–6; Felice Guarneri, *Battaglie economiche tra le due grandi guerre* (2 vols. Milan: Garzanti, 1953), I, 113–39, 146–59; Fiorentina, loc. cit., 137–45.

70 R. F. Kuisel, *Ernest Mercier, French Technocrat* (Berkeley: University of California Press, 1967), 45–88, provides the basic discussion of the Redressement that I have drawn upon.

71 Ernest Mercier, *La production et le travail* (Paris: Redressement Français, 1927), 10–16. Mercier had visited the US in 1925 and met Filene, Dennison, and other enthusiasts of scientific management. Cf. Detoeuf, *La réorganisation industrielle*, 67–80, on American rationalization. For the link with Saint-Simonian themes, cf. E. S. Mason, 'Saint-Simonism and the Rationalization of Industry', *Quarterly Journal of Economics*, August 1931.

States had achieved far more than 'a simple truce'; and another writer stated his conviction 'that there are formulas of economic and social union which enrich the whole of a country without impoverishing its poorest elements'.[72] Rationalization, its advocates believed, or at least claimed, 'promised a real social revolution'.[73] Throughout French industry enthusiasm for American neo- or super-capitalism marked the late 1920; the years that saw Lindbergh vault the Atlantic witnessed a growing adulation for Fordism as well. André Tardieu, who filled the technical ministries in the Poincaré cabinet of 1926–9, pledged the government to ship and road construction. When he succeeded to the premiership himself, he declared a five-year programme for 'national retooling'.[74]

Despite the rhetorical promises of social revolution and the sweeping vistas of modernization, the ideological implications of the new fashion were actually far less radical than those of the movements earlier in the decade. The political and economic analysis of a Mercier was obviously unlikely to indulge in any anti-capitalism. Spokesmen of the Redressement condemned not a parasitic financial network but the inefficiency of the traditional small producer. Their calls for concentration implied primarily an effort to take over middle-level manufacturers. An artisanate whose semi-luxury trades did not encroach upon industrial production could be praised as a valuable sheet-anchor of French social stability, but the small factory that resisted centralization and standardization was allegedly a threat to progress.[75] Furthermore, even the technological imagery of the rationalization movement in France was not without its pastoralism. If in Soviet Russia vast hydroelectric projects stood for revolutionary transformation, industrial and political leaders in France praised grid development for saving the small domestic producers of the countryside and slowing

---

72 Mercier, *La production et le travail*, 25; Detoeuf, *La réorganisation industrielle*, I. Among social consequences, of course, was possible unemployment, but both authors thought it would be only transitory: Mercier, 'Les conséquences sociales', loc. cit., 16, 41–2; Detoeuf, 41–2.

73 Mercier, 'Les conséquences sociales de la rationalisation', 19.

74 Rudolph Binion, *Defeated Leaders* (New York: Columbia University Press, 1960), 289–92. For the general enthusiasm: P. Bourgoin, 'La rationalisation', *Revue de France*, 15 November 1929; Pierre-Etienne Flandin, 'Le problème social, *Revue de Paris*, 1 February 1928; Edmond Giscard d'Estaing, 'Le Néocapitalisme', *Revue des Deux Mondes*, 1 August 1928.

75 On the artisanate, Mercier, 'Les conséquences sociales de la rationalisation', 32. Lucien Romier, editor of the *Journée Industrielle*, then *Le Figaro*, stressed the need to overcome excessive individualism, and was second in eminence within the Redressement. See Kuisel, *Mercier*, 64–5.

down rural depopulation.[76] Indeed, Mercier's own social analysis reflected a bourgeois conservative traditionalism, far from any right-radical *ressentiment*. The masses needed and deserved welfare benefits, but had no capacity to assume direction of the country or of its industrial plant: 'What one expects from the workers appears at first glance most simple. It is a question merely of their understanding and accepting the necessities.'[77] Labour unions had to switch from sterile political agitation to collaboration on restricted professional issues. In general, Mercier's managerial elitism emerged as a new defence of that very traditional French bulwark, the bourgeoisie; and his own parliamentary dream was the venerable Union Nationale of the centre groupings. The social policy of the Redressement faded off into the traditional justifications of capitalism by many prominent business politicians of the late twenties, including André François Poncet and Pierre-Étienne Flandin, some of whom ended up with Vichy.[78]

Rationalization in Europe, therefore, was only a stunted offspring of the American productive vision as originally conceived. It served a conservative business community seeking to exploit, first the transition to overall non-inflationary monetary conditions, then the prosperous but increasingly saturated market of the later 1920s. Gramsci's insight was thus partially correct, when at the end of the decade he wrote, 'What is today called Americanism is in large part the preemptive critique of the old strata, who are precisely the ones who will be shattered by the new order, and are already prey to a wave

---

76 On this theme: Maurice-Charles Bellet, *La politique générale de la Fédération Républicaine de France* (Paris, 1924), which saw electricity saving the French rural family, and Detoeuf, *La réorganisation industrielle*, 33.

77 Ernest Mercier, *La production et le travail*, 59–60. Cf. Mercier, 'Réflexions sur l'élite', *Revue des Deux Mondes*, 15 February 1928.

78 On Mercier's politics, Kuisel, *Mercier*, 81. For A. F. Poncet: *Réflexions d'un républicain moderne* (Paris: Grasset, 1925); for the success of American-style capitalism in solving the social question, Flandin, loc. cit., and Giscard d'Estaing, loc. cit. The business 'moderates' who embraced Fordism can be usefully set off against the more radical syndicalists; for their ideas: René Pinon, 'Les nouvelles conceptions de l'état', *Revue Economique Internationale*, October 1929. Georges Valois was a leading exponent of a syndical system that would replace the parliamentary regime. He had started as a disciple of Georges Sorel, participated uneasily in the Action Française, and organized the Faisceau in the mid-1920s, then broke with the Redressement after 1930. For Mercier's denunciation of syndicalism as 'the Soviet method', Kuisel, 72. For the concept of *synarchie* – a conspiratorial view of an elitist and semi-fascist technocracy – which has marked some French discussions of Vichy, Mercier, the 1930s 'X-crise', as well as Clémentel, see André Ullmann and Henri Ayzeau, *Synarchie et pouvoir* (Paris: Julliard, 1968). Mercier denounced syndical representation as 'the Soviet method' (Kuisel, 72). For a sample of syndical writings see Sammy Beracha, *Rationalisation et révolution* (Paris: Valois, 1930), esp. 38.

of social panic, dissolution, and desperation.'[79] In fact, the strata involved were not only the old ones, for they included the most dynamic of the entrepreneurs. Nevertheless Gramsci's conception of social defence was justified. A radical Americanism had arisen as a concomitant of war production – production, after all, without effective price and demand constraints – but in the changed conditions a decade later, its social function altered. In different ways, Tardieu and Hoover (and, it might be argued, even Stalin)[80] took over the most easily manipulated aspects of Americanism, but each came to subordinate its claims as an autonomous social vision to his own ideology. The trajectory of the technological vision ended with the Great Engineer an impotent Depression President and a querulous defender of the propertied classes.

Even at the bottom of the Depression, however, the chiliastic idea of productivity and social engineering could flare again briefly. Howard Scott's Technocracy captured the American imagination in late 1932 and struck a chord in Europe.[81] Scott, an eccentric heir of Gantt and The New Machine, had organized a so-called Technical Alliance in 1921, and sold Technocracy as a messianic prediction of energy utilization. Recalling Veblen's contrast of pecuniary manipulation and industrial production, Scott detached real energy resources from the conventions of the price system. Even as he wrote, he said, a corps of engineers was preparing a huge energy inventory that would prepare the way for an age of fabulous leisure. Because of its messianic promise and its recognition of the disequilibrium between industrial potential and real income distribution, Technocracy did respond to felt needs, but it grew not out of the flush of American economic success, but out of the crisis of capitalism; it exemplified the quackery of despair, not the vision of triumph. In fact, the conditions of the Depression necessarily undermined all Americanist industrial utopias.

79 Gramsci, *Note sul Machiavelli*, 343–4.
80 For an introduction to the story of American engineers in Russia during the plan, see Peter Filene, *Americans and the Soviet Experiment, 1917–1933* (Cambridge, Mass: Harvard University Press, 1966); W. H. G. Armytage, *The Rise of the Technocrats* (London: Routledge & Kegan Paul, 1965), 219 ff. But cf. the speech of Bukharin to Soviet engineers in February 1932, reminding them that engineers must still subordinate themselves to the dictatorship of the proletariat, not aspire to a technocracy. Cited Dorfman, *Thorstein Veblen and his America*, 514.
81 On technocracy, Dorfman, 510 ff.; Howard Scott et al., *Introduction to Technocracy* (New York: Technocracy, Inc., 1933); Allen Raymond, *What is Technocracy?* (New York: McGraw-Hill, 1933); A. M. Schlesinger, Jr., *The Crisis of the Old Order, 1919–1933* (Boston: Houghton Mifflin, 1957). European comment: Erich Kraemer, *Was ist Technokratie?* (Berlin: K. Wolff, 1933); Karl Resar, *Technokratie, Weltwirtschaftskrise und ihre endgueltige Beseitigung* (Vienna: C. Barth, 1935).

Economic contraction destroyed the postulates for class collaboration and discredited the managers of the system. At least until the second world war and its aftermath, America's model of industrial productivity lost its catalytic inspiration. Not that Roosevelt's social experimentation would not attract followers, but the supreme confidence in technology and production, in engineering as social redemption, perished with the other dreams of the twenties.

POSTSCRIPT: IDEOLOGIES OF INDUSTRIAL MANAGEMENT SINCE THE DEPRESSION

For a theoretical inquiry into the course of civilized life as it runs in the immediate present, therefore, and as it is running into the proximate future, no single factor in the cultural situation has an importance equal to that of the business man and his work.

Veblen, *The Theory of Business Enterprise*

Prescriptions for management hardly disappeared in the Depression, even if Taylorism and Fordism lost their luster. In some ways business ideologies actually became more grandiose and imperial in their implications – imperial in the sense that increasingly the task of imposing order in the factory seemed impossible unless the encompassing political economic milieu was also to be transformed. From 1910 to 1930 Taylorism, in effect, claimed that the engineer could reorder society even as he intervened to allocate tasks inside the plant. Although the Depression tarnished this project, another concept became pervasive. From the 1930s through the next decade and into the post-war years, the manager was increasingly envisaged as psychologist. His task was to make employees happy and motivated, not merely to harness workers to machines. After World War II a further claim was added: the enlightened manager was called upon to help shape national policies and values. Could he not best ensure the future of his own enterprise by influencing what happened outside its walls as well as within? Indeed, those walls seemed to become more and more porous. Thus the arenas for managerial intervention became increasingly ambitious. Taylorite managers had to govern the shop floor; managers of the 1930s had to win their employees' hearts and minds, and the idealized businessmen of the post-war period had to help shape national economic and social priorities. The continuing premise was that, if the social environment influenced the factory and its workers, managerial activists had eventually to alter society itself. The line between enterprise and capitalist environment became increasingly hazy. Managing the factory and managing society were envisaged as tasks of the same order and drawing on the same talents.

Most recently the student of managerial visions can discern an additional concept: the manager as strategist, the business leader directing corporate acquisitions or divestment in a global economic milieu. This essay can only allude to this mission, which has been increasingly in vogue since the 1960s. It differs from the earlier three concepts, for they tended to envisage the manager's role as a homeostatic one designed to preserve or restore the equilibrium of the enterprise. The assumption that a given productive unit should tend toward equilibrium, however, suggested a confidence in Western economic capacity that after a decade of inflation and stagnation tended to dissipate. In different ways each of the managerial ideologies discussed here reflected an economic confidence that in the early 1980s had at least temporarily been eroded.

Before the twentieth century a self-conscious vocation of management hardly existed in its own right. Nonetheless, business skills were becoming professionalized. American society began to train its industrialists and financiers as the Wharton School of Finance and Economy opened in 1881, to be followed by similar establishments at Chicago and the University of California – each adding instruction in commerce to augment the engineering curricula that had earlier been viewed as the academic preparation for industrialists, insofar as one had been required at all. If Veblen argued that the modern businessman too often worked for the 'derangement' and corruption of the industrial process, he remained a dissenter. By the time Schumpeter wrote his treatise on economic development, he placed the entrepreneur, who combined all needed business skills 'for the joy of creating, of getting things done,'[82] at the heart of innovation and progress.

Management, however, also entailed concern for the enterprise as a social organization and not merely as a productive unit. It drew on legacies of paternalism derived from social Catholicism on the European continent, from evangelical reform in Protestant cultures, and

82   On business education, Edward Chase Kirkland, *Dream and Thought in the Business Community, 1860–1900* (Chicago: Quadrangle, 1964), 89–100; for Veblen on 'derangement,' *The Theory of Business Enterprise*, 22, and chap. 3 for the general theme. For Joseph Schumpeter's view, *The Theory of Economic Development*, [1911], Redvers, Opie, trans. (New York: Oxford University Press, 1961), 93. On entrepreneurship see Alfred D. Chandler, Jr., *The Visible Hand* (Cambridge, Mass.: Harvard University Press, 1977); and Chandler, 'The Emergence of Managerial Capitalism,' *Business History Review*, 58, 4 (1984): 473–503; Alfred Chandler and Herman Daems, eds., *Managerial Hierarchies* (Cambridge, Mass.: Harvard University Press, 1980); Leslie Hannah, ed., *Management Strategy and Business Development* (London: Macmillan, 1976); also Jürgen Kocka's essay on Germany in *The Cambridge Economic History of Europe*, vol. VII, part 1 (Cambridge University Press, 1977), chap. 10.

from the liberals' search for rehabilitative institutions in the late eighteenth and early nineteenth centuries. The theme of concern for the moral and material welfare of employees was to linger in management doctrines, even during the heyday of Taylorism. It motivated not only conservatives, but settlement-house reformers, Fabians, and those preoccupied with the human costs of industrialism. B. Seebohm Rowntree pioneered in the ethnography of poverty in York, then ran a cocoa factory as a model plant. As his director insisted, 'The aim of management must be to render industry more effectively human, more truly a corporate effort of human beings, united for a common object and moved by a common motive.' Similarly, Edward Cadbury of the Bourneville chocolate firm insisted that his worker was 'an intelligent and capable citizen'; Cadbury organized company teams, leisure activities, and a large dining canteen – but also segregated male and female workers to preserve good morals.[83]

It was not just chocolate manufacture that encouraged such benevolent paternalism. (But see Roald Dahl's Willy Wonka in *Charlie and the Chocolate Factory* for an apposite fantasy!) Sometimes a nonconformist religious background contributed to a reformist stance. Similarly, Jewish entrepreneurs were often receptive to collaborationist models of labour relations (Filene in Boston, Olivetti of Ivrea, Alfred Mond of Imperial Chemical Industries) or to corporatist schemes for national economic planning (Rathenau of AEG and Gerard Swope of General Electric). Occasionally a utopian patriarch could institute the most modern experiments, as in the Bat'a factory community of Zlin, Moravia. One common factor was negative: the absence of representatives from heavy industry. Instead, those entrepreneurs identified with benevolent labour relations often headed light manufacturing firms, where the plant still remained a conglomeration of ateliers – for example, the famous mica room at Hawthorne – and workers might assemble small motors or packaged sweets or, in the case of Bat'a, shoes. Conversely, this style of labour relations was also compatible with the less labour intensive, continuous-flow production of the chemical industry or with far-flung electrical concerns that owned factories to assemble motors and insulators as well as generating plants that needed minimal supervision. Rarely, however, did the large iron and steel manufacturing industries that employed masses of workers

---

83 For the Rowntree approach see Oliver Sheldon, *The Philosophy of Management* (New York: Prentice-Hall, 1924), 8. Also Rowntree, *The Human Factor in Business* (London: Longmans, Green, 1921). For Edward Cadbury see *Experiments in Industrial Organization* (London: Longmans, Green, 1912); also the papers collected in Alfred D. Chandler, Jr., *Management Thought in Great Britain* (New York: Arno Press, 1979).

at semi-skilled production provide the sort of incentive for the paternalism of a Rowntree or others. That sort of standardized large-output plant suggested a more rationalized and often combative style of management. It was also the key sector of industry from 1890 to 1930.

Thus managerial ideologies did not evolve simply under the pressure of cultural or economic trends outside the firm. They also changed in response to the organizational developments within business. Taylorism and scientific management seemed to fit the iron and steel model of manufacture. Taylor himself was a metallurgical engineeer; the workers he used as the models for his incentive schemes were stolid, semi-skilled providers of heavy labor. Taylorite, then Fordist visions of industrial society postulated a centralized factory with standardized routines, where workers toiled as adjuncts of machines and the assembly line. After World War I assembly-line methods spread from the United States to European slaughterhouses, auto factories, biscuit producers, clothing manufacturers, and other industries. Thus by the 1920s the enthusiasts of scientific managment were dominating the reviews, tracts, and professional congresses as they urged rationalization of factories, offices, and even the Taylorization of leisure, the home, and the city. But even as Taylorite concepts won adherents throughout Europe, industrial organization was going beyond the centralized assembly-line plant that formed their archetypal image of the factory. The giant autoworks at River Rouge or Turin-Lingotto might capture publicists' imaginations, but innovations in the organization of corporate empires were as crucial as spectacular factories. The image of the factory remained compelling – indeed, the stylized social-realist murals of the Depression made it more pervasive – but new paradigms of management were needed.

The manager as psychologist

The advance of the corporation along with the impact of the Depression thus imposed a new managerial agenda. The world economic crisis sharpened ideological divisions between capital and labour. Appeals to a technocratic consensus were eclipsed. Instead the new influential business ideologies reflected a growing belief in the propensity toward non-rational behavior. Whether deriving from once-socialist theorists (e.g., Hendrik De Man's 1926 *Psychology of Socialism*) or from right wing images of crowd behavior, the postulates of managerial ideology became far darker. In the discussion of the 1930s, industrial man followed murky mass instincts. He was to be controlled not with rational incentives, but with appeals to collective drives and sentiments. Even at its crudest, Taylorism had addressed the incentives of individual workers, proposing a manipulated calculus of rewards for each person, not the mass. Now, however, the factory appeared as a social whole, a beehive or organism that had to be regulated as a system.

The connection between management and psychology had already been forged in several different countries. The German psychologist, Hugo Munsterberg, recruited to Harvard by William James, sought to overcome Taylor's 'helpless dilettantism' through the application of *Psychotechnik* in industry, especially by means of vocational selection. The study of psychological adjustment was coopted for frankly conservative ends of indoctrination by the right wing politicians and businessmen of the German DINTA, who sought to mould nationalist and anti-Marxist cadres among the proletariat. In Great Britain and the United States the issue of industrial 'fatigue,' with its ramifications of monotony and morale, provided the starting point for a vast elaboration of psychological approaches. From the 1915 Health of Munitions Workers Committee in Britain emerged the Industrial Fatigue Research Board, to be extended in 1921 by the National Institute of Industrial Psychology, uniting academics and industrialists, and supported by the Carnegie Trustees. The Board's avowed concern with the 'reduction of waste' along with 'selection of the most suitable workers' and the psychological aspects of labour was typical of the widespread post-war conviction that industrial society need only reduce its wasteful use of human and capital resources to assure prosperity for all.[84]

Still, these early studies did not originate in any presuppositions about the irrationality of workers. Rather psychology was intended to help employers deal with the normal process of discovering aptitudes, overcoming the physical tensions and stress that led to accidents, and smoothing unnecessary conflict. But once psychology had claimed a role it promised a far broader appeal than fatigue studies alone permitted. By the 1930s industrial psychologists ascribed to the manager the redefined mission of yoking non-rational employees together in a common enterprise. No longer was the starting point the

---

84 Besides Brady, *The Rationalization Movement in German Industry,* see the material in Peter Hinrichs and Lothar Peters, *Industrieller Friede? Arbeitswissenschaft und Rationalisierung in der Weimarer Republik* (Cologne: Pahl-Rugenstein, 1976); George H. Miles, 'The Extent and Application of Psychology and Psychological Methods in English Industrial Life,' *Harvard Business Review* (henceforth *HBR*), IV, 1 (1925–26): 138–44; Walter Bingham, 'Management's Concern with Research in Industrial Psychology,' *HBR*, X, 1 (1931–32):40–53; also Elton Mayo, *The Human Problems of an Industrial Civilization,* [1933] (New York: Viking, 1960), chaps. 1–2.

single individual, but the factory community with its own collective laws. Goetz Briefs' writings in the German-speaking world (later translated) described the proletariat as a psychological entity. And rather than designing a structure of material rewards the manager had to evoke trust, community, joy in work.[85] In the modern era these seemed especially hard to ensure. The factory was no longer an isolated community, and the influences emanating from outside were not conducive to nurturing these values within the plant. German industrialists had already declared that labour relations within a business could not partake of democracy: 'The large factory without authority is an absurdity.'[86] The difficulty was, as one industrial relations expert wrote in 1932, the worker was also a trade unionist, party adherent, and perhaps church goer:

More than ever before we can talk today of a front hostile to the factory, determined to narrow the sphere of factory life and subject it to the influence of the state and the collective right to work. All these influences of an internal and external sort increase the alienation of the worker. The factory, therefore, must exclude social disturbances as far as possible for the sake of its self-preservation.[87]

Such ideas became popular as part of a growing acceptance of irrationalist concepts of human nature – and not merely in the fascist regimes. A certain Paretan *chic* made inroads even in the United States where the *Treatise on Sociology* was translated in 1933, and the notion of the circulation of elites became a staple of historical and social analysis. In Europe, former socialist adherents as well as conservatives accepted the darker interpretation of collective behaviour. One revealing indication was the analytic reliance on the concept of 'masses' in the new treatises. Another, of course, was the left-to-right trajectory of many of the 'front generation' who became convinced that doctrinaire socialism neglected man's vitalist drives, his hunger for communal loyalties and for obedience. From Michels to de Man and thence to Emil Lederer and even into the 1940s and 1950s the disillusion with social democracy dominated sociological discourse. Politically, of course, the passage from left to right marked the New Conservatism

85 Goetz Briefs, *The Proletariat: A Challenge to Western Civilization* (New York: McGraw-Hill, 1937); also Briefs, ed., *Probleme der sozialen Werkspoltik*, 3 vols. (Munich: Duncker & Humbolt, 1930–35).

86 Albert Vögler cited in the *Berliner Börsenzeitung*, March 26, 1924.

87 Rudolf Schwenger, 'Die betriebliche Sozialpolitik im Ruhrkohlenbergbau,' *Schriften des Vereins für Sozialpolitik*, 186/1 (1932): 4; cited in T. W. Mason, 'Zur Entstehung des Gesetzes zur Ordnung der nationalen Arbeit vom Januar 1934,' in Hans Mommsen, D. Petzina, and B. Weisbrod, eds., *Industrielles System und politische Entwicklung in der Weimarer Republic* (Düsseldorf: Droste Verlag, 1974), 342–43.

in Weimar (not to claim National Socialism), the French Neo-Socialists or the rebellion of the frustrated and arrogant Oswald Mosley.

In this climate of opinion could it be any surprise that the task of the manager should also be redefined? Even before the Nazis reorganized German labour relations, commentators suggested that the provisions of Weimar legislation, conceived of as a social-democratic advance, permitted 'extensive dictatorial power' on the part of the employer. 'Employer and employee are united in one organism into a community of labour in which the latter subordinates himself freely to the command of the former for the sake of a commonly sought goal of productivity.'[88] In the perspective of the 1930s the engineer himself no longer appeared just as an efficiency expert, but as a more occult arranger, a potential ally of the new rulers in Germany or of, say, the proto-Vichyite groups in France. Jean Coutrot, *polytechnicien,* Teilhardiste Catholic, and organizer of the planning enthusiasts in the X-Crise, sought to perfect industrial administration through the application of both engineering and psychology. In the wake of 1936's labour upheavals, he urged separation of ownership and managerial administration, the latter to become a board-certified profession. And he speculated on the analogy of treating 'the psychological equilibrium within a business' as a sort of 'concentration camp conceived of as a sanatorium: provisional, with teachers and nurses, where one isolates until the end of their cure those whom one has not been able to convince so that they do not disturb others or hurt themselves.'[89]

With a less polarized political system than the Europeans, Americans could share the new management ideology with fewer authoritarian overtones. Elton Mayo began from the observations at Western Electric's light manufacturing plant at Hawthorne, Illinois, that workers responded positively to special attention. The approach to emerge would be called 'human relations.' Summarizing his work, Mayo began with the analyses of fatigue during and after the First World War, then presented the Hawthorne studies of the late 1920s and early 1930s, then turned to the difficulties of the wider society. The problem for management did not lie in any irreducible individual irrationalism; Mayo explicitly rejected Freudian ideas for an eclectic behaviourism. Nor did the problem lie in the factory alone. The disintegration of the

---

88 Otto Kahn-Freund, 'Das soziale Ideal des Reichsarbeitsgerichts,' cited by Mason, 'Zur Entstehung des Gesetzes vom nationalen Arbeit,' 344.

89 Jean Coutrot, *Les leçons de juin 1936, l'humanisme économique,* cited in Luc Boltanski, *Les cadres* (Paris: Editions de Minuit, 1982), 118–19. For German parallels see Gerd Hortleder, *Das Gesellschaftsbild des Ingenieurs. Zum politischen Verhalten des technischen Intelligenz in Deutschland* (Frankfurt am Main: Suhrkamp, 1974), 93–123.

wider society, a Durkheimian *anomie*, afflicted industrial civilization, but the same techniques might remedy the difficulties whether 'for a factory on the Volga or for another on the banks of the river Charles.' Mayo appealed to Malinowski, Piaget and Pareto among others to stress that selection of an administrative elite was the crucial need. Only the administrator could restore human collaboration within the factory and in society as a whole.[90] As Mayo's disciple, F. J. Roethlisberger, wrote at the end of the 1930s: 'The function of management, stated in its most general terms, can be described as that of maintaining a social system of the industrial plant in a state of equilibrium such that the purposes of the enterprises are realized.' The task was to align wills: Hawthorne workers had demonstrated 'neither logical nor irrational behavior. It was essentially social behavior.'[91]

Entrenched at the Harvard Business School, human relations could remain a dominant managerial theme throughout the 1950s. Outside the United States the Tavistock Institute of Human Relations and publicists such as Georges Friedmann in Paris continued the emphasis on integration. Its implications were sometimes contradictory. On the one hand, spokesmen for integration sometimes implied that the industrial system should obey its own frictionless logic, safely insulated from the surrounding social and political environment. On the other hand, it was suggested, only the transformation of political society itself, its subjection to administrative and managerial skills, might assure the harmony of the factory. Happily for the writers of the postwar decade, this seemed to be taking place. Just as a confrontational style of labour relations was disappearing within the factory, so ideological conflict was also slipping into the past: macrocosm and microcosm were converging in the benign process of modernization. The manager, as Roethlisberger suggested in 1948, in effect spanned both: 'the manager is neither managing men nor managing work . . . he is administering a social system.'[92]

Thus a reorientation of managerial ideas that took root under the

90   Mayo, *Human Problems of an Industrial Civilization*, 125–29, 161–80 (quotation, p. 139).
91   F. J. Roethlisberger and William J. Dickson, *Management and the Worker* (Cambridge, Mass.: Harvard University Press, 1939), 569, 575.
92   F. J. Roethlisberger, 'Human Relations: Rare, Medium, or Well-Done?' *HBR*, XXVI 1 (1948): 94. For the Tavistock Institute see the work of Elliot Jacques, *The Changing Culture of a Factory* (London: Tavistock, 1951); and for Georges Friedmann, see the sophisticated study with copious references: *Industrial Society: The Emergence of the Human Problems of Automation* (New York: Free Press, 1955).

impact of depression found apparent confirmation because of post–World War II prosperity. The Depression had undermined the notion that the managerial task was to harness men to machines. It fostered the conviction that the real challenge was to nurture a community of producers. Under the stress of inter-war social and political conflict, the plant could no longer be treated as the safe domain of the machine and engineer. The response could be the harsh psychological leadership inculcated by the DINTA and then legislated by the Nazi Labour Front (with the factory envisaged as a band of workers under a chief who was always obeyed, but still observed a primitive egalitarian consultation among his production team). Or it might be the *planiste* transformation suggested by X-Crise, or the collaborative evangelical paternalism advocated in Britain, or even the environmental behaviourism suggested by the Americans. In each case, though, the new emphasis required dealing with the collective mentality of employees. Harmony became as crucial as efficiency.

Just as the Depression created a new social and economic context for management ideas, so too did developments in industry itself. The auto industry, with its assembly-line production, was no longer so exclusively the archetype of an industrial plant. Now chemicals and oil and electrical generation captured the public imagination alongside iron and steel based manufacture. So, too, the idealized vision of the manager now transcended the mastery of assembly-line production. It came to involve organizing the multi-divisional firm. Even in the auto industry the change was evident in the eclipse of engineer-managers such as Charles Sorensen of Ford or William Knudsen of GM (who proved inadequate at the Office of War Production in the 1940s) as contrasted with the new eminence of Alfred Sloan. Industrial organization became far more than a Fordist concept.

The political orientations of industry also encouraged the new concepts of management. The electrical and chemical industries often became identified as special supporters of National Socialist and Italian fascist policies in the 1930s. Directors of the traditional iron and steel firms and the heads of the manufacturing concerns based on steel certainly proved happy enough to benefit from government contracts and autarkic protection, but they lost political influence. The German iron and steel industrialists had been close to the Nationalist Right in Weimar, but I.G. Farben became more central to the war-planning combinations sponsored after 1936. Likewise Giovanni Agnelli of FIAT had maintained liberal connections and the Italian steel producers had supported the pre-fascist Right, while the fascist regime turned more to chemicals and electricity.[93] Interestingly enough, however, these industries had earlier been more affiliated with liberal politics than heavy industry. In Weimar Germany, Siemens and Rathenau, both electrical magnates, had counted as politically progressive; in Britain, Alfred Mond of ICI had sought collaborative labour relations, and Elton Mayo's Hawthorne experiments were taking place within the subsidiary of an electrical firm that he described as 'definitely committed to justice and humanity in its dealings with workers.'[94] The more consistent political stance over time, in fact, emerged from the classical industries of nineteenth-century development – coal, iron and steel, and their manufacturing affiliates – which did not vault from liberal to fascist identifications but stuck with a traditional conservatism. One reason was that they remained more labour intensive and often faced strongly organized work-forces, and they relied on a style of labour relations that was patriarchal at best and often brutally anti-union. In contrast, the more process-oriented, less labour-intensive newer industries of the twentieth century tended to be either more politically reformist or else authoritarian in a new and manipulative mode. For those thinking in terms of the needs of the newer industries, the theme of organization became crucial, whether authoritarian or behaviourist and psychological.

The managerial literature that emerged under these new economic and political conditions of the 1930s through the 1950s could become naively extravagant. At the apex of the factory or the society had to be men who combined broad training and intuitive gifts. Editors demanded an expertise based upon psychological insight, but one, interestingly enough, that they did not compare with literary insight. The manager was to master a world in microcosm but no comparisons were made with Tolstoy or Flaubert or Shakespeare (not even with Prospero, who in name and role might have seemed apt) – perhaps because these writers understood that social harmony often foundered on stubborn passions, on rancour, sexuality, jealousy, and ennui. Irreducible passion did not appear in the managerial discourse; contumaciousness, accidie could all be removed. At worst a diffuse crowd

93   For the trends sketched in these paragraphs see Chandler, *Visible Hand*, chap. 14; also Alfred D. Chandler, Jr., *Strategy and Structure* (Cambridge, Mass.: Harvard University Press, 1962); Alfred P. Sloan, Jr., *My Years with General Motors* (New York: Doubleday, 1964); Valerio Castronovo, *Giovanni Agnelli* (Turin: UTET, 1971), chap. 5; Giulio Sapelli, *Organizzazione, lavoro e innovazione industriale nell'Italia tra le due guerre* (Turin: Rosenberg & Sellier, 1978); Dietmar Petzina, *Autarkiepolitik im Dritten Reich* (Stuttgart: Deutsche Verlags-Anstalt, 1968).
94   Mayo, *Human Problems of an Industrial Civilization*, 96.

mentality clouded the creatures who needed attention and care and guidance. Implicitly the managerial function became the highest that might exist. As one British spokesman wrote, recapitulating the themes of the previous quarter century:

A real philosophy of productivity should give us the right vision of a future state where the world of productive work will draw people into it, not primarily for the purpose of earning a living, but *where in fellowship as members of a team rendering a worthwhile service, they can unfold their personalities in work happily and successfully done, thereby serving their neighbours and their God.* A distant vision, it is true, and one we may never attain. Nonetheless, a vision worth striving for and one capable of drawing the best from the national team.[95]

The manager as policy activist

The notion of the manager as a psychological organizer became most pervasive after the war. Nonetheless, it had to make room for other concepts as well. The 1930s had demonstrated that the manager must consider his firm as a social system often at odds with the larger environment. As Chester Barnard had written in an authoritative statement: 'The survival of an organization depends upon the maintenance of an equilibrium of complex character in a continuously fluctuating environment of physical, biological, and social materials, elements, and forces, which calls for readjustment of processes internal to the organization.'[96] The task of a manager, in other words, was to navigate in the changing political and economic conditions of the wider world.

But might not management finally extend its purview into that wider world? Increasingly after World War II business spokesmen would call less for the responsiveness of their enterprises than for the shaping of the economic milieu. Nor did this mean just the traditional objective of securing favourable particularist policies, such as tariffs or tax relief, but rather a steady intervention on behalf of buoyant economic management. Forced to become a psychologist during the Depression, the manager was transfigured as the executive and was now to become a policy activist as well. 'We must participate in the formation of public policy even though the specific issues may not have an immediate influence on our individual businesses,' one writer argued by 1951. 'We must aim to tear down the psychological walls that have been

95   A. P. Young, *American Management Techniques and Practices and Their Bearing on Productivity in British Industry* (London, 1948?), 65.
96   Chester Barnard, *The Functions of the Executive* (Cambridge, Mass.: Harvard University Press, 1938), 6.

built around group interests. We must realize that in these matters the whole is greater than the sum of its parts.'[97]

Business leaders had to reconquer territory earlier thought outside their control. Perhaps the major group effort was the Committee for Economic Development, organized by the chairman of the Studebaker Corporation, Paul Hoffman, and designed to lobby for an active and steady interventionist role on the part of government. The CED recognized that the Keynesian 'revolution' had come to stay and feared that a return to pre–New Deal attitudes could bring a relapse into depression. In effect the Committee proposed a government–business partnership to chart out an intelligent fiscal activism, to plan a beneficial mix of government spending and tax policies to spur continued high investment. To this end the CED orchestrated a succession of meetings, the establishment of local committees, and a series of publications on such economic issues as price–wage relations, problems of small business, and proper fiscal policy. CED economists especially urged acceptance of the idea of a full-employment budget, that is, one that yielded a balance when employment was high and business prospering, but that simultaneously allowed for a counter-cyclical deficit if economic activity flagged. In some ways the CED represented an American analogue of the industrial peak associations that had long been a feature of European business organization. But it defined its task in a more upbeat and less defensive way; it presupposed, not that business was a special interest, but that, in good American fashion, business was the general interest.

In the perspective of the CED, the factory became almost an archaic concept. While the firm remained the unit of private activity, government policy was a crucial formative influence; hence businessmen had to engage in an ongoing benevolent collaboration with the state. By 1947–48 the organization of the Marshall Plan – with Hoffman becoming the head of the Washington executive agency, the Economic Cooperation Administration – became paradigmatic of the new arrangement, that is, of a public policy designed to encourage and teach economic growth abroad and at home, entrusted to a partnership of political leaders, business executives, trade union spokesmen and academics. Justifying this broad collaboration, the concept of productivity played some of the same role in political economy discourse after the second war as did efficiency after the first. Productivity was an objective that every business and labour leader could seek to maximize within his own company and it provided a national objective

97   Frank W. Abrams, 'Management's Responsibilities in a Complex World,' *HBR*, XXIX, 3 (1951): 33–34.

as well. 'Productivity', declared the CED's research director at a meeting of its trustees in October 1947, 'is a vitally needed lubricant to reduce class and group frictions. As long as we can get more by increasing the size of the pie there is not nearly so much temptation to try to get a bigger slice at the expense of others. That applies particularly to the common and conflicting interests of labour and capital. If it weren't for possibilities of increased productivity the struggle between capital and labour would be more severe and dangerous than it is.'[98]

Productivity allowed the old management concepts to be combined in a new synthesis. It recapitulated the engineer's emphasis on efficiency of the 1920s, which like productivity was the measure of a ratio: usually physical output divided by labour time. Appeals to productivity and efficiency could stress both the role of growth, the effective increase of the numerator, and the need for rationalization (as in the late 1920s), which focused on lowering the costs expressed by the denominator. But invoking productivity also suggested concern with the psychological integration that the 1930s managerial ethos had highlighted. Productivity themes also played a political role; they rallied European business leaders and the representatives of the non-communist trade unions who participated in the productivity missions and productivity councils that proliferated in Western Europe under the auspices of the Marshall Plan. The Anglo-American Council on Productivity formed one transatlantic network; in France the Commissariat du Plan created a working group on productivity that organized 450 missions to the United States. What they stressed in their reports on return was not the technological backwardness of French industry, but the lag in terms of industrial and personal relations.[99] Productivity thus served as a business strategy, as slogan for an international political coalition, and as a managerial theme that revalidated the older approaches of the inter-war period.

What code of behaviour did American business leaders suggest to European counterparts and to their own colleagues by the years of the Marshall Plan? Intelligent political activism on behalf of a progressive fiscal policy comprised only part of a broader thematic of social responsibility. As the alumni association of the Harvard Business

---

98 Ted Yntema at CED Board of Trustees, October 16, 1947. 'Minutes of Meeting,' in Paul Hoffman papers, box 40, Harry S. Truman Presidential Library, Independence, Mo.
99 Boltanski, *Les cadres*, 158–59 and chap. 2 in general: 'La fascination de l'amérique et l'importation du management'; also Chapter 3 of the present volume ('The Politics of Productivity').

School was told in June 1948, 'Today most managements operate as trustee in recognition of the claims of employees, investors, consumers, and government.'[100] Social responsibility as a managerial ideal often demanded, so friendly observers as well as critics pointed out, almost total immersion in business. The corporation claimed community participation on the part of its employees as well as the selfless loyalty of their wives. Enfolded in business as a total institution, corporate leaders could claim to serve the totality of institutions. As one of the more perceptive articulators of business aspirations, Peter Drucker, claimed in a 1951 symposium sponsored by the Advertising Council: 'We have gone a very long way in the direction of solving the basic ethical and basic political problem of an industrial society, the social and ethical harmony between the self-interest of our economic institutions and the social interests of society.' For Paul Hoffman, who chaired the symposium, America had triumphed by finding a decentralized way to collective action. 'The realization that through free non-governmental collective action in business you can not only have a better life businesswise, but also a more profitable individual business, is a comparatively modern development.'[101]

With the participation of the businessman in a fabric of social responsibility and national policy making, management ideology claimed a new inclusiveness. No longer could the managerial function be conceived in terms of the firm alone. In the era of the Cold War it involved a national mission: 'There is no higher responsibility, there is no higher duty, of professional management than to gain the respect of the general public through objective participation in, and consideration of, national questions, even though these questions in many cases do not relate directly to their business problems.'[102] In effect this attitude represented the socialization of management: the tendency to fuse factory and society. Indeed, one aspect of the new managerial claims was that the role of the manager was losing its specificity or becoming ambivalent in its meanings. 'Manager' now often implied more the concept of middle-management, the supervisor of a unit within a larger enterprise. 'Executive' was increasingly reserved as

100 Clarence Francis address, cited in Roy Lewis and Rosemary Stewart, *The Managers: A New Examination of the English, German and American Executive* (New York: Mentor, 1961), 194.
101 'Basic Elements of a Free, Dynamic Society – Part I, A Round-Table Discussion Sponsored by the Advertising Council, Inc.' (April 16, 1951), *HBR,* XXIX, 6 (1951): 57, 67.
102 Abrams, 'Management's Responsibilities,' 34.

the concept for those at the top, and this role was described as almost a super-human calling:

In many respects the role of the policy-forming executive in a business enterprise is unenviable. It is a perpetually demanding role; its rewards, both economically and socially, are rarely commensurate with the sacrifices it entails. Perhaps because of this, policy-making is an activity for which, like advanced medical research, only the exceptional and dedicated individual is truly fitted.

But top management had abdicated its leadership role to unions and government; its task was to reclaim them: 'to play, once again, the part of a leader – the kind of leader who can capture the loyalty of the employees, represent and personify the company in the public eye, and present a point of view effectively at a Congressional hearing.'[103]

By the 1950s the tone of self-satisfaction could be almost suffocating. Still, there were difficulties. Management had resolved the problem of its enterprises by integrating them within the larger socio-economic consensus of post-war productivity and growth. But within the factory alone old problems remained, including those presented by the assembly line and by Fordist production. As one critic argued, assembly-line technology perniciously influenced the assumptions about human motivation held at all levels of management, which had to learn to deal with small group production teams and not individual cogs.[104] Peter Drucker argued that management too often merely claimed its 'prerogatives'. It still had to fulfil a function, but the function required transcended the firm: how to think about plant location so cities did not become hostage to vulnerable industries, how to provide for the employment of older workers, how to encourage small business.[105] In short, management still had not solved the issues that either its earlier mission from the inter-war period or its post-war social activism had laid upon it. And in a way managerial celebrants turned towards the wider world, towards the gospel of policy activism, because only by seeking to bring in broader resources of hegemony – national mission, Keynesian macroeconomic policies, the ideological mobilization

103 Robert N. McMurry, 'Man-Hunt for Top Executives,' *HBR*, XXXII, 1 (1954): 61–62.
104 Arthur N. Turner, 'Management and the Assembly Line,' *HBR*, XXXIII, 5 (1955): 40–48.
105 Peter F. Drucker, 'Management Must Manage,' *HBR*, XXVIII, 2 (1950): 80–86; also Drucker, *The New Society: The Anatomy of Industrial Order* (New York: Harper Bros., 1950).

of the Cold War – might the persistent conflicts inherent in the business enterprise be constrained and, indeed, made manageable.

The half-century trajectory of managerial ideologies thus involved a progressive claim to subject ever broader areas of economic and cultural life, of personality and public policy to the jurisdiction of business leadership. This expansiveness was not planned from the outset. But two processes impelled the efforts at more profound stabilization within the firm and wider circles of intervention beyond its traditional boundaries. One was the search for an adequatè concept of the managerial function as the enterprise developed from simple factory into a financially linked network of multiple production or service units. The other was the increasing awareness that economic possibilities, social conflicts, and ideological dispositions were determined within the overall political economy. Ultimately the manager or executive was the man fitted to run society as a whole; indeed, he could hardly forbear from making the attempt.

To be sure, this broad thrust of management ideology remained peculiarly American and probably emerged most fully during the Eisenhower administration. Europeans remained more reserved: in Britain businessmen did not possess the cultural hegemony they had acquired in America; in France the state still claimed a major share of technocratic leadership; even in West Germany, where the American model might be received most congenially, the existence of a Social Democratic Party provided some counterweight. In Italy the dominant Christian Democratic Party responded to patronage networks in small towns and southern cities that allowed only a limited voice to spokesmen for entrepreneurship and modernization, who might dominate Confindustria or ENI, but not the regime. Nonetheless, in all these countries, engaging in the discourse of productivity meant accepting a good deal of American managerial ideals. In the United States, Charles E. Wilson, Eisenhower's Secretary of Defense designate, did not actually say that what was good for General Motors was good for the United States; he said that he always presumed that what was good for the United States was also good for GM. But the force of this patriotic productivism was the same: it affirmed the congruency of the managerial sphere within factory and society.

Still, this vision, too, was subject to erosion. By the mid 1950s there was dissent from the corporate thinking that it encouraged. Following upon David Riesman's critique of the other-directed personality, Theodore Levitt argued that the economy of abundance would produce stagnant management, a critique that echoed Schumpeter.[106]

106   Theodore Levitt, 'The Changing Character of Capitalism' *HBR*, XXXIV, 4 (1956): 37–47.

Whether the prediction was justified or not, by the late 1960s and 1970s management ideology would change again and this time towards a less celebratory mode. In this most recent phase business leadership has been cast less in terms of administration (management seems faintly derogatory) than strategy. Strategy implies the combining and recombining of portfolio assets in a somewhat Hobbesian economic environment: it implies long-term objectives, the constant presence of uncertainty, and the existence of constraints. Whether as engineer, as psychologist, or as policy activist, the twentieth-century manager entertained an implicitly homeostatic vision. His task was to preserve or restore a high-level equilibrium, within a firm buffeted by its wider environment, or within the firm and economic environment simultaneously. By the 1970s the assurance of equilibrium faded, and a new doctrine of business in constant cyclical evolution became persuasive. Despite their occasional prayer breakfasts business leaders did not evoke the Biblical imagery of Jacob's ladder; instead consultants told them to acquire 'sunrise' industries that would flourish for a while as 'milk cows', then decline as 'sunset' industries, and be cast off as 'dogs'. In the world of Japanese video recorders, Korean steel, of bleak structural unemployment in Detroit, Nancy, and Charleroi, the benign assumptions of the 1950s no longer held.

Would managerial ideologies expand once again to claim and order the international economic milieu that now impinged upon the individual enterprise; that is, could the multinationals impose a new Fordist or productivist ebullience? Or would managerial claims retreat to more mercantilist doctrines? In either case, ideologies of management could no longer presuppose entrepreneurial equilibria without concepts of development, of change not just as a random variable or a beneficial unfolding of technological potential, but change as a historic succession of economic ascendancies and decline. After a half century of relying on engineering, human relations, and growth, entrepreneurial ideologies confronted the historicity of capitalism.

2

The economics of Fascism and Nazism

An early version of this chapter was prepared for a conference at the
Kellogg Institute of Notre Dame University in April 1984 honoring
the work of Albert O. Hirschman. That contribution was published
as "The Economics of Fascism and Nazism: Premises and Performance," in Alejandro Foxley, Michael S. McPherson, and Guillermo
O'Donnell, eds., *Development, Democracy, and the Art of Trespassing:
Essays in Honor of Albert O. Hirschman* (Notre Dame, Ind.: University
of Notre Dame Press, 1986), 57–88. The original paper was proposed
as an examination of development and economic management under
nondemocratic conditions. This expanded version rests on a wider
survey of the literature and statistical material; it has a new introduction and examines some of the important controversies about the
Depression and wartime performance in greater detail. I have benefited from discussion at the Columbia Economic History Seminar, the
Harvard Economic History Workshop, and the Harvard Center for
European Studies Seminar on the State and Capitalism. Steven Marglin
pressed me to think through the issues raised by German recovery
from the Depression. Alan Milward and Tim Mason read the penul-
timate version very closely. They raised important questions and
pointed out some errors. Those that remain are my responsibility.

Introduction: two generations of studies

The economic claims of Italian Fascism and German Nazism proved
a subject of compelling interest from their inception. In the 1930s and
1940s they aroused impassioned and significant debate. Apologists
vaunted Fascism and National Socialism as political systems that
would overcome the selfishness and chaos of interwar capitalism
without recourse to a stultifying collectivism. Adversaries criticized

their apparent exploitation of wage labor, the spuriousness of their reforms, and their repressive "command economy." Sympathizers and opponents alike, however, presupposed that the two regimes were instituting a framework for capitalism that differed significantly from the market economies of the democracies.

Since the mid-1960s historians have generally reversed the argument. They have divested Nazism and fascism of particular economic characteristics.[1] Fascist policies, often ad hoc and fragmentary, appear to have been similar to the emergency interventions of the liberal capitalist states in the Depression. They allegedly prefigured the democracies' organization of production in the Second World War and even the targeting of macroeconomic variables characteristic of the postwar welfare state. Fascism was just crisis capitalism with a cudgel. There is much to recommend this view. Fascism as an ideological system emerged as a prescription for authoritarian political reconstruction. Its leaders tolerated an economic discourse but saw it as largely instrumental. Nonetheless, the ideological premises of fascism may have shaped fascist economics – institutions and performance – more than recent analysis would imply. It may be fruitful once again to open the precliometric inquiry concerning the relation of fascist ideology to economic outcomes.

Simple curiosity about the success of fascist economic experiments has also prodded this work. Recent studies have usefully advanced beyond the evaluations that contemporaries offered through the end of World War II. The older studies were rich in legal and institutional description. They were also venturesome theoretically. They penetrated the thickets of new state-coordinated cartels and agencies and proposed typologies for comprehending the systems as a coherent

1 When I use the term "fascist" – lower case and without specific reference to Italy – I am referring to Nazi and Italian fascist conditions as a group. Such a bracketing admittedly riles many historians, especially those who wish to stress that the Nazis were fundamentally anti-Semitic, the Italians only opportunistically so, that the Nazis were far more bloody and efficient, and so on. Some of the historians who bridle at the term "fascism" see the concept as a Trojan horse for a Marxist transnational class analysis. For a good résumé of this nominalist position see Gilbert Allardyce, "What Fascism Is Not: Some Thoughts on the Deflation of a Concept," *American Historical Review*, 84 (1979): 367–88. I find this position too fastidious. Typologies are justified by their utility: Several interwar regimes in Europe built political regimes upon paramilitary movements that cultivated violence, glorified war and imperialist expansion, despised both Marxian socialisms and parliamentary liberalism, condemned the rationalist traditions descended from the Enlightenment, and praised submission to personal leaders and/or to state and party collectivities. A term designed to cover this subclass of authoritarian phenomena seems useful and justified.

whole.[2] But after the 1950s many seemed old-fashioned in approach and inadequate technically. The older scholars intuitively perceived a distinction between Left and Right (virtually between light and darkness) that became more problematic as democratic socialist convictions weakened. The postwar interventionism of the welfare state made it harder to insist on the distinctiveness of the Fascist or Nazi economy. By the 1960s new and detailed historical research revealed how fascist innovations had emerged as the upshot of bureaucratic procedures; hence, their earlier presentation as components of schematic systems seemed less illuminating. The narrative replaced the organizational chart. In earlier studies, economic indices of actual performance, of growth and distribution, seemed primitive when they were offered at all. In the past two decades more refined statistical results and comparative arguments have enabled researchers to advance more complex assessments.

This essay takes the new findings as a given and attempts two other tasks. First, virtually all researchers have selected either Italy or Germany as their field of research. But if there is to be an inquiry about fascism as such – and I believe it a worthwhile objective – it must systematically canvass the recent work on both regimes. I have undertaken that review here. Second, I have attempted to rethink the connections between economic outcomes and ideological structures. Despite their technical sophistication, recent scholars have not usually sought to sustain the earlier generation's commitment to uniting political and economic analysis. In some cases they must have deemed it an impediment to a clear-headed assessment of economic results. It would be a step backward simply to reinstate the social democratic premises of those earlier works, but it is still worthwhile to reopen the bridges from econometrics to the context of politics and ideology. I have organized that effort around the issues of fascist distinctiveness, fascist performance, and the relation of ideology to outcomes.

2   For example, see Franz Neumann, *Behemoth: The Structure and Practice of National Socialism*, 2d ed. (New York: Oxford University Press, 1944); Robert A. Brady, *The Spirit and Structure of German Fascism* (New York: Viking, 1937); Brady, *Business as a System of Power* (Berkeley and Los Angeles: University of California Press, 1943); Otto Nathan, *The Nazi Economic System: Germany's Mobilization for War* (Durham, N.C.: Duke University Press, 1964); Gaetano Salvemini, *Under the Axe of Fascism* (New York: Viking Press, 1936); Louis Rosenstock-Franck, *L'économie corporative fasciste en doctrine et en fait* (Paris: Librairie universitaire J. Gamber, 1938); and Rosenstock-Franck, *Les étapes de l'économie fasciste italienne: du corporativisme à l'économie de guerre* (Paris: Librairie Sociale et Economique, 1939).

Distinctiveness: To what degree can one speak of a "fascist" economic system? Whether or not such a description is valid, what role did Italian Fascist and German National Socialist concepts of the economy actually play in shaping economic relations? Were there in fact coherent ideological approaches or just fitful initiatives justified by rhetorical appeals?

Performance: Did fascism mean, as is sometimes claimed, modernization in the sense of structural transformation? Transformation aside, how did the fascist economies perform as measured by the quantitative tests that modern Western economists often use to measure performance? And in line with the concern of so many writers, how did they perform in preparing for and then meeting the demands of war, an activity they believed was a central obligation of national existence and for which they claimed special competence.

The relation of ideology to outcomes: Were there reasons inherent in the fascist approach to the economy that account for the performance of Italy and Germany in peace and war? This inquiry, it turns out, does not lead to any fascist "program," to goals that are openly declared and pursued with more or less success. Instead, it requires thinking through the economic approaches that fascism may implicitly mandate. The connection between ideological vision and economic outcome, I believe, remains significant, but the interesting connection is not to be found at the explicit level, where it was sought for so long. The meaningful influence on economic activity arises from the implicit logic of fascist concepts and history.

The explicit content of the fascist program (productivism, corporativism, autarky)

Commentators have rightly discerned a babble of economic preachings in fascism, many of them contradictory. Fascist spokesmen preached the virtues of Darwinian struggle within a national economy but declared that their society was bound together by a common fate. They celebrated heroic entrepreneurs but condemned capitalism. They demanded a radical transformation of enterprise but promised to protect hard-pressed and often inefficient peasants and shopkeepers. They clamored for a "genuine" socialism but bitterly attacked social democracy; evoked technological progress and exuded nostalgia for rural roots. They derided state regulation but proposed an all-embracing corporative organization. Faced with these contradictions, some historians have argued that fascism in fact had no ideology worthy of the name. Fascist ideology supposedly amounted to little more than an opportunistic series of grievances that served to mobilize support on different occasions. This case is easily argued, but not really sufficient. National Socialism and Italian Fascism did present a characteristic range of economic prescriptions. Their ideas varied according to the particular stage each movement had reached, but not arbitrarily. An initial distinction can be made between the economic concepts of fascism as a movement seeking power and the programs proposed once the fascists had entrenched themselves. But even this distinction proves too clear-cut. As the litany of themes recalled above indicates, fascist spokesmen often did present conflicting ideas. Fascist leaders maneuvering for office were capable both of condemning capitalism and of claiming it needed only to be left alone for its own reinvigoration. In the critical months before seizing power, both Mussolini and Hitler went out of their way to mollify the businessmen who might remember the anticapitalist exuberance of their early oratory. In a celebrated address at Udine on September 19, 1922, and in discussions with industrialists on October 16, Mussolini stressed that fascism meant an end to the state intervention they had deplored since the war. "Basta con lo Stato ferroviere, con lo Stato postino, con lo Stato assicuratore": "Enough of the railroad state, the postal state, the state as insurance agent." Instead, one had to relearn the teachings of Smith, of Say, of Ferrara and the examples of Peel and Cavour. Indeed, fascism would create a new doctrine in the spirit of the old liberals. The accent was just an echo of what *liberisti*, such as Luigi Einaudi, had been tirelessly preaching for years.[3]

Hitler took up similar themes in his celebrated appeal to Germany's Ruhr business elite, who invited him to expound his economic ideas before the Düsseldorf Industrieklub on January 26, 1932. On this occasion, intended to overcome the distrust that lingered between many industrialists and financiers and the obstreperous National Socialist leader, Hitler praised the entrepreneurial vocation. He insisted that both businessmen and political leaders had to be men of decision, and both had to be liberated from petty restrictions on the exercise of their power. The message was similar, Walther Funk reported later at Nuremberg: Hitler was an enemy of state socialism and the planned economy. Both business leadership and political leadership legiti-

---

3 Ernesto Rossi, *I padroni del vapore* (Bari: Laterza, 1966), 46. Rossi's work, still useful for documenting fascist promises to business, represents an older quasi-conspiratorial view of the relations between Mussolini and heavy industry. Rossi, however, was not a Communist, but a Resistance liberal of independent views.

mately claimed exemption from misplaced democratic principles. Both deserved to retain the power that accrued to proven competence.[4]

Obviously these aspiring dictators, superb at sensing what their listeners wished to be told, shaped the message to the audience. Many in the audiences, however, remained skeptical. If the Milanese industrialists active in Confindustria, the Italian peak association, pressed for a coalition government in September 1922 that would include Mussolini, the Piedmontese elite, including Giovanni Agnelli of FIAT, were more reserved. If Hitler could count on the vanity of Hjalmar Schacht, the *ingénu* adulation of Fritz Thyssen, or the reactionary miscalculation of Alfred Hugenberg, other important industrialists vacillated and kept their options open.[5] The task here is not to determine how many of the industrialist community welcomed or acquiesced in the new leadership, but what concepts the Fascists and Nazis brought to their governments. Both leaders realized that they must modify their movements' earlier anticapitalist rhetoric and re-

---

4 See Alan Bullock, *Hitler: A Study in Tyranny* (New York: Harper & Row, 1952), 155. For a full analysis of Hitler's appearance at the Industrieklub (and similarly a useful demythologizing of Hitler's notorious meeting with Papen at Kurt von Schroeder's home in Cologne on January 4, 1933), see Henry Ashby Turner, Jr., *German Big Business and the Rise of Hitler* (New York: Oxford University Press, 1985), 204–19, 314–17. Turner emphasizes the fact that businessmen remained cool and uncommitted to Hitler; my point is not that they were impressed, but that Hitler shaped his ideology to woo them. For Hitler's primitive economic ideas, see ibid., 71–83. Characteristically, he declared that economics was all "a matter of common sense and willpower" (cited, p. 81). See also Henry A. Turner, Jr., "Hitlers Einstellung zu sozialökonomischen Fragen vor der 'Machtergreifung,' " *Geschichte und Gesellschaft* 2 (1976): 89–117; Avraham Barkai, *Das Wirtschaftssystem des Nationalsozialismus* (Cologne, Verlag Wissenschaft und Politik, 1977); John D. Heyl, "Hitler's Economic Thought: A Reappraisal," *Central European History*, 6 (1973): 83–96.

5 For the most careful studies, which replace the earlier crude conspiratorial ideas, see Mario Abrate, *La lotta sindacale nella industrializzazione d'Italia 1906–1928* (Milan: Franco Angeli, 1967), a well-documented though apologetic account, and – more selective, but also downplaying the connection – Piero Melograni, *Gli industriali e Mussolini: Rapporti tra Confindustria e fascismo dal 1919 al 1929* (Milan: Longanesi, 1972), esp. 9–30. Roland Sarti's *Fascism and the Industrial Leadership in Italy, 1919–1940* (Berkeley and Los Angeles: University of California Press, 1971) does not rest on business-group documentation. For the earlier views that stress fascist–business connections, besides Rossi's *Padroni del vapore*, see Franco Catalano, *Potere economico e fascismo: La crisi del dopoguerra 1919–1921* (Milan, 1967). On Germany the most revealing recent study is Reinhard Neebe, *Grossindustrie, Staat und NSDAP* (Göttingen: Vandenhoeck & Ruprecht, 1981); see also Michael Grübler, *Die Spitzenverbände der Wirtschaft und das erste Kabinett Brüning* (Düsseldorf: Beitrage zur Geschichte des Parlamentarismus und der politischen Parteien, Bd. 70, 1982). The issue has received fresh attention in light of the controversy surrounding David Abraham's *The Collapse of the Weimar Republic: Political Economy and Crisis* (Princeton, N.J.: Princeton University

assure the business establishment if they wanted to be serious candidates for power. With their cynical insight into human nature, both Mussolini and Hitler understood that some receptive industrialists nurtured the belief that the leaders might be separated from the troublesome radicals who had been their initial enthusiasts and had been needed originally to combat the Marxist parties and unions in the streets.

Nor did Mussolini and Hitler merely play on Manchesterite themes in their wooing of business leaders. They plucked deeper and more intriguing chords. Both men appealed to a technocratic impulse as they built rainbow bridges to industry. Their heroes were not financiers, but engineers and captains of industry. This dichotomy was a venerable one and appeared in many of the critiques of capitalism at the turn of the century, whether Thorstein Veblen's *Theory of Business Enterprise*, Georges Sorel's praise of engineers, or the cruder Populist (American and German) separation of the parasitic banker from the creative inventor and entrepreneur. Overtones of the distinction still persisted in Schumpeter's 1911 *Theory of Economic Development*. Debased versions would characterize the screeds of Gottfried Feder, Hitler's roustabout economic tutor in the early Munich years who preached the "breaking of interest slavery," and even Ezra Pound's paranoid pastoral written in Italian exile: *Jefferson and/or Mussolini.* Whereas Marxists indicted capitalism as a system of exploitative property relations, populistic radicalism focused on the control of credit and money as abusive. Bankers produced no real value; rather, they starved worthy farmers and small businessmen of credit for their own profits. So, too, did the organizers of monopolies or large department stores.[6]

Now respectable businessmen who sat on the boards of banks and mingled with their directors at lunch clubs would not buy this radical

---

Press, 1981), sharply criticized for slovenly and deceitful scholarship by Henry Turner and Gerald Feldman but defended as correct in substance and honest in intent, though sometimes careless in documentation, by Abraham. The attitudes of Hermann Reusch, director of the Gutehoffnungshütte concern, have become a central index in the debate. These changed over time: In the spring of 1932 the impatient Reusch thought of Hitler as an energetic candidate for a "national" coalition – not a Nazi regime – against a temporizing Brüning; later in 1932, he saw him as an unsuitable radical, too prone to work with the Communists. His temperamental views exculpate him from being an advocate of a Nazi government; they hardly establish that he was a bulwark against Hitler's rise to power.

6   To my knowledge, Neumann first pointed out the characteristic difference between the analyses of the Left and the radical Right in *Behemoth*, 320–1. For Feder's role, see Turner, *German Big Business*, 62–4, 79.

quackery that flourished in the motley undergrowth of fascism. But a more respectable version existed. This stressed the role of the "productive" industrialist, often the engineer or applier of a new technology, vis-à-vis the mere rentier. In the years preceding World War I, the Italian Nationalist Association (founded 1910), financed in large part by the Ligurian steel magnates of the Ansaldo firm, drew on fashionable Sorelian ideas to urge a national syndicalism. Alfredo Rocco, who became the draftsman of Mussolini's key judicial and labor legislation of 1925–7, was a strong advocate among the prewar Nationalists of the *marcia dei produttori*, the organization of producer groups in a national and authoritarian corporative structure. Industrial leaders supported by their loyal work force would stress discipline, authority, and economic renovation. The state would rest not on the outmoded civic ideas of 1789 and subsequent liberalism, but on individuals' functional role in the economy.[7] Concepts such as these justified imperialism and a fundamental resistance to social democracy, although they allowed alliances with independent syndicalist leaders that would be forged during the Italian debate over intervention in the First World War and would later form one of the ideological pillars of fascism. The idea of "productivism" gave Mussolini the bridge by which he could cross from his earlier volatile socialism to his opportunistic Fascism of 1919–22. Productivism, moreover, appealed to the new managerial elite and the directors of industrial peak associations. Gino Olivetti, the most able spokesman for Confindustria, and his more authoritarian successor, Antonio Benni, tirelessly propagated the gospel of the technocratic industrialist. "Interference in authority is not possible," insisted Benni. "The only possible hierarchy in the factory is the technical one required by the productive order. . . . Industry is not personified by the capitalist or by the stockholders, but by its directors, its chiefs, and by the organizers of the enterprise."[8] These technocratic appeals played a continuing role among the less intransigent Fascists. Massimo Rocca argued that technocratic *gruppi di competenza* should replace the squads as the cadres of the new regime. Fascism would draw on those with economic or technological

---

7   See Paolo Ungari, *Alfredo Rocco e l'ideologia giuridica del fascismo* (Brescia: Morcelliana, 1963).
8   Benni to the Grand Council, March 1926, in Segreteria Particolare del Duce, 242/R, Gran Consiglio, National Archives microfilm T586/1122/074296-309. For Olivetti, see, Frank Adler, "Italian Industrialists and Radical Fascism," *Telos*, no. 30 (1976–7): 193–201; and Adler, "Factory Councils, Gramsci and the Industrialists," *Telos* 31(1977): 67–90. On some of the context of these managerial ideas in the 1920s see Chapter 2 of this volume.

expertise no matter what their earlier party preferences. Rocca lost out to the militants' insistence on the party's leading role during the Matteotti crisis of late 1924, but Giuseppe Bottai, the later minister of corporations, would sponsor similar plans. They remained an important motif of fascist economic thinking during the interwar period. Even if these ideas never seriously threatened the position either of the economic elite or the party hierarchs, they continued to appeal to some of the intellectuals, at least until the cultural stultification that afflicted the regime after the mid-1930s.[9]

Some analogous currents influenced German intellectuals. Rathenau's collaborator at German General Electric (AEG), the engineer Wichard von Moellendorff, called for a "conservative socialism" that would combine technical knowledge with an austere dedication to national duty and work. Oswald Spengler's "Prussian Socialism" similarly envisaged a Fichtean collectivism based on national labor and the collaboration of the engineer with political leaders. The Verein deutscher Ingenieure remained dedicated to the notion of an apolitical technocracy, which, they initially believed, National Socialism would help realize. Likewise the movement for *Schönheit der Arbeit*, growing out of the Neue Sachlichkeit of the late 1920s, sought a sober modernism and technological aesthetic even within the unpromising framework of National Socialism, with its other emphases on blood and race.[10]

These notions influenced ideas of industrial management. Pre–world war factory discipline began to be restored during the mid-1920s, and theorists of management proposed concepts of labor control that the Nazis had hardly to improve on. The *Führerprinzip* in the factory was grafted onto an encroaching authoritarianism that drew on imported Taylorite and Fordist appeals to scientific management and social engineering. Similarly, the Nazis' resort to compulsory arbitration de-

9 For syndicalist "productivism" see David D. Roberts, *The Syndicalist Tradition and Italian Fascism* (Chapel Hill: University of North Carolina Press, 1979), 257–60; also Alberto Aquarone, "Aspirazioni technocratiche del primo fascismo," *Nord e Sud*, 11, no. 52 (April 1964): 109–28; Sabino Cassese, "Un programmatore degli anni trenta: Giuseppe Bottai," *Politica del Diritto*, 3(1970): 404–47.

10 See Wichard von Moellendorff, *Konservativer Sozialismus* (Hamburg: Hanseatische Verlagsanstalt, 1932); Gerd Hortleder, *Das Gesellschaftsbild des Ingenieurs* (Frankfurt am Main: Suhrkamp Verlag, 1970); Karl-Heinz Ludwig, *Technik und Ingenieure im Dritten Reich* (Düsseldorf: Droste, 1974); Anson Rabinbach, "The Aesthetics of Production in the Third Reich: Schönheit der Arbeit," *Journal of Contemporary History*, 11(1976): 43–74; and Jeffrey Herf, *Reactionary Modernism* (Cambridge University Press, 1985).

veloped out of the Weimar arbitration courts that had already been turned into promanagerial authorities since 1930.[11]

To summarize, fascist doctrines could combine a neoliberal emancipation of the businessman coupled with a technocratic justification of his vocation. Productivism and an appeal to innovation and managerial engineering constituted the modern message that Fascists and Nazis conveyed to the Italian and German economic elites. These themes were cultivated after the respective seizures of power and remained recurring if not dominant motifs. But these ideas could not constitute the total of fascist notions about economic leadership. Although industrialists would be wooed with a technological gilding of their role in a profit system, their support was crucial only at certain moments, especially during the process of coming to power and then establishing a regime. The seizure and consolidation of power might require respectability. The earlier step, however, of making the party a plausible contender required a different strategy. It called for mobilizing enough broad-based support to make the movement seem the indispensable instrument for popular control. This objective required playing on the grievances of agriculture and the *ceti medi* (or *Mittelstand*). To this end both movements encouraged corporative utopias. Italian Fascist syndicalists advanced plans for organizing the economy into "corporations" that would reward dynamic businessmen but also guarantee everyone's economic niche. Nazi propagandists elaborated the small-business and agrarian corporative longings that had long characterized German economic organization.[12]

An important distinction persisted, however, between Italian and German corporativist programs. Italian theories urged corporative organization as a remedy for economic backwardness, as compensation for the fragmentation of the Italian economy, and as a step toward modernization. "The problem of the State thus becomes a formidable

---

11 See Otto Neuloh, *Die deutsche Betriebsverfassung und ihre Sozialformen bis zur Mitbestimmung* (Tübingen: Mohr, 1956); Johannes Ewerling, *Vom Einigungsamt zum Treuhänder der Arbeit* (Düsseldorf: Dissertations–Verlag E. H. Nolte, 1935); T. W. Mason, "Zur Entstehung des Gesetzes zur Ordnung der nationalen Arbeit vom 30. Januar 1934: Ein Versuch über das Verhältnis 'archäischer' und 'moderner' Momente in der neuesten deutschen Geschichte," in Hans Mommsen et al., eds., *Industrielles System und politische Entwicklung in der Weimarer Republik* (Düsseldorf: Droste Verlag, 1974), 322–51.
12 The Catholic industrialist Clemens Lammers offered a discerning critique early on of the leading economic ideas of Nazism; see his *Autarkie, Planwirtschaft und berufständischer Staat?* (Berlin: Heymann, 1932), cited in Turner, *German Big Business*, 251.

problem of *organization* by means of subordinating to the State all its reciprocally coordinated social elements."[13] In Germany, however, corporative advocates spoke more in terms of social protection, not modernization. Small business, handicraft, and the peasantry would be shielded from the competitive and oligopolistic tendencies that were pressing them toward bankruptcy. Italian national syndicalists and corporatives aspired to the very organization that seemed to make the German economy so vigorous; German corporativists sought to insulate the *Mittelstand* from the oppressive domination of big business and the threats of organized labor. Italian corporativists could thus easily endorse the proindustry thrust of "productivist" rhetoric. (Occasionally, however, they did become angry with the industrialists' efforts to evade control by the Fascist corporations. The 1925 debate over what economic sectors were to be included in the new corporations showed that industrialists wanted to remain unregulated.)

Whether corporativist aspirations sprang from modernizing or defensive impulses, they had limited results. After long discussion in 1925–6, Mussolini outlined six corporative sectors that would serve as counterparts to the national fascist labor corporations. He appointed a minister of corporations to oversee the structure, but with few budgetary or organizational resources to vie with the established bureaucracies of the ministries of Finance and National Economy. This provisional framework still assumed contrasting representation for labor and for capital. Disputes between the two would be resolved at the ministerial level or in the field of labor by the Magistratura del Lavoro (following the guidelines of the 1927 Charter of Labor). In 1930 the National Council of Corporations was instituted, and in 1934 the government called into being the "corporations" for particular economic sectors. They were theoretically designed as self-governing organs for planning and administration, but since they included labor representatives, landlords and industrialists resisted their claims to real authority. Even as hollow shells they served Mussolini some latent functions. They allowed him to claim that Fascism did incorporate an economic model that set it apart from liberal capitalism, which else-

13 Giuseppe Bottai, "Ancora dello stato corporativo," *Critica Fascista*, June 15, 1928, pp. 221–2, now included in Anna Panicali, ed., *Bottai: Il fascismo come rivoluzione del capitale* (Bologna: Cappelli, 1978), 140. Compare Pietro Grifone, *Il capitale finanziario in Italia*, 2d ed. (Turin: Einaudi, 1971), 111: "The economy regulated and disciplined by the state becomes the idea of the decisive classes of finance and economy. Henceforth [1929–33] they have acquired the firm conviction that it is impossible to overcome the crisis and move toward decisive recovery of business without recourse to the permanent and organic assistance of the state apparatus." This analysis is that of a Confindustria employee in 1940.

where seemed so discredited by the contemporary slump. The corporations also provided a project for the second decade of Fascist rule, which seemed to have completed its initial historical achievement of stabilization by virtue of the 1929 reconciliation with the Vatican. Fascist intellectuals, such as Ugo Spirito, made the round of conferences preaching the virtues of a postcapitalist fascism and in fact tried to nudge the structure in a "leftist" direction by calling for more collective control and even corporative ownership of the economy. Mussolini looked abroad to find that Franklin Roosevelt was merely seeking to emulate Italy's innovations. Actually, the corporations never achieved real regulatory power, much less ownership of assets. "Homo corporativus, the corporative economy, the corporative state and all the other irridescent formulae, object of such lively discussion and such ample study for a good twenty years, remained a dead letter."[14] Insofar as state intervention increased, it did so through the organization of the state holding company, IRI, establishment of the funds for land reclamation (Bonifica Integrale), the creation of national offices for controlling prices and production in cotton, paper, and cellulose, regulation of the banking system, and the buildup for war.

Corporativist initiatives had even fewer substantive results in Germany. Peasants did win virtually a return of hereditary entail, but within a year the early corporative initiatives had fallen into desuetude (a development analogous in a sense to the fate of the NRA under the New Deal). Kurt Schmitt, Hugenberg's successor as minister of economics after July 1933, retreated on measures that would have enhanced small-business organization. He halted initiatives, for example, that would have regulated the prices charged by the large integrated steel concerns to the smaller finishing industries. This was a setback, not to handicraft, but to smaller industries; however, other regulatory efforts also succumbed, such as plans to curtail department stores and to inhibit consumer cooperatives. Chambers of the handicraft sector and guilds won some relief from discount price competition, although they could not freeze their suppliers' prices, nor could

14 Sabino Cassese, "Corporazione e intervento pubblico nell'economia," in Alberto Aquarone and Maurizio Vernassa, eds., *Il regime fascista* (Bologna: Il Mulino, 1974), 325–56 (citation, p. 351). Compare in the same volume Silvio Lanaro, "Appunti sul fascismo 'di sinistra': La dottrina corporative di Ugo Spirito," 357–388. For the political context see Renzo De Felice, *Mussolini il Duce: Gli anni del consenso 1929–1936* (Turin: Einaudi, 1974). For the limited achievement of corporativist approaches in labor disputes see Gian Carlo Jocteau, *La Magistratura e i conflitti di lavoro durante il fascismo 1926/34* (Milan: Feltrinelli, 1978). The corporative structure was ostensibly completed in 1939 with the transformation of the parliament into a chamber of corporations.

they win any continuing authority to impose uniform prices on their members. The same compromise results regulated issues of vocational training. The grievances caused by the advance of large-scale capitalism were thus partially attenuated, but *Mittelstand* organizations did not capture the control they had hoped for. The number of handicraft firms fell by 153,000, or approximately 9 percent of the original 1.65 million.[15]

Corporativism thus yielded few of the socially protectionist results its adherents hoped for in Germany and few of the modernizing results its propagandists trumpeted in Italy (few results, too, in terms of integrating labor with capital). In different ways, it promised what neither regime was prepared to deliver – at least not outside agriculture. Corporativism envisaged a sort of producers' equality, but neither the large firms nor the state authorities were willing to cede real control over substantive policies. Corporatism as an informal accumulation of power among producer groups certainly remained a continuing tendency of twentieth-century political economies. Bureaucratic state intervention in Germany and Italy could delay its advance or establish agencies of countervailing corporatist power, but these new state-affiliated centers of economic authority had little to do with the formal agencies designed to transform the allegedly atomized individual of 1789 into man-the-producer.

Finally, as the armaments boom heated up in the late 1930s, the corporative structures installed for labor tended to crumble. By 1940, according to one recent study, state and industry were preparing themselves actually to accept some de facto collective bargaining, or else to grant the wartime labor authorities the power to exert even more coercion than that which Nazi labor law guaranteed on paper.[16] Beyond the spurious Labor Front, the choice would have to be either unions or the Gestapo.

If corporativism proved less important to fascism than ideologues

---

15   Arthur Schweitzer, *Big Business in the Third Reich* (Bloomington: Indiana University Press, 1964), 110–238.

16   See Rüdiger Hachtman, "Die Krise der nationalsozialistischen Arbeiterverfassung: Pläne zur Anderung der Tarifgestaltung 1936–1940," *Kritische Justiz*, 17 (1984): 281–300. The tensions within the Labor Front created by excess demand for labor have led Tim Mason to postulate a crisis for Nazi rule – see his *Arbeiterklasse und Volksgemeinschaft* (Opladen: Westdeutscher Verlag, 1975) and *Sozialpolitik im Dritten Reich* (Opladen: Westdeutscher Verlag, 1977) – which helped push Hitler into a decision to wage war. But in response, see Ludolf Herbst, "Die Krise des Nationalsozialistischen Regimes am Vorabend des Zweiten Weltkrieges und die forcierte Aufrüstung – eine Kritik," *Vierteljahrshefte für Zeitgeschichte*, 26 (1978): 347–92. The difficulties that did arise, the breakdown of a supposedly prolabor corporatism and the need either to make real concessions or use greater force, also emerged in Italy.

had originally proposed, national self-sufficiency became more so. In National Socialism autarkic concepts were always implicit in the visions of *Lebensraum*. Italian Fascism turned toward autarkic policies at two major points. By the mid-1920s Mussolini departed from his earlier *liberista* policies, replaced the laissez-faire Alberto De' Stefani as minister of finance with the Venetian shipping magnate and industrialist Giuseppe Volpi di Misurata. He initiated a more dirigiste control over banking and foreign exchange, initiated the "Battle for Grain" with its tariffs and subsidies, and sought stabilization of the lire at an exchange rate – the Quota 90 (90 lire per pound) – that rudely challenged the preferences of the dynamic export industries. The program rallied the southern landlords, grateful for the protection of grain prices and the revaluation of the government bonds they held, and helped create a new network of dependent industries. Above all, the chemical and electrical concerns would start to look toward the protection and contracts government provided. Depression difficulties prodded national self-sufficiency even further. The government established two public holding companies, the IRI (Istituto per la Ricostruzione Industriale) and the IMI (Istituto Mobiliare Italiano), as public bail-out agencies. The major steel companies passed into state receivership: Ilva, Terni, and Siac (Ansaldo and Cornigliano) under the IRI umbrella; Cogne, directly. Autarky was openly proclaimed a national objective in 1936 as a consequence of the Ethiopian war and League of Nations sanctions.[17] The official goals of autarky allowed the triumvirate of public steel managers, Arturo Bocciardo, Oscar Sinigaglia, and Agostino Rocca, the chance to press plans for technical modernization and centralized control over investment. With encouragement from Mussolini and the military, sectoral planning progressed in 1937 and 1938. But preparations for war and the need to achieve maximum production in the short term allowed private-sector firms to reclaim authorization for their own expansion. Long-term plans for integrated production were only partially fulfilled. They were renewed more effectively after the war when Alcide de Gasperi supported Sinigaglia's ambitious plans

17 For the organization of the banking system, the state holding companies, and the shift toward autarky, all of which constituted a major reorientation of political economy and involvement of the regime in the economy, see Gianni Toniolo, *L'economia dell'Italia fascista* (Bari: Laterza, 1980), 197–341; the conference volumes issued by the Banco di Roma, *Banca e industria tra le due guerre* (Bologna: Il Mulinio, 1981), esp. vol. 2, *Le riforme istituzionali e il pensiero giuridico*. More general accounts that cover this period include the still valuable memoir by Felice Guarneri, *Battaglie economiche tra le due grandi guerre*, 2 vols. (Milan: Garzanti, 1953); also G. Gualneri, *Industria e fascismo in Italia* (Milan: Vita e Pensiero, 1978); and Grifone, *Il capitale finanziario in Italia*, 148–211.

for modernization. Sectoral planning, therefore, did not require fascism; it did help to have IRI as stockholder and, later, Marshall Plan assistance. Given government control, any overriding public objective could allow the spokesmen for modernization to make some headway against those with investments already committed to outmoded technologies and small-production units.[18]

In Germany the beneficiaries of autarky were primarily the chemical industries, who profited from the encouragement to develop synthetic fuel. Without a "synfuel" program and state contracts, I. G. Farben could not have recouped the huge costs of hydrogenation development.[19] The impulse toward an avowed policy of autarky followed upon the continuing dispute between the Ministry of Agriculture, the army, and Farben on one side and the Ministry of Finance under Schacht on the other. The army and its supporters sought higher military expenditures and greater purchases of foreign raw material; Schacht remained concerned about balance-of-payments difficulties, the stability of the reichsmark, and the inflationary effect of rapidly growing public expenditure. For Hitler economic constraints were not insuperable; rearmament was a central priority, and political will could prevail over alleged economic obstacles. In a memorandum prepared at the Obersalzburg in August 1936, he wrote that every other consideration must be subordinated to achieving the world's largest army for the struggle against Marxism and Judaism. This meant developing the synthetic fuel industry within eighteen months. It further required the development of the low-grade Salzgitter iron-ore mines, which were to be restructured as the basis for the new Reichswerke Hermann Goering: "The Volk does not live on behalf of the economy, its economic leadership, or economic and financial theories, but rather, finance and economy, economic leadership, and every theory exist only

18 See Franco Bonelli, A. Carparelli, and M. Pozzoboni, "La riforma siderurgica: Iri tra autarchia e mercato (1935–1942)," in Franco Bonelli, ed., *Accaio per l'industrializzazione* (Turin: Einaudi, 1982), 215–333; Paride Rugafiori, *Uomini macchine capitale: L'Ansaldo durante il fascismo* (Milan: Feltrinelli, 1981).

19 Thomas Parke Hughes, "Technological Momentum in History: Hydrogenation in Germany, 1898–1933," *Past & Present*, 44 (1969): 106–32. See also W. Birkenfeld, *Der synthetische Treibstoff 1933–1945: Ein Beitrag zur nationalsozialistischen Wirtschafts- und Rüstungspolitik* (Göttingen: Musterschmidt Verlag, 1964). For Farben's pre-Machtergreifung concerns about Nazi hostility to their enterprise and their fears of losing export markets see Turner, *German Big Business*, 246–8; and for a detailed account that stresses the limited benefits and great uncertainties for Farben in the era of autarky, see Peter Hayes, *Industry and Ideology: I. G. Farben in the Nazi Era* (Cambridge University Press, 1987), esp. Part 3.

to serve in the struggle for our people's self-determination."[20] Results, it shall be seen in more detail below, belied the Führer's rhetoric. Political control was centralized under Goering's nominal leadership as head of the Four-Year Plan, and Schacht was pushed toward retirement. Still, production quotas were barely advanced by 1938, and by 1939 the economy would be prepared to fight only a brief war, not a protracted struggle for national existence. Some of the constraints derived from persisting shortages of important natural resources. In part, however, the difficulty lay in the fact that the new economic superstructure was imposed on an economy that was already highly organized by firms and trade associations that resisted new interventions. Had the regime simply provided the resources for additional hydrogenation development or for expansion of low-grade ore utilization, progress might have been swifter. Ruhr steel industrialists such as Ernst Poensgen and Albert Vögler of the Vereinigte Stahlwerke remained distrustful of Goering's new steel empire. In contrast to the Italian steel sector, the German Four-Year Plan did not allow a nucleus of technocrats to clear the way for decisive modernization. It seems only to have augmented the opportunity for internecine conflict.

Autarky thus was a policy with clear winners and losers. It moved both regimes beyond liberal economics and proclaimed them to be activist participants in a mixed capitalism. It established a new, artificially protected role for agriculture. It frayed the support of the traditional private mining and metallurgical industries that had earlier applauded authoritarian measures.[21] In return it drew on the efforts of newer managers who saw politics as an instrument of technocratic intervention (and personal opportunity). Nonetheless, it would be wrong to suggest that state intervention and autarky severely cost either regime the support of industrialists as a group. If private managers lost the freedom to invest in new plant without approval, in return they had already won an unprecedented degree of authoritarian control over labor, whose independent unions had been a preeminent concern since the First World War. They also often secured tariff protection or other subsidies. Giovanni Agnelli, for example, head of

---

20 Dietmar Petzina, *Autarkiepolitik im Dritten Reich: Der nationalsozialistische Vierjahresplan* (Stuttgart: Deutsche Verlags-Anstalt, 1968), 50–1; R. J. Overy, "Heavy Industry and the State in Nazi Germany: The Reichswerke Crisis," *European History Quarterly*, 15 (1985): 313–40.

21 For some of the relative losers, see the instructive industry study by John R. Gillingham, *Industry and Politics in the Third Reich: Ruhr Coal, Hitler and Europe* (London: Methuen, 1985), 51–2 and 68–87.

FIAT, was one of Italy's more liberal industrialists, but faced with the Model A in the late 1920s, he was grateful for protectionist policies.[22]

Let us pull together the ideological aspects of the Fascist and Nazi economic programs. Both Mussolini and Hitler called for freeing industrialists from state regulation in the crucial months before and after attaining power. Fascist and Nazi rhetoric drew upon a virtual engineering romanticism that was widely diffused in the decades before the World Depression. Each distinguished technological and industrial innovation from financial manipulation. Each included plans for corporative protection that would cut across class lines, although corporativism could have a modernizing thrust in Italy and a socially defensive one in Germany. Corporativism, however, had a limited impact in either case. The Nazis dropped their emphasis on rescuing the *Mittelstand* and exploited the concept primarily to seek *Gleichschaltung* of the trade associations already of long standing. The Italian regime instituted corporative structures step by step but withheld real authority from them, entrusting power to ad hoc instruments for sectoral intervention. Finally, if it advanced any economic program, fascism proposed an economy geared for national self-sufficiency and war. Autarkic policies represented a natural outgrowth of their political premises. They seemed all the more attractive to the dictators as ways to cut through contradictory interests at home. Faced with a tug of war among conflicting priorities and bureaucratic agencies, Mussolini in 1925 and 1936 and Hitler in 1935–6 seized upon autarky to impose a more comprehensive authority over disputing factions. Because the Italian economy was less advanced in many sectors, autarky could provide the sanction for more substantive efforts at modernization. In the German situation it tended to open up a new set of bureaucratic conflicts.

To be sure, this account has not stated what, along with nationalist economic objectives, remained the premise of both movements: the destruction of an independent labor movement. Between 1925 and 1928, Mussolini's government effectively undermined the socialist and Catholic trade unions and imposed a fascist confederation of unions as the official voice of labor. Finding in turn that this new structure was potentially too powerful, Mussolini subdivided it. The Nazis dissolved the old unions and imposed a Labor Front under party auspices. In both countries, the factory cadres (*commissioni interne* and NSBO cells) that more boldly represented labor interests, even when in fascist

---

22 Valerio Castronovo, *Giovanni Agnelli* (Turin: UTET, 1971), 457–62.

hands, were decisively weakened. The suppression of labor remained far from complete, but it was certainly thorough enough to win the adherence of most industrialists, even as the regimes moved toward degrees of intervention and regulation they otherwise mistrusted. To a large extent, despite their technocratic veneer, the repression and authoritarian control of organized labor remained the mission of these movements.

In a larger sense, fascist economics was not really economics at all. As Hitler wrote, economic issues were problems to be overcome by political will. The original appeal of fascism consisted in part of its promise that ordinary people need not be powerless against what often seemed inevitable and overpowering economic trends. German voters chose National Socialism not for its economic program, but from dismay at what the autonomy of the market and of economic laws had supposedly wrought – whether the formation of a militant working class or the formidable influence of monopolistic industries, banks, and department stores. Hitler promised, in Tim Mason's phrase, "the primacy of politics" over what became despised as "the system."[23] In Italy, decisive political will seemed important for converse reasons. Italian businessmen and commentators felt that their economy was insufficiently organized; throughout the early twentieth century, they aspired to emulate German achievements. Political authority appeared necessary to impose organization on a ramshackle capitalism. In both Italian and German situations, the underlying message stated that the economy was responsive to political will and not irresistibly subject to iron constraints or selfish interests. Very few major democratic statesmen in the West (outside of Franklin Roosevelt) offered a message that might compete with this counsel: Neither laissez-faire conservatives nor doctrinaire social democrats really believed in political reform for capitalism.[24] Fascists and Nazis exploited their failures of imagination.

23 T. W. Mason, "The Primacy of Politics – Politics and Economics in National Socialist Germany," in Stuart Woolf, ed., *The Nature of Fascism* (New York: Vintage, 1969), 165–95.
24 It is revealing that World War I economic accomplishments colored New Deal rhetoric and that many of the New Deal agencies drew inspiration from the American innovations of 1917–18. See William Leuchtenburg, "The New Deal and the Analogue of War," in John Braeman, *Continuity and Change in Twentieth-Century America* (Columbus: Ohio State University Press, 1964). For the passivity of social democrats see Robert Skidelsky, *Politicians and the Slump: The Labour Government of 1929–1931* (New York: Macmillan, 1967), and Harold James, "Rudolf Hilferding and the Application of the Political Economy of the Second International," *Historical Journal*, 24 (1981): 847–69.

Performance: the issue of modernization and development

The fate of the publicly controlled iron and steel sector raises a more general question: In what sense was fascism a force for economic modernization? The issue is raised occasionally for Germany, more often with respect to Italy. Hitler, after all, inherited an economy recognized as one of the two or three most technologically advanced, even if its farming population (as in the United States) was far higher than that of Britain or Belgium. The task facing the National Socialists was to resume and accelerate industrial output, not necessarily to transform the structures of production. Hence, the question of fascism as a force for modernization must really be addressed to Italian Fascism. The interpreter who has most strongly insisted it was is A. James Gregor, who has declared Italian Fascism to be a precursor of the nationalist modernizing ideologies that seemed prevalent through much of the "Third World" in the 1950s and 1960s. In contrast, Nazism is often labeled an archaic effort to arrest the consequences of modernization, a utopian railing against rationalization.[25] The debate is often conducted in confused terms. It rarely distinguishes political or societal from economic modernization; it usually fails to distinguish between different indices of transformation; and almost inevitably it fails to ask what the plausible trajectory of development would have been had the respective regimes remained nonauthoritarian. As one of the few Marxist analysts sympathetic to the claim of fascist modernization writes: "Under Fascist rule, Italy underwent rapid capitalist development with the electrification of the whole country, the blossoming of automobile and silk industries, the creation of an up-to-date banking system, the prospering of agriculture. . . . Italy's rapid progress after World War II . . . would have been unimaginable without the social processes begun during the Fascist period."[26] But for analyses of development as for other events, *post hoc, ergo propter hoc* is flawed reasoning.

An argument for social or political modernization is easier to make than one for economic modernization. Ralf Dahrendorf has argued that, whatever visions of an archaic *Gemeinschaft* the Nazis may have invoked, their major political contribution was to pulverize the older elites through persecution and war, so that on the debris of fragmented hierarchies the pluralist society of the Federal Republic could be built

25 See A. James Gregor, *The Ideology of Fascism* (New York: Free Press, 1969); and Henry A. Turner, Jr., "Fascism and Modernization," *World Politics*, 24 (1972): 547–64.

26 Mihaly Vajda, "The Rise of Fascism in Italy and Germany," *Telos*, 12 (1972): 3–26 (citation, p. 12).

more easily.[27] In this sense, of course, every political movement that persecutes its enemies lays the groundwork for modernization. National Socialism opened up new positions of influence, some to paranoid mediocrities who organized the SS, others to talented entrepreneurs who earlier would have remained petty businessmen, such as Paul Pleiger, machinist, then small manufacturer of mining equipment, regional NSDAP activist, and finally head of the Reichswerke Hermann Goering.[28] It can be argued that the Nazis' contempt for older, honorific establishments (as in academics), or their decimation of nobility and civil servants after the July 20, 1944, assassination attempt, eliminated future opponents of a modern democracy, even while the official ideology supposedly invoked values deriving from older, organic communities. But collaboration may ultimately have discredited the older elites more than persecution thinned them out.

Italian Fascism pulverized less. It left the monarchy intact and made a treaty with the Church. Dealing with existing elites, whether the industrial leadership or the political brokers of the Mezzogiorno, the Fascists suborned rather than smashed. Nonetheless, Mussolini and the Fascists appealed less frequently to what might be called *Vergangenheitsmusik* than did the Nazis. Certainly they did not like liberal democracy and socialism, but they did not glorify handwork and guilds, even if they periodically praised rural roots. They suggested that corporativism as a functional arrangement for political economy was the wave of the future. They destroyed the Left's unions but did not try to reverse the concept of collective labor relations. In a sense they tried to impose an authoritarian carapace over socioeconomic changes underway, though this often meant political reaction. The decisive episodes of Italian political modernization followed thick and fast between 1911 and 1922: The advent of universal male suffrage made political party overhaul necessary; the bitter controversy over entering World War I, the impressive mobilization of the work force and resources between 1915 and 1918 (more successful than during the Second World War), and finally the quasi–civil war in the North

27 See Ralf Dahrendorf, *Society and Democracy in Germany* (New York: Doubleday, 1967); a similar argument emerges in David Schoenbaum, *Hitler's Social Revolution* (New York: Vintage, 1963). Mancur Olson, *The Rise and Decline of Nations: Economic Growth, Stagflation and Social Rigidities* (New Haven, Conn.: Yale University Press, 1982), 74–80, makes a similar case to explain postwar German economic growth. The argument underestimates the continuities that persisted in German associational life across the 1945 rupture.
28 See Matthias Riedel, *Eisen und Kohle für das Dritte Reich: Paul Pleigers Stellung in der NS-Wirtschaft* (Göttingen: Musterschmidt, 1973).

between 1919 and 1922 all contributed as much or more to political modernization than the subsequent Fascist *ventennio*.

Nor did Mussolini's rhetoric and the other velleities of technocracy make fascism a modernizing ideology as such. It remained a prescription for ruling a society riven by internal cleavages. Perhaps one can rescue a weak connection between fascism and modernization in the sense that Kenneth Organski sought to claim fifteen years ago, when he argued that fascism was "a last-ditch stand by the elites, both modern and traditional, to prevent the expansion of the [domestic political] system over which they exercise hegemony. This attempt always fails and in some ways the fascist system merely postpones some of the effects it seeks to prevent."[29] This argument implies, however, that fascism is the result of sociopolitical bottlenecks in the process of modernization, and not the cause of the process. The view has some similarity to the longer-term schema proposed by Barrington Moore, Jr. The fascist recourse, Moore suggests, arose in societies (Germany and Japan) whose elites had earlier imposed economic modernization – tantamount to the introduction of market society – while limiting political democratization. In this view, fascism emerged from the Right's recognition that a channeled and plebiscitary mass mobilization was required if a more authentic democratic representation was to be forestalled.[30]

The issue of economic modernization is addressed even less incisively in the literature. Some scholars have cited overall rates of economic growth, as if the vicissitudes of the interwar world economy did not have any bearing on these national statistics. Others cite indices of industrialization without asking what the appropriate trend lines might be. To establish a connection between fascism and economic modernization or development, however, more precise indices are needed. If overall growth rates are potential evidence, they must be compared not only with respect to fascist and nonfascist economies in any period, but also with the growth rates before and after. At the same time, a long-term developmental trend must be proposed so that the effect of the wars and the Depression can be discounted. This is hardly a simple procedure. Economic historians, for example, have suggested two basic trend lines for German economic development: One would be the secular growth and employment tendencies from, say, 1900 to 1960. The other would treat the interwar period as one

29 A. F. K. Organski, "Fascism and Modernization," in Woolf, ed., *Nature of Fascism*, 41.
30 Barrington Moore, Jr., *Social Origins of Dictatorship and Democracy* (Boston: Beacon, 1964), chap. 8.

Table 1. *Per capita growth rates of selected countries and Western Europe as a whole*

Country	1897–1913 (%)	1922–38 (%)
Italy	2.7	1.9
Germany	2.6	3.8
United Kingdom	1.9	2.2
Sweden	3.5	4.1
Western Europe	2.1	2.5

Source: Gianni Toniolo, *L'economia dell'Italia fascista* (Bari: Laterza, 1980), 6.

of "delayed catching up," which is allegedly the normal process after a major war. The Nazi record seems more impressive in the first case, less exceptional in the second. Unless it is resolved which model should indicate the normal trend, it is hard to evaluate the contribution.[31] Finally, one must avoid oversimplified notions of what the development process entails. To measure only the decline of the agrarian sector can be misleading. Both Nazism and Fascism argued that the countryside must not be further depopulated. Their vision of modernization included maintenance of a significant agrarian sector. The appropriate measures to apply, then, might include per capita farm output, but not just the percentage of farmers in the population.

Granting these qualifications, we can examine a few rudimentary indices. Starting with per capita growth of real GNP, we can compare Italy and Germany with other Western European nations (Table 1).[32] The Italian economy thus progressed under fascism, but one can hardly credit a performance superior to that of the prewar Giolittian period and of course inferior to that of the decades 1950–70, in which real growth averaged 5 to 6 percent per annum. Nor can one claim that Fascist Italy distinguished itself in comparison with European standards during the interwar period.

31 For the secular trend evaluation see Knut Borchardt, "Trend, Zyklus, Struktur-brüche, Zufälle: Was bestimmt die deutsche Wirtschaftsgeschichte des 20. Jahr-hunderts?" in Borchardt, ed. *Wachstum, Krisen, Handlungsspielräume der Wirtschafts-politik* (Göttingen: Vandenhoeck & Ruprecht, 1982), 100–24. For the catch-up model (*verzögerte Rekonstruktion*), see Werner Abelshauser and Dietmar Petzina, "Krise und Rekonstruktion: Zur Interpretation der gesamtwirtschaftlichen Entwicklung im 20. Jahrhundert," in Abelshauser and Petzina, eds., *Deutsche Wirtschaftsgeschichte im Industriezeitalter* (Königstein/Taunus: Athenäum, 1981), 47–93.
32 No single source of statistics has been used for the various data cited in this chapter; hence, there may be some discrepancies. Nonetheless, each individual comparison – e.g., growth rates, manufacturing indices – has been drawn from a single source and should provide a valid measure of cross-national performance.

Does the record suggest better results in terms of structural change? If one examines agricultural output, which was a target sector of the regime, the results are not encouraging. Mussolini focused on "the battle for grain" as he sought to redress the balance of payments and reduce the heavy burden of grain imports caused by the poor harvest of 1924. Wheat was the major import whose output could be raised domestically. The battle of grain would also overcome class differences in the countryside and unite landlords and peasants as government clients.[33] A grain tariff was restored in July 1925 after a decade of suspension, and Arrigo Serpieri, one of the most impressive technocratic civil servants of the era, was placed in charge of extensive land reclamation schemes (the *bonifiche integrali*). Malarial swamps were drained, and major investment was committed to agricultural production. But agricultural productivity slowed despite the effort: Per worker growth of agricultural output declined from 2.2 to 1.6 percent in the years from 1921 to 1938, then rose in the postwar years (1949–67) to 6.2 percent.[34] The reclamation program underway after 1928, especially the commitment of state funds for landlords who undertook agrarian modernization, produced ambiguous results. The land area given over to grain cultivation rose about 9 percent, especially in the South, but this was not necessarily a rational allocation of national resources, especially since agrarian diversification did not advance. If grain imports no longer burdened the balance of payments, exports of wines, tomatoes, olive oil, and citrus stagnated. Yields per hectare increased in response to investment, but regional yields did not rise. Rural labor continued to leave the reclamation areas, which ran counter to the hopes for the program.[35] The contribution of agriculture to the national economy was not always thought through. The tariff was

33 Still useful is Carl T. Schmidt, *The Plough and the Sword* (New York: Columbia University Press, 1938), 45ff. For the political motivation see Piero Bevilacqua, *Le campagne del Mezzogiorno tra fascismo e dopoguerra: Il caso della Calabria* (Turin: Einaudi, 1980), 175–9.

34 Toniolo, *L'economia dell'Italia fascista*, 9. Data drawn from G. Fuà, *Formazione, distribuzione e impiego del reddito dal 1861: Sintesi statistica* (Rome: ISCO, 1972).

35 J. S. Cohen, "Un esame statistico delle opere di bonifica intraprese durante il regime fascista," in Gianni Toniolo, ed., *Lo sviluppo economico italiano 1861–1940* (Bari: Laterza, 1973), 351–73. Statistics on hectare yields in Giuseppe Tattara, "Cerealicoltura e politica agraria durante il fascismo" in Toniolo, *Lo sviluppo economico italiano*, p. 379. Even before the battle for grain the wartime growth of the chemistry industry led to more intensive use of fertilizers in the developed Po Valley region during the postwar years. See also A. Cadeddu, S. Lepre, and F. Socrate, "Ristagno e sviluppo nel settore agricolo italiano," *Quaderni Storici*, 29–30 (1975), cited in Toniolo, *L'economia dell'Italia fascista*, p. 62.

designed to encourage expansion of grain output, and indeed grain prices remained relatively shielded from the effects of the World Depression (the tariff was periodically raised in gold-lire units, hence rose ad valorem from about 25 percent in 1928 to almost 300 percent in 1934, as world market prices tumbled).[36] Only because food consumption, especially consumption of foodstuffs rich in protein, actually dropped after 1927 could the new costs be absorbed. Finally, government-guaranteed loan funds made their way disproportionally to the *latifondisti.* The social structures of the South were only reinforced as expansion of cultivated land benefited nobles and agrarian elites. When the architect of the program, Arrigo Serpieri, sought to impose requirements for the landlord beneficiaries to commit their own funds as well as state loans for improvements, he lost his job.[37]

Agricultural self-sufficiency motivated Italian Fascist policies earlier than German ones. Nazi policy sought at first more to stabilize a threatened farming population than to expand output. Reestablishing a form of peasant entail, the Reichserbschaft, was one approach; maintenance of grain prices was another. Antiinflationary concerns after 1936, however, kept the Nazis from supporting meat and dairy prices, with the result that farmers cut back on herds to grow rye.[38] Similar distortions, however, arose in many of the efforts at agricultural price stabilization pursued in different countries through the Depression. Canada, France, and the United States instituted policies to centralize the purchase of grains and support prices. Farmers proved to exercise decisive political leverage. To create reformist coalitions in democratic societies, such as Sweden and the United States, the parties of the Left had to subordinate the long-standing interest of their working-class constituents in cheap food and seek rural votes with plans for raising farm prices. The German Social Democrats singularly

---

36 See Toniolo, *L'economia dell'Italia fascista,* 148–9.
37 Jon S. Cohen, "Rapporti agricoltura-industria e sviluppo agricolo," in Piero Ciocca and Gianni Toniolo, eds., *L'economia italiana nel periodo fascista* (Bologna: Il Mulino, 1976), 379–407; also Jon S. Cohen, "Fascism and Agriculture in Italy: Policies and Consequences," *Economic History Review,* 2d ser., 32 (1979): 70–88. On the limits of the program and the social consequences in the South, see Bevilacqua, *Le campagne del Mezzogiorno,* pp. 200–1, 294–7. Without the bonifica program, investment would have fallen as sharply in agriculture during the Depression as it did in the other sectors of the economy. But if net investment in agriculture claims a higher proportion of national investment in the 1930s than before or after, does this suggest success for the agricultural program or just the attrition of industrial capital formation?
38 J. E. Farquharson, *The Plough and the Swastika: The NSDAP and Agriculture in Germany 1928–1945* (Beverly Hills, Calif.: Sage, 1976), 166ff., 223–7.

Table 2. *Average annual outputs of steel and electrical power in Italy*

	1901–10	1911–20	1921–30	1931–40	1941–50	1951–55
Steel	367,000	961,000	1.52m	1.96m	1.65m	3.94m
(indexed),	(= 100)	(= 262)	(= 414)	(= 534)	(= 450)	(= 1,074)
metric tons						
Electrical	750m	3,190m	7,640m	14,158m	19,165m	33,277m
power,	(= 100)	(= 425)	(= 1,187)	(= 1,888)	(= 2,555)	(= 4,437)
kilowatt-hours						

Source: Statistics from Rosario Romeo, *Breve storia della grande industria in Italia* (Bologna: Cappelli, 1963), Tables 12 and 17.

rejected such a strategy at the end of the 1920s, and radicalized German farmers turned decisively to the NSDAP from 1930 on.

Did industry make notable strides in Italy? Again, the results suggest progress, but no particular improvements over earlier or later periods, nor a record that was any better than that of other countries. Manufacturing output rose approximately 4 percent per annum between 1921 and 1937, as compared with 4.6 percent in Germany, 4.1 in France, 5.3 in the United Kingdom, 6.6 in Sweden, and 3.9 in the United States, where the Depression took its greatest toll (− 20.6 percent between 1929 and 1932). Output per worker climbed modestly; the engineering industry (*meccanica*, which includes machine tools, autos, and metal fabrication in general) and the chemical industry, however, grew as robustly in Italy as anywhere else. These sectors, moreover, created employment. If 1929 employment is indexed at 100, by 1939 the steel industry index had climbed to 166, the engineering industry to 170, whereas the aggregate for manufacturing stood at only 107. The autarky program that Mussolini proclaimed in March 1936 probably contributed to the most dramatic sectoral advances.[39]

Nonetheless, growth in output was more spectacular before the First World War and after the Second. The key indices of steel production and electrical power generation listed in Table 2 reveal these patterns. The rhythm of Italian industrial development does not, therefore, seem particularly tied to the Fascist regime. Italian growth has comprised

39   G. Tattara and G. Toniolo, "L'industria manifatturiera: Cicli politiche e mutamenti di struttura (1921–37)," in Ciocca and Toniolo, eds., *L'economia italiana nel periodo fascista*, 103–69, esp. 103–9, 140–3, 160 (tavola A.1). For the progress made in some key plants such as the Cornigliano steel works or FIAT's Mirafiori complex and the general technological enthusiasm of the 1930s, see Giulio Sapelli, *Organizzazione lavoro e innovazione industriale nell'Italia tra le due guerre* (Turin: Rosenberg & Sellier, 1978), 261–70.

a progression of spurts and slowdowns, surges of technical transformation that have yielded to the constraints of a more refractory social structure, then to be followed in turn by a resumption of rapid growth, often in the wake of decisive liberalization or dirigiste intervention. The Giolittian decade brought sustained development; the hothouse industrialization during World War I led to postwar crisis, but then to rapid export-led growth during the early, *liberista* phase of the regime from 1922 to 1925. Slowdown in the latter 1920s – induced in part by the excessive revaluation of the lira – introduced the doldrums of the Depression era, which hit Italy harder than often depicted.[40] Finally after a decade of often painful reorientation toward the domestic market, state investment stimulated renewed growth on the basis of autarky in the late 1930s, a period that helped lay down the infrastructural basis for the renewed spurt of the 1950s. If there is an argument for structural change, it lies with the growing role of IRI and the investments in steel, the engineering industries, and the chemical industries as Italy pressed forward toward national self-sufficiency and then war from 1938 to 1942.[41] Over the lifetime of the regime, however, Fascist interventions were part of a longer pattern

---

40 See Pierluigi Ciocca, "L'economia italiana nel contesto internazionale," in Ciocca and Toniolo, eds., *L'economia italiana nel periodo fascista*, 36. (The article as a whole provides a useful evaluation of the Italian performance in the international setting.) Cf. Toniolo, *L'economia dell'Italia fascista*, 139–46, esp. Tables 4.2 and 4.3. With an index of 100 for 1929, per capita GNP in 1933 was 95.9 in the United Kingdom, 93.0 in Germany, 95.1 in Europe generally, and 95.2 in Italy. But this setback was concentrated in manufacturing, not agriculture. The manufacturing indices for 1932 were 89.8 in the United Kingdom, 60.8 in Germany, and either 85.6 (ISTAT estimate) or 74.9 (OECD criteria) in Italy. W. Arthur Lewis, *Economic Survey 1919–1939* (London: Allen & Unwin, 1949), 61, suggests a sharper drop for industrial production: With 1929 = 100, 1932 output was 84 for the United Kingdom, 67 for Italy, and 53 for Germany and the U.S. Unemployment reached almost 16% in 1931 and 1932 but had dropped to less than 4% by 1935, and full employment prevailed from 1937 on (Toniolo, *L'economia dell'Italia fascista*, 276, n. 18).

41 Renato Covino, Giampaolo Gallo, and Enrico Mantovani, "L'industria dall'economia di guerra alla ricostruzione," in Ciocca and Toniolo, eds., *L'economia italiana nel periodo fascista*, 171–270, esp. 214–37. Even those who stress wartime destruction and backwardness of equipment, the authors argue, must credit the organizational changes, such as the work of IRI, that took place under Fascism (p. 234). Cf. P. Saraceno, *Ricostruzione e pianificazione (1943–1948)*, P. Barucci, ed., 2d ed. (Milan: Giuffré, 1974), 58–60, 76. But see in the Ciocca–Toniolo volume the formal model that stresses how modest growth and productivity gains remained: Renato Filosa, Guido M. Rey, and Bruno Sitzia, "Uno scheme di analisi quantitativa dell'economia italiana durante il fascismo," 50–101. For the ambiguous results of development see also Ester Fano Damascelli, "La 'Restaurazione antifascista liberista.' Ristagno e sviluppo durante il fascismo," *Il Movimento di Liberazione in Italia*, no. 104 (July–Sept. 1971): 47–100; also E. Fano, "Problemi e vicende dell'agricoltura italiana tra le due guerre," *Quaderni Storici*, 29–30 (1975): 468–96.

of periodic public initiatives. When these put power in the hands of intelligent entrepreneurs and engineers, they meant progress. When they responded to entrenched or politicized constituencies, they led to slowdown. In this sense Fascist leadership resembled the clientelistic approach of its liberal predecessors and its Christian Democratic successors.[42]

Performance: employment, wages, and recovery

Italian Fascism, the above discussion proposes, encouraged spurts of development when it came to power and as it switched to autarky. The fascist experience produced few results in terms of modernization that other governments might not have achieved. Although the Nazi performance gives an initial impression of greater progress, it is arguable that it, too, brought no great qualitative changes in the German economy. Productivity gains were meager in comparison with those scored in the United States, and even in Italy. The German lag, moreover, persisted at the phase of early recovery in the business cycle, when it is usually easiest to register such gains. Growth in productivity also lagged in comparison with the pre-1914 or post-1950 achievement.[43]

Structural change aside, recovery from the Depression was an accomplishment in its own right. In a world that found it difficult to utilize productive resources, how did the German record stack up? Since the trough of the Depression occurred six months before Hitler was summoned to the chancellorship, the Nazis might be considered more to have been beneficiaries of an economic revival that had its own autonomous impulses. Nevertheless, if one grants the National Socialists credit for the continuation of recovery, how should we evaluate their performance? Along with the United States, Germany was the country that suffered most catastrophically in the economic crisis. It emerged, of course, far more quickly. Nor was it likely that rearmament triggered this success, although rearmament helped sustain and advance the boom after 1935.[44] Admittedly, there were other

---

42   See Mariuccia Salvati, *Stato e industria nella ricostruzione: Alle origini del potere De-mocristiano (1944/49)* (Torino: Einaudi, 1982).

43   See R. J. Overy, *The Nazi Economic Recovery 1932–1938* (New York: Macmillan, 1982), 54–6; L. Rostas, "Industrial Production, Productivity and Distribution in Britain, Germany and the United States, 1935–7," *Economic Journal*, 53 (1943): 39–55.

44   Harold James, *The German Slump: Politics and Economics 1924–1936* (Oxford: Clarendon, 1986), 382–6, however, maintains that rearmament expenditures over 1933–5 amounted to 5.2% of GNP, a significant stimulus, as General Thomas certainly believed, and that they look small only in comparison with the later appropriations.

"Keynesian measures" undertaken under the "Immediate Program" (conceived under the Papen government and committing RM 600 million, or $150 million) and the Reinhardt program of 1933–4, including the construction projects for the Autobahn. Between 1933 and 1936 the government appears to have committed about RM 3 billion for work-creation projects and, allowing for related spending, perhaps RM 5.2 billion.[45] This was only 1 percent of GNP, but a large number of jobless were quickly absorbed during 1933 and 1934, first in house repairs, then construction. Recovery in fact soon outpaced whatever contribution deficit spending might have accounted for, even presupposing a generous multiplier effect.[46]

The impulses that led to German recovery remain difficult to explain.[47] Foreign demand did *not* provide a major stimulus. Exports rose again but at their peak in 1937 remained less than half the money

---

Some of these funds were spent on infrastructure. Still, the effect on employment would depend on the degree to which deficit finance was involved, not merely the size of the contracts. Unfortunately, the James book does not propose a general model for economic recovery.

45 Dietmar Petzina, *Die deutsche Wirtschaft in der Zwischenkriegszeit* (Wiesbaden: Franz Steiner Verlag, 1977), 112–13. For the major account of business-cycle policies, which stresses that recovery preceded rearmament, see C. W. Guillebaud, *The Economic Recovery of Germany From 1933 to the Incorporation of Austria in March 1938* (London: Macmillan, 1939).

46 Knut Borchardt argues that the 1932 shortfall in national income vis-à-vis the potential full-employment situation was RM 30 billion. Even a large deficit program would have comprised only RM 2 billion. See Borchardt, "Zwangslagen und Handlungsspielräume in der frühen dreissiger Jahre," in Borchardt, ed., *Wachstum, Krisen,* esp. 174, 270–1, n. 29, and 276–9, nn. 59, 63. Petzina's statistics (see footnote 31, above) suggest that during 1933–4, the government was spending about RM 2 billion per annum. Looking at government expenditure over the first five years of Nazi power, Costantino Bresciani-Turroni arrived at a multiplier of only 1.5; see "The Multiplier in Practice," *Review of Economics and Statistics,* 20 (1938): 76–88. Jeffrey Sachs and Barry Eichengreen, "Exchange Rates and Economic Recovery in the 1930's," *Journal of Economic History,* 45 (1985): 925–46, suggest that, in all countries, currency devaluation played a more effective role in the recovery than did Keynesian policies, which were intermittent (as in the United States), feeble (as in Britain), or late in coming on stream (as in Sweden). Germany, however, did not devalue the reichsmark; it resorted to bilateral agreements to pay for imports and reflated at home. See James, *The German Slump,* 395–7.

47 I follow here much of Overy's account, *Nazi Economic Recovery,* 28–38, including the limits of external demand (p. 30). Overy, however, may overstress public investment as the motor of recovery, especially encouragement of the Autobahns and a belated motorization (with all the linkages of these industries). The key, I think, is an effective government guarantee against a rapid rise of real wages, as had occurred in Weimar. This is apparently James's view, too. See *The German Slump,* 413–18.

value of those of 1928; the often noted bilateral trade with southeastern Europe comprised only about a tenth of this, and it had to be thrust upon the Balkans to cover Germany's needed imports (e.g., oil) rather than being generated by Bucharest or Budapest autonomously. But assuming that the source of demand had to be overwhelmingly internal, private economic forces seemed notably feeble. Of course, government policies had to facilitate reflation by loosening monetary policy, which (as in the United States) had become so restrictive during 1931. The Papen cabinet of summer and fall 1932 already began to abandon Brüning's intensely deflationary policies. It disguised an initial deficit financing of industrial recovery through the issue of Mefo notes – bills of exchange for the metallurgical industry that the Reichsbank would discount and the treasury would accept in lieu of taxes. By 1937 these bills and allied methods allowed significant expansion of the money supply.

Still, although monetary expansion permitted investment, it could not provide a positive impulse in its own right. Whence did that impulse derive? The resurgence of investment goods and production goods (the Germans distinguished these two sectors of nonconsumer items) rapidly outpaced that of consumer goods. Private net capital formation, however, does not seem to have contributed to recovery until 1935. Certainly public investment was a necessary spur, as was public expenditure in general: It rose 84 percent over 1933 levels by 1936, whereas national income rose only 46 percent.[48] This spending

---

48 The argument on the paucity of net private investment is made most persuasively by Samuel Lurie, *Private Investment in a Controlled Economy: Germany, 1933–1939* (New York: Columbia University Press, 1947), 22–38. Overy, *Nazi Economic Recovery*, 36, borrows Lurie's figures (p. 23) for net private investment and public investment (lines 4 and 5 of the tabulation below) but derives higher statistics for total private

	1928	1932	1933	1934	1935	1936
1. Total private investment (Overy; presumably with inventories and before depreciation)	9.7	0.3	3.2	4.7	7.2	9.2
1a. Total private investment without inventories, before depreciation (Lurie)	3.6	0.7	0.8	1.4	2.0	2.6
2. Inventory investment (estimate derived from 1 − 1a)	6.1	−0.4	2.4	3.3	5.2	6.6
3. Less depreciation (Lurie)		−1.8	−1.6	−1.6	−1.6	−1.6	−1.6
4. Net private investment, i.e., exclusive of inventories and after depreciation (Lurie)		1.8	−0.9	−0.8	−0.2	0.4	1.0

flowed to new public and party jobs (classified as public investment), to housing, transportation, including the Autobahns and railroad improvements, and, increasingly after 1935, rearmament.[49] In the industrial sector caution prevailed; "animal spirits" apparently lagged behind animal politics.

Given the tremendous underutilization of resources in Depression era Germany, it was perhaps not surprising that private industry held back from new capital investment, especially since the rationalization movement of 1927–9 had seen considerable capital deepening. Businessmen instead began restocking in 1934, eventually rehiring labor to operate the machines put into service during the previous decade. Insofar as investment did revive, restocking in the private sector and construction, sponsored by public authorities as well as private sources, seem to have been critical (see the Addendum).

If the new regime could not immediately spur private industry to undertake capital investment, it certainly signaled that labor might be rehired without earlier rigidities. Whether justifiably or not, German industrialists felt that labor demands had placed them in a crippling profit squeeze by the end of the late 1920s. The rapid wage increases of the postinflationary years (1924–9), the workers' exploitation of compulsory arbitration procedures, and the imposition of new social

---

investment. His results would seem to imply high inventory investment, since total private investment includes net private investment plus restocking of inventories and an allowance for depreciation. Subtracting Lurie's estimate for depreciation, RM 1.6 billion per year, allows a calculation for presumed inventory investment (line 2). But these derived estimates are higher than the direct statistics of company balance sheets indicate. (Granted, only public corporations, AGs, were tallied in the direct statistics, not all firms; see Table 6 in the Addendum for presentation of those findings.

49 For the prerearmament components of government spending see R. J. Overy, "Cars, Roads, and Economic Recovery in Germany, 1932–8," *Economic History Review*, 2d ser., 28 (1975): 466–83; G. F. F. Spenceley, "R. J. Overy and the Motorisierung: A Comment," *Economic History Review*, 32 (1979): 100–6; and Overy, "The German Motorisierung and Rearmament: A Reply," *Economic History Review*, 32 (1979): 107–12. I think that Spenceley is correct to insist on the initial impulse of building, including subsidies for home improvements. James discounts the role of investment in housing and suggests that new party jobs were a significant component of public "investment" (*The German Slump*, 414). But the significant variable for recovery is not whether 1935 investment and employment in the industry had reached 1929 levels; it is the increase over Depression levels. See Walter Fey, *Leistungen und Aufgaben der deutschen Wohnungs- und Siedlungsbau* (Berlin: Institut für Konjunkturforschung, 1936), for the estimate that housing employed 750,000 workers by 1934. Government subsidies and second mortgages provided RM 750 million of 2.2 billion for housing during the period from January 1933 to April 1934. Public construction was an even larger sector. See the Addendum.

insurance charges convinced German businessmen that they faced higher labor costs than their competitors. Above all they blamed the Weimar state for this handicap. Its provisions for arbitration and workers' representation, the leading role that the Social Democratic Party had played in its establishment, its weakness in the face of Allied reparations demands all tainted the entire constitutional order. So long as "the system" remained intact, industrialists reasoned, social democracy and labor unions would always be able to press for wages and benefits that precluded adequate profits and investment. Even Chancellor Brüning's use of decree power to impose deflationary policies and the exclusion of the SPD from the circles of government could not appease their distrust of the republic. A coalition that included the National Socialists along with conservatives promised a more durable redress.[50] The destruction of the social democratic trade unions, the change in arbitration results from prolabor to promanagement decisions, the failure of even the autonomous Nazi shopfloor delegates (the NSBO) to hold their own against the centralized and bureaucratic Labor Front, and the legislation of 1934 that defined the manager as the "leader" of a community of work meant a revolution in industrial relations.

Real-wage behavior also confirmed business hopes. In the late 1920s investment (so-called rationalization) became attractive, less as a means to take advantage of a buoyant market than as a way to lower unit labor costs and standardize jobs. Real wages rose, however, and because of rapidly falling prices, they continued to rise throughout the slump until mid-1932. Then monetary reflation allowed real wages to fall so that by the mid-1930s labor was again becoming relatively less expensive. The Nazis did not have to decree wage cuts as Mussolini had. They took advantage of the Depression that had predated their regime. Thereafter, they essentially stabilized real hourly wages at 1930 levels, indeed benefited from a further 6 percent decline in hourly real wage rates between 1932 and 1939; money wage rates were to remain more than 20 percent below their pre-Depression high. Until

50 Borchardt's essays, cited in footnotes 31 and 46, have generated heated controversy in Germany – and have won considerable support – by implying (1) that there were no feasible alternatives to Brüning's deflationary policies during the economic crisis and (2) that real wages really were excessive during Weimar and that industrialists understandably could see no remedy within the democratic system. For an opposing view and a review of the literature, see Charles S. Maier, "Die Nicht-Determiniertheit ökonomischer Modelle: Ueberlegungen zu Knut Borchardts These von der 'kranken Wirtschaft' der Weimarer Republik," *Geschichte und Gesellschaft*, 11 (1985): 275–94. See James, *The German Slump*, 190–245, for a judicious presentation of wage movements and how they were perceived.

the approach of war, with the "overemployment" and the wage drift of the rearmament boom, labor costs remained remarkably stable.[51] Likewise, the wage and salary share of national income also dropped from its 66 percent quotient of 1932 to about 55 percent by 1938, whereas the share of profits rose inversely.[52] As unemployment benefits declined with recovery, moreover, social welfare payments could decline from 9.3 percent of GNP in 1929 to 6.0 percent in 1938. They also dropped in the same period from 43.9 to 21.0 percent of the direct taxes and social security payments collected from taxpayers.

These significant changes in the division of national income were not easily perceived, however, against the backdrop of recovery from the Depression; the regime was always concerned about working-class hostility. General economic recovery let workers log longer weeks so their pay packets could increase. As labor costs became proportionally less onerous during the 1930s, the government also superintended a growing trend toward wage differentiation. Pay discrepancies increased between the skilled and unskilled. Male workers could win raises, whereas women continued to receive low pay. Exploitation of these lines of division could defuse any reaction, especially when no independent union movement existed to emphasize the stagnation of basic hourly wage rates.[53] In effect, the Nazi regime ensured that as

---

51 Gerhard Bry, *Wages in Germany, 1871–1945* (Princeton, N.J.: Princeton University Press and National Bureau of Economic Research, 1960), 233–65. Average hourly real-wage rates in all industry went from 100 in 1932 to 99.4 (1933), 96.8 (1934), 95.2 (1936), 93.9 (1937), 93.6 (1938), 94.0 (1939). Weekly earnings, however, rose from 100 (1932) to 113.7 (1936) to 126 (1939) (ibid., p. 262, Table 67). The fact that so much capacity was idle suggests that businessmen could rehire workers without having to add new capital, so the wage cost and its likely trend would be critical in considering profit margins. The fact that productivity remained relatively low (in a phase during which it should have risen) suggests, too, that capital investment seemed postponable and wage bills cheap Cf. Overy, *Nazi Economic Recovery*, 54 6).

52 Wage share cited by Borchardt, "Zwangslagen und Handlungsspielräume," in Borchardt, ed., *Wachstum, Krisen*, 281. For the source see Rainer Skiba and H. Adam, *Das westdeutsche Lohnniveau zwischen den beiden Weltkriegen und nach der Währungsreform* (Cologne: Bund Verlag, 1974), 108, Figure 8, for the quotients of labor's share of GNP, corrected for changes in occupational structure over time.

53 For this policy of wage differentials see Tilla Siegel, "Lohnpolitik im nationalsozialistischen Deutschland," in Carola Sachse, Tilla Siegel, Hasso Spode, and Wolfgang Spohn, eds., *Angst, Belohnung, Zucht und Ordnung: Herrschaftsmechanismen im Nationalsozialismus* (Opladen: Westdeutscher Verlag, 1982), esp. 109–29. The percentage figures for social insurance are from Konrad Eisholz, "Der Sozialhaushalt des Bundes," *Bulletin des Presse- und informationsamtes der Bundesregierung*, no. 25 (1960), 240, cited in Siegel, "Lohnpolitik," p. 107.

national income recovered and increased it could flow toward profits and investment, and rearmament.

Management, however, would find that it might recover profit margins, but not investment autonomy. Increasingly firms had to use their renewed earnings to purchase government securities and had to seek approval for expansion and new projects according to the competing priorities of state agencies, as in the Four-Year Plan. Nonetheless, the restrictions proved vexatious only later in the 1930s. They probably mattered less to businessmen than did the new availability of contracts and their recovery of unchallenged control within the enterprise.[54]

Whatever the impulse toward recovery and expansion, the national economy achieved an average annual 8.2 percent rate of growth from 1933 to 1939. By the later 1930s, rearmament was a major spur. If the 1939 national income exceeded that of 1936 by a third, the increment went increasingly into military expenditures. Still, even more impressive than the increase in output – by 1937–8 the British economy had also risen 20 percent over 1932 output – was the pace of reemployment, which seems to have been the most rapid in the West. By 1938 as Germany approached labor scarcity, the United States still had an unemployment rate of 20 percent, and the United Kingdom 10 percent.[55]

The Italian Fascists imposed similar restrictions on the role of labor. They undermined the old unions and then in 1928–9 undercut the autonomy of the Fascist replacements. Real wages were compressed, as in Germany, but without an equivalent contribution to growth of GNP. First of all, the high revaluation of the lira curtailed the export-led growth of 1922–5, and until the mid-1930s no domestic demand surged forth to replace foreign purchases. Still, the government did not rely on market slack alone to lower prices. Once inflationary pressure rose again after the revaluation of the lira, Mussolini decreed a 10 percent wage cut in May 1927 and, in October, a further reduction to bring the cumulative cut to 20 percent. Further reductions of about 7 to 12 percent each followed in 1930 and 1934, as real wages threatened to rise. In each case the government announced that it was trying to keep purchasing power constant as prices descended, although the wage reductions probably led the fall in prices. Only after 1938, as Italy moved toward rearmament, did wage pressure (and the possi-

---

54   On these policies see René Erbe, *Die nationalsozialistische Wirtschaftspolitik 1933–1939 im Lichte der modernen Theorie* (Zurich: Polygraphischer Verlag, 1958); also Lurie, *Private Investment*, esp. 98ff.

55   Petzina, *Die deutsche Wirtschaft*, 108.

Table 3. *Indexed real wages in Italy (based on 1938 lire)*

Year	Daily wages	Hourly wages	Hours worked	Year	Daily wages	Hourly wages	Hours worked
1913	100	100	10	1929	110	157	7.0
1918	90	81	11	1930	109	162	6.7
1919	118	147	8	1931	110	168	6.5
1920	130	162	8	1932	110	170	6.4
1921	135	179	7.5	1933	118	176	6.7
1922	128	160	7.8	1934	119	179	6.6
1923	133	164	8.2	1935	107	175	6.1
1924	132	155	8.5	1936	105	173	6.05
1925	126	148	8.5	1937	109	176	6.2
1926	123	143	8.6	1938	106	175	6.05
1927	125	162	7.7	1939	116	184	6.3
1928	112	161	6.9	1940	145	182	8

Source: Data from Vera Zamagni, "La dinamica dei salari nel settore industriale," in Piero Ciocca and Gianni Toniolo, eds., *L'economia italiana nel periodo fascista* (Bologna: Il Mulino, 1976), Tables 1–3.

bilities for working-class representation) resume.[56] Until then considerable slack in the economy remained, and it was possible to keep employment relatively stable (except for 1931–4) only by putting many workers on short time. Work seems to have been spread, not created (see Table 3).[57]

Fascism in each country thus performed at least one common economic role. Both Fascists and Nazis came to power after a period of rapidly rising money wages had been ended by a deflationary crisis. In Italy the sharp recession of 1921–2 ended the giddy pay increases of the postwar years. The layoffs of 1921–2 contributed in fact to the weakness of the working class in the face of Fascist violence. In Germany the end of the 1923 inflation had led to a sharp stabilization crisis and heavy unemployment. Real wages were stabilized at a level

56 On the resumption of fascist trade-union pressure see Giuseppe Parlato, "La politica sociale e sindacale," in Gaetano Rasi, ed., *Annali dell'economia italiana*, vol. 8, part 1, *1930–1938* (Milan: IPSOA, 1983), 302–5; and "La politica sociale e sindacale," in *Annali*, vol. 9, part 1, *1939–1945*, 413–29. In both regimes the rearmament boom strained official labor structures and threatened to force a resumption of *de facto* collective bargaining. Cf. the sources cited in footnote 16.

57 Vera Zamagni, "La dinamica dei salari nel settore industriale," in Ciocca and Toniolo, eds., *L'economia fascista nel periodo fascista*, offers the most recent and reliable résumé of wage movements, pulling together and evaluating earlier series by Salvemini, Buozzi, Mortara, Vannutelli, the Confindustria, and others.

far lower than that of 1913; however, wages jumped rapidly during the prosperity of the late 1920s. Whereas unit labor costs in Germany lagged behind Britain's in the mid-1920s, by the end of the decade they had overtaken them. German entrepreneurs looked for a way to cap the rise of money wages and despaired of finding it within the framework of republican politics. While the Depression broke the momentum of wage increases, the Nazis enforced wage stability for the renewed post-1932 expansion. Now it did not require fascist institutions to contain wage pressure; in Great Britain wages remained low despite major union offensives. But in Italy and Germany the "opening" of the political system in the postwar period and the tumultuous advent of mass political parties and powerful unions seemed to preclude similar stabilization. Fascism seemed to provide the necessary political framework.

There were differences, however. They may have derived from the inherent strength of the two economies, but they also depended on historical timing. Italy did not benefit from the rapid recovery that Germany enjoyed before the rearmament boom. Whereas the National Socialists could exploit the recovery to achieve a relatively painless redistribution of national income shares away from labor, the Fascists could not. Moreover, whereas declining real wage rates in the period from 1932 to 1936 probably stimulated the German recovery, the money wage cuts decreed in Italy did not have a comparable effect.[58] In effect, the Italian Fascists had to steer their economy through the worst shoals of the World Depression, while the Nazis could ride the recovery. Mussolini had coasted on the world economic recovery from 1922 to 1925; he did not get another equivalent opportunity.

Performance: mobilization and war

The final test of the fascist economies was preparation for the war they helped bring about. Their performance, especially that of Germany, has been the subject of many controversies. Both countries devoted significant shares of national income to preparation for the Second World War (Table 4). By 1939 Germany was directing about 23 percent of its GNP to military expenditures. Even Italy apparently allocated an impressive 10 to 12 percent to military preparations, al-

---

58 Either neoclassical or Keynesian theory could account for this. Neoclassical theory would argue that the Italian money wage cuts were not sufficient to compensate for the fall in prices, so real wages fell insufficiently. Keynesian theory would argue that cutting money wages was bound to diminish aggregate demand. The path to lower real wage rates must be through higher prices, i.e., the German outcome.

Table 4. *Comparative military expenditures*

Country	1935	1936	1937	1938	1939
Italy[a]	$999m	1,175m	672m	796m	—
	L 12.2b	16.1b	12.6b	15.0b	28.1b
	= 12.0%	15.0	10.0	10.9	18.4
Germany	$2,415m	4,352m	4,704m	6,908m	—
	RM 6b	10.8b	11.7b	17.2b	30b+
	= 8.1%	13.0	12.6	16.4	23+
France	$835m	906m	859m	840m	—
	Fr 12.7b	14.9b	21.2b	28.9b	92.7b
	= 5.7%	5.8	7.0	8.5	—
Britain	$671m	924m	1,265m	1,944m	—
	£ 137m	186m	256m	398m	719m
	− 3.3%	4.2	5.6	8.3	14.4

Note: Data are expressed in U.S. dollars, in national currency, and as a percentage of national income.
[a]Italy's budget figures are 1935–6, 1936–7, 1937–8, etc.
Source: MacGregor Knox, *Mussolini Unleashed 1939–1941* (Cambridge University Press, 1982), 293–6, and calculated from diverse sources, including, for Germany, Berenice Carroll, *Design for Total War: Arms and Economics in the Third Reich* (The Hague: Mouton, 1968), 184. For Italy see Renato Covino, Giampaolo Gallo, and Enrico Mantovani, "L'industria dall'economia di guerra alla ricostruzione," in Piero Ciocca and Gianni Toniolo, eds., *L'economia italiana nel periodo fascista* (Bologna: Il Mulino, 1976), 189–96. Combining their Table 4 (189) with the indirect expenditure percentages reported on p. 195, one reaches ratios of military costs to gross national income of about 33% (1941), 43% (1942–3), and 57% (1944). The last seems implausibly high, however. For the French difficulties – George Bonnet's fiscal orthodoxy in 1937, the woeful industrial infrastructure even when funds were voted, the delays in construction after authorization – see especially Robert Frankenstein, *Le prix du réarmement français 1935–1939* (Paris: Publications de la Sorbonne, 1982), 163, 234, 289–9. On British fiscal conservatism in the 1930s, G. C. Peden, *British Rearmament and the Treasury 1932–1939* (Edinburgh: Scottish Academic Press, 1979).

though it is hard to calculate how much went to the Ethiopian war and how much to rearmament for a European conflict. In any case the commitment declined for two years after the Ethiopian war. (The percentage shares listed in Table 4 might be compared with the approximately 10 percent proportion of GNP that the NATO powers targeted in the early 1950s and the 5 to 6 percent devoted to military expenses today.)

The view that tended to dominate from the work of Burton Klein to that of Alan Milward denigrated German military efforts and argued that at best Hitler prepared only for quick blitzkrieg campaigns. Hitler, it has been suggested, hesitated to impose too severe an austerity on

German society; he feared a reenactment of the revolution of 1918. The theme of 1918's surrender and revolution appear frequently in Hitler's oratory, as he repeatedly insisted that the Second World War would not end as the first had. Nonetheless, the finding that the Nazis spared civilian consumption more than did the other major belligerents has since been challenged by Berenice Carroll, R. J. Overy, and others. A great deal depends on the index chosen. Conversion of the economy for "total war," Overy argues, was planned from the outset, not suddenly improvised. ("Total war," however, remained a widespread rhetorical trope in nationalist circles. What policies it might actually entail was hardly clear.) If the production targets of 1939 seem undistinguished, it was because government planning usually projected the initiation of war only after 1940. Nonetheless, commitment of national resources to war increased from the late 1930s until Allied bombing and invasion finally dislocated the German economy. How great the real burden was is not easy to decide, however. Recent estimates suggest a powerful conversion effort from 1939, but a large share was tribute exacted from the occupied countries. Table 5 provides some breakdown of the national effort.

Moreover, as Overy argues, in the areas of housing and automobiles, cutbacks *were* significant. Since, however, this curtailment of civilian consumption had already been initiated before the war, wartime conversion may have appeared less drastic.[59] Carroll's figures suggest that the pace of British conversion to military expenditure was steeper than Germany's – not only did the United Kingdom begin later, but

59 R. J. Overy, "Hitler's War, and the German Economy: A Reinterpretation," *Economic History Review*, 2d ser., 35, no. 2 (1982): 272–91. For the older views see Burton H. Klein, "Germany's Preparation for War: A Re-Examination," *American Economic Review*, 38 (1948): 56–77; and Klein, *Germany's Economic Preparations for War* (Cambridge, Mass.: Harvard University Press, 1959); Alan S. Milward, *The German Economy at War* (London, Athlone, 1965); and the original source for this view, the United States Strategic Bombing Survey, *The Effects of Strategic Bombing on the German War Economy* (Overall Economic Effects Division: October 31, 1945). Klein was assistant director of the staff, J. K. Galbraith the director. For an estimate of how successfully the Germans could extract resources from abroad see Alan S. Milward, *The New Order and the French Economy* (New York: Oxford University Press, 1970); and Milward, *War, Economy and Society, 1939–1945* (Berkeley and Los Angeles: University of California Press, 1979), 135–65. Milward estimates that payments from France to Germany comprised 11% (1940), 19% (1941), 21% (1942), 37% (1943), and 28% (January to June 1944) of French GNP and that these represented from 3 to 9% of German GNP in the respective years. In addition Germany extracted underpriced goods and services for the francs extracted and underpriced labor from the French workers who labored in Germany. France's total contribution represented about 42% of what Germany drew from all the occupied countries as a group. Fritz Federau, *Der Zweite Weltkrieg: seine Finanzierung in Deutschland* (Tü-

Table 5. *German military expenditure and national income*

Year [a]	National income [b]	Military expenses [c]	Civilian spending	Sources of Reich income			
				Taxes	Other [d]	Credits	Levies [e]
1939–40	98	41.2	22.3	24.9	6.3	29.1	0.7
1940–1	120	60.2	27.0	28.7	6.3	44.7	10.6
1941–2	125	77.5	32.2	33.0	6.9	56.0	16.3
1942–3	134	91.1	45.9	44.6	9.8	63.0	24.6
1943–4	130	110.8	50.0	33.9	10.7	85.0	24.7
1944–5	—	64.2	35.0	19.5	5.0	97.6	8.0

Note: All data represent billions of reichsmarks.
[a] For all categories but national income (which presumably goes from midyear to midyear) the years run from September 1 through August 31. For 1944–5, the figures apply up to May 8, 1945.
[b] The national income estimate is from Overy as cited in the source note, below. The other data are from Federau, as cited in the source note.
[c] Military expenses include direct Wehrmacht expenses and support for families, which declined over time from about 8 to 6 percent of the whole.
[d] Other income here includes that from railroads, state corporations, levies on internal state authorities, etc.
[e] Levies include the sources derived from the occupied countries and territories. These include levies from the General-Government, Bohemia-Moravia, and other regions annexed within the Grossdeutsches Reich, intergovernmental revenues provided by occupied states still in being (the Western and Scandinavian countries; Italy after 1943), and revenues from occupied Russia.
Source: The data are derived primarily from Fritz Federau, *Der Zweite Weltkrieg: Seine Finanzierung in Deutschland* (Tübingen: Wunderlich, 1962), 32, 59, 63. Federau has interpolated from German fiscal years (April 1 to March 31) to get war years. He has also evidently combined domestic *"sonstige"* receipts from Poland and Bohemia-Moravia with other occupation costs. Federau's war costs (after deducting military family allowances) are roughly comparable to those provided by R. J. Overy, "Hitler's War and the German Economy: A Reinterpretation," *Economic History Review*, 2d ser., 35, no. 2 (1982): 272–91, Table 1, p. 283. For the most recent estimates, see Willi A. Boelcke, *Die Kosten von Hitlers Krieg* (Paderborn: Schöningh, 1985).

its expenditures peaked by 1942, a year or two before Germany's. However, the final demands of the wartime economy were apparently not so different in London and Berlin. Each adversary ended up claiming above 60 percent of GNP for military expenditure (the United

bingen: Wunderlich, 1962), 30, 32, 62, 63, estimates that income from the occupied countries (not counting forced labor of foreigners in Germany) amounted to RM 85 billion, or 46% of the 185 billion in taxes the Germans raised from their own population, 27% of their public revenues, and 13% of budgeted war costs.

States remaining below 45 percent).[60] During the war Germany and Italy added significantly to their productive capacity – investment that might serve purposes of war or peace but meant significant social saving. Allied air attacks on factories did little more than compensate for the installation of new plant.[61]

Obviously these Axis efforts were not sufficient. Could a rational calculation have suggested that they might be? A great deal of the German expenses in the late 1930s went to constructing barracks, air-fields, and other infrastructural items that compliance with the Treaty of Versailles until 1935 had precluded building. The raw-material balance sheet in terms of iron ore, manganese, petroleum, and many other essential supplies was discouraging. The Reichswehr understood clearly that if the projected attack on Poland developed into a full-scale war with the Western Allies, the German economic situation would become precarious. Only 44 percent of imported foodstuffs, 33 percent of necessary raw-material imports, and 40 percent of aggregate imports, for example, came from adjacent territories. The greater share was subject to interdiction by blockade. Although a Greater German or middle European economic realm did seem to promise sufficient foodstuffs, industrial raw materials, the army argued, required at least control of Scandinavia as well as Southeast and Eastern Europe. As late as August 22, 1939, Hitler conceded that Germany did not yet have the economic potential for a long war.[62] The logic of risking a long war in 1939 was deeply flawed.

60 Berenice Carroll, *Design for Total War: Arms and Economics in the Third Reich* (The Hague: Mouton, 1968), 184–5, and appendix, 262–7. The British effort peaked at about 57% of GNP vs. 64% of national income; the German effort apparently peaked at more than 61% of GNP. Carroll finds military investment (including military hardware but not pay) to be significantly greater than Klein's estimates, especially if infrastructural items are included (p. 188).

61 See R. Krengel, *Anlagevermögen, Produktion und Beschäftigung der Industrie im Gebiet der Bundesrepublik von 1924 bis 1956* (Berlin: Duncker & Humblot, 1958), 94. Italy, too, saw some notable increments in productive capacity in the steel, engineering, and chemical sectors between 1938 and 1942 but a continuing underutilization of this growing capacity until the postwar period. For a detailed sectoral analysis see Covino, Gallo, and Mantovani, "L'industria dall'economia di guerra alla ricostruzione," 171–270, esp. 214–37.

62 Hans-Erich Volkmann, "Die NS Wirtschaft in Vorbereitung des Krieges," in Militärgeschichtliches Forschungsamt, ed., *Das Deutsche Reich und der Zweite Weltkrieg* (Stuttgart: Deutsche Verlags-Anstalt, 1979), vol. 1, esp. 350–5, 366. However, despite the shortfalls in Four-Year-Plan targets, raw-material shortages apparently did not cause general economic difficulties until 1944. (Whether the foreseeable constraints might have preemptively shaped military strategy and arms efforts so as to avoid earlier emergencies is not clear.) See Rolf Wagenführ, *Die deutsche Industrie im Kriege 1939–1945*, 2d ed. (Berlin: Duncker & Humblot, 1963), 52 (based on Wagenführ's 1945 manuscript); also cited by Dietmar Petzina, "Vierjahresplan und Rüstungspolitik," in Forstmeier and Volkmann, eds., *Wirtschaft und Rüstung*, 79.

But the rationality of the wager is not the concern here. Given that there was war, how did the German (and Italian) economy respond with the resources it could muster? The question has remained a difficult one, because the economy had to be organized under increasingly adverse and hazardous conditions.[63] It is also hard to resolve because mobilization of resources in quantitative terms was not the only important variable. Let us grant that Germany's mobilization in terms of national product reached levels that despite the slackening of pace in 1940–1 became as high as any other power's. Two important questions remain: Could more resources have been mobilized; and could resources have been used more efficiently? There is still reason to believe that mobilization of labor and the diversion of productive resources were relatively lackadaisical. Reserves of female labor went unused, and the number of German women employed may actually have dropped slightly. Consumer goods were hardly cut back until 1942 (from 28 to 29 percent of net output in 1939–41 to 25 percent in 1942, 23 percent in 1943, and 22 percent in 1944); and caloric intake remained high.[64] In sum, the Germans waged an inconsistent war effort characterized by (1) a massive thrust toward rearmament that came primarily out of the *reemployment* of resources from 1935 to 1940; (2) a slackening of pace during 1940–1 (while the British pushed ahead); and (3) an impressive harnessing of resources from 1942 to 1944 coupled, however, with an unwillingness to increase female labor, convert small-unit, middle-class production, or infringe on food consumption (though extraction from the occupied countries obviated those sacrifices).

Efficient use of resources also seems to have been impaired. If there is any consistent report about the German and, even more, the Italian war production effort, it is one of administrative confusion and bu-

---

63 Airplane production illustrates the difficulty of assessing achievements and underlying problems. In 1940 Germany turned out 10,247 planes, the United States 12,804, Russia 10,565, and Britain 15,049 – up from 7,940 the previous year. In 1944, the year of maximum production, Germany produced 39,807 planes, compared with Britain's 26,461, the Soviet Union's 40,300, and the United States's 96,318. This remains an impressive, if hopeless, effort. True, the Western powers were able to work more efficiently as well as produce more. In 1941, German workers produced aircraft at 81% of the volume of American workers; by 1942 they dropped to 69% recovered to 80% in 1943, and by 1944 had fallen to 45%. However, "efficiency" may just reflect the disruption of German factories by aerial bombardment. See R. J. Overy, *The Air War 1939–1945* (London: Europa, 1978), 150, Table 12, and 168.

64 Dietmar Petzina, "Soziale Lage der deutschen Arbeiter und Probleme des Arbeitseinsatzes während des Zweiten Weltkriegs," in Waclaw Dlugoborski, ed., *Zweiter Weltkrieg und soziale Wandel* (Göttingen: Vandenhoeck und Ruprecht, 1981), 65–86; and Ludolf Herbst, *Der totale Krieg und die Ordnung der Wirtschaft* (Stuttgart: Deutsche Verlags-Anstalt, 1982), 118–26.

reaucratic ineptitude. General Thomas on the German side, General Favagrossa on the Italian documented the quarrels between agencies and the flawed decisions. Thomas complained that Goering's Four-Year Plan left him inadequately provisioned with steel and other raw material. Labor allocations were insufficient. For Italy new weapons were produced at best in prototype; army units remained skeletal and underequipped. Delusion about strength and modernity were cultivated by Mussolini and permeated the defense establishment.[65]

Such conflicts, to be sure, beset all the war economies, and participants in many countries complained about the slow pace of conversion. After all, the story of war production everywhere must be a history of bottlenecks. It is hard to know whether the German effort (leaving aside the Italian deficiencies, which seem of a different order) was really so much less efficient. The major German deficiency may have been the reluctance to shake out inessential labor, such as from domestic service, or to convert more plants to multiple shifts. Instead, the Reich resorted to levies of foreign workers. Almost 30 percent of the Reich's industrial workers and 22 percent of farm workers had been dragooned from abroad by mid-1944.[66] Their availability allowed the Nazi party apparatus to resist Speer's efforts at more effective mobilization.

How can the nonexpert adjudicate the overall controversy? Preparation for war was impressive and clearly outpointed that of the democracies. Overy's insistence on this accomplishment is a useful one, although what total war ought actually to have mandated he leaves obscure. Still, it was natural enough that rearmament should have been impressive. Preparing for some war was the Nazi collective project. Accepting major economic sacrifices during war was a different matter. When they were imposed after 1942, Germany came around to making them; on that point Carroll makes sense. But Klein and Milward still remain persuasive that, during 1940 and 1941, the German leadership envisaged the war effort as a relatively painless one and seriously underestimated the demands of their Russian or Anglo-American conflicts. Was success in Poland and the West too cheap?

65 Carlo Favagrossa, *Perché perdemmo la guerra* (Milan: Rizzoli, 1946); Fortunato Minniti, "Il problema degli armamenti nella preparazione militare italiana dal 1935 al 1943," *Storia Contemporanea*, 9, no. 11 (1978): 5–61; General Georg Thomas, *Geschichte der deutschen Wehr- und Rüstungswirtschaft* (1918–1943/5) (Boppard am Rhine: Schriften des Bundesarchivs, no. 14, 1966).

66 Edward Homze, *Foreign Labor in Nazi Germany* (Princeton, N.J.: Princeton University Press, 1967), 234–5; Clarence D. Long, *The Labor Force under Changing Income and Employment* (Princeton, N.J.: Princeton University Press, 1958), 202–14; and Sidney Ratner, "An Inquiry into the Nazi War Economy," *Comparative Studies in Society and History*, 12, no. 4 (1970): 466–73.

Or would a quicker and more drastic mobilization have collided with too many entrenched positions and ideological preferences? Let us accept that societies so geared toward military achievement showed notable hesitancy in imposing the controls needed for streamlined war production. The explanatory task does not require demonstrating that Germany performed noticeably less well than the democracies. It requires accounting for the deviations from what might have been expected from a militarized authoritarian regime.

Inefficiency is sometimes cited, but the term is too vague. It may be used to cover a failure of will or foresight: a disbelief that more effort had to be made than was made by 1940. It may apply to the internal structure of the regime: its "polycratic" rivalries and infighting or its fear that asking too much of its citizens might endanger its authority. It may apply to more ordinary sources of friction, such as beset most states that have to convert to war production: managerial inefficiency.[67] The fact that the fascist states had contemplated rearmament for years before the war may have diminished the incentive of the military to work with industry. The generals relied on their own expertise and links with traditional suppliers. Only when Fritz Todt and then Albert Speer wrested control of the war economy in 1942–3 could a successful turnabout be improvised. Its essence was "industrial self-administration," which meant getting rival ministries, party *Gauleiter*, and, after May 1942, even the army's Economic and Armament Office (the Wirtschafts- und Rüstungsamt, now largely dismantled and reconstituted within Speer's munitions ministry) out of the procurement business. Instead, the military planning agencies would channel their requests, via Speer's bureaucrats, to committees of industrialists who would take charge of producing the materiel, distribute orders to firms, and authorize the use of labor and raw materials. Cutting across these committees (but with the same businessmen often serving in both) were the "rings" that were organized by the industrial sector to take charge of procuring the needed raw material. By 1944, the system of rings and committees had grown into a sprawling network with cross-cutting tasks and jurisdictions. Speer's central planning office employed only about six hundred functionaries, but tens of thousands now had positions in hundreds of overlapping committees. They worked well at getting hold of submarines, tanks, or motors, but not at making overall production choices. Speer's achievement was less to organize an overall planning organization – although he did gut the rival agencies of the army and the Four-Year

---

67   A revealing case study is provided by Edward L. Homze, *Arming the Luftwaffe: The Reich Air Ministry and the German Aircraft Industry, 1919–39* (Lincoln: University of Nebraska Press, 1976), esp. 261–7.

Plan – than to shield business and engineering talent from bureaucratic interference, even as he upgraded his own ministry. In this sense, as in so many others, the capacity for improvisation proved more useful for modern war than did the skills of long-term planning.[68]

Granted, improvisation and planning do not have to be at odds. Nevertheless, despite the massive apparatus on paper for planning in Germany, until 1942 effective planning was fragmentary at best. Too many agencies collided inside government circles; too many jealous hierarchs saw their power and prerogatives at stake; too much revery was allowed the dictators.[69] In contrast, Great Britain, whose economy remained the most resistant of any to governmental intervention during the 1930s, proved more successful at wartime planning. In part Britain could not afford to harbor any illusions of swift victory or a short war. British constraints in terms of labor supply and necessary imports, moreover, were so overwhelming that all economic process could be maximized in terms of labor and/or shipping.[70] In a sense London faced a much simpler programming problem. Once it determined its wartime needs in terms of shipping and or labor, its administrators might harness resources more efficiently than its adversaries on the Continent. Furthermore, the system of committees and joint boards that Britain developed proved flexible and resistant. Todt and Speer organized the functionally equivalent ring and committee system only belatedly, and it too became unwieldy. "Planning" proved to be an ambiguous term. It might signify a national mobilization of resources and harnessing of effort, but for Germany, even more so for Italy, it often amounted only to a proliferation of decrees and exhortations the effect of which rapidly dissipated beyond the walls of government ministries.

---

68 See Gregor Janssen, *Das Ministerium Speer* (Frankfurt am Main: Ullstein Verlag, 1968), 42–55, 168–76; Carroll, *Design for Total War*, 232–50; Albert Speer, *Inside the Third Reich: Memoirs by Albert Speer*, Richard and Clara Winston, trans. (New York: Macmillan, 1970), 189–229; A decree of September 2, 1943, further transformed the Ministry of Munitions into a more powerful Reich Ministry for Arms and War Production (RMRuK), opposed by a weakened Economics Ministry, an ambitious SS, and the Nazi party *Gauleiter*.

69 On organization see, Herbst, *Der totale Krieg*, 111–18, 255–75; Hans-Erich Volkmann, "Zum Verhältnis von Grosswirtschaft und NS-Regime im Zweiten Weltkrieg," in Dlugoborski, ed., *Zweiter Weltkrieg*, 89–100.

70 See D. N. Chester, ed., *Lessons of the British War Economy* (Cambridge University Press and National Institute for Economic and Social Research, 1951); H. M. D. Parker, *Man Power: A Study of War-time Policy and Administration* (London: HMSO, 1957), esp. 101ff. Ironically, Germany had a less severe human resource constraint (because of the exploitation of foreign labor), but it became the source of much greater conflict, especially between Speer and Sauckel.

Ideology and the limits of fascist economic performance

What were the successes of the fascist economies? Wherein lay their failures? They produced indifferent records of development, if development is taken to mean a structural modernization that leads to greater productivity per worker or to an evolving industrial base, and not merely the resumption of earlier growth. The Italian economy probably underwent more qualitative change under fascism than did the German. First of all the regime lasted a decade longer. Second, the Italian Fascists took charge of a country still dualist in structure, still ripe for the major transformations associated with industrialization. Nevertheless, the Fascists did not really succeed in pushing through structural changes outside the regions already on their way to development. Moreover, the governments before and after the Fascist era chalked up more impressive records. The Italian Fascists, in effect, presided over further advances, at a moderate pace, in the already modernized regions of the country. Likewise, their performance in terms of quantitative growth rates was typical of other eras. The regime enjoyed two growth spurts, 1922–5 and 1935–9; between the two, the Fascists suffered from the same stagnation that afflicted all the capitalist economies and that had repeatedly hobbled long-term Italian growth.

The Nazis' major achievement was the rapid reduction of unemployment and then, toward the end of the 1930s, a hothouse investment in projects that were geared toward war. Sometimes these could mean modernization of infrastructure, as in the case of the hydroelectric and steel plants that were constructed in Austria after the Anschluss. Expansion of plant remained impressive way into the war, such that despite the bombardment there was as much industrial capacity by the end of the war as at the beginning. This was a result also achieved by the often belittled Italian economy.[71] Of course, it still paled before the American achievement, but then the continental United States lay far beyond the range of aircraft.

For both regimes, control of labor might count as the clearest achievement. It is unclear whether the accomplishment was unique

71 Austrian authors like to insist that the Anschluss cost their country more than it gained; however, the Germans endowed the Ostmark with an expanded steel industry, engineering works, and electrical power plants that raised capacity 80%, from 1,406 million to 2,520 million kilowatt-hours. The major losses followed less from wartime destruction than postwar Russian dismantling, but the electrical installations could not be so easily trucked away and remained as infrastructure for postwar growth. See Norbert Schauberger, *Rüstung in Österreich 1938–1945* (Vienna: Verlag Brüder Hollinek, 1970), 175–85.

to fascism. Postwar Germany and Italy enjoyed labor compliance that was just as great – especially if measured by wage stability – but they were postfascist, not merely nonfascist. They might have benefited from their predecessors' bludgeoning of unions. Liberal Britain, in contrast, had already contained labor demands in the 1920s through deflation and unemployment. There were alternative rigors available.

One result, therefore, is that fascism did not produce economic achievements or introduce an economic system that was different in kind from the interventionist capitalism that other Western countries improvised in the Depression and/or during the war. Fascism legitimated the ad hoc intervention that massive unemployment or wartime requirements evoked elsewhere. It offered an ideological justification, a mix of technocratic visions, autarkic and corporativist aspirations, for state controls. Fascism never aspired to public ownership as a matter of principle, though it pragmatically accepted state takeovers of key industries – for example, under the aegis of the IRI or by organization of the Reichswerke Hermann Goering – to achieve overriding goals and satisfy bureaucratic ambitions. But one errs in looking for a fascist economic vision as such. Stuart Woolf's conclusions still hold: From the contemporary's perspective, the drive for national self-sufficiency, the command economy, and the disregard of price or market rationing might make fascist economic systems a true species distinct from Western capitalism. In a longer-term perspective, however, the distinctiveness fades.[72] Fascism remained the expression of a political ideology and a political drive. Its economic expedients were byproducts of a political vision, and they had mixed results. Even when fascism might seem to offer decisive advantages, as in the regimentation of labor, the results hardly measured up to fears or expectations, and the British produced more rationalized human resource policies than did Nazi Germany. What is more, as many commentators have noted, fascism's highly charged political vision ensured that nonrational considerations were interjected. Only the Nazi leadership would use scarce troops to make an epic battlefield movie as its own military fronts were falling back. Only the Nazis would devote immense planning and scarce transportation resources to exterminating groups that could have been exploited (even simply worked to death) far more productively.

Even if one credits the fascists with better than average results in pulling out of the World Depression, both regimes revealed special

72 Cf. Stuart Woolf, "Did a Fascist Economic System Exist?" in Woolf, ed., *Nature of Fascism*, 142–5.

difficulties in mobilizing for war. The evidence still supports the view that the Germans powerfully mobilized resources for a military economy (say, 25 percent of GNP) before 1940. Whether they ultimately intended to reach the plateau of "total war" (e.g., more than 50 percent of GNP) as Overy says was in the offing, they certainly did not rush to complete this conversion before battlefield reverses began. And given their enthusiasm for military efforts and the authoritarian resources at the disposal of the regime, in many ways they were less effective in utilizing resources than they might well have been – less effective not so much in terms of expenditures levels, but in terms of coordinating efforts and setting priorities. This changed with Todt's and Speer's innovations of 1942, but why did a regime that so prided itself on its capacity to make war adopt such expedients so belatedly? In this respect the Klein–Milward view of a laggard performance still requires an explanation.

The answer, I believe, returns us to ideology, not in the sense of any explicit program, but as an underlying orientation guiding political action. I would propose tentatively that both as a set of attitudes and as a guide to governance and political economy fascism proved less successful than liberalism at operations that required a clear and early ordering of priorities. Granted all the efficiency of specialized agencies within the regime – the army, the Organization Todt, or Eichmann's Sonderkommando – the latent ideology of fascism best guided those tasks that involved moving from a situation of underutilization of resources to one of fuller utilization. But once near the threshold of capacity, neither fascist ideology nor the institutional procedures that came in its wake indicated how to make necessary choices.

The ideology of fascism was a non-zero-sum doctrine that celebrated the national state or the racial people. Most Western political orientations accepted trade-offs and sacrifices as inherent in historical development. They presupposed conflict and faction at home. Liberalism envisaged a middle-class or bourgeois triumph at the expense of old elites; social democracy projected a working-class victory over private property holders. Fascism, in contrast, rejected a vision of domestic losers. Instead, it called for subordinating all traditional cleavages at home, especially class conflict, to the maximization of national power and energy, presumably by overcoming fictitious internal enemies (the Jews) or outside adversaries: Bolshevism, Zionism, or the British Empire. Fascism and Nazism were not ideologies that provided guidance for situations in which, so to speak, Paretian optimality had already been achieved or further gains must come at someone's cost.

In addition, the institutional structure that the implicit ideology of fascism helped to establish also militated against clear trade-offs. It consisted increasingly, especially in Germany, of official satraps who competed for the approval of the Führer. The problems thus became ones of both governmental structure and the dictators' psychology. When conflict between agencies seemed beyond compromise, the dictators tended to create a new body that would subordinate the former contenders, such as the Four-Year Plan or Speer's upgraded Ministry of Rearmament and War Production. This does not imply that the dictators could make no decisions. Instead, they impulsively reasserted authority when there was no alternative but resisted choices so long as painful trade-offs could still be avoided. Faced with a revolt inside the Fascist Party during the Matteotti affair, Mussolini had decisively embraced authoritarian governance. Confronted with the Russian counterattack before Moscow in December 1941, Hitler insisted on holding the line rather than retreat. Short of such an unavoidable dilemma (which meant accepting a momentous alternative even were no action taken), Mussolini and Hitler were reluctant to resolve the choices that constantly presented themselves. Mussolini grew so demoralized that he abandoned even his normal posturing, allowed himself to be removed from power by a vote of the Grand Council, then to be reestablished as a German puppet. Hitler fell back on assertions that sufficient willpower could achieve any objective, then retreated to the Obersalzburg or to his bunkers, planning new conquests or a new chancellery, refusing even to visit the bombed cities that might reveal his failure.

Once, however, the expansionist recourse of fascism led to war, choice became unavoidable. If war sets any challenge, it is that of collective choice. With resources strained to the utmost, modern warfare demands setting priorities. Hitler and Mussolini found the task of choosing unfamiliar, for they had come to power less by making choices than by overriding them or by crashing through traditional restraints. But these had been the restraints set by liberals and social democrats, the restraints of nineteenth-century European civilization. The constraints set by total war did not yield so easily. Nor did these difficulties depend simply on the peculiar psychology of the dictators. The awkwardness in resolving alternatives was a natural outgrowth of the fascist "operational code," of its *Einstellung* (disposition), and of its implications for arranging the political process. Thus fascism, which might convince an economic community that it could costlessly climb out of a depression (and which could also enforce the classic remedy of lower real wages to facilitate the process), did not do as well in meeting the task it always claimed as its own. Fascist economics was not an autonomous doctrine or systematic approach. It was an adjunct of fascist politics. Fortunately, the politics proved incapable of mastering the situations that it insisted upon loosing on the world.

Addendum: recovery and industrial investment

The question of what forces in Germany promoted recovery from the Depression remains a difficult one and merits greater consideration than can be accommodated in the main essay. The Statistisches Reichsamt published three reports on the balance sheets of German private corporations in the 1930s.[73] What do they reveal? Capital investment (*Anlagen*) continued to increase into 1930 for a year and a half after the peak of business activity because of long-term construction, especially in electrical works. When investment did begin to fall, the effect was disguised in the balance sheets in part by the transfer of funds from internal reserves – a procedure German firms had long cultivated. As recovery gathered strength after 1932, the opposite procedure applied. Even as investments began to be undertaken, write-offs disguised the recovery so that profits could be concealed and hidden reserves reconstituted.[74] Write-offs were especially heavy during the accounting year 1934–5 because of new tax legislation that made depreciation particularly advantageous.

Thus "creative" accounting disguised the slowing of investment as business collapsed and, conversely, tended to underreport the actual increases for investment that took place once business recovered.[75] Nonetheless, plant investment seems to have been slow in any case. In the mining and raw-materials sector, plant assets declined by RM 104 million in 1936–7. In the major processing and manufacturing (*verarbeitenden*) industries, plant investment rose by RM 103 million. This result included one major area of expansion, RM 139 million of plant investment for synthetic fuel production (a government-sponsored activity) and one major offset item, RM 104 million for the financial restructuring of AEG: overall, therefore, an indifferent investment pattern aside from hydrogenation. Laggardness in expansion of plant continued, despite profitability in almost all sectors and an

---

73 "Abschlüsse deutscher Aktiengesellschaften 1933/34 und 1934/35," *Statistik des Deutschen Reichs*, Bd. 493 (1936); "Abschlüsse deutscher Aktiengesellschaften 1934/35 und 1935/36," *Statistik des Deutschen Reichs*, Bd. 504 (1937); and "Abschlüsse deutscher Aktiengesellschaften 1935/36 und 1936/37," *Statistik des Deutschen Reichs*, Bd. 525 (1938).

74 *Statistik des Deutschen Reichs*, Bd. 493, pp. 4–5; Bd. 525, pp. 16.

75 In 1950 prices, the gross investment capital of German firms declined only from RM 52.8 billion in 1928 to RM 50.4 billion in 1932 (to reach RM 72.7 billion by 1944). In fact between 1928 and 1932 there was absolute decline (disinvestment) in only two sectors. Raw-material production, mining, and production goods fell from RM 27.4 billion to 25.3 billion, investment goods declined from RM 11.1 billion to 10.6 billion. See R. Krengel, *Die langfristige Entwicklung der Bruttoanlageinvestitionen der westdeutschen Industrie von 1924 bis 1955/56*, *Vierteljahreshefte zur Wirtschaftsforschung*, Neue Folge 42 (1957): 16, 168ff.

Table 6. *Major balance sheet items for German Aktiengesellschaften (AGs)*

Balance year	Plant less renewal funds	Inventories	Net change	Shares in own or other AGs	Orders, pre-payments, loans
1928–9	18.117	5.479	—	7.203	39.309
1930–1	18.183	4.582	− 897m	8.215	38.316
1931–2	18.307	3.631	− 951m	7.748	32.540
1932–3	15.897	2.727	− 904m	7.119	32.071
1933–4	16.371	2.828	+ 101m	7.601	31.140
1934–5	15.639	3.356	+ 528m	8.375	30.936
1935–6	16.029	4.091	+ 735m	9.320	30.783
1936–7	15.989	4.257	+ 166m	9.620	30.145

Note: Items represent about 90% of German Aktiengesellschaft capital; figures represent billions of reichsmarks. Major restocking comprised semicompleted products, above all in manufacturing industries. The decline in plant in 1936–7 was due to especially heavy write-offs, including the financial restructuring of AEG (General Electric). Major real investment in plant in 1936–7 included RM 139 million in domestic petroleum production – a project obviously keyed to the needs of rearmament (see *Statistik des Deutschen* Reichs [1938], Bd. 525, p. 9). Firms bought significantly on the stockmarket during 1932 in part to recover control of their own shares, in part to cushion price declines, then used the profits during recovery to reconstitute reserves.

increasing volume of day-to-day transactions.[76] Firms used their profits to reconstitute reserves, but they were also increasingly under obligation to buy government debt.

In contrast to the conservatism apparently governing investment in plant, the inventory assets on corporate balance sheets showed greater fluctuation from peak to trough and again from trough to peak than any other item. If 1932 were set at 100, inventories dropped from a value of 170 in 1928–9 and then rose again to 130 by the end of 1935 as restocking accelerated. Clearly, inventory movements can have different meanings: Piling up one's own product is a sign of recession; stocking up needs from another provider is an indication of buoyancy. The pattern of the recovery suggested expansion, as raw-material stocks fell while semifinished goods were restocked.[77] Tables 6 and 7 summarize these results.

The figures in Table 6 reduce considerably the inventory investment worked out as residuals from R. J. Overy's data (see footnote 48). Assuming that the direct data provided by the corporate balance sheets

76 *Statistik des Deutschen Reichs*, Bd. 525, pp. 11–12.
77 Ibid., Bd. 493, p. 8; Bd. 504, p. 7; Bd. 525, pp. 8–9.

Table 7. *Quarterly changes in plant, inventory, and accounts receivable*

	1933		1934				1935				1936				1937	
	III	IV	I	II	III	IV	I	II	III	IV	I	II	III	IV	I	II
	−5.4	−5.6	−10.0	−5.7	−5.0	−3.9	−6.6	−1.6	−3.6	−0.9	−1.6	−1.2	−3.9	+0.1	+2.0	−2.0
	−12.7	−0.7	−2.4	+9.1	+22.5	+13.5	+30.4	+22.9	+20.9	+12.9	−2.2	−14.8	+4.8	+9.0	+5.5	+5.7
	−4.9	−2.0	−3.0	−1.6	−2.7	+6.8	−1.9	+7.2	+1.2	+2.7	−2.8	+2.5	+9.8	+9.5	−3.4	+6.7

Note: Data represent percentage of change from the beginning of the period to the end.

are more accurate, the new result suggests that, although restocking remains the investment item that changed most in percentage terms, it was hardly a massive locomotive for recovery. Given the earlier wave of investment attendant upon the "rationalization" movement of the late 1920s, it is not surprising that plant investment did not reemerge as a major item on corporate accounts so long as labor could be reabsorbed without capital commitments. Indeed, the conservatism of German business was noted by private and governmental sources deep into 1935.[78] What, then, was the source of recovery? Spenceley proposes housing subsidies as a major early impetus. According to the figures of the Reichskreditgesellschaft, cited by Lurie and Spenceley, construction rose from RM 3.2 billion in 1933 to RM 5.7 billion in 1934, 7.5 billion in 1935, and 9.0 billion in 1936. Public construction provided the major source for this investment (RM 1.7 billion, 3.5 billion, 4.9 billion, and 5.4 billion), and German sources estimated that the increase in construction accounted for virtually half of the reemployment of German workers from 1933 through 1936 (a result not unlike the British pattern). Highway building and related construction, along with increased automobile production (in a sense catching up to the level Britain and France had reached in the 1920s) provided a second stimulus. Finally, rearmament and investment in plant under the auspices of the Four-Year Plan ensured that Germany did not lapse into a significant slowdown in 1937, as happened in the United States and as first-quarter 1937 accounts receivable suggested was still possible.

78 See Spenceley, "Overy and the Motorisierung," 106; also Costantino Bresciani-Turroni, "The Multiplier in Practice," 76–88; Lurie, *Private Investment*, 24.

3

The politics of productivity: foundations of American international economic policy after World War II

The theme introduced here has been taken up by other authors, especially in regard to Italy. See Pier-Paolo D'Attorre, "Aspetti dell'attuazione del Piano Marshall in Italia," in Elena Aga Rossi, ed., *Il Piano Marshall e l'Europa* (Rome: Instituto della Enciclopedia Italiana, 1983), 163–80; and Mariuccia Salvati, *Stato e industria nella ricostruzione: Alle origini del potere democristiano* (Milan: Feltrinelli, 1982). On the impact on trade unions see the essay by Federico Romero, "Postwar Reconversion Strategies of American and Western European Labor," European University Institute Working Paper, no. 85/193 (San Domenico di Fiesole, September 1985). Since this article appeared, I have continued a study of the United States and postwar reconstruction in Europe, which will develop further the argumentation and evidence introduced here.

The ground rules of a liberal international economic system may establish formal equality among participants but they also reflect the disparity of power and resources. Just as significant, they reveal the inequalities and conflicts within the dominant national societies of the system. The primary objective of this chapter is to suggest how the construction of the post–World War II Western economy under United States auspices can be related to the political and economic forces generated within American society. A second focus must be to demonstrate how those American impulses interacted with the social and political components of other nations, both European and Japanese.

The close of World War II brought American policy makers a rare and heady opportunity to reshape the guidelines of the international economic order. The pretensions of the Axis powers to organize continental Europe and East Asia had collapsed. Soviet Russia seemed preoccupied with its own huge tasks of reconstruction and the establishment of a glacis in Eastern Europe. Great Britain depended upon Washington's assistance to maintain its own international role and could not durably oppose American policies. Spared the losses incurred by the other belligerents, the United States inherited a chance to secure Western economic ground rules according to its own needs and visions.

What determined those needs and visions? Historians and political scientists have often argued that they represented either an enlightened idealism or a nationalistic and capitalist expansionism. Thus polarized, the debate remains inconclusive because the same policies could serve both aspirations. Washington's neo-Cobdenite mission did aim at higher world levels of exchange and welfare. Simultaneously, it was intended to benefit American producers who could compete vigorously in any market where the "open door" and the free convertibility of currencies into dollars facilitated equal access.[1] Both the defenders and the critics of American objectives, moreover, have recognized the traumatic legacy of a Depression that only wartime orders finally overcame. Indeed, Donald Nelson of the War Production Board and Eric Johnston of the Chamber of Commerce encouraged the Soviets to believe that American businessmen wanted their orders lest mass unemployment recur after the wartime stimulus ended. Nor was international commerce solely an economic objective: trade restrictions, argued New Deal spokesmen, brought political hostility. "Nations which act as enemies in the market place cannot long be friends at the council table," said Assistant Secretary of State William Clayton, a wealthy cotton dealer sympathetic at first hand to the needs of exporters.[2] He echoed Cordell Hull's assessment that the establishment of a closed trading bloc comprised an essential aspect of Fascism: "The political line up followed the economic line up."[3] Thus, a compelling objective in 1945 was to do away with protected trading areas outside the United States, thereby to banish domestic depression and international conflict. The United States would lead the United

---

1 For critical analyses, Lloyd C. Gardner, *Economic Aspects of New Deal Diplomacy* (Madison: University of Wisconsin Press, 1964); Gabriel Kolko, *The Politics of War: The World and United States Foreign Policy, 1943–1945* (New York: Random House, 1968); William Appleman Williams, *The Tragedy of American Diplomacy* (New York: Dell Publishing Co., 1962).

2 For Johnston and Nelson, see John Lewis Gaddis, *The United States and the Origins of the Cold War, 1941–1947* (New York: Columbia University Press, 1972), pp. 176–77, 185–89. Clayton cited in Thomas Paterson, *Soviet-American Confrontation: Postwar Reconstruction and the Origins of the Cold War* (Baltimore: The Johns Hopkins University Press, 1973), p. 4.

3 *The Memoirs of Cordell Hull*, 2 vols. (New York: Macmillan Co., 1948), Vol. I, p. 364.

Nations to a lofty plateau of peaceful intercourse and economic expansion.

This eschatology of peaceful prosperity – with its amalgam of nationalist and universal aspirations usefully termed "Wilsonian"[4] – is not sufficient, however, to account fully for the ideological sources of American foreign economic policy. (Nor, I hope to show, is growing anti-Communism a sufficient ideological explanation.) American concepts of a desirable international economic order need to be understood further in terms of domestic social divisions and political stalemates. United States spokesmen came to emphasize economic productivity as a principle of political settlement in its own right. They did this not merely because of the memory of harsh unemployment, nor simply to veil the thrust of a latter-day "imperialism of free trade,"[5] nor even because wartime destruction abroad made recovery of production an urgent objective need. Just as important, the stress on productivity and economic growth arose out of the very terms in which Americans resolved their own organization of economic power. Americans asked foreigners to subordinate their domestic and international conflicts for the sake of higher steel tonnage or kilowatt hours precisely because agreement on production and efficiency had helped bridge deep divisions at home. The emphasis on output and growth emerged as a logical result of New Deal and wartime controversies, just as earlier it had arisen out of inconclusive reform movements.

The domestic sources of American economic concepts

In retrospect, it is easy to point out that the international economic arrangements the United States sought in the years after the Second World War would benefit a capital-intensive and resource-rich economy. Wartime leadership and British dependence brought the opportunity to press for the Treasury and State Department's preferred multilateralism. These policies had not originally been ascendant. At its inception, the New Deal had adopted a course of monetary unilateralism as Roosevelt refused cooperation with the London Economic Conference in 1933 and embarked upon the almost capricious gold

---

4 To see the implications of Wilsonianism, see N. Gordon Levin, Jr., *Woodrow Wilson and World Politics. America's Response to War and Revolution* (New York: Oxford University Press, 1970).

5 For the earlier analogue: John Gallagher and Ronald Robinson, "The Imperialism of Free Trade," *Economic History Review*, 2nd series, 6 (1953): 1–15; objections in D. C. M. Platt, "The Imperialism of Free Trade: Some Reservations," *Economic History Review*, 2nd series, 11 (1968): 196–306, and "Further Objections to an 'Imperialism of Free Trade,' 1830–1860," *Economic History Review*, 2nd series, 26 (1973): 77–91.

purchases of 1934. Such initiatives represented, in part, a reaction to Britain's floating of the pound and regrouping of a Commonwealth trading bloc in 1931–1932. They also reflected the Democrats' distrust of the New York banking elites (the Federal Reserve leadership and J. P. Morgan, Co., etc.) that had sought to work with the British toward monetary stabilization in the 1920s and seemed to emphasize international cooperation rather than domestic growth. Nonetheless, a common British and American need to limit competitive devaluation after France departed from the gold standard led to a Tripartite currency agreement in 1936. The danger of Nazi expansionism further impelled Neville Chamberlain to solicit Washington's cooperation and conclude the Anglo-American trade agreement of November 1938.[6] With the advent of World War II, Britain had to become even more insistent a suitor. For its Lend-Lease assistance, Washington pressed for further dismantling of the Commonwealth trading bloc. London finally had to rely upon shared political values and plucky sacrifices to temper American demands for the liquidation of its international financial position.[7]

Noisy disputes sometimes obscured the underlying thrust of United States policy, but foreign economic objectives generally reflected Cordell Hull's unceasing emphasis upon the virtue of lowering tariff barriers. This program was consistent with the lessons of comparative advantage and a universalist vision of economic advance, even as it served to encroach upon the British Commonwealth. Roosevelt needed Hull because of his excellent relations with Congress; and the official who offered an alternative program of international commodity bartering, George Peek, the Administrator of the Agricultural Adjustment Act, resigned in late November 1935. The disputes between Hull and Henry Morgenthau, Jr. at the Treasury appear more those of bureaucratic rivalry than fundamental policy disagreements. Hull was originally willing to allow the British monetary flexibility in return for free-trade commitments; in 1935 he dissented from the dollar's competitive devaluation against the pound. But while Hull afterward urged

6   Benjamin M. Rowland, "Preparing the American Ascendency: The Transfer of Economic Power from Britain to the United States," in *Balance of Power or Hegemony: The Interwar Monetary System*, Benjamin M. Rowland, ed. A Lehrman Institute Book (New York: New York University Press, 1976), pp. 195–224, and, in the same volume, Harold van B. Cleveland, "The International Monetary System in the Interwar Period," esp. pp. 54–56; Lowell M. Pumphrey, "The Exchange Equalization Account of Great Britain," *American Economic Review*, 32 (December 1942): 803–16.

7   Richard N. Gardner, *Sterling-Dollar Diplomacy: Anglo-American Cooperation in the Reconstruction of Multilateral Trade* (Oxford: Clarendon Press, 1956), offers the best account of this relationship.

the postwar elimination of the Westminster system as a condition for Lend-Lease, Morgenthau was less insistent. The Treasury emphasized economic leadership through a pivotal role for the dollar. Rather than impose Section VII of the Lend-Lease agreement which committed Britain to move toward free trade, the Secretary of the Treasury sought to extract London's agreement not to rebuild its foreign currency reserves during the period of American aid.[8] Nonetheless, the Treasury's quest for monetary leadership was not fundamentally inconsistent with the State Department's stress on the "open door" and the importance of free trade. Both policies envisaged using the American abundance of food and cotton and the productivity of labor to establish a benign economic dominance that would raise the welfare of all nations. Neither agency had reason to sanction an exhausted Britain's maintaining imperial pretensions at US expense. Both policies derived from a Wilsonian globalism. In Morgenthau's concepts, for example, a Britain prosperous but on reduced monetary tether accompanied a Germany shorn of its heavy industry and a Russia reconstructed with American credits.[9] The premise for all policy makers was American economic preeminence. This preeminence was felt to arise naturally from the nation's energy and resources, not from the exercise of coercion.

Yet this very emphasis on economic potential itself emerged from deeper divisions. The productivist view of America's postwar mission arose naturally out of the domestic modes of resolving social conflict, or, rather, the difficulty of resolving conflicts cleanly. Neither an insistence upon conflict nor upon consensus adequately conveys the dialectical interplay of both social conditions, such that unresolved disputes brought contestants to apolitical areas of common endeavor. Most immediately, the emphasis on the benevolent mission of America's productive leadership reflected the stalemate of New Deal reform and even wartime politics. By the late 1930s, the New Deal thrust to displace economic power from private capital to either corporatist National Recovery Administration (NRA) institutions or to countervailing private forces (i.e., labor unions) was rapidly dissipating. The severe recession of 1937–38 intensified political infighting between "spenders" such as Harry Hopkins, Harold Ickes, Marriner Eccles, and Leon Henderson and those such as Morgenthau who urged tax cuts for business. Outside the White House, the Democratic coalition began

---

8 Rowland, "Preparing the American Ascendancy," pp. 202–04, 213–15.
9 For Morgenthau's ideas, see John Morton Blum, ed., *From the Morgenthau Diaries,* Vol. 3: *Years of War 1941–1945* (Boston: Houghton Mifflin Company, 1967), pp. 228–30, 324–26, 333ff; cf. Kolko, *Politics of War* pp. 323–40.

to fray and the President failed to persuade Congress to enact several key proposals during 1938–39. In November 1938 Republicans won 81 new seats in the House and eight in the Senate. As the political situation in Europe became more preoccupying, it provided a further incentive for the President to turn back to a business community that a few years earlier he had labelled "economic royalists." Harry Hopkins, newly installed as Secretary of Commerce in early 1939, chose Averell Harriman as a close advisor, in part to reconstruct bridges to business leadership. Edward Stettinius, Jr. of US Steel, James Forrestal of Dillon Reed, Donald Nelson of Sears Roebuck, and William Knudsen of General Motors were only a few of the "tame millionaires" the Administration summoned to run the ever-shifting agencies designed to coordinate defense production. With Pearl Harbor, Roosevelt could announce that "Dr. Win the War" was replacing "Dr. New Deal."[10]

The infusion of industrialists, however, could not automatically adjourn old conflicts over social and economic policy. Critics of business found the new organizers unimpressive and laggard in the task of converting industry to wartime production. The new participants from banking and industry regarded the inveterate New Dealers as partisan and woolly-headed. As Forrestal reported about the provocative Henderson in July 1941: "He is trying to use the Office of Civilian Requirements to get a foothold and control of the defense effort and incidentally to fight a social as well as a military war."[11] The role of labor was particularly controversial. The Office of Production Management (OPM) and its successor, the War Production Board, resisted the policies of the trade union Left. The CIO and AFL sought representation in the key industry divisions of the OPM but had to be content with participation in the less central labor advisory committees. Labor delegates did become important on the War Manpower Committee, but after a production crisis in 1943, Roosevelt's solution of placing James Byrnes in charge of an overarching Office of War Mobilization again kept labor spokesmen from the center of decisions.[12]

10   William E. Leuchtenburg, *Franklin D. Roosevelt and the New Deal, 1932–1940* (New York: Harper and Row, 1963), pp. 243ff.; J. Joseph Huthmacher, *Senator Robert F. Wagner and the Rise of Urban Liberalism* (New York: Atheneum, 1971); Robert Sherwood, *Roosevelt and Hopkins* (New York: Harper & Brothers, 1948), pp. 110–11.

11.   Letter to Averell Harriman, July 7, 1941, in James Forrestal papers, Princeton University Library, Box 56. For a liberal, journalistic account of Washington wartime economic conflicts, see Bruce Catton, *The Warlords of Washington* (New York: Harcourt, Brace, 1948).

12   Paul A. C. Koistinen, "Mobilizing the World War II Economy: Labor and the Industrial–Military Alliance," *Pacific Historical Review*, 42 (November 1973): 443–78, esp. 446–60. Cf. Barton J. Bernstein, "America in War and Peace: The Test of Liberalism," in *Toward a New Past: Dissenting Essays in American History*, Barton J. Bernstein, ed. (New York: Random House-Vintage, 1968).

From one perspective these struggles were bureaucratic rivalries with multi-million-dollar appropriations and unprecedented regulatory control as the important stakes. Yet it would be misleading to forget the ideological implications. The war imposed a common task upon all contenders but could not nullify the profound struggles over business and labor power that had continued for over a decade. Nor could it cleanly resolve them. Symptomatic of the continuing ideological and social disputes was the stormy career of Henry Wallace. By 1942 Wallace had established himself as the spokesman for a messianic liberalism of abundance; America's war was an act of millennial liberation that would usher in "the century of the common man." Not merely a visionary, the Vice-President and his aides had accumulated key economic supervisory positions. But the State Department resented the inroads of Wallace's Bureau of Economic Warfare. And the long, public quarrel with Jesse Jones, the conservative Texas millionaire who served as Secretary of Commerce and directed the Reconstruction Finance Committee (RFC), finally led Roosevelt to abolish the Bureau of Economic Warfare, limit the RFC's role, and establish a new Foreign Economic Agency under Jones's protege, Leo Crowley. The struggle was a bureaucratic and personal one but its upshot disheartened the New Deal Left and set back potential precedents for future economic regulation and planning. At Thanksgiving 1942 Wallace had approached FDR "in the spirit of Queen Esther approaching King Ahasuerus, only I was going to speak on behalf of the liberals rather than the Jews."[13] He did not recall that since the laws of the Medes and the Persians were immutable, the Jews won only the right to defend themselves, not the cancellation of the attacks already ordered.

In Congress the fate of New Deal reform under wartime conditions was also problematic. Price controls and rationing under the Office of Price Administration (OPA) remained a sore point for conservatives, especially since OPA became a refuge for New Deal exponents such as Henderson and Chester Bowles. Senator Robert Wagner, chairman of the Banking and Currency Committee, managed to renew the OPA and price-control legislation. He failed, however, to secure passage of the Wagner–Murray–Dingell bill, which would have enacted an equivalent of Britain's Beveridge Plan if it had not remained a dead letter in 1943, 1944, and 1945. When the National Resources Planning Board, deeply influenced during the war years by Harvard Keynesian

---

13 John Morton Blum, ed., *The Price of Vision: The Diary of Henry A. Wallace, 1942–1946* (Boston: Atlantic-Little Brown, 1973), p. 137. See also Norman D. Markowitz, *The Rise and Fall of the People's Century: Henry A. Wallace and American Liberalism, 1941–1948* (New York: Free Press, 1973), pp. 47ff.; Frederick H. Schapsmeier and Edward L. Schapsmeier, *Prophet in Politics: Henry A. Wallace and the War Years, 1940–1945* (Ames, Iowa: The University of Iowa Press, 1970), pp. 55–71.

Alvin Hansen, brought forward its 1943 proposals for continued welfare reforms and countercyclical spending, it won applause from *The New Republic*. Congressional conservatives, on the other hand, responded by gutting the agency. By 1944, with further Republican gains at the polls, Congress reflected a taut division between Liberals and Conservatives. The result was typified by the fate of the Liberals' proposed full-employment bill. Originally designed to mandate government spending to prevent joblessness, it emerged, after much horse-trading, as the Employment Act, which merely targetted maximum feasible job levels. With the creation of the Council of Economic Advisors it remained more a technical than a political measure.[14]

This stalemate of forces precluded any consistent social-democratic trend for the American political economy. Coupled with the impressive record of the domestic industrial plant as the "arsenal for democracy," it made it easier for American leaders to fall back upon the supposedly apolitical politics of productivity. The theme of productivity as a substitute for harsh questions of allocation was a venerable one. It had emerged in the Progressive Era and pervaded the War Production Board of 1918. It was championed by Herbert Hoover under the form of a business "associationism" that would transcend wasteful competition, and be given institutional expression once again in the NRA concept of industrial self-government. The recurrent ideas all stressed that by enhancing productive efficiency, whether through scientific management, business planning, industrial cooperation, or corporatist groupings, American society could transcend the class conflicts that arose from scarcity. The coinage of politics – power and coercion – was minted only in the kingdom of material necessity and would have no function in the realm of abundance.[15]

Although the Depression discredited the claims to foresight and acumen on the part of America's business elites, the wartime experience suggested again that the United States could enjoy productive abundance without a radical redistribution of economic power. The

---

14 Bernstein, "America in War and Peace," for Congressional conservatism; Markowitz, *Henry Wallace*, pp. 57–65, on the NRPB; Huthmacher, pp. 285–302; Stephen Kemp Bailey, *Congress Makes a Law: The Story behind the Employment Act of 1946* (New York: Columbia University Press, 1950).

15 See Ellis Hawley, "Herbert Hoover, the Commerce Secretariat and the Vision of an 'Associative State,' 1921–1928," *The Journal of American History*, 61 (June 1974): 116–40; also Hawley's own essay in *Herbert Hoover and the Crisis of American Capitalism*, Ellis Hawley et al. (Cambridge, Massachusetts: Schenkman, 1973); Barry D. Karl, "Presidential Planning and Social Science Research: Mr. Hoover's Experts," *Perspectives in American History*, 3 (1969): 347–409. See also Chapter 1, this volume, "Between Taylorism and Technocracy."

neo-Progressives in the business community organized a Committee on Economic Development (CED) to urge continuing governmental responsibility (including advantageous tax benefits) for maintaining high investment and employment. Charles E. Wilson of General Electric and the War Production Board and Paul Hoffman of Studebaker, later head of the Economic Cooperation Administration, became major CED spokesmen for the new government-business partnership.[16] Not surprisingly, it was the emergency priorities of wartime that rendered this celebration of a business-oriented commonwealth initially acceptable to American Liberals. The wartime celebration of production and output, its rehabilitation of the large corporation, and its evocation of an overarching national commitment, all facilitated a new consensus on interventionist planning. As Harriman noted in his first unofficial press conference after becoming Secretary of Commerce in October 1946, "People in this country are no longer scared of such words as 'planning.' . . . people have accepted the fact the government has got to plan as well as the individuals in the country."[17]

It is important to emphasize, however, that planning was accepted only in a restricted sense. During the 1930s, the Department of Agriculture under the guidance of Rexford Tugwell and Mordecai Ezekiel, the National Resources Planning Board as influenced by Gardiner Means, and the Tennessee Valley Authority (TVA) had emerged as foyers for the planning enthusiasts. But the impact of the would-be planners was concentrated in natural resource issues; for in questions of environmental resources, providing ever-normal granaries, or halting erosion, planning could claim a conservation-related justification it could not in industry. Likewise, planning seemed more acceptable on the regional level: TVA became a New Deal showcase not merely because of its cheap power but its incubation of local democracy. Its exuberant director, David Lilienthal, foresaw TVA-like developments helping to leapfrog the more exploitative and wasteful stages of growth outside the United States as well:

There seems to be a definite sequence in history in the change from primitive or non-industrial conditions to more highly developed modern industrial conditions. Whether all of those steps have to be taken and all the intervening

16   Karl Schriftgeisser, *Business Comes of Age: The Story of the Committee for Economic Development and its Impact upon the Economic Policies of the United States* (New York: Harper and Row, 1960); also Herbert Stein, *The Fiscal Revolution in America* (Chicago: University of Chicago Press, 1969), Chapters 8–9; Robert Lekachman, *The Age of Keynes* (New York: Random House, 1966).
17   Secretary of Commerce files in W. Averell Harriman papers, Washington, National Press Club Luncheon, October 15, 1946.

mistakes made is open to question. . . . Don't we have enough control over our destinies to short-cut those wasted steps?[18]

The same buoyant belief in the power of economic rationality would mark Marshall Plan administrators. But precisely because they and other American Liberals usually envisaged planning as a step toward productive efficiency, it became apolitical. Planning would overcome the waste that CED industrialists saw in restrictive labor practices or needless competition, that Lilienthal measured in overpriced kilowatt-hours, or that Keynesians perceived in idle savings and unemployed workers. In each case, the mission of planning became one of expanding aggregate economic performance and eliminating poverty by enriching everyone, not one of redressing the balance among economic classes or political parties. When they turned to European difficulties after 1945, American advisors enjoyed greater opportunity to reshape the ailing economies abroad than to influence the domestic one. But even in confronting European needs, they reaffirmed the general premises of American economic thinking. United States aid was designed to remove "bottlenecks," and to clear away the obstacles left by war and political demoralization by temporary coal shortages and transitory dollar gaps. Prosperity was available for Europeans too, once the impediments to production were limited. The true dialectic was not one of class against class, but waste versus abundance. The goal of economic policy, abroad as at home, was to work toward the latter.

American opinion generally viewed the transition to a society of abundance as a problem of engineering, not of politics. Nonetheless, as Americans ended the Second World War, they recognized one major institutional impediment to peacetime prosperity – monopoly. Denunciation of monopoly was a recurring ideological theme. John Taylor of Caroline, Andrew Jackson, the Progressives, and the New Deal successively assailed monopoly as an affliction of democracy. The criticism of monopoly presented the same rhetorical advantages as the stress on productivity and efficiency. Instead of depicting po-

18 *The Journals of David E. Lilienthal*, Vol. I: *The TVA Years, 1939–1945* (New York: Harper & Row, 1964), p. 471, entry of April 14, 1942. On the conservation justification, see Robert F. Himmelberg essay in Hawley et al., pp. 63–82; for planning in the '30s: Ellis W. Hawley, *The New Deal and the Problem of Monopoly* (Princeton: Princeton University Press, 1966), pp. 122–27, 130–46; Lewis L. Lorwin and A. Ford Hinrichs, *National Economic and Social Planning* (Washington: GPO, 1935); Charles F. Roos, *NRA Economic Planning* (Bloomington, Indiana: Principia, 1937); Charles Merriam, "The National Resources Planning Board: A Chapter in American Planning Experience," *American Political Science Review*, 38 (December 1944): 1075–88.

litical society as subject to complex interest cleavages, it posited a rallying of all productive elements against one isolated enemy. Spokesmen for reform found it easier to lead a crusade against monopoly than persevere in, or even fully confront the implications of, a contest against the more pervasive inequalities of power and wealth.

By the mid-1930s, the theme of monopoly became preoccupying anew on several grounds: the new literature on imperfect competition and oligopoly,[19] the relapse into severe recession-in 1938, and, finally, the American diagnosis of the nature of Fascism. In his study for the Secretary of Agriculture, *Industrial Prices and Their Relative Inflexibility*, Gardiner Means contrasted the competitive market in agriculture with the administered markets where prices were not allowed to fall with slackening demand.[20] The result was reduced purchasing power that might explain persistent depression. When manufacturing prices rose faster than wages, Henderson and Ezekiel both correctly predicted renewed recession.[21] The setback to New Deal hopes prompted Roosevelt to propose a major investigation of the economic obstacles to recovery. An attack on monopoly was not only relatively cost-free in political terms; it seemed appropriate in the light of the latest economic analysis. In April 1938 the President asked Congress to open a major inquiry into American economic structures with a message that stressed the inequality among corporations (less than 0.1 percent of corporations owned 52 percent of the assets) and attributed unemployment to rigid administered prices.

Monopoly, Roosevelt suggested further, was politically dangerous: "The liberty of a democracy is not safe if the people tolerate the growth of private power to a point where it becomes stronger than their democratic state itself. That, in its essence, is Fascism – ownership of government by an individual, by a group, or by any other controlling private power."[22] This warning naturally reflected the anxieties of 1938. The *Anschluss* had taken place a month earlier. The idea also fit in

19 Joan Robinson, *The Economics of Imperfect Competition* (London: Macmillan, 1933); Edward H. Chamberlain, *The Theory of Monopolistic Competition* (Cambridge, Massachusetts: Harvard University Press, 1938).
20 US Congress, Senate, *Industrial Prices and their Relative Inflexibility*, by Gardiner Means. Sen. Doc. 13, 74th Congress, 1st. Sess. 1935; cf. Adolph Berle and Gardiner Means, *The Modern Corporation and Private Property* (New York: The Macmillan Co., 1937); also Maurice Leven, Harold G. Moulton, Clark Warburton, *America's Capacity to Consume* (Washington: The Brookings Institution, 1934), pp. 126–28.
21 David Lynch, *The Concentration of Economic Power* (New York: Columbia University Press, 1946), pp. 1–34; Hawley, *The New Deal and the Problem of Monopoly*, pp. 404–19.
22 Temporary National Economic Committee, *Hearings*, Vol. I, appendix, p. 105.

with Cordell Hull's view of the German threat, which the Secretary interpreted as a political outgrowth of strivings for autarky. In syllogistic terms, Hull argued that economic nationalism reduced living standards, led to unemployment and despair, and, finally, provoked the use of political violence as an alternative to disorder.[23]

By the late 1930s Liberals thus connected Fascism with monopolistic economic tendencies. The Depression had obviously been instrumental in bringing Hitler to power. In addition, remarked Thurman Arnold, the new head of the Anti-Trust division of the Justice Department, the effort to protect special-interest groups, which the New Deal had pursued misguidedly under the NRA, had also been an objective of the ill-fated Weimar Republic.[24] When Roosevelt listened to Morgenthau plead for a cut in business taxes to restore industry's confidence, the President backed away. Appeasing business "would put a man in as President who," as he called it, "would be controlled by a man on horseback, the way Mussolini and Hitler are. . . . This simply would mean that we would have a Fascist President."[25]

It was foreordained that the anti-monopoly theme would weaken at home with economic mobilization. On the one hand, Keynesians themselves came to stress that persistent unemployment lay in the failure to invest and not with rigid prices or inadequate consumer power. The Temporary National Economic Committee (TNEC) hearings laboriously continued, producing dozens of monographs on industries, patents, and taxation, but without much legislative result. The Committee had begun with the assumption that a conflict-free solution to unemployment, price rigidity, and unhealthy concentration of power might be found in attacking monopoly. Instead, they encountered complexity and uncertainty about the relation of size to efficiency or monopoly to depression. Thurman Arnold's vigorous antitrust prosecutions languished as the War Production Board insisted that price competition had to be relaxed for the duration.[26]

Nonetheless, the theme of monopoly continued to play a strong role in the analysis of European developments. Robert Brady, who had earlier analyzed the Nazi regime and the German rationalization movement, which also involved growing mergers and concentration, spotlighted the political role of the leading industrial interest groups

23 *The Memoirs of Cordell Hull*, I, p. 364.
24 Lilienthal, *TVA Years*, p. 324, entry of May 22, 1941.
25 John Morton Blum, ed., *From the Morgenthau Diaries*, Vol. 1: *Years of Urgency, 1938–1941* (Boston: Houghton Mifflin Company, 1965), p. 20.
26 Lynch describes the TNEC results; for antitrust see Hawley, *The New Deal and the Problem of Monopoly*, pp. 420–25.

in his *Business as a System of Power.* Franz Neumann's *Behemoth* helped to make a quasi-Marxist analysis of National Socialist power the intellectual basis for much of American planning for the postwar occupation of Germany. These and similar discussions in the press continued to elaborate Roosevelt's 1938 conclusions that Fascism was essentially an outgrowth of modern private economic power.[27]

Thus by 1945 the two themes of productivity and monopoly formed the conceptual axes along which Americans located economic institutions. At home there was the inconclusive confrontation between the popularly mandated New Deal and the long-sanctioned tradition of free enterprise, between the wartime rehabilitation of industrialists and the distrust of monopoly. This domestic stalemate made recourse to metapolitical notions of economic organization natural and appealing. Monopoly explained political and economic setbacks; productivity promised advance.

Nevertheless, the conjugate themes would be applied to different areas. The politics of productivity beckoned originally in the non-Axis countries. The inefficiencies of production that would be vexing in Europe after 1945 did not appear as a result of concentrated power but as the consequences of a hidebound traditionalism attributed to small and backward businessmen. Moreover, the indices of production and growth allowed supposedly apolitical criteria for dealing with the rivalries among the postwar contenders in France, Italy, and elsewhere. They provided a justification for separating constructive growth-minded labor movements (Social-Democratic or Christian) from divisive and allegedly self-seeking Communist ones.

Americans would draw upon the anti-monopoly orientation, on the other hand, in establishing plans for transforming the political economies of defeated Germany and Japan. Until 1948–49, the Occupation authorities imposed decartelization in their German zone and moved to break up the Zaibatsu across the Pacific. As Edwin Pauley's reparation mission concluded in the months after V-J Day:

Japan's Zaibatsu (literally, 'financial clique') are . . . the greatest war potential of Japan. It was they who made possible all Japan's conquests and aggressions. . . . Not only were the Zaibatsu as responsible for Japan's militarism

---

27 See three books by Robert Brady, *The Rationalization Movement in German Industry* (Berkeley and Los Angeles: University of California Press, 1933); *The Spirit and Structure of German Fascism* (New York: The Viking Press, 1937); *Business as a System of Power* (New York: Columbia University Press, 1943); Franz Neumann, *Behemoth: The Structure and Practice of National Socialism* (Toronto and New York: Columbia University Press, 1942). Cf. Lutz Niethammer, *Entnazifierung in Bayern: Säuberung und Rehabilitierung unter amerikanischer Besatzung* (Frankfurt am Main: S. Fischer Verlag, 1972), pp. 37ff.

as the militarists themselves, but they profited immensely by it. Even now, in defeat, they have actually strengthened their monopoly position. . . . Unless the Zaibatsu are broken up, the Japanese have little prospect of ever being able to govern themselves as free men. As long as the Zaibatsu survive, Japan will be their Japan.[28]

Not only did the anti-monopoly concepts find service in the Occupation, but some of the trust-busters themselves left the unpromising Justice Department to pursue their work in defeated Germany and Japan.[29] The Axis powers offered a laboratory in which to pursue the reforms that had been shelved at home. Within a few years, of course, they would be shelved abroad. Faced with the Cold War, Americans ultimately would actually carry out one further dialectical transformation. They would subordinate their crusade against monopoly in the ex-Fascist powers precisely to advance the cause of productivity. Just as during the war the Administration had dropped antitrust prosecutions for the sake of industrial mobilization, after 1948, policy makers would tacitly abandon the anti-monopoly drive in Germany and Japan in order to spur the non-Communist economies as a whole. By that time, however, Americans had already constructed the scaffolding of the Western economic order they were seeking.

The arena for American policy

"Americans are inclined to believe that the period at the end of the war will provide a tabula rasa on which can be written the terms of a democratic new order. The economic and political institutions of 1939 and before are clearly in suspension and need not be restored intact after the war."[30] This assessment, which was offered during an October 1942 study group session of the Council on Foreign Relations, was typical of much American thinking. And by 1945, looking at Berlin and Warsaw, or Caen, who could doubt that Europe was a tabula rasa?

In fact, however, Europe was not a blank slate, and the economic policies that the United States thrust upon it could not avoid partisan implications even when they were deemed apolitical. The major issues

28 Jerome B. Cohen, *Japan's Economy in War and Reconstruction* (Minneapolis: University of Minnesota Press, 1949), p. 427.

29 For the embittered reaction of one see James Stewart Martin, *All Honorable Men* (Boston: Little, Brown, 1952).

30 Council on Foreign Relations: Studies of American Interests in the War and the Peace, Memoranda of Discussion; Economic and Financial Series, E-A 36, October 27, 1942.

Washington sought to influence in economic reconstruction concerned new monetary arrangements and trade agreements (the whole complex structure of multilateralism) and the role of foreign assistance. Also at issue were the nature of labor representation (specifically, how to organize trade union support for plans consonant with American leadership) and the total reconstruction possible in West Germany and Japan. Each of these massive and perplexing sets of issues tested the American postulates of productivity.

Multilateralism and monetary reorganization

The return to a system of stable exchange rates was high on the agenda for both American and British leaders from the beginning of US involvement in the war. Yet, within the Anglo-American alliance, there were sharp differences of interest. If Congress or the United States Treasury were going to endorse unprecedented foreign aid first in the Lend-Lease agreements, then in the $3.75 billion loan of 1945–46, they saw no reason not to compel London to give up commercial advantages that excluded American producers. Section VII of the Lend-Lease agreement had insisted upon postwar trade liberalization (although specifics remained omitted). The Treasury did not want British reserves to rise, and American negotiators criticized Britain's reliance on the dominion credits held in sterling in London. The British, on the other hand, invoked the notion of "equality of sacrifice" in the common war effort. What Washington was being asked to bear appeared small in comparison to their losses, financial and otherwise.

It would be wrong to bifurcate the positions too absolutely. After their own devaluation decisions during 1933–34, Roosevelt and his advisors agreed that high employment should take precedence over the stability of international exchange. Veterans of the 1930s understood that they could not allow the cost of stable currency parities to be a wrenching deflation of the home economies. This meant that as natural postwar leader and source of the potential key currency, the United States would bear a special responsibility. It must be prepared to rediscount the deficits in international account of the weaker economies and to provide the international liquidity that would get its own goods abroad. Was Washington ready for that responsibility? And if Roosevelt himself, bound by ties of sentiment and flattery to Churchill, was, would Republican Conservatives and Western Democrats endorse the policies?

The record was mixed. From the outset the differences between Keynes's plan for a postwar clearing union and Harry Dexter White's proposed stabilization fund reflected the divergent national interests.

In Keynes's concept, the burden of currency stabilization was to be shared with the creditor nation (much as later the United States would pressure West Germany and Japan for upward revaluation of their respective exchange rates). Keynes envisaged a large pool of international reserves, which, like later Special Drawing Rights (SDRs), could be created as needed. To discourage countries from maintaining an undervalued currency he proposed that the large creditors of the clearing union pay interest along with the debtors. This was a suggestion that most of his colleagues saw as more playful than serious. Finally, Keynes envisaged automatic overdraft rights on the clearing union by national banks, much as British businessmen might overdraw their own accounts. The United States plan included only a modest fund without overdraft rights; but by mid-December 1942 White proposed a "scarce currency" clause that would have allowed debtor nations to discriminate in trade against a creditor nation that persisted in piling up balances with the stabilization fund. "The Americans," noted Roy Harrod, who felt the concession truly epochal, "have, happily, played a card which according to the rules of the game we could not play."[31] The scarce currency provision was actually accepted by the Congress in the Bretton Woods Act of July 1945. This action suggested that the majority understood it could not demand that an exhausted Europe simultaneously "buy American" and maintain currency stability. In contrast with the 1920s, this represented a significant insight, or concession, on the part of the United States, albeit a limited one. The International Monetary Fund (IMF) remained inadequately funded and entrusted with procedures that enforced a deflationary unorthodoxy upon debtors; and Washington was to keep up pressure on Britain to restore the pound to a disastrous convertibility.

The ambivalent pattern of pressure and support on the West Europeans remained characteristic of United States policy from the war until the 1950s. Increasingly, the more restrictive policies became identified with the Treasury while those more sympathetic with European reflationary needs influenced the Marshall Plan administration. The policy makers in these agencies had to confront a variety of European monetary initiatives after 1945. For all the countries the root problem was the same: apportioning the costs of the war by cancelling various claims to wealth and income. In Belgium and Holland a resolute amputation of bank accounts and monetary claims facilitated quick reconstruction of stable currencies. This was a solution that

31 Cf. Gardner, *Sterling-Dollar Diplomacy*; Rowland, "Preparing the American Ascendancy," pp. 213–22; Paterson, pp. 159–73; Roy Harrod, *The Life of John Maynard Keynes* (New York: Harcourt, Brace, 1951), p. 547 (letter to Keynes, March 2, 1943).

America and Britain would impose upon West Germany three years later.[32] In France, equivalent measures were proposed by Pierre Mendès-France but met opposition from a Communist Party in search of middle-class votes and found no support from De Gaulle. Instead, France muddled through with a chronic inflation that amounted to a disguised capital levy. Italy's postwar financial policy initially followed the pattern of French irresolution, for the liberation of Italy restored a group of traditionalist *liberisti* economists as policy makers. They were untainted by Fascism but retained the laissez-faire convictions of the pre-1925 era. Once the Left had been forced out of the governing coalition in 1947, they embarked upon a severe scheme of monetary stabilization. Their restrictions of private credit indeed halted the inflation that had shrunk the lira to one-seventieth of its 1938 value, but also provoked a recession that bottled up potential labor in the South and left existing industrial capacity badly underutilized. Recent monetarists have judged the results as a necessary cleansing for the heady growth of the 1950s. However, Economic Cooperation Administration (ECA) critics of the time (and subsequent Keynesian-type analysts) sharply condemned a policy that seemed to waste Marshall Plan resources on building up currency reserves.[33] The heirs of Franklin Roosevelt did not really wish simply to restore the counterparts of Herbert Hoover.

On the other hand, there was American consensus on the general value of multilateral exchange and as much currency convertibility as possible. The creation of intra-European payment mechanisms that were to culminate in the European Payments Union of 1950 appeared

---

32   Leon H. Dupriez, *Monetary Reconstruction in Belgium* (New York: The Carnegie Endowment for International Peace and the King's Crown Press, 1947), esp. Chapters 3–4; Fritz Grotius, "Die europäischen Geldreformen nach dem 2. Weltkrieg," *Weltwirtschaftliches Archiv*, Vol. 63 (1949 II): 106–52, 276–325; J. C. Gurley, "Excess Liquidity and European Monetary Reforms," *The American Economic Review*, 43 (March 1953): 76–100; Hans Möller, "Die westdeutsche Wahrungsreform von 1948," in *Wahrung und Wirtschaft in Deutschland 1876–1975*, Deutsche Bundesbank, ed. (Frankfurt am Main: Fritz Knapp GmbH, 1976), pp. 433–83.

33   For criticism, Marcello De Cecco, "Sulla politica di stabilizzazione del 1948," *Saggi di politica monetaria* (Milan: Dott. A. Giuffrè Editore, 1968), pp. 109–41; Economic Cooperation Administration, *Country Study (Italy)* (Washington, 1950); Bruno Foa, *Monetary Reconstruction in Italy* (New York: The Carnegie Endowment for International Peace and King's Crown Press, 1949); favorable judgments in George H. Hildebrand, *Growth and Structure in the Economy of Modern Italy* (Cambridge, Massachusetts: Harvard University Press, 1965), Chapters 2 and 8. On France, see Maurice Parodi, *L'économie et la société française de 1945 à 1970* (Paris: Armand Colin, 1971), pp. 66ff. For general coverage of postwar policies, A. J. Brown, *The Great Inflation, 1939–1951* (London: Oxford University Press, 1955), pp. 227–48.

just the logical steps toward an expansion of trade that all desired. These clearing mechanisms, however, raised new conflicts with London. Authorities there feared that the intra-European accounts would expose Britain's hazardous reserve position to further depletion, as had occurred when, under Washington's pressure, the pound had been made convertible for several weeks in the summer of 1947. Belgium especially, by dint of its early currency reform and the continuing influential role of its orthodox central bank, had achieved the strongest balance-of-payments position within Europe; London feared that Brussels might present its accumulation of sterling for conversion. British Labour spokesmen Stafford Cripps and Hugh Gaitskill also feared a renewal of Washington's earlier efforts to break into the sterling area. They felt that the United States sought to undermine the currency restrictions that allowed Britain to pursue socialist experiments without worrying about a flight from the pound. After a mini-crisis in June 1950, a compromise agreement between American negotiators and London limited the convertibility of intra-European claims, and Brussels and Washington spared London the burden of converting Belgium's accumulated sterling.[34]

The record of American policy thus remains ambivalent. On the one hand, United States negotiators pressed Britain to renounce its special protection for the pound and for its trade. This occurred between 1941 and 1945, again in 1946–47, and during 1950. On the other hand, credits did come through and the American demands were repeatedly modified in practice. US Treasury authorities pursued a rigid Bretton Woods multilateralism most vigorously, perhaps because key Treasury officials of the Truman years came not from academic economics (as had Harry Dexter White) or gentleman farming (as had Morgenthau) but from the world of banking. John Snyder (succeeding the cautious Southerner Fred Vinson) emerged from a mid-West banking milieu. His special assistant for international finance and later US executive director of the International Monetary Fund, Andrew Overby, had also begun as a banker and then served as a Vice-President of the New York Federal Reserve. In contrast, the Marshall Plan authorities who dealt with the individual European countries after 1948 derived from a more expansionist industry background and had endorsed Keynesian-type reflation. They also included labor union representatives to work with European trade union leaders. The debate between Treasury and Marshall Plan officials thus tended to reflect the unresolved differences between Keynesians and conservatives at home, between the New Deal and its critics.

Another indication of the same disputes and policy ambiguity was provided by American resistance to ratification of the International Trade Organization (ITO) draft charter. It was signed at Havana in March 1948, but it finally had to be removed from Congressional consideration by Truman in December 1950. The scuttling of the ITO, however, did not mean that the United States was turning its back on the laborious efforts to lower trade barriers; indeed the country remained committed to the interim General Agreement on Tariffs and Trade (GATT) concluded in 1947. But the more ambitious architecture of the ITO sought also to regulate commodity agreements and to make allowances for the weaker partners in the international economic system. American business critics felt it had the disadvantage of committing the United States to free trade while allowing escape clauses for less robust countries. Especially disturbing was the fact that the ITO would have allowed nations to keep exchange controls and continue inflationary policies to avoid the recessions that might attend a return to full convertibility. If American businessmen were to prolong the US commitment to low tariffs, they wanted Hull's implicit compact: the open door at home would be compensated for by the open door abroad.[35]

Foreign aid

Crudely summarized, American policy sought to maximize currency stability and international trade. This would enhance the welfare of all and the predominance of the United States. The price of Bretton Woods, however, had to be foreign assistance. Initially, Americans did not realize or confess the full extent of support they would have to provide. Only after two years of false starts did they face up to the problem of Europe's dollar gap in its full magnitude. But the issue of expanding foreign aid beset their postulates with new difficulties. Originally an apolitical aid was thought to secure the broad range of American objectives. Once, however, the Soviet Union was acknowledged as a threat, the liberals' image of a healthy political economy became strained. It was no longer clear that simple maximization of output adequately answered American interests. Increasingly, policy makers rejected those forms of international assistance which provided no direct political dividend, such as the UN Relief

---

35 On this issue, see William Diebold, Jr., *The End of the ITO*, Princeton University, Department of Economics and Social Institutions, Studies in International Finance (Princeton: Princeton University Press, 1952).

and Rehabilitation Administration (UNRRA). Harriman and others criticized this form of aid early on.[36] On the other hand, foreign aid could not become purely subordinate to politics, for it followed from all the earlier axioms that problems of political stability and capitalist recovery were resolved by efficient and neutral applications of planning or social engineering.

The difficulties became significant when Léon Blum came to plead for coal and funds in Washington during March 1946. As the American Ambassador in Paris warned, a rebuff to Blum would benefit the Communists significantly. Assistant Secretary of State Clayton endorsed generous assistance on behalf of the State Department. In the meetings of the National Advisory Council on International Monetary and Financial Problems, however, Marriner Eccles objected that "he would dislike to have the Government accused of undertaking to buy a foreign election." (This was a scruple soon to vanish.) Clayton answered that "he had great difficulty in separating political from economic conditions in thinking about Europe. If he thought that country X was in danger of economic and social chaos he would favor a loan if it were reasonable in amount and there were a reasonable chance of repayment." Secretary of Commerce Henry Wallace was also willing to go along, provided that a "bad" loan would not be extended merely to stabilize political conditions.[37] Hesitation about using loans for partisan or anti-Communist goals was expressed in Council on Foreign Relations discussions as late as December 1946. Some speakers felt that Washington should decide on the groups it favored and extend aid selectively. Others found Dean Acheson's food policy "exerting too much direct pressure on European politics."[38]

It is notable that a selective policy still raised controversy at the end of a year of growing tension over Germany and Eastern Europe, atomic weapons, Iran, and the role of Communism in general. Nonetheless, the rationale for foreign aid now involved both Cold War objectives and the commitment to productivity. When George Kennan's Policy Planning Staff worked up a paper on aid to Western Europe in May 1947, it argued that "it does not see Communist activities as the root of the difficulties of Western Europe." Blame was instead placed on the effects of the war and the "profound exhaustion of physical plant and of spiritual vigor." Thus, it advocated "that American effort in

36　Paterson, pp. 94–98.
37　US Department of State, *Foreign Relations of the United States*, 1946, V, 440–43. (Minutes of the Twenty-Fourth Meeting of the National Advisory Council on International and Monetary Problems, Washington, May 6, 1946.)
38　Council on Foreign Relations archives, Records of Groups, XII G.

aid to Europe should be directed not to the combatting of Communism as such but to the restoration of the economic health and vigor of European society."[39] When the European Recovery Program was launched, it was theoretically offered to the Communist states as well, although most in Washington probably did not expect Soviet adhesion and were probably relieved when Molotov quit the preliminary talks. But at least the Marshall Plan allowed American liberals to endorse an implicitly anti-Communist aid program on the older grounds of economic assistance. Aid could remain simultaneously apolitical in motive and political in result. The point is not to deny that the antagonism with Soviet Russia deeply influenced American objectives. It is easy to catalogue the Cold War initiatives of the period (whether ultimately they were taken in response to Soviet threats is not the issue here): they included firmness over Iran, formation of the Bizone, and exclusion of the Communists from the coalitions in France, Belgium, and Italy. Wrangling at the Foreign Ministers' Conferences, the Truman Doctrine, moving toward establishment of a West German state, and limiting Socialist outcomes in the Western zones were other important milestones. This escalation confirmed the division of Europe and Asia and the formation of a United States hegemony in "the West." Nonetheless, if the politics of the Cold War in a sense took over the economic rationale of American policy, it also logically continued the politics of productivity. Both were efforts to align universalist aspirations with United States preponderance.

The issue of European labor

The politics of productivity, as it set the guidelines for American policy during the formative postwar years, had necessarily to include a trade union dimension. Ultimately, the American prescriptions for Europe postulated that economic relations could be free of conflict, hence, could transcend earlier class divisions. This was never really true in the US, although observers during the war might be excused for thinking class antagonisms had been superseded. More accurately, the challenge of American labor had not shaken the society's consensus on the value of private enterprise as in Europe. After 1945, the view of Europe as a tabula rasa suggested an equivalent opportunity to build consensus there as well.

What such a perspective suggested was that those labor groups willing to endorse growth and productivity should continue as a component of the European coalitions. Those who dissented were held to be regrettably partisan, obstructionist, and by 1947, subversive.

---

39 US Department of State, *Foreign Relations of the United States*, 1947, III, 224–25.

During the period of liberation, it was precisely the French and Italian Communists who insisted upon the imperatives of production and summoned striking coal miners and workers back to their jobs. At the same time, Catholic, Social-Democratic, and Communist labor representatives strenuously worked to unify their trade unions as they emerged from an era of Fascist suppression. But this unity proved ephemeral and broke down on both the political and the trade union levels.[40] In France Communist Party acquiescence in policies of wage restraint provoked criticism from left-wing militants as the harsh Winter of 1946–47 set back economic recovery. Following hesitating support for a strike of Renault workers, the Party was excluded from the French government, and, in constant touch with the State Department, De Gasperi performed analogous surgery in May of 1947.[41]

In the flurry of messages over American aid in the Spring of 1947, the issue of Communist participation in government had emerged as implicitly critical. It was not surprising that by the Fall of 1947, the Communist labor confederations should make rejection of the Marshall Plan a major issue in the demonstrations and strikes that shook France and Italy. The strike movement, however, further crystallized the internal divisions within the trade union movements. Non-Communist members had already organized their own journal in France, *Résistance Ouvrière*, now redubbed *Force Ouvrière*. By late 1947 acceptance of the Marshall Plan became the major touchstone of division between the non-Communists and Communists, and Force Ouvrière leaders felt that the Communists had engaged labor's sacrifices to support a policy dictated by Moscow. At the end of 1947 they left the Confédération Générale du Travail (CGT) to organize their own federation the following April. In Italy, Catholic and socialist trade unionists left their federation, the General Confederation of Italian Labor (CGIL), a few months thereafter.[42]

Throughout this interval United States officials and AFL leaders

40   Trends can be followed in Georges Lefranc, *Le mouvement syndical de la libération aux événements de mai–juin 1968* (Paris: Presses Universitaires de France, 1969), pp. 41–76; Fabio Levi, Paride Rugafiori, Salvatore Vento, *Il triangolo industriale tra ricostruzione e lotta di classe 1945/48* (Milan: Feltrinelli, 1974); Adolfo Pepe, "La CGIL della ricostruzione alla scissione (1944–1948)," *Storia Contemporanea*, 5 (1974): 591–636; Alfred J. Rieber, *Stalin and the French Communist Party, 1941–1947* (New York: Columbia University Press, 1962), Chapter 14.

41   Besides the above, see Ambassador Caffrey's report to the State Department in *Foreign Relations of the United States, 1947*, III, p. 703, and Ambassador Dunn (Rome) on May 28, 1947, in ibid., pp. 911ff.

42   Lefranc, pp. 51–76; Sergio Turone, *Storia del sindacato in Italia (1943–1969)* (Bari: Laterza, 1973), pp. 177–89; Daniel L. Horowitz, *The Italian Labor Movement* (Cambridge, Massachusetts: Harvard University Press, 1963), pp. 214ff.

encouraged the non-Communist unions to secede and establish their own federations. CIA agent Thomas Braden later estimated that $2 million was channeled to the pro-Western elements.[43] Ambassador Caffery in Paris condemned the CGT as "the fortress" of the French Communist Party. Ambassador James Clement Dunn in Rome saw the local working class demand for factory councils as a "Communist framework for fomenting disorder and attacking the authority of the state."[44] American CIO leaders were initially reluctant to join in the concerted pressure against the unified labor federations and for a while resisted official pleas that they enlist against the Communists. But by late 1948 the CIO was wracked by the struggle against Communist-led unions within its own ranks, and its leaders felt a greater Communist danger. Secretary James Carey also served on the Harriman Committee that helped outline the European Recovery Program after Marshall's famous address of June 1947, and he became angry over the obstruction to the plan that the fellow-traveling Secretary-General of the World Federation of Free Trade Unions seemed to be raising. By the Spring of 1949, the CIO and the AFL met with the Force Ouvrière and the British Trade Union Congress to charter a new non-Communist international labor federation.[45]

The Marshall Plan thus irrevocably split the European labor movement between 1947–49. More precisely, it sealed a division that was probable in any case; but it did so on the questions of economic recovery that Americans found easiest to defend. Given the United States axioms, what men of good will could legitimately reject the concept of assistance to stimulate investment and production? The Communists, in a sense, placed themselves outside the continuum of normal politics. On the other hand, the premises of the Marshall Plan, as well as the make-up of the Truman Administration, imposed limits on the political reaction of 1947–49. No Democratic Administration in the United States, especially one facing a challenge from its Left, could have alienated labor. Nor would it thereafter have been able to work with any anti-Communist government abroad that needed to preserve some working-class support. From this derived the imperative of constructing a Social-Democratic center, even if this strategy meant, as Dunn argued from Italy, that socialization would be accelerated.[46] The British Labour Party, finally, remained a key

---

43 *The New York Times,* May 8, 1967, p. 1, for Braden revelations.
44 *Foreign Relations of the United States,* 1947, III, 690–91 (Caffery cable, February 19), and 747–48 (Dunn report, December 11, 1948), III.
45 Evolution of the CIO leadership can be followed in *Foreign Relations of the United States,* 1948, III, 847–48, 867 (reports of March 10 and 24).
46 *Foreign Relations of the United States,* 1948, III, p. 863 (March 28, 1948).

factor in organizing a "third force," and its members believed, in the words of Dennis Healey, that Europe could be reconstructed only as Democratic Socialist or Communist.[47] Far from turning out to be an infinitely malleable society, Europe and its divisions forced the American politics of productivity in a clear centrist direction.

Germany and Japan

The influence that Washington exerted through foreign aid in most of Europe could be imposed directly in the two societies that would later form the strongest building blocks of the Western economy along with America, specifically West Germany and Japan. During the very months that the division of Germany was becoming irremediable (Spring 1947 to Spring 1948), the future political economy of the West German state was also being decided. The outcome depended upon a complex interplay between a number of groups and individuals. General Lucius Clay was proconsul of the American zone. The Department of the Army in Washington supported Clay. The Department of State heeded the Paris Embassy's warnings about the dangers of compelling the shaky French government to accept too quick a German recovery. Finally, the British government controlled the industrial heartland of North-Rhine-Westphalia. It was clear that Clay would seek to limit Socialist initiatives inside the *Länder* of the American zone. The formation of the Bizone, moreover, allowed him to determine effectively the outcome within North-Rhine-Westphalia as well, even though it lay inside the British administrative sphere. During 1947 Clay forestalled British Labour Party intentions to establish the Ruhr mines under public German control. Once Clay's views prevailed in Washington, French and British dependence upon American aid precluded their resisting his framework for a capitalist and federalist West German state. The implications for future West German politics were crucial; for coupled with the diminishing chances for reunification, the new constraints on West German collectivism effectively condemned the left wings of the SPD and of the CDU to a political desert. Who remembers today the vibrant Christian Socialism of the North-Rhine-Westphalian CDU before 1949?[48]

---

47 Ibid., p. 855 (March 17, 1948).
48 For Clay's opposition to British plans, and Washington discussions, see *Foreign Relations of the United States*, 1947, II, pp. 910–11, 924ff; also Jean Edward Smith, ed., *The Papers of Lucius D. Clay: Germany 1945–1949*, 2 vols. (Bloomington, Ind.: The Indiana University Press, 1975), Vol. I, pp. 341–43, 352–63, 411–13. For German political ramifications see, among others, Hans-Peter Schwarz, *Vom Reich zur Bundesrepublik. Deutschland im Widerstreit der aussenpolitischen Konzeptionen in den Jahren der Besatzungsherrschaft 1945–1949* (Neuwied and Berlin: Luchterhand, 1966), pp. 297–344, 551–64; also Eberhard Schmidt, *Die verhinderte Neuordnung 1945–1952* (Frankfurt am Main: Europäische Verlagsanstalt, 1970).

Comparable developments took place in Japan. The revival of trade unionism that Occupation authorities originally encouraged became unwelcome when labor protested against the deterioration of living conditions that had occurred after the end of the war and that had reached a crisis (in all countries) during the Winter of 1946–47. When the militant, Communist-oriented Sambetsu union federation announced a general strike for February 1, 1947, MacArthur prohibited the demonstration. The Socialist Party won a plurality in the April elections (the Liberals and Democrats had not yet consolidated) and participated in the government during 1947–48. It was the last time for a generation that they were to do so. Both Japanese business and the Supreme Allied Command-Pacific endeavored successfully to encourage a schism in the Sambetsu. They achieved a secession by the moderates and the formation, by 1950, of the Sōhyo federation. This was analogous to the contemporary formation of Force Ouvrière in France or the Social Democratic Party in Italy.[49]

In both Germany and Japan the policy of industrial deconcentration was slowly jettisoned. By the Fall of 1947, the Harriman–Draper mission to Germany recommended a new emphasis on rebuilding German industry and protests rose against dismantling and reparations (even to the Western allies). Draper visited Japan in early 1948 and made similar recommendations. He was followed by Secretary of the Army Kenneth Royall and by fiscally orthodox Detroit banker Joseph Dodge in early 1949. The campaign against the Zaibatsu faltered as did the effort to reorganize durably the German iron and steel industry.[50] The logic of the new policy was persuasive. If the United States were to commit itself to a great effort to restore economic production in Europe and Asia, how could it plausibly persevere in crippling the most productive centers of those continents?

Indeed, West Germany and Japan remained the states where the United States' politics of productivity could be transplanted most triumphantly. Perhaps because of the visible destruction all around or the labor pool formed by the immigrants from the East, German

---

49 Jon Halliday, *A Political History of Japanese Capitalism* (New York: Pantheon Books, 1975), pp. 206–19, is useful from a Marxist perspective. See also Eitaro Kishimoto, "Labour-Management Relations and the Trade Unions in Post-War Japan (1)," *The Kyoto University Economic Review* Vol. 38, No. 1 (April 1968): 1–35, which emphasizes the role played by "seniority wages" in encouraging enterprise unions at the expense of more class-oriented labor coalitions; also Iwayo F. Ayusawa, *A History of Labor in Modern Japan* (Honolulu: East-West Center Press, 1966), pp. 257–75, 281–301, 315–23; Koji Taira, *Economic Development and the Labor Market in Japan* (New York: Columbia University Press, 1970), pp. 183–87.

50 Halliday, *A Political History of Japanese Capitalism*, pp. 182–90; John Gimbel, *The American Occupation of Germany, 1945–1949* (Stanford, Calif.: Stanford University Press, 1968), pp. 147ff., 163ff., 174–85.

labor demonstrated consistent restraint. The Social Democratic Party (SPD) did not press its program in Bizonia. Indeed, it reverted to the opposition. The trade union federation (DGB) accepted a far more circumscribed co-determination law than it originally wanted. As German industrial and banking leaders would themselves testify, trade union wage restraint became a major component of the economic miracle.[51] The post-Korea take-off in Japan condemned the Left in that country to a noisy but marginal status.

American policy in Germany and Japan was thus a resounding success. The whole thrust of Washington's effort in the emerging Federal Republic, the new Japan, and the members of the Organization for European Economic Cooperation (OEEC) – later the Organization for Economic Cooperation and Development (OECD) – was to ensure the primacy of economics over politics, to de-ideologize issues of political economy into questions of output and efficiency. The two occupied states offered the most promising ground for accomplishing the conversion of politics into economics. Especially in West Germany, the political structure developed as a scaffolding for economic reconstruction; the Federal Republic emerged as a proto-state built upon organs for economic administration. Even today both the Federal Republic and Japan are nations which represent massive economic forces that lack concomitant political weight. From states in which military-bureaucratic establishments, pursuing objectives of prestige and expansion, called upon the resources of production for statist ends, they have become political economies in which the concept of state has become virtually otiose.

In the last analysis, the politics of productivity that emerged as the American organizing idea for the postwar economic world depended upon superseding class conflict with economic growth. By bringing West Germany and Japan into a community of nations as dynamos of wider regional recovery, the United States aided other societies to adjourn their own distributive conflicts and to move from scarcity to relative abundance. By helping to establish West Germany and Japan as nexuses of economic transactions and the most efficient accumulators of capital, rather than as centers of political power, America most completely carried out its postwar economic postulates.

The success of this politics of productivity can be judged by the fact that the 1950s and the 1960s turned out to be periods of unparalleled growth and capital formation. Investment was a major objective of

51   See, for example, Herman Abs's presentation to the Council on Foreign Relations, December 5, 1949, Council on Foreign Relations Archives, Records of Meetings, Vol. 10.

Table 1. *Gross national capital formation*

	1950–58 (%)	Previous maxima (%)
UK	16.2	14.0 (1900–14)
German Federal Republic	26.8	24.1 (1891–1913)
Italy	19.8	17.3 (1901–10)
United States	18.4	21.9 (1889–1908)
Sweden	21.4	c. 20.4 (1941–49, inferred)
Japan	30.2	15.3 (1927–36)

Source: Simon Kuznets, *Modern Economic Growth: Rate, Structure, and Spread* (New Haven: Yale University Press, 1966), pp. 236–39.

the European Recovery Program. Without capital formation, American aid might ease immediate balance-of-payment crises but would have to continue indefinitely, whereas the premise of the Marshall Plan as presented to Congress was that after four years Europe's self-sufficiency would be restored. By 1948–49, it was clear that Europe was investing 20 percent of its GNP, whereas from an equal social product in 1938, its societies had ploughed back only 12 percent. (And military expenditures in 1948–49 were only 1 percent less than 1938's 6 percent.) Indeed, the ambitious British investment levels of 1948–49, when gross domestic capital formation (less overseas deficit) reached 22.8 percent (1948) and 21.4 percent (1949), or roughly twice that of 1938, seemed excessive to American Keynesians. The memory of the Depression, when aggregate demand did not keep pace with productive capacity, sobered the observers of British efforts under the Marshall Plan.[52]

Insofar as much of post–World War II politics can be viewed as a debate between growth and equality, between collective investment or public consumption, at least until the late 1960s, the argument was largely resolved so as not to endanger investment. This can be inferred not only from electoral returns that excluded the Left, but from the slow percentage growth of wage shares as a component of national income. In the stately half-century decline of the return on capital, the 1950s represented a decade of redress. Reviewing the reverses of Socialism in 1959, Richard Titmuss found increasing privilege, inequality, and concentrations of power.[53] The other side of the story

52 Howard Ellis, *The Economics of Freedom* (New York: Harper, 1952), pp. 129, 135.
53 Richard Titmuss, "The Irresponsible Society," *Essays on the Welfare State* (Boston: Beacon Press, 1969).

was unparalleled economic growth (albeit outside Great Britain) and the rise of real incomes. Germany and Japan, above all, achieved record growth and accumulation. These were, of course, precisely the arenas in which the American politics of productivity could be most thoroughly instituted.

In retrospect the 1950s, and even the 1960s, must be judged a great era for the stabilized growth capitalism of the West. Conservative governments ruled in London, Bonn, Rome, for a time in Paris, and certainly in Washington. This was not right-wing leadership, but solid men of the center committed to growth after wartime destruction and exhaustion with ideological conflict. The United States encouraged this trend but did not have to impose it. Had these impulses not been present it seems unlikely that Americans could have built a breakwater in Europe any more than they were able to dam up different aspirations in Asia. On the other hand, the social basis for the politics of productivity was present in Europe, as it was not in mainland Asia. The war and Nazi occupation had shaken, but not uprooted, a prevailingly bourgeois society with broad middle-class patterns of ownership and culture.

The limits of American hegemony

Perhaps the best term for the postwar Western economy would be that of consensual American hegemony. "Consensual" can be used because European leaders accepted Washington's leadership in view of their needs for economic and security assistance. Hegemony derives from Washington's ability to establish policy guidelines binding on the West. In what respects, however, did hegemony really mean influence exerted to alter European policies that might otherwise have turned out differently? Certainly in the years 1944 to 1947 the emphasis on free convertibility of currencies and stable exchange rates, as stipulated in the Bretton Woods arrangements and aid to Britain, were designed, in part, to limit London's capacity to organize a separate trading bloc. Pained British protests made American *force majeure* abundantly clear, although they did not necessarily justify British preferences in terms of broader criteria of economic welfare. In the years after 1947, when the objectives of some American policy makers became more politically conservative, Washington's continuing pressure on behalf of the dollar as an international currency, the political signals which accompanied its foreign aid, and its direct intervention in West Germany and Japan could inhibit leftist experiments in societies that might have tried alternative principles of economic organization. These would in turn have ultimately been less susceptible to United States influence. Usually Washington did not have brutally to abort a series of promising Socialist initiatives. Instead, it more subtly rewarded a generation of centrist "Atlantic" oriented European leaders (and Japanese Liberal Democrats) who found the American preferences rational and humane. Moreover, the United States could benefit from some of the economic arrangements generated in wartime Europe and Japan. For if the wartime experiences provoked a left-wing resistance mystique, paradoxically they reinforced corporatist patterns of social bargaining that persisted afterward. Labor relations in Germany, Japan, the Netherlands, and other countries were to bear the wartime impression, and the United States would ultimately benefit from the collaborative tendencies thus bequeathed.[54] In the last analysis, the means of exercising hegemony may be as critical as the fact of dominance itself: the architects of the American-sponsored international economic order exerted a gentlemanly persuasion. Moreover, it was one enjoying most of the mystical aura of an "invisible hand," which usually attends smoothly running cybernetic systems, much as had been the case with the Gold Standard before World War I.[55]

Hegemony remains successful, however, only when it achieves advances for the whole international structure within which it is exercised. Hegemony imposed in a zero-sum cockpit, that is, at the expense of the secondary members of the system, must finally prove less durable. (Alternatively, it requires overt force; viz., Hungary, 1956, and Czechoslovakia, 1968.) The quarter-century of relatively frictionless American domination depended partially upon the fact that the technologies of the era (including the capitalization of agriculture) permitted the growth that was its underlying premise. Ironically, too, the destruction left by World War II allowed rapid catch-up recovery that could be attributed to the American role. The result was that the

54 These continuities in Europe comprise a major theme of my own current research; for the Japanese case, see Taira, p. 188, drawing upon the Japanese work of Ryohei Magota.

55 For the issue of whether international monetary systems do or do not require "hegemonic" leadership, see the essays in Rowland, ed., *Balance of Power or Hegemony;* also Stephen D. Krasner, "State Power and the Structure of International Trade," *World Politics* Vol. 28, No. 3 (July 1976): 317–43. Insights into the regulatory capacity of the earlier system are derived from Arthur Bloomfield, *Short-Term Capital Movements under the Gold Standard*, Princeton University, Department of Economics and Social Institutions, International Studies No. 16 (Princeton, N.J., 1952), esp. pp. 72ff.; Peter Lindert, "Key Currencies and Gold, 1900–1913," *Princeton Studies in International Finance*, No. 24 (Princeton, N.J.: Princeton University Press, 1969).

politics of productivity rested upon the reality of productivity. The system paid off.

Indeed, once the system ceased to pay off, it began to founder. Between 1944 and 1971 the structures of American leadership could serve the United States in one of two ways: one accepted as legitimate and one as less legitimate by the secondary participants. Insofar as the United States was prepared to furnish European societies goods and services without real economic counterpart, it could ask policy compliance in return. This was the situation of the "dollar gap" in the late 1940s and early 1950s, when Washington provided more than $20 billion of assistance and secured more open trading areas. The other way that Americans could utilize the Bretton Woods framework was precisely the reverse: by exacting tribute through seignorage, i.e., accumulating dollar liabilities abroad and purchasing European assets with an overvalued currency. This was the situation of the late 1960s when, in effect, the United States taxed its allies for part of the costs of the Indochina War (combined with other public commitments) by trying to insist upon the unaltered reserve status of an eroding dollar. Since, however, the system remained one of consensual hegemony (contrasted, for example, with the German organization of continental Europe between 1940 and 1944), the United States could not easily enforce the power of unlimited overdrafts. The French refused to pay the levy from 1965 on, and it was primarily the special West German dependence upon US security presence that enabled the Bretton Woods framework to last as long as it did. (That West German need, both objective and subjective, in turn reflected the special circumstances in which the Federal Republic of Germany had emerged under US auspices.)

With the partial relinquishing of American claims to leadership, divergent patterns of foreign economic policy became more visible. While Washington's politics of productivity helped to reorient the Western economies in the postwar era, characteristic national preferences and approaches persisted. Of course, as American predominance relaxed, it would have been logical for the secondary countries to revert to a more mercantilist conduct in the absence of forceful leadership. Such trends, though, were to be further reinforced by traditional historical patterns of economic policy making. For all its economic vigor, for example, the business leadership of West Germany continued to reemphasize the primacy of exports and only secondarily the importance of domestic purchasing power and expansion. Italian and Japanese policy makers likewise tended to pursue policies in which relatively cheap labor played a major role. The American politics

of productivity applied abroad had originally encouraged labor restraint to secure ultimate economic growth. As American leadership
became more diffuse, entrepreneurs and political leaders in Europe
tended to emphasize the restraint more than the growth.

Perhaps it is ungracious to ask whether what was originally a successful and, I believe, broad and generally beneficial policy had serious
costs. But all grand policy structures must at least exclude alternatives,
and this particular international economic system probably served to
stabilize the inequalities of income and power within each society of
the West and Japan. A contrast with the British imperial structure
before 1914 may help to reveal the mechanism and also establish its
proportions. Britain's financial preponderance rested upon real growth
but also upon the society's willingness to live with sharply skewed
distributions of income and wealth. Had there been sharper challenges
to domestic inequality over the half-century before World War I, it
might have proved far more difficult to generate the social savings
that established the reserve position of sterling. By the 1920s, the costs
of continuing were excessive, even for a society as cohesive as the
British. American hegemony, on the other hand, was a child of Wilsonianism and the New Deal. Politically, it could not demand renunciation on the part of the American working classes for the sake of
providing the liquidity of the West. Nor, initially, did it have to; the
discrepancy in productivity and output between Europe and the US
left by the Second World War made American leadership relatively
painless in domestic terms. Conservatives complained about taxes,
but the sacrifice even to support the Marshall Plan was comparatively
slight. It was not the fiscal burden, but the departure from political
traditions that represented the major domestic hurdle. When, by the
end of the 1960s, real sacrifices at home in terms of taxation or restrictions on use of the dollar abroad might have been necessary to
restore credibility in the dollar's reserve status, the Nixon Administration chose to renounce a degree of economic primacy.

Yet the contrary-to-fact query remains. Might the progress of re-
ducing inequality within the United States as well as Europe not have
been faster or surer without the quarter-century of economic domination? It is impossible to be confident. While periods of quick growth
do not usually reduce income disparities, neither does stagnation,
which might have been the result of a less forward American policy.
Nonetheless, the question must be posed. "Welfare" criteria apply,
most easily, to whole societies. Alone they cannot measure the costs
of hegemony on particular components but can only confirm the
triumph of productivity for the aggregate. But this, indeed, was all

Americans sought to know. The cohesiveness of our politics lay in the reluctance to suggest alternative questions. In the terms that all significant sectors of opinion would have posed the issue, US foreign economic policy was beneficial as well as potent. This judgment should not be surprising; it followed from the ideological beliefs that rescued national cohesion in a society of great material differences.

4

The two postwar eras and the conditions for stability in twentieth-century Western Europe

This chapter was originally drafted during tenure of a fellowship from the National Endowment for the Humanities to pursue research on the United States and European reconstruction after World War II. Earlier versions benefited from conversation with Duke University colleagues as well as from discussion at seminars at the University of Wisconsin in Madison, Princeton University, Harvard University, and the European Studies Center at the University of Chicago, and at Werner Conze's seminar for social and economic history at Heidelberg. A semi-final draft was presented as a paper at the Ninety-Third Annual Meeting of the American Historical Association, held in San Francisco, December 1978. I am grateful to Leonard Krieger, Richard Kuisel, and Carl Schorske for their comments at that session. The version reprinted here is especially indebted to the suggestions of Professor Kuisel, the subsequent critiques by the anonymous referees for the *American Historical Review*, and the comments of Patrick Fridenson of the Ecole des Hautes Etudes en Sciences Sociales, Paris. I have not reproduced here the comments by Charles P. Kindleberger and Stephen Schuker that were published along with the original article, nor my rebuttal.

Broadcasting over the BBC in November 1945, A. J. P. Taylor assured his listeners, "Nobody in Europe believes in the American way of life – that is, in private enterprise; or rather those who believe in it are a defeated party and a party which seems to have no more future than the Jacobites in England after 1688."[1] Taylor proved to be wrong, or at least premature, about the end of private enterprise. The question here is why, at least in Western Europe, there was less transformation than he envisaged. Posed in broader terms, how did Western Europe

1 Taylor, "The European Revolution," *Listener* (London), November 22, 1945, p. 576.

153

achieve political and social stability by the mid-twentieth century after two great, destructive wars and the intervening upheaval.

Historians often treat stability as a passive coming to rest or a societal inertia that requires no explanation. In fact, stabilization is as challenging a historical problem as revolution. It can emerge dramatically. As one historian who has focused on the process wrote, "Political stability, when it comes, often happens to a society quite quickly, as suddenly as water becomes ice."[2] Stabilization, moreover, does not preclude significant social and political change but often requires it. Certainly the two world wars broadened democracy in Britain and stimulated economic transformation in France. World War II finally removed the contradictions between modernity and reaction in Germany, thereby facilitating a meritocratic pluralism. Yet, despite the transformations, earlier liberal and elitist arrangements that governed the distribution of wealth and power either persisted or were resumed after authoritarian intervals. And at least until the end of the 1960s the societies of Western Europe seemed more cohesive, humdrum, and routine than either those who feared change or those who longed for it would have predicted.

The key to this stability lies in both postwar eras, the period after World War I as well as that after World War II. Although the years after the first war did not bring enduring stabilization, neither did they produce the radical economic and social change that Left and Right had expected. Outside Russia the first war opened the way only to limited upheaval, conservative reconstruction, or, in some cases, counterrevolution. With the end of the second war, as Taylor's prognosis suggested, many observers again anticipated a major social transformation. This time the postwar years brought not only an ebbing of radicalism but at least a generation of political and economic stability as well. Yet that midcentury stability rested upon the cumulative achievements of both postwar eras. Together the postwar intervals comprised two chapters in a single half-century effort by reform-minded and conservative elites to exploit postwar circumstances for a successful restructuring of the hierarchies they dominated.

Given the objective of historical comparison, the two periods are usefully envisaged as complementary and parallel alike. Complementary (as is stressed below) in that each made its own distinct but partial contribution to the process of channeling change. Parallel in that key

2   J. H. Plumb, *The Origins of Political Stability: England, 1675–1725* (Boston, 1967), xvii.

political and economic developments tended to recapitulate themselves. The recurring elements after both wars demonstrate that, although many problems were different, the same underlying political cleavages, enduring class and industrial conflicts, and continuing economic dilemmas remained. As in earlier postwar transitions, each period witnessed a swing from radical challenge to political consolidation. Such a trajectory had marked Europe in the aftermath of the wars of the French Revolution and Napoleon, Russia following the Crimean War, Italy, Prussia, and Austria after the wars of unification, the United States after its Civil War, and France again in the wake of 1870, Spain after 1898, and Russia after 1905. The periods after the two world wars likewise reveal certain parallels.

Consider, first, the comparable political developments. Just as radical or reformist forces of the Left seemed ready to impose extensive changes and then lost their impetus between 1918 and 1921, so the Resistance-born coalitions of Communists, Socialists, Catholics, and liberal democrats initiated reforms but collapsed by 1947–48. In both cases this disarray followed early polarization within the working-class parties and unions. From the viewpoint of the moderates, Soviet-oriented leaders grew ruthlessly opportunistic and sectarian; reverse the perspective and Social Democrats appear preoccupied with Bolshevism or communism. After both wars, too, the respective Catholic parties – the German Zentrum and the Italian Popolari after 1918, the diverse Christian Democrats after 1945 – also retreated from their earlier commitments to boldly proclaimed economic reforms. Catholic trade-union leaders and left intellectuals lost out to spokesmen for middle-class stability, the Church hierarchy, or "social-market liberalism."

A careful distinction is necessary here. After 1945, plans to supersede capitalism yielded to efforts to reinvigorate economic liberalism. Yet liberal party organizations continued the long-term decline that had originated even before World War I. This attrition hurt both right- and left-wing variants of liberalism, although the Right could fall back upon the economic interest groups it dominated and the Left still controlled influential journalistic outposts. Electoral support, however, was a different story. Voting results were prevailingly disappointing. In 1946 Italian laissez-faire Liberals and the reformist Actionists together polled no more than 8 percent of the electorate. The French non-Marxist, non-Catholic Left had brilliant writers but few voters. Belgian Liberal deputies were returned at roughly half of their prewar strength with about 9 percent of the popular poll, and the revived Liberal Democratic party in West Germany (today's Free Democrats), with its 9.5 percent in Landtag elections and 12 percent of the first

Bundestag, remained comparable to voting results of the combined Democratic (Staatspartei) and People's parties in the late Weimar Republic.[3]

Just as striking as the draining of energy on the Left in the respective postwar years was the recapitulation of key industrial and monetary developments. Certainly the economy of the era after 1948 became far more robust than the ephemeral prosperity of the late 1920s. Nonetheless, some of the same dilemmas and solutions marked both recoveries. By the mid-1920s Americans were finally helping ease Europe's postwar balance-of-payments difficulties by the enthusiastic purchase of European bonds. At the same time, leading bankers on both sides of the Atlantic pressed for currency stabilization and monetary convertibility on the basis of the gold-exchange standard: the Reichsmark was anchored in late 1924, sterling in April 1925, the lire in 1927, and the French franc (legally re-established exclusively on a gold base) in 1928. The laboriously negotiated tariff compromises and trade treaties of the latter 1920s along with such interindustry agreements as the Entente Internationale de l'Acier advanced the integration of the major Continental steel and chemical producers. Agreements between industries across frontiers encouraged mergers and concentration within the component national economies. In a similar sequence after World War II, the European Recovery Program of 1948–51, and subsequent Mutual Security assistance provided American credits to compensate for Europe's massive dollar deficit. The European Payments Union, the product of negotiations extending from 1948 to 1951 worked toward renewed currency convertibility. The Coal-Steel Community of the early 1950s reinforced the capitalist revival of the second postwar period.[4]

3 For a useful tabulation of voting results, see Derek W. Urwin, ed., *Elections in Western Nations, 1945–1968*, University of Strathclyde, Survey Research Center, *Occasional Papers*, nos. 4–5 (Glasgow, n.d.).
4 For the negotiations of the 1920s, see Charles S. Maier, *Recasting Bourgeois Europe: Stabilization in France, Germany, and Italy in the Decade after World War I* (Princeton, 1975), 516–45; and Jacques Bariéty, "Das Zustandekommen der Internationalen Rohstahlgemeinschaft (1926) als Alternative zum misslungenen 'Schwerindustriellen Projekt' des Versailler Vertrages," in Hans Mommsen *et al.*, eds., *Industrielles System und politische Entwicklung in der Weimarer Republik* (Düsseldorf, 1974), 552–68. For the negotiations between coal and steel producers after World War II, the material in the steel trusteeship papers at the Koblenz Bundesarchiv [hereafter, BA], B 109/97, is revealing; these papers are complemented by the memoranda of meetings included in the archives of the Compagnie de Pont-à-Mousson at La Châtre [hereafter, PAM], boxes 70669, 70671, 70690–91, 77042. Also see William Diebold, Jr., *The Schuman Plan: A Study in Economic Cooperation, 1950–1959* (New York, 1959). For monetary negotiations, see Stephen V. O. Clarke, *Central Bank Cooperation, 1924–1931* (New York, 1967); Sir Henry Clay, *Lord Norman* (London, 1957); L. V. Chandler, *Benjamin Strong, Central Banker* (Washington, 1958); W. A. Brown, Jr., *England and the New*

Obviously, there were crucial differences between the two postwar eras; to discern parallels is not to claim identities. After the First World War, to cite just a first salient difference, the political Right emerged more militant than before 1914. Fascism drew upon a striking force of veterans inured to violence and contemptuous of civilian virtues. After the Second World War, fascism was discredited and even traditional conservative nationalism rejected. The psychological impact of the fighting did not create nuclei of Arditi, Free Corps recruits, or others addicted to paramilitary violence. For most soldiers the second war impelled instead a search for private fulfillment: "the happy obscurity of a humdrum job and a little wife and a household of kids," according to Bill Mauldin, or, a front away, the return to "the mountains of the Caucasus, the exciting blue smoke of the foothills . . ., the sweet faces of loved ones."[5] What analogue existed after 1945 to the *trinceismo*, the glorification of the trenches of World War I, was the partisans' mountain ordeal: a trial that Resistance spokesmen claimed was moral justification for a new elite, although without any encouragement for a continuing cult of violence. Indeed, the distinction in 1914–18 between front soldiers mired down in brutalizing combat and male civilians at home who sometimes enjoyed cushy, protective berths – the so-called *embusqués* or *imboscati* – dissolved in 1939–45 with the rapid movement of troops, the air attacks on civilian targets, and the hardships of occupation. Almost 50 percent of Europe's dead in the second war were civilians, compared to about 5 percent in the first.[6] These factors all contributed to limiting the po-

Gold Standard, 1919–1926 (New Haven, 1929), and *The International Gold Standard Reinterpreted, 1914–1934*, 2 vols. (New York, 1940); Donald E. Moggridge, *British Monetary Policy, 1924–1931: The Norman Conquest of $4.86* (Cambridge, 1972); and Gerd Hardach, *Weltmarktorientierung und relative Stagnation: Währungspolitik in Deutschland, 1924–1931*, Schriften zur Wirtschafts- und Sozialgeschichte, vol. 27 (Berlin, 1976). For post-1945 negotiations, see William Diebold, Jr., *Trade and Payments in Western Europe* (New York, 1952); J. Kummell, *De Ontwikkeling van het Internationale Betalingsverkeer* (Leiden, 1950); Robert Triffin, *Europe and the Money Muddle* (New Haven, 1957); and Raymond F. Mikesell, *Foreign Exchange in the Postwar World* (New York, 1954).

5　As quoted in John Morton Blum, *V Was for Victory: Politics and American Culture during World War II* (New York, 1976), 70, 73. For the attitudes and political organization of veterans, only a minority of whom became radically antidemocratic, see James M. Diehl, *Paramilitary Politics in Weimar Germany* (Bloomington, Ind., 1977); Volker R. Berghahn, *Der Stahlhelm, Bund der Frontsoldaten, 1918–1935* (Düsseldorf, 1966); Robert G. L. Waite, *Vanguard of Nazism: The Free Corps Movement in Postwar Germany, 1918–1923* (Cambridge, Mass., 1952); Giorgio Sabatucci, *I combattenti nel primodopoguerra* (Bari, 1974); and Antoine Prost, *Les Anciens combattants et la société française, 1914–1939*, 3 vols. (Paris, 1977), esp. volume 3: *Idéologies et mentalités*.

6　Gordon Wright, *The Ordeal of Total War, 1939–1945* (New York, 1968), 264.

tential of any veterans-based right radicalism. Except for the recurring but small German nationalist splinters, achieving at best 8 to 10 percent electoral support at the Land level (and about 2 percent in national polls), the search for right-wing movements after 1945 yields only ambivalent possibilities: the Gaullism of 1947 and the Uomo Qualunque of southern Italy, a sort of pre-Poujadism that rejected the moralistic claims of the Resistance Left. This failure of the neofascist Right to emerge in greater strength was a major surprise of postwar European politics.[7]

Only in retrospect is it discernible that even under the collaborationist regimes conservative elements had to rethink the economic role of the state and the future relationship of capital and labor. To cite just the French situation (although analogues existed in the Netherlands and the Salò Republic), awareness that the Vichy regime was doomed and mass upheaval likely prompted the industrialists summoned by the Conseil Supérieur de l'Économie Industrielle et Commerciale to search for a "factory community" that would provide a "balanced solution" between "yesterday's capitalism" and "collectivism." Such explorations, however, could build upon more than fear of postwar revolution. They carried forward some of the heterodox notions of economic planning that dissenting socialists and conservative intellectuals alike had outlined in the 1930s.[8]

A major condition for a more flexible Right was the fact that the Left too debarked differently after the second war. Between 1918 and 1921 the European working classes had first surged into spontaneous demonstrations, had then waged long, disciplined mass strikes, and had finally retrenched in frustration and divided. Much of their insurrection followed from the intensified labor discipline the war imposed as well as progressive ideological alienation from its national objectives. The second war imposed some of the same ordeals within the factory, but the German occupation made the factory a less central source of oppression. The heirs of the working-class leadership that

---

7   For the Gaullism of 1947, see Jean Touchard, *Le Gaullisme, 1940–1969* (Paris, 1978), 98–133. On Uomo Qualunque, see Sandro Setta, *L'Uomo Qualunque, 1944/48* (Bari, 1975). And, for post-1945 Germany, see Kurt P. Tauber, *Beyond Eagle and Swastika: German Nationalism since 1945*, 2 vols. (Middletown, Conn., 1967).

8   Conseil Supérieur de l'Économie Industrielle et Commerciale, Commission Nr. 4, Procès-Verbal de la séance du 5 novembre 1943, PAM, box 70411; and Report to the Minister, July 17, 1944, *ibid.* Also see Richard Kuisel, "Vichy et les origines de la planification économique (1940–1946)," *Le Mouvement Social*, 98 (1977): 77–101; Jacques Amoyal, "Les Origines socialistes et syndicalistes de la planification en France," *ibid.*, 87 (1974): 137–69; and, on the labor issue, Jacques Julliard, "La Charte du Travail," in Jeanine Bourdin, ed., *Le Gouvernement de Vichy, 1940–1942: Colloque de la Fondation Nationale des Sciences Politiques* (Paris, 1972), 157–210.

had come to oppose the first war by 1917 urged active resistance to the Germans after June 1941, so that the second war was less an alien upper-class cause than an arduous wait for liberation. Its conclusion thus brought a different tempo of working-class cooperation and protest. Western Communists played down any radical economic transformation that outran the broad Resistance consensus on purges and the nationalization of key industries or those tainted by their owners' collaboration. Instead Communist leaders stressed anti-Nazi unity (until the final defeat of Germany) and continuing production, even at the cost of harsh industrial discipline. "The bonus per ton is evil," wrote one CGT leader in March 1945 about detested pay differentials, "but coal is necessary." Maurice Thorez insisted to coal miners at Waziers in July 1945 that production itself was a demonstration of solidarity, militancy, and working-class power.[9] "Only by working, only by working hard will we be able to overcome this situation [of hardship]," the secretary of the Milan Chamber of Labor told the factory council of Magneti Mirelli in early 1946. "We all seek socialism. But do you believe that we can socialize poverty?" Communists, warned Jacques Duclos, as he condemned the 1946 Socialist-supported strikes of French civil servants, had to demonstrate "that democracy is a regime of order, a regime of tranquility and of work."[10]

The open question in France, Belgium, and Italy (to the extent that the Anglo-American occupation would have permitted) was whether an angry and long-repressed working class would explode in a spontaneous radicalism with plant seizures, local "socialization," and summary trials. Communist pressure for carrying through purge procedures probably helped contain grass-roots grievances. In fact, whether in France, Italy, Belgium, Holland, or Bavaria (under American auspices), the purges became more and more restricted. Categories of guilt seemed to blur hopelessly, and moderates came to grasp that trying business leaders for cooperation with the Germans could have radical consequences, or, in the words of one *Esprit* intellectual

9   L. Delfosse, in *La Tribune des Mineurs*, March 18, 1945, as quoted in Jean Bouvier, "Région et Nation: Inflation, reformes de structures, nationalisation des houillères, et crise sociale," *Actes du Colloque de l'Université de Lille III, 2–3 novembre 1974: La Libération du Nord et du Pas-de-Calais, 1944–1947* [hereafter, *Colloque de Lille*], in *Revue du Nord*, 57 (1975): 609. For Communist policies, see J.-P. Hirsch, " 'La Seule voie possible': Remarques sur les communistes du Nord et du Pas-de-Calais de la Libération aux grèves de novembre 1947," *ibid.*, 563–78, which contains an extensive discussion of Thorez's celebrated Waziers appeal, July 21, 1945.

10 Milanese secretary of the Chamber of Labor, as quoted in Febo Guizzi, "La Fabbrica italiana Magneti Marelli," in Luigi Ganapini *et al.*, *La ricostruzione nella grande industria: Strategia padronale e organismi di fabbrica nel Triangolo, 1945–1948* (Bari, 1978), 280; and Duclos, as quoted in Alain Bergonieux, *Force Ouvrière* (Paris, 1975), 55.

who advocated it, "The purge of the economic sector entails over-turning all property relations."[11] Purges were thus wound down short of any major upheaval, and the emphasis upon sifting individuals probably diverted effort from institutional transformation – although originally the Left had envisaged *épuration* as a mode of collective change.

Perhaps, however, the major force for preventing ideological polarization after World War II was neither the chastened Right nor the tempered Left but the new Christian Democratic parties of the center. For the crucial three years after 1944, left Catholicism with its declared hostility to liberal capitalism seemed ascendant. The appearance was deceptive in the long run, but it served well to contain otherwise radical currents in the flux of the immediate postwar period. Konrad Adenauer could swallow and survive the radical-sounding Ahlen Program of the Westphalian Christian Democrats in 1947, understanding that it kept the CDU from appearing reactionary; Alcide De Gasperi ultimately profited from the mass base organized by Catholic labor leader Achille Grandi; and the French MRP accepted nationalization but, except for collaborators, insisted upon compensation.[12] In Italy and Belgium the prolonged controversy over the fate of the discredited monarchs helped the Catholic parties accommodate both Left and Right. As the American embassy reported from Brussels, the Christian

11   G. Zérapha, "Le Problème politique français," *Esprit*, December 1944, as quoted in Michel Winock, *Histoire politique de la revue "Esprit"* (Paris, 1975), 260. On the purges, see Peter Novick, *The Resistance versus Vichy* (New York, 1968); Robert Aron, *Histoire de l'épuration*, 3 vols. (Paris, 1967–75); D. Laurent *et al.*, "Sur l'épuration dans le Nord et le Pas-de-Calais," *Colloque de Lille*, in *Revue du Nord*, 57 (1975): 365–80, 623–36; Lutz Niethammer, *Entnazifizierung in Bayern: Säuberung und Rehabilitierung unter amerikanischer Besatzung* (Frankfurt a/M. 1972); and Marcello Flores, "L'E-purazione," in Instituto Nazionale per la Storica del Movimento di Liberazione in Italia, *L'Italia dalla liberazione alla repubblica; del convegno internazionale . . . 26–28 marzo 1976* (Milan, n.d.), 413–67. Also see Guizzi, "La Fabbrica italiana Magneti Marelli," 245–72; and Valerio Castronovo *Giovanni Agnelli* (Turin, 1971), 671–88. Also see the reports from U.S. diplomats on the slowing of the Belgian and Dutch purges, National Archives, Washington, Record Group 59 [hereafter, NA-RG 59], including the report by Charles Sawyer, May 29, 1945, NA-RG 59,855.00/5-2945; by Theodore Achilles, June 11, 1946, *ibid.*, 855.00/6-1146; and by J. Webb Benton from the Hague, August 15, 1946, *ibid.*, 856.00/8-1546.

12   For Adenauer's views, see Sozialausschuss der CDU, February 21–22, 1947, in Friedrich-Ebert-Stiftung, Bonn, Hensler Nachlass, 16. Also see Gerold Ambrosius, *Die Durchsetzung der sozialen Marktwirtschaft in Westdeutschland, 1945–1949* (Stuttgart, 1977); and Konrad-Adenauer-Stiftung, *Konrad Adenauer und die CDU der britischen Besatzungszone, 1946–1949* (Bonn, 1975), 46–47, 288–89. On Grandi, see Benedetto de Cesaris, "Cattolici, eredità 'popolare' e nuovo stato," in *Problemi del movimento sindacale in Italia, 1943–1973: Annali della Fondazione Giangiacomo Feltrinelli*, 16 (1976): 229–39. For the MRP stance see *Colloque de Lille* in *Revue du Nord* 57 (1975): 596–7.

Social party, by defending the rights of Leopold III, could retain the allegiance of Belgian conservatives, even while letting its trade unionists champion social reform, and could thus provide "all things to all men who believe in the Roman Catholic religion."[13] This capacity naturally undermined the radical élan of Christian democracy but did allow the movement to serve as an integrating force for moderation.

Domestic party developments obviously took place under the shadow of the great powers. The overwhelming difference between 1918 and 1945 was the continuing intervention of the United States and the Soviet Union in their respective spheres of influence. But in Western Europe, American aid, with its attendant pressure, was only one of many factors abetting liberal reconstitution. The discrediting of the European Right, the fear of Communist motives and the Soviet Union that replaced Popular Front effusions, and the desire on the part of both Christian Democrats and Social Democrats to establish moderate welfare states were powerful impulses on their own. They alone sufficed to make 1945 different from 1918.

Different, but not separate. Both postwar periods, as noted, formed part of a continuing effort at stabilization, a search that was sufficiently active and persistent (and rewarded finally with sufficient success) to comprise a major theme of twentieth-century Western European history. Stabilization, however, for whom? And of what? Stabilization meant not so much preserving liberal procedures as re-establishing the overlapping hierarchies of power, wealth, and status that can be loosely termed "capitalist." In an age of mass suffrage, these challenged hierarchies had to be defended less in terms of custom than results – that is, their performance for society as a whole. Increasingly, performance included the maintenance of economic welfare. The Depression led voters to shatter the Western political coalitions of the 1920s even when it did not destroy democratic regimes. Distress forced governments in the 1930s to become employers of last resort; by the 1950s they were called upon to assure continuing economic growth as well as high employment at a given level of national income. Stabilization thus entailed a dual task. It meant re-establishing the contested legitimacy of European social and economic elites – buttressing the hierarchies that even in an age of mass voting still presupposed that only small minorities could share the prerogative of directing human labor. Justifying inequality, in turn, required satisfying criteria of economic performance: figuratively and literally delivering the goods. Although they had to broaden their recruitment and recognize

13   Jefferson Patterson to the Department of State, August 20, 1945, NA-RG 59,855.00/ 8-2045.

new spokesmen for organized labor, by and large the elites super-
intending Western society met these related conditions for stability –
those of legitimation and those of production. But they did not meet
both conditions at once.

Instead, Europe's elites resolved their difficulties seriatim, such that
each effort of postwar stabilization overcame one of the two challenges.
With the 1920s came not a total, but a nevertheless impressive, response to the ideological attack upon the legitimacy of capitalist hierarchies as hierarchies. That is, the leaders of the 1920s rallied with
persuasive justifications of capitalist entrepreneurship. They ended
up rejustifying not so much ownership *per se* as a hierarchy of managerial power that preserved the essentials of control. Nonetheless,
the 1920s did not solve the economic dilemma of ensuring continuous
production and high employment. That task was left to the second
postwar period. Only by the 1950s were the afflictions that undermined capitalist stability effectively overcome as a whole. The cumulative achievement required the institutional flux that was left in
the wake of not one but two wartime upheavals.

In what sense can it be maintained, however, that developments
of the 1920s served durably to reinforce the legitimacy of European
capitalism? In light of mass unemployment, the taint of wartime collaboration, and the wave of socialist aspirations incorporated in the
Resistance, did not capitalism seem as shaken, vulnerable, and problematic after World War II as ever before – hence A. J. P. Taylor's
verdict? In fact, however, the Left's programs after World War II did
not often go so far as the challenges of 1918–21.[14] This does not mean
that the Left was universally stronger earlier. Although in Germany
and Italy social revolutionary outcomes had been more feasible after
the First than the Second World War (if only because no occupying
forces were present), had it chosen to exploit its power, the French
Left possessed a more commanding position in late 1944 than it had
controlled in 1918. In Britain the protests of 1918–19 that looked toward
a syndicalist socialism were succeeded in 1945 by the more solid, if
more moderate, triumph of the Labour party. In short, the relative
strength of the Left in the respective postwar periods depended to a

---

14 On this point, see some of the recent surveys of this period, including Francis
    Carsten, *Revolution in Central Europe, 1918–1919* (London, 1972); Charles L. Bertrand,
    ed., *Revolutionary Situations in Europe, 1917–1922: Germany, Italy, Austria-Hungary*,
    Proceedings of the Second International Colloquium of the Interuniversity Center
    for European Studies (Montreal, 1977); and *Rivoluzione e reazione in Europa, 1917/
    1924: Convegno storico internazionale, Perugia, 1978* (Rome, 1978).

great extent upon the particular national situation. The programs of the Left, however, often remained a less clearcut challenge after 1944 than they were after 1918. They aspired less to overturn bureaucratic and economic control than to attain public ownership of key industries. By 1945, however, ownership was a less crucial issue than earlier for many sectors that the Left targeted for nationalization. The earlier socialist challenge that followed in the wake of the Bolshevik Revolution with its innovation of soviets was probably more fundamental. What the participants in the massive strikes and insurrections of 1918–21, the militants at party and union congresses, and the remarkable socialist theorists of the early 1920s urged in aggregate was not merely the centralization of important industries in the hands of the state; this demand came from moderate Social Democrats. Instead, they criticized managerial control of the workplace and of production regardless of ownership; and, by extension, they challenged the chains of command of the Western economies from top to bottom.

These movements failed in the West for many reasons. They were rooted in the shop steward organizations of the Clydeside, the factory grievance committees established during the war to smooth labor relations, which in turn helped generate the *consigli di fabbrica* of Turin and the *Räte* in Germany and Austria. Some spokesmen for these councils envisioned a syndical reorganization of the economy and politics. But often their militancy derived from the more conservative impulses of defending the work skills and artisanal independence still conserved under factory roofs against degrading standardization of tasks and wartime "dilution" (the hiring of unskilled replacements, sometimes women).[15] Moreover, the councils comprised a strong movement only in a few industrial regions, and their revolts exploded out of phase with each other. The movement, moreover, appears to have evoked the least resonance in France, which would still have had to be the keystone of any general West European transformation. In France, reformist socialists as well as industrial leaders restricted the mandate of factory delegates, while after the armistice radicals

---

15 On the resistance of skilled workers, see James Hilton, *The First Shop Stewards' Movement* (London, 1973); Bertrand Abhervé, "Les Origines de la grève des métallurgistes parisiens, juin 1919," *Le Mouvement Social*, 93 (1975): 75–85; and David Montgomery, "The 'New Unionism' and the Transformation of Workers' Consciousness in America, 1909–1922," *Journal of Social History*, 7, (1974): 509–29. Also see Carmen J. Sirianni, "Workers' Control in the Era of World War I: A Comparative Analysis of the European Experience," *Theory and Society*, 9 (1980): 29–88; and Martin Clark, *Antonio Gramsci and the Revolution that Failed* (New Haven, 1977).

spilled into street demonstrations that were militant but diffuse and finally settled on a program for nationalization of the railroads.[16] Likewise in Britain, Labour militants came to focus upon takeover of the coal industry. In Germany, the councils emerged during revolution but often just to take charge of factories, regiments, or towns in which central authority crumbled. When German council champions took up explicitly socialist goals, they incurred drastic repression, as in Munich in April 1919 or in the Ruhr after the Kapp Putsch.[17]

Trade-union leaders, moreover, remained cool toward alternative modes of representation, fearing that the new councils would undercut their long, patient struggle to speak for labor. Bourgeois politicians such as David Lloyd George in 1919 or Giovanni Giolitti in 1920 deflected protests into cumbersome committees, which finally generated compromise proposals for co-determination that commanded no adherence and were soon shelved (like the more recent Bullock Commission in Britain). Supple industrial leaders, such as Milanese banker and electrical magnate Ettore Conti or Rhenish lignite industrialist Paul Silverberg, similarly exploited such spurious concessions.[18]

Still, given the limitations of the movement, the council episodes suggested that bourgeois concepts of rational economic and political authority were all terribly vulnerable. The dramas staged at Fiat or Renault or the mines of Essen were frightening not primarily because they may have attained an ephemeral success but because they suggested that only force, not consensus, stood in the way of a collectivist alternative. At stake, therefore, was bourgeois legitimacy as well as naked control. Bourgeois response, thus, had to go beyond mere

16 Abhervé, "Les Origines de la grève des métallurgistes parisiens"; Nicholas Papyanis, "Masses révolutionaires et directions reformistes: Les Tensions au coeur des grèves des métallurgistes français en 1919," *Le Mouvement Social*, 93 (1975): 51–73; and Gilbert Hatry, "Les Délégués d'atelier aux Usines Renault," in Patrick Fridenson, ed., *1914–1918, l'autre front: Cahiers du "Mouvement Social"*, 2 (Paris, 1977): 221–35. Also see the older surveys, Roger Picard, *Le Mouvement syndical durant la guerre* (Paris, 1927); and William Oualid and Charles Picquenard, *Salaires et tariffes, conventions collectives, et grèves: La Politique du Ministère de l'Armament* (Paris, 1928).

17 On Britain, in addition to Hinton's *The First Shop Stewards' Movement*, see Branko Pribicevic, *The Shop Stewards' Movement and Workers' Control* (Oxford, 1959); Arthur Marwick, *The Deluge* (New York, 1970), 56–76, 203–09; and G. D. H. Cole, *Labour in the Coal-Mining Industry, 1914–21* (Oxford, 1923). On Germany, see Eberhard Kolb, *Die Arbeiterräte in der deutschen Innenpolitik, 1918–1919* (Düsseldorf, 1962), and "Rätewirklichkeit und Räte-ideologie in der deutschen Revolution von 1918–1919," in Kolb, ed., *Vom Kaiserreich zur Weimarer Republik* (Cologne, 1972), 165–84; Reinhard Rürup, ed., *Arbeiter- und Soldatenräte im rheinisch-westfälischen Industriegebiet Märzrevolution im Ruhrgebiet*, vol. 1 (Frankfurt a/M, 1970), and *Märzrevolution 1920*, vol. 2 (Frankfurt a/M, 1973); and Georg Eliasberg, *Der Ruhrkrieg 1920* (Bonn, 1974).

18 See Charles S. Maier, *Recasting Bourgeois Europe* (Princeton, 1975), chap. 3.

repression. Counterstrategies had to operate on plant and national planes, micro- and macro-levels simultaneously. The need to reassert authority within the factory gave renewed impetus to plans for scientific management, which would further centralize factory authority by differentiating tasks "down to the tiniest detail," as some French sponsors defined their Taylorite efforts.[19]

Acceptance of this technocratic functionalism required conservative flexibility, and business as well as political milieux divided between progressives and reactionaries. The reactionaries distrusted industry-wide organization and insisted on the prerogatives of ownership, asserting what German critics called their *Herr-im-Hause* domination. But the more fruitful approach was to build upon the potential for cooptation that wartime labor-management agreements and the unavowed brotherhood of wage-price spirals had encouraged after 1914.[20] As might be expected, the industrial "progressives" were less fixated on ownership, more concerned with managerial expertise; they were multi-divisional foxes rather than single-factory lions. Building upon his wartime organizational efforts, Walther Rathenau forcefully defended entrepreneurial leadership, while outlining complex schemes for capitalist self-government and planning. Later in the decade, Alfred Mond, organizer of the Imperial Chemical cartel and Ernest Mercier, an architect of French electrical networks, pursued related visions (as did Herbert Hoover in the United States).[21] Other spokesmen throughout the 1920s derived from the important interindustry associations – less businessmen than their organizers and lobbyists: André François Poncet of the Comité des Forges with his defense of technocratic inequality; Gino Olivetti of Confindustria, who from even before the war was to emphasize that only the industrialist could

19 "Concours pour l'application du Système Taylor dans les Mines et Usines de la Société de Pont-à-Mousson: Préamble," PAM, box 18936.
20 Gerald Feldman, "German Business between War and Revolution: The Origins of the Stinnes-Legien Agreement," in Gerhard A. Ritter, ed., *Entstehung und Wandel der modernen Gesellschaft: Festschrift für Hans Rosenberg zum 65. Geburtstag* (Berlin, 1978), 312–41, and *Iron and Steel in the German Inflation, 1916–1923* (Princeton, 1977), 91; Charles A. Gulick, *Austria from Habsburg to Hitler*, 2 vols. (Berkeley and Los Angeles, 1948), 1:150–57; and Chapter 5, this volume, "The Politics of Inflation in the Twentieth Century."
21 Walter Rathenau, *Von kommenden Dingen* (1916), and *Die neue Wirtschaft* (1917), volumes 2 and 3 of his *Gesammelte Schriften* (Berlin, 1918); Alfred Moritz Mond, *Industry and Politics* (London, 1927); Hector Bolitho, *Alfred Mond, First Lord Melchett* (London, 1933), 313–18; and Richard Kuisel, *Ernest Mercier, French Technocrat* (Berkeley and Los Angeles, 1967). Also see Martin Fine, "L'Association Française pour le Progrès Social (1927–1929)," *Le Mouvement Social*, 94 (1976): 3–29, and Chapter 1, this volume.

"technically order the factory according to a pre-established plan"; his successor Antonio Benni, who insisted that industry was "not personified by the capitalist or the stockholder but by its directors, by its chiefs, and by the organizers of the enterprise."[22] Industry, moreover, became the paradigm for political society in general, as, for instance, when Ernest Mercier sought to rally managerial expertise in the above-party Redressment Français or Alfred Mond organized the Mond-Turner talks with trade-union leaders in the wake of the British General Strike.

These initiatives and self-justifying notions were hardly widespread enough to reorder industrial organization, any more than the council movement had revolutionized the workplace. Nonetheless, celebrators and critics alike felt that scientific management represented a decisive economic and social breakthrough,[23] and the economic circumstances of the late 1920s powerfully reinforced this new legitimation of capitalism. The stabilization of currencies on the gold-exchange standard, renewal of intense international competition, and concern about saturation of home markets all made "rationalization" more urgent. Rationalization was a concept that comprised market-sharing agreements across frontiers and within domestic economies plus parallel efforts to lower the burden of wages and other costs through investment, technical improvements, and mergers. At the same time industrial leaders sought legitimation for their power, whether it derived from the right to lay off workers in a cyclical downturn or from their collaboration with an authoritarian regime as in Italy. The managerial mystique evoked widespread enthusiasm, assumed a truly cultic importance precisely because it was a modern and supposedly class-neutral alternative to the immediately preceding socialist attack on industrial hierarchies.

"This Taylorization is connected with the problem of lowering overall costs," noted Marcel Paul, a Pont-à-Mousson manager, when

---

22   André François Poncet, *Reflexions d'un républicain moderne* (Paris, 1925); Olivetti, as quoted in Franklin Adler, "Factory Councils, Gramsci, and the Industrialists," *Telos*, 31 (1977): 79; and Benni, as quoted in Maier, *Recasting Bourgeois Europe*, 567. Also see Franklin Adler, "Italian Industrialists and Radical Fascism," *Telos*, 30 (1976–77): 193–201.

23   For André Philips's analysis of the central role of scientific management in American economic achievement, see his *Le Problème ouvrier aux États-Unis* (Paris, 1927). For the enthusiasm evoked by what I call the "managerial mystique," see Edmond Giscard d'Estaing, "Le Néocapitalisme," *Revue des Deux Mondes*, August 1, 1928; Paul Devinat, *Scientific Management in Europe*, ILO Studies and Reports, ser. B, no. 17 (Geneva, 1927); and *La Prospérité: Revue trimestrielle de l'organisation scientifique* (1928–), an ebullient magazine that was briefly published by Michelin.

his firm embarked upon the venture in the late 1920s.[24] Scientific management supposedly promised a painless method of cost cutting, although it often just meant speed-ups or extra hours. The unions, however, had already exhausted their capacity for resistance during fruitless labor struggles, in France during 1920, in Italy from 1920 through 1922 and less overtly in 1924–26, in Germany after the inflation and again by 1928, and in Britain during 1921 and 1926. By the late 1920s, moreover, a generation of moderate labor spokesmen emerged who honestly believed in collaboration: trade unionists in Germany and the United States, the aging Albert Thomas at the Geneva International Labor Office, the younger Walter Citrine, and Ernest Bevin, who saw his job of "the large scale organization of labor" as akin to that of the industrial manager.[25]

The Left never again challenged the premise that production was a question for managers and engineers with the same vigor that they had immediately after the first war. Even when the close of World War II seemed to offer renewed opportunity, plans to reorganize the factory and control production remained relatively undeveloped. In France, workers revolted against the coerciveness of the Occupation and sought to oust patrons they identified as both collaborators and exploiters. But their efforts yielded only limited success, and the bitterness of the later strikes in 1947 and 1948 testified to the frustration of aspirations raised at the Liberation. The Communists did support new schemes for a workers' voice in the tripartite management boards (representing management, labor, and the state) for the nationalized industries, urged by Minister of Industry Marcel Paul. But they had

---

24 Marcel Paul to Jean Cavalier, May 19, 1928, PAM, box 41595. On the thrust of rationalization, see Robert Brady, *The Rationalization Movement in German Industry* (Berkeley and Los Angeles, 1933); Giulio Sapelli, "L'Organizzazione 'scientifica' del lavoro e innovazione tecnologica durante il fascismo," *Italia Contemporanea*, 28 (1976): 3–28; and Paola Fiorentini, "Ristrutturazione capitalistica e sfruttamento operaio in Italia negli anni '20," *Rivista Storica del Socialismo*, 10 (1967): 134–54.

25 "The opposition of leaders of labor to bonafide scientific management has practically disappeared, and during recent years there has been noteworthy cooperation between scientific management leaders and labor leaders"; H. S. Person, "Scientific Management," Industrial Relations Committee Report, February 15, 1928, AFL Papers, Florence Thorne Collection, 117/8A, box 18, State Historical Society of Wisconsin, Madison, Wisc. Also see Milton J. Nadworny, *Scientific Management and the Unions, 1900–1932* (Cambridge, Mass., 1955); Philips, *Le Problème ouvrier aux États-Unis*, 556; Martin Fine, "Albert Thomas: A Reformer's Vision of Modernization, 1914–1932," *Journal of Contemporary History*, 12 (1977): 545–64; Madeline Rebérioux and Patrick Fridenson, "Albert Thomas, pivot du reformisme français," *Le Mouvement Social*, 87 (1974): 85–97; and Alan Bullock, *The Life and Times of Ernest Bevin*, volume 1: *Trade Union Leader, 1881–1940* (London, 1960), 396.

to retreat in the face of MRP and Socialist countermeasures to ensure a more technical supervision; nor was it clear that the PC had really wanted more than its own industrial barony.[26] Italian workers were perhaps most consistent in reviving factory representation through the *consigli di gestione*. Communist spokesmen, however, came to define these councils as a structure for giving the workers a stake in production. They were not intended to replicate Gramsci's revolutionary factory councils.[27] And, in Germany, while co-determination as sought in the mining and metal industries may well have represented a creative and innovative demand, it still remained an effort more to share in the control of traditional managerial functions rather than to overthrow them. The left-wing SPD spokesman Viktor Agartz developed the most extensive concepts of "economic democracy" but quickly declined in influence in his own party once the Federal Republic was constituted.[28] In short, the second postwar era did not resume the fundamental ideological challenge to managerial control of twenty-five years earlier. The first postwar restoration had largely confirmed the premise that the modern industrial order must operate under hierarchical chains of command, like an army or bureaucracy. The presumption of technical rationality legitimized the economic power that ownership alone could not.

Subduing labor's bid to control the organization of production and, by extension, to make economic authority democratic was not sufficient, however, to stabilize a political economy that faced great inherent strains after the First World War. If the defenders of interwar capitalism proposed a social bargain – the increasing satisfaction of material wants in return for a restoration of industrial authority – they

26 See Etienne Dejonghe, "Les houillères à l'épreuve, 1944–1947," *Colloque de Lille*, in *Revue du Nord*, 57 (1975): 643–66. On nationalization schemes, see Mario Einaudi *et al.*, *Nationalization in France and Italy* (Ithaca, N.Y., 1955), 96–105.

27 For Emilio Sereni's exhortation, see Guizzi, "La Fabbrica italiana Magneti Marelli," 252; and, on the role of post-1945 councils, see Paride Rugafiori, "La 'Ricostruzione' in una grande azienda IRI in crisi: L'Ansaldo (1945–1948)," in Ganapini *et al.*, *La Ricostruzione nella grande industria*, 428–444; and Giulio Sapelli, "Industriali e lotta di classe a Torino (1945–1947)," *ibid.*, 445–527. Also see Liliana Lanzardo, *Classe operaia e partito comunista alla Fiat: La Strategia della collaborazione* (Turin, 1971). For a good survey, see F. Levi *et al.*, *Il Triangolo industriale tra ricostruzione e lotta di classe. 1945–1948* (Milan, 1974).

28 Ernst Ulrich Huster, *Die Politik der SPD, 1945–1950* (Frankfurt a/M, 1978), 35–41. Also see Erich Potthoff, *Der Kampf um die Montanmitbestimmung* (Cologne, 1957); and Eberhard Schmidt, *Die verhinderte Neuordnung, 1945–1950* (Frankfurt a/M, 1970), 182–200.

had to be able to pay up. In the interwar period, however, many difficulties precluded paying up for more than a brief period.

Two interlocking flaws especially undermined sustained prosperity: constraints imposed by the international economy and by domestic conflicts. Once currencies were stabilized under the gold-exchange standard, balance-of-payment concerns, especially in light of the postwar creditor position of the United States, seemed to mandate relatively low European wages so that Britain and the Continent could maintain exports, compete internationally, and preserve their exchange rates. Reparation obligations for Germany and war debts for the Allies just made these constraints more demanding. At the same time, within each country, economic leaders remained preoccupied with potential saturation of the market and limits of profitability – what the Germans term *Rentabilität*. Industry spokesmen felt that profits were faltering, capital accumulation and investment was imperiled, and, in turn, international competitiveness endangered. They sharply attacked what they perceived as the politically determined costs of labor and of new social-insurance obligations.[29]

But, while European businessmen fretted about impediments to accumulation, the relatively high rates of investment in the late 1920s may have outpaced the purchasing power that would sustain the return to capital. Although wages may not have lagged proportionally behind returns to capital,[30] urban and rural disposable incomes did not necessarily grow sufficiently to justify the continued "rationalization" of the 1920s. In formal terms, what had to be attained was a "warranted growth" path of capital and incomes that allowed the expansion of each to call forth and absorb the increments of the others. Only satisfying the two constraints together allowed each to be resolved in its own right. Only securing the two simultaneously, moreover, was likely to reconcile the major organized interest groups of the European economies.

Reading backward, one can say, of course, that the 1930s did not find the warranted growth path; and the original statements of the difficulty reflected the somber outcome in their pessimistic depiction of a "knife edge" that a dynamic economy had to tread if it was not to falter. Later theory, perhaps reflecting the generation of post-1950 growth, has suggested that in fact equilibrium growth is relatively

---

29 For the best recent discussion of these attitudes in Germany, see Bernd Weisbrod, *Schwerindustrie in der Weimarer Republik* (Wuppertal, 1978).
30 Peter Temin has insisted on this, for the U.S.-European indices can be read in different ways; Temin, *Did Monetary Forces Cause the Great Depression?* (New York, 1976), 32.

easy to generate: technological substitutions, public spending, population growth, and income redistribution have all been shown to make ascent of the knife edge far less chancy.[31] Indeed, the dilemma of equilibrium growth at the end of the 1920s was in part self-imposed by the reigning preoccupation with capital shortages and by the brakes placed on national income growth by the neomercantilist policies of the years following currency stabilization. There were dissenters to prevailing policy, such as John Maynard Keynes. But Keynes remained a gadfly and not always consistent in his recommendations. By the 1930s Keynes and like-minded adherents of purchasing-power doctrines pointed to the state as the agency that could assure high aggregate demand. Their intellectual task became simplified when they urged that their societies more or less disconnect from the international market and seek higher employment levels autarkically – that is, that they cease to fret about exchange rates. Indeed, abandonment of old currency parities followed almost by *force majeur* after 1931. In the long run, Keynes also felt, capital accumulation should become a less preoccupying task, for capital would become more plentiful in relation to the need for it.[32]

Today these simplifying premises appear more problematic. Indeed, contemporary Western economic dilemmas suggest partial parallels with the difficulties perceived at the end of the 1920s. United States economic concepts for the postwar international economy largely precluded the welfare-state self-sufficiency that Keynes suggested. This meant further that his vision of satiated investment needs, with its resultant "euthanasia of the rentier," was likewise premature. Industrial societies in a world market arena can hardly allow investment to atrophy without losing real income to new competitors. Even to apply Keynesian macroeconomic stimulus to assure full employment may bring deteriorating balances of trade and, if no foreign subsidies

31 For the "knife-edge view" of the warranted growth path, see R. F. Harrod, "An Essay in Dynamic Theory," *Economic Journal*, 49 (1939): 12–33, 377. Also see Evsey D. Domar, "Capital Expansion, Rate of Growth, and Employment," *Econometrica*, 14 (1946): 137–47. James Tobin and Robert M. Solow allowed for various tenable rates of growth with factor substitutability; see Tobin, "A Dynamic Aggregative Model," *Journal of Political Economy*, 63 (1955): 103–15; and Solow, "A Contribution to the Theory of Economic Growth," *Quarterly Journal of Economics*, 70 (1956): 65–94. For a recent optimistic summary that sees supply normally generating demand (with the 1930s as an exceptional catastrophe), see John Cornwall, *Growth and Stability in a Mature Economy* (London, 1972).

32 For Keynes's views concerning the decreasing scarcity of capital, see his *The General Theory of Employment, Interest, and Money* (London, 1960), 375–77; and, concerning the advantages of going it alone, see his *Essays in Persuasion* (1931; 2d ed., New York, 1963), 271–96, and "National Self-Sufficiency," *New Statesman and Nation*, July 8, 15, 1933.

are found, declining welfare. Some of the constraints that vexed the 1920s have thus re-emerged and, with them, the distributive conflicts between the interests of wage earners and the spokesmen for capital. The difference is that, in the 1920s, the difficulties were rooted in too limited a confidence in mass consumption as a force for growth, whereas in the 1970s they may have derived from too excessive a reliance.

What remains historically remarkable is that from the late 1940s into the 1970s the constraints of the interwar period eased as a twin reorientation took place. First, the United States developed a commitment to European prosperity; second, the political and economic calculations of Europeans themselves changed so that they felt less locked into a distributive contest. Both changes together eased the iron framework of wages, profits, state claims, and international payments.[33]

How could this reorientation take place so easily after 1945? For one thing, it was silently underway before that date. The Depression had certainly discredited the old orthodoxies. The war also demonstrated to British and American financial planners that states could impose levels of expenditure far beyond what the budget-balancers of the 1920s or British Treasury officials of the 1930s had imagined was safe and feasible.[34] Certainly the role of the United States was transformed: the credits of the 1920s had been extended via private banks and had remained hostage to the differential rates of return in Europe and New York; the grants of the late 1940s represented political decisions on the part of Washington. The new American policy did not come instantaneously or automatically. Just as between 1922 and 1924 the New York banking community accepted the need to intervene in Europe,so, as the newly opened records of the U.S. National Advisory Council on International Monetary and Financial Policies help

33 The conflict between international competitiveness and demand stimulus at home has been brought out especially by the "Scandinavian" models of two-sector open economies. See Odd Aukrust, "Inflation in the Open Economy: A Norwegian Model," in Walter S. Salant and Lawrence B. Krause, eds., *Worldwide Inflation: Theory and Recent Experience* (Washington, 1977), 107–53; and Jeffrey Sachs, "Wages, Profits, and Macroeconomic Adjustment: A Comparative Study," *Brookings Papers on Economic Activity,* 2 (1979): 269–319.
34 On the fiscal conservatism of the Treasury, see R. A. C. Parker, "Economics, Rearmament, and Foreign Policy: The United Kingdom before 1939 – A Preliminary Study," *Journal of Contemporary History,* 10 (1975): 637–47; Robert Paul Shay, Jr., *British Rearmament in the Thirties: Profits and Politics* (Princeton, 1977), 73–79, 136–55, 242–46; and Susan Howson, *Domestic Monetary Management in Britain, 1919–38* (Cambridge, 1975), 120–26. For the transformation of attitudes, see Donald Winch, *Economics and Policy: A Historical Survey* (London, 1972), chap. 12; and Herbert Stein, *The Fiscal Revolution in America* (Chicago, 1969), chap. 8.

show, Washington became increasingly willing to exploit foreign aid for political purposes: from the coy hesitation about extending loans to the Léon Blum mission in early 1946, to the vigorous European Recovery Program and the almost importuning support for noncommunist unions and parties by 1948, to the funds rushed to Yugoslavia after Tito's break with the Cominform.[35]

The Marshall Plan signaled a political decision that the resources of the United States would be available for the reconstruction of a welfare capitalism in Europe. But in quantitative terms the role of American aid had to be limited. For the major European economies from 1948 through 1951 it probably contributed no more than 10 to 20 percent of capital formation during the first two emergency years, then tapered off to below 10 percent.[36] Washington's assistance served more as capital-liberating than as capital-transfusing. "The basic ele-

35 Minutes of the Meetings of the National Advisory Council on International Monetary and Financial Policies, meetings 23, 24 (May 6, 1946), 89 (March 18, 1948), 112 (December 3, 1948, on Japan), 115–16 (January 7, 13, 1949), etc., Office of the Secretary of the Treasury, NA-RG 56.

36 The tabulation below provides the ratio of grants and loans made by the United States to the gross domestic capital formation of the respective countries. Gross domestic capital formation (converted here into dollars at current exchange rates) is a more relevant measure for the postwar years than net investment, for the replacement of depreciated plants meant qualitative improvement. (For Italy in 1948 and 1949, only net figures are available.) Grants extended during 1948 include "interim aid." The judgment on the limited role of U.S. funds amends my original statement that the aid amounted to little. In fact, it comprised a transfer of about 2% of GNP.

Country	1948	1949	1950	1951
United Kingdom $\dfrac{\text{U.S. Aid}}{\text{GDCF in \$}}$	$\dfrac{\$\ 937m}{\$10,400m} = 9\%$	$\dfrac{\$1,009m}{\$9,000m} = 11\%$	$\dfrac{\$\ 629m}{\$6,400m} = 10\%$	$\dfrac{129m}{\$6,300m} = 2\%$
France $\dfrac{\text{U.S. Aid}}{\text{GDCF in \$}}$	$\dfrac{\$\ 781m}{\$\ 5,600m} = 14\%$	$\dfrac{766m}{\$6,400m} = 12\%$	$\dfrac{\$\ 465m}{\$4,460m} = 10\%$	$\dfrac{\$\ 421m}{\$5,380m} = 7\%$
West Germany $\dfrac{\text{U.S. Aid}}{\text{GDCF in \$}}$	$\dfrac{1,130m}{\$\ 3,600m} = 31\%$ (est.)	$\dfrac{\$\ 948m}{\$4,340m} = 22\%$	$\dfrac{470m}{\$4,400m} = 11\%$	$\dfrac{362m}{\$5,300m} = 7\%$
Italy $\dfrac{\text{U.S. Aid}}{\text{GDCF in \$}}$	$\dfrac{\$\ 399m}{\$\ 1,500m} = 27\%$ (net)	$\dfrac{\$\ 437m}{\$1,300m} = 34\%$ (net)	$\dfrac{\$\ 257m}{\$2,700m} = 10\%$	$\dfrac{\$\ 261m}{\$3,000m} = 9\%$

Note: All figures in millions of current (1948–51) dollars; only net figures are available for Italy in 1948 and 1949, and only an estimate can be made for West Germany in 1948, since the available statistics do not give figures for the first half of that year.

ments in Western Europe's economic crisis . . .," the staff of the Eaton-Herter Select Committee on Foreign Aid accurately emphasized, "converge and appear in their most conspicuous aspect as a deficit in the balance of payments with the dollar area."[37] By easing balance-of-payments constraints and freeing key bottlenecks for specific goods, American aid allowed the European economies to generate their own capital more freely, certainly without returning to the deflationary competition of the 1930s. U.S. aid served, in a sense, like the lubricant in an engine – not the fuel – allowing a machine to run that would otherwise buckle and bind.

This calculation suggests that a modulated judgment on the role of American capital would be appropriate. Ultimately, the real sources of Europe's postwar growth had to derive from the Continent's own energies. Indeed, some recovery was apparently already underway by late 1946, even for the battered West German economy.[38] Had not the fearsome winter of 1946–47 paralyzed transportation, impeded food and fuel deliveries, and radicalized workers into politically explosive wage demands, recovery might have continued. In that case, without the emergency American response the ongoing European economic performance might well have resembled, say, British growth in the late 1930s: more protectionist and less spectacular than was to be racked up under American auspices in the 1950s, but still respectable.

In this regard, the American economic role in restabilization after World War II paralleled the political role. Europe would probably not have "gone Communist" or collectivist even if the United States had not intervened with the same resolution. The European middle classes remained socially anchored; the German occupation had hardly struck or aimed at them as a group, nor had it attacked their economic values. But both the political and economic development of the 1950s would doubtless have been less resolutely capitalist and market-oriented, less justified by dynamic success. Throughout the first three postwar years, in fact, there was less decisive purpose than confused experimentation and uncertain initiatives. Business recovery was not held

---

Sources: Totals of American aid have been taken from *Statistical Abstract of the United States, 1954*, 898–902; British GDCF, from *Statistical Abstract for the United Kingom*, no. 87 (1948–49); Table 294, no. 88 (1950): Table 296, and no. 89 (1952): Table 288; and, other 1948–49 statistics, from *Statistisches Jahrbuch fur die Bundesrepublik Deutschland, 1952*, 454–55; *Annuaire Statistique de la France*, 59 (1952): 335; and *Annuario Statistico Italiano*, ser. V, 3 (1951): 590. Non-British GDCF estimates for 1950 and 1951 are taken from United Nations, *Yearbook of National Accounts Statistics* (1957).

37 U.S. Congress, House Select Committee on Foreign Aid, *Final Report on Foreign Aid* (May 1, 1948), 80th Cong., 2d sess., House Report no. 1845, p. 24.

38 Werner Abelshauser, *Wirtschaft in Westdeutschland, 1945–1948* (Stuttgart, 1975), 167–70.

back by ideological sympathies for socialism but by the fear of risky venture, the hesitation finally to write off the losses of the war years. Between 1945 and late 1947, for example, the French and the Italians, then the West Germans along with their American occupiers, avoided imposing the deflationary reforms that helped invigorate capitalist growth.[39] Nor were they prepared to abandon the fuzzy political compromises, which found expression in the tripartite Catholic–Socialist–Communist governing coalitions but seemed less and less likely to mandate either socialism or renewed capitalist growth. Only in 1947–48, when ideological and economic threats appeared potentially catastrophic, did the spokesmen for West Europe's middle classes and elites, and their American sponsors, resolve upon the liberal capitalist mandate that might best be described as a new "wager upon the strong."

Economic analysts have proposed several theories for the remarkable growth that followed. Structural explanations include the sharp increase in agricultural productivity achieved by tractors and fertilizers, the resultant supply of labor released for industry (a supply already augmented by the migrants from eastern Germany and the Italian South, among other areas), and the special efficiency of investment in the context of postwar damage and renewal. Monetarist accounts attribute success to rigorous stabilization programs in Germany, Italy, and Japan. The historian can point to the wage restraint that Dutch, German, and Italian workers demonstrated because of labor's commitment to reconstruction and, perhaps, to mere exhaustion after fascist repression and war.[40] On the managerial side, new business confidence and technocratic impulses gradually prevailed. The example of Pont-à-Mousson suggests that once public policy makers, such as

39 For the French rejection of deflation, see Richard Kuisel, *Modernization and the Managed Economy: The State and Capitalism in France, 1900–1950* (Cambridge and New York, 1981), chap. 7. For the Italians, who in 1947 embarked upon deflation, see George H. Hildebrand, *Growth and Structure in the Economy of Modern Italy* (Cambridge, Mass., 1965), chaps. 2, 8; Marcello De Cecco, "Sulla politica di stabilizzazione del 1948," in his *Saggi di politica monetaria* (Milan, 1968), 109–41; and Camillo Daneo, *La politica economica della ricostruzione, 1945–1949* (Turin, 1975), chap. 7. On the American and German hesitation to impose early currency reform, see Edward A. Tennenbaum, "The German Mark," book draft, chaps. 11–12, Tennenbaum Papers, box 3, folder 5, Truman Library, Independence, Mo. Belgium was the outstanding exception to the general inflationary languor at the end of the war. For the reforms of Camille Gutt, see Léon H. Dupriez, *Monetary Reconstruction in Belgium* (New York, 1947).

40 For examples of structural approaches, see Ingvar Svennilson, *Growth and Stagnation in the European Economy* (Geneva, 1954); U.N. Economic Commission for Europe, *Economic Survey of Europe in 1961*, part 2: *Some Factors in Economic Growth in Europe during the 1950's* (Geneva, 1961); and Charles Kindleberger, *Europe's Postwar Economic Growth: The Role of Labor Supply* (Cambridge, Mass., 1967). For an example of the monetarist approach, see Hildebrand, *Growth and Structure in the Economy of Modern*

Jean Monnet or Robert Schuman, made commitments to supranational institutions, a new generation of expansionist entrepreneurs could find support for pressing vigorous investment plans within their own firms.[41]

The upshot was that both the major restraints that had corseted the economy of the 1920s could be loosened together. U.S. aid helped overcome the deflationary pressures resulting from defense of the balance of payments. But these pressures also remained minimal because a new generation of Keynesian-influenced administrators were willing to take international deficits in stride. Establishment of European-wide clearance schemes and the willingness of intra-European creditor countries, such as Belgium and even Italy, to hold sterling or other European currencies as a *quid pro quo* for American aid also eased the strains on the economies tending toward balance-of-payments deficits. Washington policymakers certainly did not like the impediments to currency convertibility that Europeans kept in force, and they continued to press for the removal of these obstacles to the free circulation of dollars. U.S. Treasury officials and American delegates to the International Monetary Fund insisted stubbornly on convertibility even at the cost of deflationary policies. In contrast, American officials with the Marshall Plan administration (the ECA) tended to accept compromise arrangements that permitted Europeans to prolong shielding their international accounts; and even the stern Treasury disciplinarians had to accept British cancellation of sterling convertibility after the disastrous attempt during the summer of 1947. They likewise were compelled to acquiesce in French creation of a two-tiered currency market in 1948, which allowed scope for floating exchange rates, and they accepted restrictions upon full convertibility in the European clearance unions from 1949 through 1951. Preaching that all currencies should be fully tradable for dollars, Washington officials nonetheless lived with a compromise monetary regime.[42]

Italy. Angus Maddison has emphasized policy factors, including a Western internationalism attributed to the Cold War; see his "Economic Policy and Performance in Europe, 1913–1970," in Carlo Cipolla, ed., *The Fontana Economic History of Europe,* 5 (Glasgow, 1976): 442–508. For a general treatment, see M. M. Postan, *An Economic History of Western Europe, 1945–1964* (London, 1967).

41 See, for example, the debate on expansion of coking facilities and Roger Martin's advocacy of investment, October 16, 1951, PAM, box 70671. Also see Richard Kuisel, "Technocrats and Public Policy: From the Third to the Fourth Republic," *Journal of European Economic History,* 2 (1973): 53–99.

42 For debates on convertibility, see Minutes of the Meetings of the National Advisory Committee on International Monetary and Financial Policies, meetings 70, 79–81, 83–84, 134, 153, 158, 171, Office of the Secretary of the Treasury, NA-RG 56. For the EPU, see William Diebold, Jr., *Trade and Payments in Western Europe* (New York, 1972), 64–69; and Albert O. Hirschman, "The European Payments Union: The Negotiations and the Issues," *Review of Economics and Statistics,* 33 (1951): 49–59.

The second major inhibition that had undermined continuing expansion in the 1920s also disappeared: the precarious "knife edge" equilibrium growth path for wages and investment broadened into an easy highway. If policymakers no longer wished to sacrifice living standards on the altar of fixed exchange rates, labor showed sufficient wage restraint such that investment could soar. Rather than relatively high labor costs impelling capital substitution, relatively low labor costs permitted capital expansion. The statistics of the 1950s reveal not only the familiar growth of national income but unprecedented rates of capital formation as well: 30 percent in Japan, 27 percent in Germany, 20 percent in France and Italy, 16 percent in the United Kingdom, 18 percent in the United States.[43] In contrast, the wages share of national income remained stable or even dropped slightly, as in Western Germany: a decade's halting of the slow but otherwise prevailing trend of the twentieth century. The expansion and harmony that businessmen had sought in the 1920s was finally achieved in the 1950s.

This result, of course, required the cooperation of those labor leaders who shared the premises of a growth-organized welfare capitalism – the commitment that I have elsewhere termed the "politics of productivity."[44] "The improvement of productivity, in its widest sense, remains the fundamental problem of Western Europe," declared the Organization for European Economic Cooperation, and it echoed the themes of the managerial mystique of the 1920s as it reported, "Great emphasis is placed in the United States . . . upon public relations efforts by management in acquainting workers with their plant, its problems, and its place in the economy."[45] For society as a whole, the politics of productivity meant simply the adjournment of conflicts over the percentage share of national income for the rewards of future economic growth. As one West German official explained to business and labor representatives in the remarkable Königstein discussions of February 1949 (which, in effect, adumbrated West German economic strategies up to the present day), anyone who could renounce some

---

43   Simon Kuznets, *Modern Economic Growth: Rate, Structure, and Spread* (New Haven, 1966), 236–37; and U.N. Economic Commission for Europe, *Some Factors in Economic Growth in Europe during the 1950's*, chap. 2, pp. 16–22. For the wage share of national income, see U.N. Economic Commission for Europe, *Incomes in Postwar Europe: A Study of Policies, Growth, and Distribution* (Geneva, 1967), chap. 2, pp. 30–31.

44   See Chapter 3, this volume: "The Politics of Productivity: Foundations of American International Economic Policy after World War II."

45   Organization for European Economic Co-Operation [hereafter, OEEC], *Europe: The Way Ahead: Towards Economic Expansion and Dollar Balance*, 4th Annual Report of the OEEC (Paris, 1952), 195. Also see Roger Grégoire, "European Productivity Agency," in OEEC, *At Work for Europe* (5th ed., Paris, 1960), 139–52.

consumption had to renounce it. "He had to save, whether or not he wanted, because he cannot be permitted to evade the common tasks of reconstruction."[46] As an explicit principle of consensus, economic growth – the notion of continuously higher levels of national product – came into its own at the end of the 1940s. The earliest public celebration of its virtues may well have been Leon Keyserling's speeches as chairman of the Council of Economic Advisers during 1949;[47] but the less precise concepts of sustained high purchasing power or simply "reconstruction" or "production" served to rally labor as well as businessmen from the end of the war on.

Throughout 1945 and 1946 Communist labor leaders themselves seemed ready to accept the trade-off between present consumption and future growth. The increasing hardship of their rank and file during the winter of 1946–47 and the threat of militant unions on their left flank (aside from any guidance that Moscow may have urged as the dispute with the United States deepened) impelled them to abandon their collaborative stance. The French Communists' reluctant sponsorship of the Renault strike, which likewise led to their dismissal from the governing coalition (and, similarly, the Belgian Communists' refusal to accept coal price increases), best revealed their shifting priorities. No less anti-communist an AFL representative than Irving Brown, who felt that the successive strikes revealed the Communists' "complete desire to destroy the government even at the cost of permanently destroying France," understood that a socialist movement could hardly recapture leadership within the CGT if it participated in a cabinet seeking to freeze wages.[48] Despite the admitted difficulty in

---

46 Statement of Dr. Troeger, Königstein, January 4, 1949, BA Koblenz, Z 13/63. The labor minister of the Bizone, Halbfell, dissented, arguing against unplanned investment, but was in a clear minority.

47 Keyserling, "Prospects for American Economic Growth," Address in San Francisco, September 18, 1949, Truman Library, President's Secretary's File 143: "Agencies: Council of Economic Advisers."

48 Brown, "Report on Greece, France, and England," July 7, 1947, State Historical Society of Wisconsin, AFL Papers, Florence Thorne Collection, 117/8A, box 17, F. 3A. On the events of 1947, see Wilfried Loth. "Frankreichs Kommunisten und der Beginn des kalten Krieges: Die Entlassung der kommunistischen Minister im Mai 1947," *Vierteljahrshefte für Zeitgeschichte*, 26 (1978): 9–65, and "Die französischen Sozialisten und der Marshall-Plan," in Othmar Haberl and Lutz Niethammer, eds., *Die europäischen Linke und der Marshall-Plan* (Frankfurt/Main, 1986). Also see Vincent Auriol, *Journal du Septennat*, ed. Pierre Nora and Jacques Ozouf, volume 1: *1947* (Paris, 1970), *passim*; and Alfred Rieber, *Stalin and the French Communist Party, 1941–1947* (New York, 1962), 331–57. On Belgium, see NA-RG 59,855.00/3-1147 (no. 372), 855.00/3-2147 (no. 1069), 855.00/3-3147 (no. 1097).

reconstructing a mass base for the socialists, by 1947–48, American policymakers, AFL emissaries, and European businessmen diligently encouraged the formation of social democratic unions in the Latin countries and pressed for the purge of Communist sympathizers from British, German, and American federations. The moderates of Force Ouvrière, the TUC, or the Italian Catholic union federation (CISL) became all the more essential as interlocutors for labor. "The trend in Europe is clearly toward the Left," noted one of the Department of State's leading European analysts shortly after tripartism collapsed. "I feel that we should try to keep it a non-communist Left and should support Social-Democratic governments."[49] The axis of the politics of productivity thus had to fall right in the center of the labor movement: "politically speaking the break must come to left of or at the very least in the middle of the [French] Socialist party. Translated into labor terms, the healthy elements of organized labor must be kept in the non-Communist camp. Otherwise the tiny production margin of the fragile French economy would vanish and the ensuing civil disturbances would take on the aspects of civil war."[50]

The economic premises that the "healthy elements" of labor subscribed to remained precisely those of the trade-union leaders who had pioneered collaborative labor relations in the late 1920s. Union spokesmen such as Ernest Bevin had then joined progressive industrialists for talks on enhancing productivity. By the late 1940s they were serving in high office. Their integration testified to the postwar

---

49 John Hickerson to H. Freeman Matthews, June 25, 1947, NA-RG 59, Office of European Affairs, box 3. For European policies of the AFL, see International Labor Committee, Minutes of the Meeting of November 11, 1947, AFL Papers, Florence Thorne Collection, 117/8A, box 17, F. 3C. Also see Matthew Woll to Thorne, April 6, 1948, and the attached "Confidential Report," *ibid.*, F. 4. And see Ronald Radosh, *American Labor and U.S. Foreign Policy* (New York, 1969); Ulrich Borsdorf, "Erkaufte Spaltung: Der Marshall-Plan und die Auseinandersetzung um die deutschen Gewerkschaften," in Haberl and Niethammer, eds., *Die Linke*; Horst Lademacher, "Die Spaltung des Weltgewerkschaftfundes als Folge des beginnenden Ost-West Konfliktes," *ibid.*, and Lutz Niethammer, "Strukturreform und Wachstumspakt," in Heinz Oskar Vetter, ed., *Vom Sozialistengesetz zur Mitbestimmung: Zum 100. Geburtstag von Hans Böckler* (Cologne, 1975), 303–58. On the French unions, see Bergonieux, *Force Ouvrière;* and André Barjonet, *La C.G.T.* (Paris, 1968), 49–51. On Italy, see Daniel L. Horowitz, *The Italian Labor Movement* (Cambridge, Mass., 1963), 208–73; and Adolfo Pepe, "La CGIL dalla ricostruzione alla scissione, 1944–1948," *Storia Contemporanea,* 5 (1974): 591–636, and the works cited in n. 31. Also see the reports from Paris and Rome to the Department of State in *Foreign Relations of the United States, 1947,* 3 (Washington, 1972): 690–91, 695–99 (on the CGT), 847–48, 863–68 (on Italian labor).

50 Robert Lovett to Ambassador Caffrey, Paris (based on a memo by Hickerson), October 25, 1947, NA-RG 59,851.00/10-2447.

years' fulfilment of the second criterion for stabilizing the welfare capitalist economies of the West. The new cooperation, along with America's underwriting, ensured that capital accumulation and wages and welfare benefits could increase in tandem, thus overcoming the fatal impediments to sustained growth in the 1920s. As Western leaders looked more and more to economic growth, increasingly presupposed, first, as automatic and, second, as the major index of a society's welfare, the stakes of politics narrowed. Communism increasingly became a permanent and sullen opposition, to be analyzed, in the spirit of the 1950s, as inherently pathological. At the same time, the appeal of neofascism or Gaullism remained fitful, largely consigned to the regions that paid for dynamic growth elsewhere with their own relative backwardness. In the political center Christian Democrats (or Tories in Britain) either shared power with Social Democrats or alternated officeholding in a consensual politics that debated only whether the anticipated dividends of economic growth should be devoted to social-welfare consumption or ploughed back into private investment. Residual colonial or religious and ethnic issues – not the baselines of political economy – remained the major sources of passion and controversy.

Repression, cooptation, and the success of the managerial mystique with its vogue of productivity had reconsolidated the bureaucratic organization of industrial work in the 1920s. The economic accomplishments of the period after 1948 completed the second half of the stabilization assignment. They seemed to eliminate the vulnerability of economic life and enhanced legitimacy with output and growth. Despite the tragic waste of the Great Depression, the immense destructiveness of two world wars, and the countless lives scattered like dry autumn leaves throughout Europe, Western leaders recovered more of their prosperity and liberalism, retained more of their privileges and prerogatives, than they would have dared predict.

Successful systems of political equilibrium must remain isolated (as did Tokugawa Japan) or be international in scope. The notable eras of European stabilization – the generation after Utrecht, for example, or the half-century after Vienna – have been periods of class equilibrium and international compromise simultaneously. The configurations of power among states tend to second those within societies. The Vienna settlement consisted of adjustments between states but also comprised a restoration of old and new landed classes along with a strengthened bureaucracy. *Pax Britannica* assimilated bourgeois elements to this international coalition and added resources outside Europe to equilibrate strains at home. Fully to comprehend the period from 1918 to 1950 as a search for stabilization on the part of old upper and middle classes, now augmented by a reformist working-class leadership, requires looking at the international architecture as well as domestic structures. Obviously, the Cold War had a decided influence on internal outcomes after World War II. But to register this connection hardly reveals the principles of interaction. The Cold War did not, in itself, determine the logic of the international system for domestic stability.

The surprising centers of growth in the 1950s and 1960s were West Germany, Japan, and, though a smaller economy, Italy. West Germany and Japan, above all, became virtual engines of capital accumulation. As such, they played a critical role in U.S. encouragement of an international coalition of liberal polities with mixed capitalist economies. Although, as of 1944, the U.S. Treasury resoundingly rejected the idea that a German economic contribution would be vital for European prosperity, Congressmen, the Harriman mission (to prepare for Marshall Plan aid), and industrial leaders by 1947 viewed German recovery as doubly critical, both for its own sake and for the economic linchpinning of the wider region.[51] If integrated into a West European system of exchange, German skilled labor, technological virtuosity, and coal would benefit all her neighbors. Without German recovery and integration, their economies must operate less efficiently. The same calculation came to hold for Japan and its role in America after the Communist takeover in China and hostilities in Korea.[52] Opponents of a punitive treatment for Germany had emphasized their European economic vision from the outset, and by the summer of 1947 their concept had quickly become the main theme of the influential spokesmen for German recovery. The lesson was not lost on industrial interests in the emerging state: when German firms petitioned to raise their output or rebuild their rolling mills, their directors unabashedly

51   U.S. Treasury Memorandum, "Is European Prosperity Dependent upon German Industry?" September 7, 1944, Mudd Library, Princeton University, Harry Dexter White Papers, box 7, F. 22e: "In short, the statement that a healthy European economy is dependent upon German industry was never true, nor will it be true in the future." For the turnabout, see "Records of Conferences," Harriman mission, summer 1947, W. A. Harriman's papers, Washington, D.C. Also see John Gimbel, *The Origins of the Marshall Plan* (Stanford, 1976), and *The American Occupation of Germany, 1945–1949* (Stanford, 1968), 147–58, 163–69, 174–85.

52   Joyce Kolko and Gabriel Kolko, *The Limits of Power: The World and United States Foreign Policy, 1945–1954* (New York, 1972), chaps. 11, 19; Jon Halliday, *A Political History of Japanese Capitalism* (New York, 1975), 182–90; and John Dower, *Aftermath of Empire: Yoshida Shigeru and the Japanese Experience, 1878–1954* (Cambridge, Mass., 1979), chaps. 9–10, and manuscript essays on "The Reverse Course."

pleaded the cause of good Europeans.[53] Nor was recovery only the demand of businessmen. German trade unions and the AFL, which supported them, strongly advocated industrial reconstruction.[54] Rehabilitation of the German economy thus emerged as critical for the United States's wager on productivity.

Was it just an accident that the countries that forged ahead so brilliantly and then came to serve as international poles of growth even beyond expectation were the exfascist powers? This question must be confronted, despite its harsh implications. Did Washington, in effect, reap the final benefit from the discipline and coercion of labor that the Axis states had earlier imposed? Not directly, of course. But the American-sponsored international economy may have ultimately benefited from the fact that the working classes within the defeated countries had been atomized by political repression, wartime sacrifices, and the mere tasks of survival. Labor leaders who returned from concealment, prison, or exile faced sufficient challenge just in rebuilding their shattered movements. Stressing the necessity of production appeared to them less a contribution to restoration than the premise for the patient work of reorganization.[55] In addition, defeat and occupation clearly permitted the United States more direct intervention than was possible elsewhere. Occupation authorities in all three countries could limit the organization of political unions, postpone nationalization, and halt strikes. Allied fiscal control – exerted perhaps most consistently by Joseph Dodge in Japan[56] – ultimately reinforced those who advocated rapid capital formation, although businessmen often resisted at first. Harder to measure, but just as important, was the yearning for private goals in countries where fascists had sought to politicize all aspirations and relationships. The United States, after

---

53 See, for example, Akten des Verwaltungsamtes für Eisen und Stahl, BA Koblenz, Z 41/23: "Vorschlag zur Wiedereinschaltung der August Thyssen Hütte in der europäischen Stahlplanung . . . 9 Februar 1950."

54 For example, see the works council of Robert Bosch, AG's protest against decartelization proceedings, March 17, 1948, Deutscher Gewerkschaftsbund Archiv, Düsseldorf: "Wirtschaftspolitik, Dekartellierung 1948–49." For similar objections to controls on German industry, see BA Koblenz, B 109/345: "Stellungnahme der Gewerkschaften zum Ruhrstatut vom 7. Januar 1949." For a specimen of AFL support, see William Green to President Truman, November 24, 1947, AFL Papers, William Green Collection, 117A/11C, box 7F (Marshall Plan).

55 For an example of this organizational effort, see [Hans Böckler] "Bericht der Deutschlandreise, 6. März bis 30. April 1946," Deutscher Gewerkschaftsbund Archiv, Düsseldorf.

56 Detroit Public Library, Joseph Dodge Papers, Japan Assignment, box 1, F: "Budget: Ikeda Interviews," and Japan Assignment, 1950, box 3, F: "Correspondence, Marquat."

all, was gambling on the renewed persuasiveness of individual well-being.

Germany, however, had hitherto repeatedly resisted integration into an international productive coalition. Insofar as the international divisions of the period from 1914 to 1950 had an economic dimension, they involved conflict less between capitalist societies and a Bolshevik challenger than among different capitalist alternatives. Anglo-American disagreements over the organization of a global economy persisted and raised bitter recriminations on each side. The issue remained whether the international economy should maximize multilateral trade and welfare, but thereby reward the most massive and technologically productive economy, or whether as the British desired, it should be based upon regional systems of dominion that guaranteed international markets to the weaker power.[57] Still, the British dominion alternative seemed to be a limited challenge, whereas the German threat to the open international economy had been more ominous and, just as critical, the emanation of an ugly political regime.

This is not to argue that Nazism was menacing because of its international economic policies – the autarky and bilateralism that so angered Cordell Hull. Instead, the connection between politics and economics was central to the very way Nazism was interpreted as a regime. American commentators viewed Nazism as an abusive political economy: a cartel of monopolists who subordinated the public sphere to private forces.[58] Although Hjalmar Schacht's bilateral treaties yoked Eastern Europe into a German-dominated economic bloc, trade access to this area was hardly a crucial stake in itself. Nevertheless, a Germany that was enrolled in a system of international exchange with the West, as the Weimar Republic had been from 1924 to the Depression,[59] naturally appeared a safer and more decent participant in a liberal international order.

Hence the central conflict defining the international political economy from World War I until about 1950 was not that between American and Soviet alternatives, between capitalism and communism. The

---

57   Richard Gardner, *Sterling-Dollar Diplomacy: Anglo-American Cooperation in the Reconstruction of Multilateral Trade* (Oxford, 1956); and Benjamin M. Rowland, "Preparing the American Ascendancy: The Transfer of Economic Power from Britain to the United States," in Rowland, ed., *Balance of Power or Hegemony: The Interwar Monetary System* (New York, 1976), 195–224.

58   See Chapter 3, this volume, pp. 131–3. Roosevelt's own message calling for the Temporary National Economic Committee investigation on monopoly, April 29, 1938, defined fascism as "ownership of government by an individual, by a group, or by any other controlling private power," an interpretation that linked the attitudes of the "second" New Deal with the concern about Nazi expansionism.

59   Werner Link, *Die amerikanische Stabilisierungspolitik in Deutschland, 1921–1932* (Düsseldorf, 1970); and Gerd Hardach, *Weltmarktorientierung und relative Stagnation: Währungspolitik in Deutschland, 1924–1931* (Berlin, 1976), 152–62.

Soviet–American antagonism after World War II, in effect, imposed a framework on international politics but did not exhaust the issues. Viewed over the whole half century, the American international economic effort of the era of stabilization centered on overcoming British, Japanese, and especially German alternatives to a pluralist, market-economy liberalism. In the case of Germany, these alternatives were incorporated first in Berlin's vision of Mitteleuropa during Ludendorff's regime of 1917–18 and then in Hitler's expansionist Reich. Defeating these German projects, however, could be only the first stage in erecting a stable alternative. To assure liberal, pluralist stability within each West European country, as well as for the Atlantic region as a whole, required the further step of integrating German economic dynamism into an international system of exchange: perhaps the preeminent Western diplomatic task in each postwar reconstruction period.

These respective postwar tasks, however, took more than just German defeat; they also required that the United States assume the burden of funding Germany's international deficits – including reparations – after the two wars. American reluctance to take on this responsibility until 1924 (and then only indirectly) helped produce the impasses of the five years after Versailles. U.S. willingness to take on the burden after 1947 facilitated the stabilization of the 1950s and 1960s. But American readiness was no automatic decision. As one minor Department of State official wrote before victory in Europe, "It seems certain that Germany has lost the war; but it appears that Dr. Schacht has a very good chance of winning the peace."[60]

In light of these developments, the international corollary of the era of domestic stabilization may be viewed as a German–American (or perhaps a trilateral German–American–Japanese) association achieved only after two world wars. Success for this policy was registered not by the rubble of Berlin but by the frustration of such postwar German leaders as Jakob Kaiser of the CDU and Kurt Schumacher of the SPD, both of whom sought unsuccessfully to maintain under democratic auspices a less capitalist and less exclusively Western-oriented German society.[61] Their very setbacks testified to the triumph of stabilization in West Germany, Western Europe, and the noncom-

---

60 Joseph Fuqua to Woodrow Willoughby, December 21, 1944, National Archives Record Group 59, International Trade Papers, Box 19, Folder: "Article VII. United Kingdom – General."

61 Hans Peter Schwartz, *Vom Reich zur Bundesrepublik. Deutschland im Widerstreit der aussempolitischen Konzeptionen in den Jahren der Besatzungsherrschaft, 1945–1949* (Berlin, 1966), 297–344; Werner Conze, *Jakob Kaiser: Politiker zwischen Ost und West, 1945–1949* (Stuttgart, 1969); Lewis J. Edinger, *Kurt Schumacher: A Study in Personality and Political Behavior* (Stanford, 1965); and Ernst Nolte, *Deutschland und der Kalte Krieg* (Munich, 1974), 208–14, 322–3.

munist countries as a whole. Just as the end of the second war against Germany resolved the international issues left undecided after the close of the first, so the strengthening of Western pluralism after the second war completed the European domestic institutional restructuring begun after the first. Stabilization meant an end to the German problem. It likewise meant winning the adherence of a large enough segment of the working classes to preserve the scope for private economic power and hierarchy that defined liberal capitalism. The achievement was not simply restorative, for the new, very real guarantees of social welfare and social-democratic political participation contributed change even as they purchased continuity.

This suggests that the major sociopolitical assignment of the twentieth century paralleled that of the nineteenth, which saw the incorporation of the middle classes and European bourgeoisie into the political community. The international corollaries of the earlier development were the paralysis and reduction of Metternichian Austria within Europe and the extension of overseas empire. The international corollaries of the new development were the linking to the West of at least part of Germany and the recession of overseas empire: the trajectory from grandeur to welfare. The institutional device for the nineteenth century was parliamentary representation; the institutional foci for the twentieth-century achievement included trade unions, ambitious state economic agencies, and bureaucratized pressure groups – the components of what I have termed elsewhere "corporate pluralism."

Observers have often failed to note the magnitude of the twentieth-century accomplishment because the costs were so distressing. Certainly this essay should not be read as an argument that, because stability resulted, the intervening tyranny, warfare, sacrifice, and resistance lose their historical significance. Still, to ask about significance is to search for meaning, which is just one task of history. To trace the structural principles of collective life must remain an equally valid historical enterprise; and that pursuit compels us to admit that even catastrophic events do not always durably alter the trajectory of institutions any more than the constant slow renewal that proceeds in the absence of disaster. Indeed, that continuing change best facilitates the analysis of earlier patterns. If now the institutional solutions of the second postwar era show signs of wear and tear, if the social compromises of the welfare state become precarious as economic growth falters, if the stability of the past generation appears perhaps to have rested on exceptional and transitory advantages, such as the consensus on postwar reconstruction or the ease of securing resources from outside Europe, then we can better begin to understand the recent era not merely as events but as history.

Part II

Collective preferences and public outcomes

5

The politics of inflation in the twentieth century

The literature on this theme has ballooned in the years since the publication of this article. For essays on recent inflation see Leon Lindberg and Charles S. Maier, eds., *The Politics of Inflation and Economic Stagnation* (Washington, D.C.: Brookings Institution, 1985), and the collection in which this chapter first appeared: Fred Hirsch and John H. Goldthorpe, eds., *The Political Economy of Inflation* (London: Martin Robertson; Cambridge, Mass.: Harvard University Press, 1978). For historical résumés of Latin American monetary experiences through the 1970s, see Rosemary Thorp and Laurence Whitehead, eds., *Inflation and Stabilisation in Latin America* (London: Macmillan, in conjunction with St. Antony's College, Oxford, 1979). A useful, focused volume emerged from a colloquium at the Institute for International Economics in December 1984: John Williamson, ed., *Inflation and Indexation: Argentina, Brazil and Israel* (Washington, D.C.: Institute for International Economics, in conjunction with MIT Press, Cambridge, Mass., 1985). A major collective project on the German inflation of the 1920s in comparative and historical perspective has been edited by Gerald D. Feldman, Carl-Ludwig Holtfrerich, Gerhard A. Ritter, and Peter-Christian Witt. Volumes include *The German Inflation Reconsidered: A Preliminary Balance* (Berlin: de Gruyter, 1982) and *The Experience of Inflation: International and Comparative Studies* (Berlin: de Gruyter, 1984). Related studies include Carl-Ludwig Holtfrerich, *The German Inflation 1914–1923: Causes and Effects in International Perspective*, Theo Balderston, trans. (Berlin: de Gruyter, 1986); and Gerald D. Feldman, ed., *Die Nachwirkungen der inflation auf die deutsche Geschichte 1924–1933* (Munich: Oldenbourg, 1985). A major social history of the German inflation by Professor Feldman is currently near completion.

I published a brief contrast of two major inflationary periods: "Inflation and Stabilization in the Wake of the Two World Wars: Comparative Strategies and Sacrifices," in Feldman et al., *The Experience of Inflation*, 106–29. That piece sought to apply some of the more general typologies of the essay included here. It argued that the coalitions behind stabilization policies after World War II were more willing to wipe out rentier or savers' claims, less preoccupied by protecting bond holders, and more concerned with keeping economic activity at a high level than were coalitions after World War I. A major reason was the lesson learned from clinging to outmoded exchange rates in the Depression; another important factor was the greater power of working-class representatives after 1945 and the partial triumph of Keynesian policies in the United States and Great Britain. I also argued that the United States had changed its role after the 1940s and 1950s, when it subsidized those countries who undertook stabilization but still encouraged them to pursue high-employment nondeflationary policies. In the 1960s, in contrast, the United States used the reserve-currency status of the dollar, in effect, to exact subsidies from its allies through international seignorage. Foreign central banks (outside France) were still pledged to accept dollars at overvalued exchange rates, and Washington deficits also acted as an engine of international monetary expansion.

The text of this essay is presented here as originally published, with a few minor additions to the notes. The contemporary trends described in the last section describe the economic circumstances of the mid-1970s. I have made no attempt to rewrite that section, because any revision would itself become outdated relatively quickly. Furthermore, the historical analysis of more or less pro-inflationary coalitions, I hope, is still useful. Describing their elements was the major objective of the paper.

The final discussion of indexation in this essay turned out, as of the mid-1980s, not to be wrong, but inapplicable. An era of inflation has been ending since the early 1980s – the Argentinian, Italian, and Israeli stabilization efforts of 1985–86 completing the cycle that began with the U.S. recession of 1981. (Brazil's stabilization of 1985–86 remains in question as of early 1987.) Part of this stabilization involved fiscal and monetary changes, but part also involved dismantling the indexation that was so strongly rooted in these societies. Had, in effect, the systemic international economic climate not changed, it is doubtful that these societies could have loosened the ratchet mechanism of indexation. In social class terms, dismantling indexation means that key party or labor union leaders are themselves finally won over to a stabilization coalition. In part their shift has reflected a long-term evolution in the structure of the labor force they represent. It is revealing that, when the Italian Communist Party sponsored an early 1986 national referendum against weakening wage indexation, it suffered a major rebuff.

The essay here does not compare its interest-group and class explanations with economic theories of inflation. The latter explain mechanisms, not preferences. Thomas J. Sargent's stimulating essay, "The End of Four Big Inflations" (National Bureau of Economic Research Paper Washington, D.C., August 1980), sought to buttress "rational expectations" theory with the data from selected hyperinflations. Sargent argued that expectations are crucial and that turning these around depends on installing a new monetary "regime." The historian must respond that a new monetary regime depends on a new political regime – or at least a significant change in coalitions. Readers who wish to pursue the issue of what insights the inflation of the 1970s provides for contending theoretical explanations – "sociological," on the one hand, economic (monetarist, Keynesian, etc.), on the other – are referred to the introduction and conclusion in the Lindberg and Maier volume cited earlier. This essay is reprinted by permission of the publishers and Basil Blackwell, Oxford, Ltd., from *The Political Economy of Inflation*, Fred Hirsch and John H. Goldthorpe, editors, Cambridge, Mass.: Harvard University Press and Oxford: Martin Robertson Ltd. Copyright © 1978 by Ruth Hirsch and John H. Goldthorpe.

Introduction: The limitations of the economic models

Of the more than sixty years since the outbreak of World War I over half have comprised periods of sharply rising prices: 1914 to 1921 or to 1926 (the terminal date depending upon the particular economy), 1938 to 1953 (with 'creeping inflation' still prevailing from 1953 to the late 1960s), and 1967 or so to the present. Nonetheless, political scientists have only recently begun serious analysis of inflation, while historians of politics and society have been even more laggard. Even economic historians strictly speaking have contributed few studies, although this is not surprising. Until recently most economic historians concentrated on questions of development and growth, and above all on industrialization. Inflation, however, presents an urgent problem of welfare and allocation. Sometimes it involves distributing the dividends of economic growth, but often it serves as the mechanism for sharing out the costs of stagnation and decline. All the more central a theme it should be, therefore, for historians of twentieth-century politics and society. Their investigations cannot avoid the political bitterness that has arisen in epochs when growth faltered or fell. In that distributive conflict, inflation has played important roles, either easing or exacerbating the struggle over shares.

The historian can draw only limited assistance from the economic models proposed to understand inflation.[1] On one level they provide the raw material for a history of ideas; they indicate how strongly theoretical systems are influenced by refractory problems and policy dilemmas of the day. Quantity theory served economists writing on the inflationary experiences of the 1920s. They might differ as to whether balance-of-payments difficulties or internal budget deficits prodded currency emissions, but they attributed inflation to growing monetary circulation and in France at least tended to define inflation as the increasing volume of currency, not the rise in prices.[2]

The Keynesian analysis turned from the quantity of money to levels of income and expenditure. But, as interpreted by those whom Coddington termed 'hydraulic' Keynesians, the problem presented by potential excess demand was viewed as a mirror image of insufficient demand. An implicit theoretical parity suggested that if the $C+I+G$ streams of demand (consumption, investment and government spending) produced an inflationary gap, macroeconomic adjustments could reduce them easily to a full-employment non-inflationary equilibrium. This extrapolation from a world of depression to one of inflation was too simple, and for the historian of economic ideas, the development of Phillips-curve analysis after World War II can be interpreted as a defensive retreat on the part of the Keynesians. They abandoned the presumed mirror-image symmetry between deflation and inflation and fell back on the more intractable trade-off. Yet even the Phillips-curve redoubt has come under heavy bombardment from Friedmanite critics and earlier defenders are themselves uncertain of its soundness.[3]

Although the historian can trace these theories as they have de-

1   Robert J. Gordon, "The Demand for and Supply of Inflation," *Journal of Law and Economics*, 18 (1975): 807–36.
2   James Harvey Rogers, *The Process of Inflation in France 1914–1927* (New York: Columbia University Press, 1929), 91–128; Albert Aftalion, *Monnaie, prix et change* (Paris: Sirey, 1927); Frank D. Graham, *Exchange, Prices, and Production in Hyper-inflation: Germany 1920–1923* (Princeton, N.J.: Princeton University Press, 1930); Howard Ellis, *German Monetary Theory, 1905–1933* (Cambridge, Mass.: Harvard University Press, 1934); Costantino Bresciani-Turroni, *The Economics of Inflation*, Millicent Sayres, trans. (London: Allen & Unwin, 1937).
3   Alan Coddington, "Keynesian Economics: The Search for First Principles," *Journal of Economic Literature*, 14 (1976). For summaries of the monetarist school, see Milton Friedman, "The Quantity Theory of Money – A Restatment," in Milton Friedman, ed., *Studies in the Quantity Theory of Money* (Chicago: University of Chicago Press, 1956); Don Patinkin, "The Chicago Tradition, the Quantity Theory, and Friedman," *Journal of Money, Credit and Banking*, 1 (1969): 46–70; Robert L. Teigen, "A Critical Look at Monetarist Economics," *Federal Reserve Bank of St. Louis Review* (January 1972): 10–25.

veloped since the 1930s, they do not offer an effective starting point for his or her own sociopolitical analysis. Monetarism focuses on the keepers of the printing press and summons them to abstinence, but rarely explains what pressures sustain or overcome their resolution. Keynesian analysis tends to look at consumption decisions on the part of the generality or sometimes postulates the coherence of a class of wage earners. Conservatives, regardless of theoretical camp, postulate gloomy secular changes in a society undermined by 'growthmania,' dark-skinned immigrants or Caucasian egoism.[4] The point is that the actors posited by the economists are not the agents a historian or social observer will find critical. Each economic model usually implies a particular sociological model, but not all are useful. Refinement of the implicit sociology can make possible decisive advances in economic theory: one of the basic claims of *The General Theory* (1936) was that the group behaviour alleged by classical orthodoxy did not correspond to actual decision-making in the collectivity. A finer breakdown of savers and investors (at least as roles if not as separate individuals) explained why the presumption of full employment was ill-founded. Keynes did not propose an equivalent sociology of inflation, probably because he felt its origins were more centrally determined by war finance.[5] Nor do I think that economic models since Keynes have allowed a sufficiently plausible sociology of inflationary propensity, in part because the different class roles vary in different societies, and in part because class alignments themselves evolve in the course of inflation. Social and political structure helps to shape inflation; conversely inflation alters collective social roles. No economic theories, so far as I know, incorporate these reciprocal influences.

Some economic models, however, have begun from assumptions of institutional or class behaviour and not from the postulates of pure competition or marginal-choice rationality. Analyses of cost-plus or other administered pricing go back to Gardiner Means, Joan Robinson and Edward Chamberlin in the 1930s, were incorporated by Franklyn Holzman in his 1950 analysis of inflationary wage price spirals, and recently have been accredited by William Nordhaus after being elab-

---

4   E. J. Mishan, "The New Inflation: Its Theory and Practice," *Encounter* 42 (May 1974): 12–24.
5   John Maynard Keynes, *How to Pay for the War* (London: Macmillan, 1940); Sidney Weintraub, "The Keynesian Theory of Inflation: The Two Faces of Janus," *International Economic Review*, 1 (1960): 143–55; James A. Trevithick, "Keynes, Inflation, and Money Illusion," *Economic Journal*, 85 (1975).

orated by French and German economists as well.[6] Marxist concepts, which link political alignments and economic outcomes even more closely, offer two major theoretical lines of development. James O'Connor and Ian Gough stress the contradictory burdens placed upon the public sector in capitalist society – the state's need to bear all the 'externalities' of the profit system, even while it must provide sufficient welfare payments to prevent social upheaval. (Their analysis here converges with many points made by free-market critics of the mixed economy.) This Marxian concentration on the budgetary process derives from Goldscheid's fiscal sociology of the early twentieth century. Goldscheid did not break down the different class and sectoral claims impinging on the state but emphasized growing public indebtedness *vis-à-vis* private accumulation, and he called upon the state to 'reappropriate' the assets it had allowed capitalists to assemble.[7]

Other Marxian models look less at the state than at the clash of class claims directly in a society where state and economy have largely interpenetrated. Hilferding's concepts of 'organized capitalism' and the 'political wage' pointed to the connection between political strength and market power in the raw pluralism of the Weimar Republic.[8] Labour's success in wage negotiations depended upon the German Social Democratic Party preserving the ground-rules for collective bargaining and arbitration; in turn the SPD could remain powerful only so long as its affiliated trade unions retained leverage in the labour market. Similar ideas, of course, have been offered by liberal theorists who stress interest-group rivalry, from Bentley to McConnell and Lowi.[9] In what Beer terms the collectivist age and what I have elsewhere

6   Franklyn D. Holzman, "Income Determination in Open Inflation," *The Review of Economics and Statistics*, 32, (1950): 150–58; Pierre Biacabe, *Analyses contemporaines de l'inflation* (Paris: Sirey, 1962), 247–50; Horst Georg Koblitz, *Einkommensverteilung und Inflation in kurzfristiger Analyse* (Berlin: de Gruyter, 1971).

7   James O'Connor, *The Fiscal Crisis of the State* (New York: St. Martins Press, 1973); Ian Gough, "State Expenditure in Advanced Capitalism," *New Left Review*, 92 (1975); Rudolf Goldscheid, "Staatssozialismus oder Staatskapitalismus," [1917], and "Staat, öffentlicher Haushalt und Gesellschaft," [1926], in R. Goldscheid and Joseph Schumpeter, *Die Finanzkrise des Steuerstaates*, R. Hickel, ed. (Frankfurt/M: Suhrkamp, 1976).

8   Rudolf Hilferding, "Arbeitsgemeinschaft der Klassen?" in *Der Kampf*, 8 (1915); and "Die Aufgaben der Sozialdemokratie in der Republik," *Sozialdemokratischer Parteitag, Kiel 1927* (Berlin, 1927).

9   Arthur Bentley, *The Process of Government*, Peter H. Odegard, ed. (Cambridge, Mass., Harvard University Press, 1967); Grant McConnell, *Private Power and American Democracy* (New York: Alfred Knopf, 1966); Theodore J. Lowi, *The End of Liberalism: Ideology, Policy, and the Crisis of Public Authority* (New York: Norton, 1969).

termed corporate pluralism or just corporatism, several developments may facilitate inflation.[10] The state has become 'spongier,' more extensive in function and reach but less distinct in administration *vis-à-vis* private interests. The modern economy seems to increase the disruptive possibilities for organized groups – not necessarily because schoolteachers, dustmen and even truck-drivers are more crucial today than railroad workers half a century ago, but because we seem to feel more uncomfortable when they withhold their services, perhaps because the legitimacy of a pluralist system depends precisely upon the appeasement of grievances short of a group's actual walkout. (How else can we explain the potency of student strikes?) In any case, the brokerage of group demands may seem less painful than showdown; as Tobin argues, 'Inflation lets this struggle proceed and blindly, impartially, and nonpolitically scales down all its outcomes. There are worse methods of resolving group rivalries and social conflict.'[11]

While this sort of analysis can remain empty or trivial, it does suggest that the state is no longer just an umpire (even a biased one) but a player deeply enmeshed in the game of social and economic bargaining. This player possesses one trump: control of the money supply. But in its control of money and credit (sometimes shared with central bank authorities who achieve genuine independence), the state does not act qualitatively differently from other groups. Each competing interest under inflationary conditions seeks in effect to monetize the assets it controls, whether by means of commodity currency keyed to agricultural products thereby stabilizing the income of farmers, control of interest rates on the part of banks, or index wages that would make labour time the unit of value. Rapid inflation involves the search for constant income shares and thus the attempted coinage of each group's respective scarce goods. Coinage, however, has been a traditional prerogative of sovereignty. Inflation thereby tends to erode sovereignty. Likewise it usually accompanies the devolution of state regulatory capacities upon private interests and, even more generally, dissolves the very sense that an effective public authority exists to enforce the same rules on haves and have-nots together. The loss of commonwealth is, I would argue, one of the severest tolls of inflation, but a cost that the usual welfare functions of economists cannot accommodate.

10 Samuel H. Beer, *British Politics in the Collectivist Age* (New York: Random House, 1967); Charles S. Maier, *Recasting Bourgeois Europe* (Princeton: Princeton University Press, 1975), 9–15, 580–86.
11 James Tobin, "Inflation and Unemployment," *American Economic Review*, 62 (1972).

The analysis of group bargaining thus begins with a tautology, namely that the granting of price and wage claims beyond the given money value of the national product produces inflation. But this recognition, derived from either Marxian or liberal theories of group rivalry, at least assists in demystifying inflation and understanding it as one of the major forms of distributive conflicts in contemporary society. This at least provides the starting point for linking political and social analysis to economic outcomes. For the specification of particular group conflicts and outcomes, case-by-case analysis is required.

Levels of inflation and the configuration of interests

Efforts to infer a sociology or politics of inflation have often foundered on their over-generalization and their formalism. However, inflation is not a uniform phenomenon; it may rather be a syndrome of very different group conflicts. At the risk of over-simplification we can establish a typology of three inflationary plateaus and a deflationary process as well. They are labelled here: 'hyperinflation', 'Latin inflation,' 'creeping inflation' and 'the stabilization crisis.' These are represented in Figure 1. The first three cases are analysed in this section, the stabilization crisis in the following section. Each case, I submit, is characterized by one or two different configurations of interests and group alignments.

Table 1 summarizes the respective inflationary types and their associated socio-political alignments. Table 2 provides some examples of inflation rate in selected time periods. It is important to note that the differing levels of inflation may be more or less stable. There is no inevitable slide from creeping inflation to Latin inflation or thence to hyperinflation; significant alterations in group attitudes and/or group behaviour are necessary for these step-changes. On the other hand, hyperinflation involves such a great destruction of the real value of money in circulation that it usually provokes an economic crisis deep enough to regroup political forces and impel currency reform. Hyperinflations are the super novas of the monetary firmament, exploding furiously outward only to collapse into the dark neutron stars of economic contraction. Likewise a stabilization crisis cannot continue indefinitely although deflationary pressures can remain prolonged, as from 1930 to 1933.

It is natural to ask whether the coalitions associated with different levels of inflation actually help cause the inflation or merely result from it. Of course, incipient inflation can encourage the crystallization of groups whose very demands will thereupon aggravate the inflationary pressure. But even beyond this recursive scenario, the align-

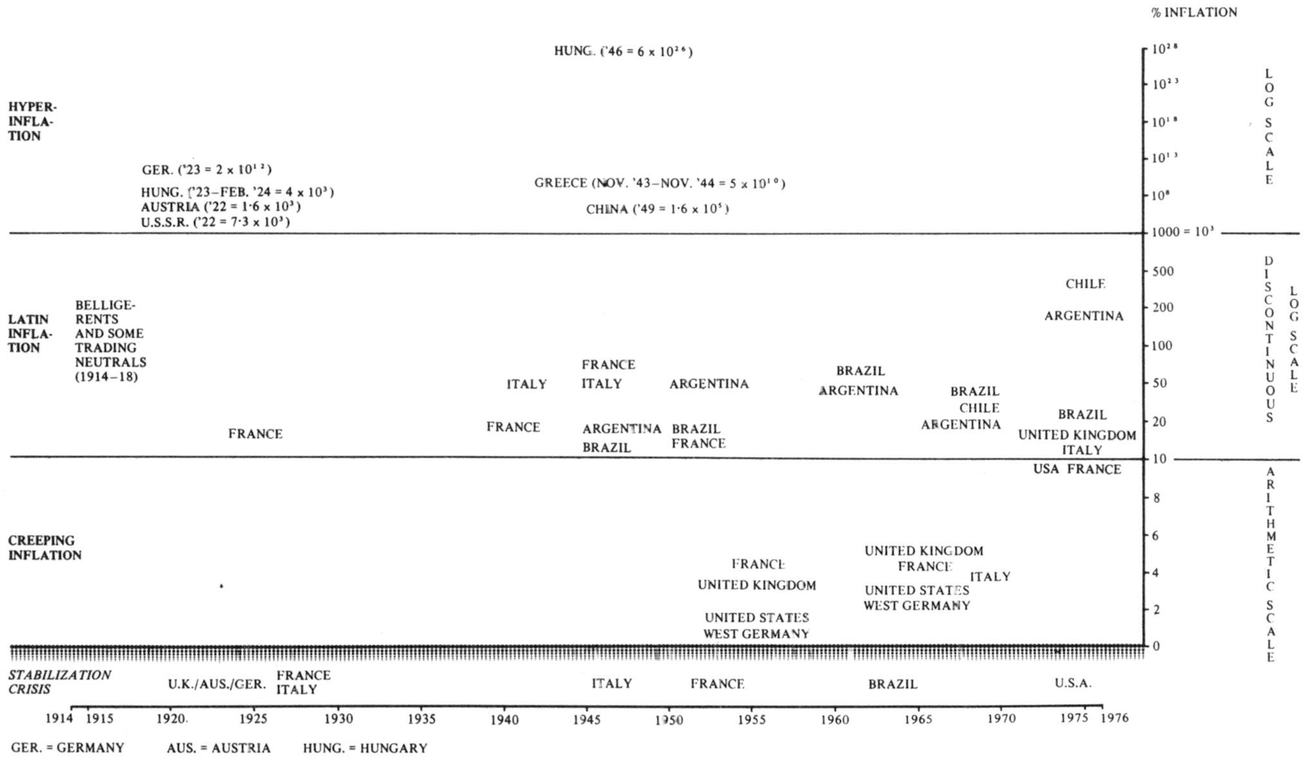

% INFLATION

HYPER-INFLATION

HUNG. ('46 = 6 × 10¹⁴)

GER. ('23 = 2 × 10¹²)
HUNG. ('23–FEB. '24 = 4 × 10³)
AUSTRIA ('22 = 1·6 × 10³)
U.S.S.R. ('22 = 7·3 × 10³)

GREECE (NOV. '43–NOV. '44 = 5 × 10¹⁰)
CHINA ('49 = 1·6 × 10⁵)

LOG SCALE

10^{14}
10^{13}
10^{12}
10^{11}
10^{9}
$1000 = 10^{3}$

LATIN INFLATION

BELLIGE-RENTS AND SOME TRADING NEUTRALS (1914–18)

DISCONTINUOUS LOG SCALE

500 — CHILE
200 — ARGENTINA
100
50 — BRAZIL / ARGENTINA (CHILE, ARGENTINA)
20 — BRAZIL / UNITED KINGDOM / ITALY

ITALY / FRANCE
FRANCE / ITALY / ARGENTINA / BRAZIL FRANCE
FRANCE / ARGENTINA BRAZIL

ARITHMETIC SCALE

10 — USA FRANCE
8
6
4
2
0

CREEPING INFLATION

UNITED KINGDOM
FRANCE ITALY
UNITED STATES
WEST GERMANY

FRANCE
UNITED KINGDOM
UNITED STATES
WEST GERMANY

ITALY
FRANCE
BRAZIL
U.S.A.

STABILIZATION CRISIS

U.K./AUS./GER. FRANCE ITALY

FRANCE

1914 1915 1920 1925 1930 1935 1940 1945 1950 1955 1960 1965 1970 1975 1976

GER. = GERMANY   AUS. = AUSTRIA   HUNG. = HUNGARY

Figure 1. The positions show the average annual rate of inflation for the timespan indicated. For simplification, only the maximum annual rates have been used for the hyperinflations. The plottings are approximate only, and are designed to show the relative position of each country within the particular episode.

Table 1. *The coalitions of inflation*

	Economic characteristics	Coalitions
Hyperinflation (over 1000%/year)	Initial economic expansion; crisis of credit and production in final stage.	*De facto* industralist–trade-union collaboration on basis of wage–price spiral, export premium, hostility to foreign power. Relative expropriation of rentiers, unorganized salaried employees, eventually small businessmen. The inflation of the producers.
Latin inflation (10–1000%/year)	Either real growth and development, or unproductive subsidies of export sector and services. Side-by-side persistence of modern and pre-modern sectors.	Strong interest-group disaggregation and working-class–bourgeois conflict. Redistribution of resources toward working classes, and/or key resistance of middle-class and upper-class elements *qua* consumers and savers. Effort to avoid direct taxes by broad evasion, export of capital. Bourgeois leverage precludes early fiscal redress.
Creeping inflation (up to 10%/year – typically, creeping inflation up to 7%)	Real growth.	General consensus of all classes on high employment and welfare. Remains under control only so long as real increases do not require cutting back any sector in absolute terms.
Stabilization and/or deflation	Initial crisis and recession; then expansion or weak recovery with periodic crises.	Initial collaboration of middle-class *qua* consumers and savers with entrepreneurial spokesmen on basis of capital formation. Can lead to middle-class alienation because of inadequate revaluation of assets, stringent credit, or higher taxes.

ments themselves appear to me causative in important ways. At the least they help determine the extent and duration of an inflationary experience, even if the initial shock to the system is provided by an exogenous event such as the need to finance a war, the changes in prices of key imports or the sudden cashing in of domestic currency balances held abroad. Thereafter internal coalitions – not always prepared in advance but quickly, if sometimes unwittingly, woven across existing party lines according to patterns of wealth, income and industrial affiliations – themselves generate inflationary impulses of

Table 2. *Selected annual rates of inflation*

Creeping inflation: the experience of the 1960s
Mean annual percentage increases in consumer prices, 1961–71

United States	France	Germany	Britain	All OECD countries
3.1	4.3	3.0	4.6	3.7

Latin inflation: some major episodes
Percentage increases in consumer prices

	1914–18	1919	1920	1921	1922	1923	1924	1925	1926	1927
France	138.0	21.0	37.7	−21.6	−1.0	17.8	9.6	13.0	27.2	−6.3

	1938–44	1945	1946	1947	1948	1949	1950	1951	1952
France (retail food prices only)	182.0	36.7	71.1	62.2	58.7	9.4	14.3	17.4	8.5

	1919	1920	1921	1922	1923	1924	1925	1926	1927
Italy	1120.0	95.9	18.0	62.4	5.7	1.7			
Argentina	—	20.7	17.1	12.2	13.0	32.7	24.6	37.2	38.1
Brazil	—	—	27.3	5.8	3.5	6.0	11.4	10.8	20.4

	1958	1959	1960	1961	1962	1963	1964	1965	1966	1967
Argentina	31.4	113.9	27.3	13.5	28.1	24.0	22.1	28.6	31.9	29.2
Brazil	17.3	51.9	23.8	42.9	55.8	80.2	86.6	45.5	41.2	24.1

Table 2. (continued)

Latin inflation: some major episodes (continued)

	1968	1969	1970	1971	1972	1973	1974	1975	1976
France	4.6	6.1	5.9	5.6	5.9	7.4	13.6	11.8	9.6
Italy	1.3	2.7	4.9	5.1	5.4	10.8	19.1	17.2	15.7
Britain	4.7	5.4	6.4	9.5	7.1	9.2	15.9	24.2	16.8
Argentina	16.2	7.6	13.6	34.7	58.5	62.5	23.4	171.2	486.0
Brazil	24.5	24.3	20.9	18.1	14.0	12.6	27.5	29.0	41.7
Chile	27.9	28.9	35.3	20.1	77.9	319.5	586.0	380.0	229.5

Hyperinflation: two Central European cases
Percentage increases in internal prices

	1914–18	1919	1920	1921	1922	1923 (to November)
Germany	140	223	68	144	5,470	75×10^9

Percentage increases in government cost-of-living index

	1914–18	1919	1920	1921	1922 (to October)
Austria	1,226	197	87	797	1,603

Sources: For "creeping inflation": OECD, *Economic Outlook*, December 1974; "Latin inflation": IMF, *International Financial Statistics*, January, 1948, January, 1954, October, 1973, and August, 1977. See also Albert Sauvy *Histoire économique de la France entre les deux guerres*, 2 vols. (Paris: Fayard, 1965), I; Thomas Skidmore, "The Politics of Economic Stabilization in Postwar Latin America," in James Malloy, ed., *Authoritarianism and Corporatism in Latin America* (Pittsburgh, Penn.: University of Pittsburgh Press, 1976); also Susan M. Wachter, *Latin-American Inflation* (Lexington, Mass.: Lexington Books, 1976). For "hyperinflation" see Constantino Bresciani-Turroni, *The Economics of Inflation*, Millicent Sayres, trans. (London: Allen & Unwin, 1937); and J. van Walré de Bordes, *The Austrian Crown: Its Depreciation and Stabilization* (London: P. S. King, 1924). [German statistics should now be updated from Carl-Ludwig Holtfrerich, *The German Inflation* (Berlin: de Gruyter, 1986).]

varying intensity. Likewise, the stabilization crisis is often triggered by signals from abroad that the time for 'responsibility' has come. The signals include outflows of reserves (under fixed exchange rates), currency depreciation (under flexible rates) or admonitions from the IMF. Nevertheless, while such pressure from guardians abroad is often needed to persuade domestic policy makers to undertake stabilization or to provide politically weak but deflation-minded civil servants with useful symbols of national emergency, the ensuing course of stabilization is still associated with a characteristic domestic structure of interests and classes. Foreign bankers reinforce domestic interests.

Clearly, the classifications proposed here are over-simplified. The initial approach to sorting inflations according to their magnitude represents an effort to rank the 'intensity' of these economic experiences. However, the level of inflation may be less politically relevant than the acceleration of inflation. A rapid slide from an inflation rate of 5 per cent to one of 12 per cent or more, as in the major market economies during 1974, may be more destablizing than a long period of continuing 50 to 75 per cent inflation as in Brazil. For the hyperinflationary experience, the distinction tends to collapse since only very great accelerations of inflation can produce the astronomic magnitudes that are recorded. Conversely in 'creeping' inflation the rate of change of inflation must be very low or the level of inflation itself would quickly become worrisome. But in the middle range it is possible that what is politically important is the second and not the first derivative of prices with respect to time. Yet the continuing, if stable, high rates of inflation in a country like Brazil do suggest underlying class cleavages of a strong and characteristic type. A society with prolonged but steady Latin inflation has different inner conflicts from a society with prolonged creeping inflation.

Hyperinflation

Hyperinflation is, of course, the most sadly picturesque deterioration of purchasing power. Cagan, who has presented a systematic monetarist treatment, dates the appearance of hyperinflation from the month in which price rises reached 50 per cent.[12] Extended steadily over a year's time this rate would yield 130-fold price increases. Societies in recent times that have lived through hyperinflation by this measure include Austria, Hungary, Germany, Poland and Russia in the wake of World War I; Hungary again, Rumania, Greece and China during and after World War II. The highest rate of inflation

12 Phillip Cagan, "The Monetary Dynamics of Hyperinflation," in Friedman, ed., *Studies in the Quantity Theory of Money*, 25–117.

was achieved not by Weimar Germany (which stabilized its new currency at 10^{-12} prewar marks), but by Hungary between August 1945 and July 1946. After a year of frantic issues of Milpengö (10^6 pengö), bilpengö (10^{12}), then tax pengö based on astronomic index numbers, Budapest finally stabilized a new forint at the rate of 4×10^{29} pengö, or about 400 times a billion cubed.[13]

Effectively, such a degree of inflation destroys money in circulation and substitutes foreign currencies or book-keeping units. Keynes estimated that a government could double the supply of money every three months without entirely destroying its use in retail transactions; the Germans first exceeded this multiple between September and November 1922 and then vastly accelerated by mid-1923.[14] Introduction of a new currency or index-money can in fact accentuate depreciation. The Soviets issued a chervonets in November 1922 and allowed the original rouble and successive heavy roubles to sink until a final conversion ratio was established in early 1924. The German authorities consciously drove down the mark in the last two weeks before stabilization in November 1923 in order to prepare the ground for the forthcoming Rentenmark.

What is the political context of such currency disasters? As in other inflations, weakness of the state is an underlying general condition. But that alone specifies little. In certain circumstances hyperinflation accompanies outright civil war, as in Russia from 1917 to 1921 or China between 1945 and 1949. Austria and Germany after World War I, Hungary after World War II were sharply divided polities. Secondly – and as also is the case in other inflations – an important incentive may exist for major socio-political interests to avoid early stabilization. The Bolsheviks felt they might exploit inflation against their class enemies; the Hungarian Communists in the coalition of 1945–7 could likewise perceive political and economic advantages: German exporters learned about the advantages of dumping, and the German Right in general could see that the inflation effectively paralysed the reparations

13 F. Falush, "The Hungarian Hyperinflation of 1945–46," *National Westminster Bank Review* (August 1976); Bertrand Nogaro, "Hungary's Recent Monetary Crisis and Its Theoretical Meaning," *American Economic Review*, 38 (1948). [For post–World War I hyperinflations in Central Europe, see most recently the studies by Hans Kernbauer and Fritz Weber, "Die Wiener Grossbanken in der Zeit der Kriegs- und Nachkriegsinflation"; Elizabeth A. Boross, "The Role of the State Issuing Bank in the Course of Inflation in Hungary between 1918 and 1924"; Jonathan Bloomfield, "Surviving in a Harsh World: Trade and Inflation in the Czecholslovak and Austrian Republics 1918–1926"; and Zbigniew Landau and Jerzy Tomaszewski, "Poland between Inflation and Stabilization 1924–1927" – all in Gerald Feldman, Carl Ludwig Holtfrerich, and Peter-Christian Witt, eds., *Die Erfahrung der Inflation* (Berlin: de Gruyter, 1984), 142–294.]
14 John Maynard Keynes, *A Tract on Monetary Reform* (London: Macmillan, 1923), 55n.

system they hated. Thirdly – and this seems a distinguishing aspect in societies with a cohesively organized working class – common economic advantages of an inflationary policy bind industrialists and labour together, even if politically they remain at daggers drawn.

None of this is to deny that hyperinflation is proximately generated by massive fiscal dislocations. Hyperinflation is amplified by wage–price spirals, but at any one time the increase in money supply represents in effect a frenzied effort at tax collection. Preobrazhensky pointed this out to the Soviets in 1921,[15] and two years later Keynes wittily explained that the diversion of purchasing power to the state amounted to a mode of taxation: 'The income-tax receipts which we in England receive from the Surveyor, we throw into the wastepaper basket; in Germany they call them bank-notes and put them into their pocket-books; in France they are termed Rentes and are locked up in the family safe.'[16]

This taxation operates differently, however, according to the rate of inflation. While double-digit inflation under a progressive tax system will increase government revenues by pushing income earners into higher brackets, hyperinflationary conditions destroy the normal tax framework. The delay between levying a tax bill and collection wipes out much of the value of the receipt with the important exception of weekly withholding. By March 1923, 95 per cent of German income taxes derived from those wage-earners and employees subject to withholding – a situation the General Trade Union Federation (ADGB) vigorously protested.[17] In addition the state cannot usually raise the price of public services quickly enough to avoid a massive subsidy. German freight rates were a noted example. Replacing conventional taxes by currency emissions provides a heady though ultimately self-defeating alternative. In the hyperinflations that Cagan reviews, the tax yield of new currency issues ranged from 3 to 15 per cent of national income, except for the Soviet state which had a return below one per cent. But as the real value of cash balances declines, the yield must fall unless the government can issue paper ever more rapidly; and it is never rapid enough to keep the money supply and tax base from shrinking to a tiny fraction, inadequate for commercial needs or for public revenue.[18]

Critical to the unleashing of runaway inflation, therefore, is the fail-

15 Alexander Erlich, *The Soviet Industrialization Debate* (Cambridge, Mass.: Harvard University Press, 1967), 43n.

16 Keynes, *Tract*, 42.

17 Karl-Heinz Harbeck, ed., *Das Kabinett Cuno 22. November 1922 bis 12. August 1923: Akten der Reichskanzlei, Weimarer Republik* (Boppard am Rhein: H. Boldt, 1968), 228–31.

18 Cagan, "Monetary Dynamics of Hyperinflation," 89.

ure of the normal fiscal system. Unexpected demands of war finance usually trigger such note issues in some degree, but political factors determine how far the community will thereafter choose direct sacrifice or continued levies through inflation. Soviet finance revealed a situation where an inflationary levy seemed actually purposeful and not just an expedient. After the fact, the Soviets justified their drastic depreciation of the rouble as a way of expropriating the bourgeoisie. During the era of War Communism, Soviet theorists could likewise celebrate a reversion to a moneyless economy characterized by direct requisitioning and provision of goods and services to workers. Even as over 10,000 employees printed roubles (the total value of which by 1921 was no more than a thousandth of the money stock in November 1917), the state pared rents, sought moneyless payments between its agencies and envisaged the elimination of taxes. Still, the monetary collapse remained, it seems, a result of desperation, not calculation in advance.

The advent of the New Economic Policy in the spring of 1921 ended the anti-monetary revery. 'State capitalism' required money and book-keeping criteria of efficiency. Budgeting, which had been largely ignored, was revived, and the expected deficit was reduced from about 85 per cent of government expenditure in 1920 and 1921 to 40 per cent for the first three quarters of 1922. In the same period conventional taxes rose from 1.8 to 14 per cent of government revenue, while the levy derived from the note issue fell from 90 to 56 per cent (with payments in kind making up the remainder). While the old rouble and periodic successors continued to collapse, the chervontsi of November 1922 provided a stable accounting unit until the final currency reform in 1924. In retrospect the Soviet inflation possessed a certain unwitting, costly and ruthless logic for an era of civil war. Ideologists may have made a virtue of necessity when they praised demonetization as an indicator of socialism, a fervour soon after discarded as 'infantile.' But at the price above all of urban–rural exchange, inflation did permit a harsh and coercive control over the allocation of goods and services.[19]

More relevant for other Western countries are the German and the Austrian hyperinflations. Both societies had a cohesive, organized urban working class enjoying critical political influence after the revo-

19 E. H. Carr, *The Bolshevik Revolution, 1917–1923*, 2 vols. (London: Macmillan, 1952), II, 256–68, 345–59; S. S. Katzenellenbaum, *Russian Currency and Banking* (London: P. S. King, 1925); L. M. Yurovsky, *Currency Problems and Policy of the Soviet Union* (London: Leonard Parsons, 1925); and on Lenin's apocryphal remarks about debauching the currency as a path to revolution, see Frank W. Fetter, "Lenin, Keynes, and Inflation," *Economica*, 44 (1977).

lutions of 1918–19. At the same time conservative élites were not uprooted and ably resisted incursions into their real property and prerogatives. To carry on the Weimar Republic required the appeasement, if not originally of diehard Junkers, then of the industrialists whose leadership seemed essential for recovery and to meet reparation demands. Successive governments in Berlin reflected either a stalemate among different interests – the Joseph Wirth–Walther Rathenau cabinets of 1921–2 sought to keep Social Democratic support and business cooperation simultaneously – or else they reflected the conventional wisdom of the industrial and financial community as under Wilhelm Cuno (1922–3). The price of industry's toleration was fiscal paralysis. If in Russia monetary debasement was a weapon of civil war, in Central Europe it became its surrogate. Moreover, recourse to the printing press seemed more attractive because of a widely-shared unwillingness to meet reparation charges from national income. Until the last months, hyperinflation was virtually welcomed by many business leaders and bureaucrats as providing a demonstration that without a change of policy in Paris, the German monetary disaster could only injure British and American commerce.[20]

From May 1921 through to the summer of 1923, the Wirth and Cuno ministries by and large accepted the view of the industrial leadership that further increases in the floating debt represented the only possible fiscal option. When stabilization came under consideration in the fall of 1922, leading industrialists such as Hugo Stinnes raised the spectre of serious recession. Stabilization would indeed impose transitional costs, which might involve unemployment for the working class and real taxes for industry and personal income. The question facing the political system was which group would pay more. Inflation had disguised the levies and at first had imposed them on middle-class households, although its results later hit labour too. Finally the government and representatives of industry accepted a stabilization programme once the alternative appeared grave Communist-led unrest and once depression threatened as credit dried up in the summer and fall of 1923. In addition, the export premium that inflation had provided ended in the summer of 1923 as domestic price increases outran the mark's depreciation in terms of foreign currency. (In effect all prices became set in terms of the daily dollar or pound rate plus a hefty

20   In addition to the new sources cited at the beginning of this chapter, see Peter-Christian Witt, "Finanzpolitik und sozialer Wandel im Krieg und Inflation 1918–1924," in Hans Mommsen et al., eds, *Industrielles System und politische Entwicklung in der Weimarer Republik* (Dusseldorf: Droste Verlag, 1974); Maier, *Recasting Bourgeois Europe*, chaps. 4 and 6; Gerald D. Feldman, *Iron and Steel in the German Inflation, 1916–1923* (Princeton: Princeton University Press, 1977).

mark-up for the expected depreciation to follow – a self-defeating form of indexation.) Industry still understood how to alleviate its own costs and the liquidity crisis accompanying stabilization by imposing longer working hours and a disadvantageous calculation of stable-money wages upon the unions. The inflation and Ruhr conflict had almost totally undermined their financial and organizational capacity for resistance.[21]

Still, the trade unions had accepted the inflation with surprisingly little labour unrest, even before the French occupation of the Ruhr imposed a patriotic front. But then, demand remained strong and employment high, and Germany was spared the brief but severe depression of 1920–1. In part, too, business and the government allowed union wages to keep relative pace with rising prices, although there were painful lags in 1921 and 1922 and growing misery as real income for the society dropped sharply in 1923.

The German Social Democrats and the bourgeois left did indeed suggest alternative fiscal policies between 1919 and 1923. The Catholic Centre leader, Matthias Erzberger, then Social Democratic ministers and advisors, proposed mild capital levies. But even when taxes were theoretically stiffened, as with Erzberger's reforms of 1919–20 and the 'tax compromise' of 1922, they came to nought because payment was stipulated in rapidly depreciating paper marks. Instead of winning needed fiscal reform, working-class representatives won relative wage protection, though not without recurring losses of real income. And by the end of 1923 and early 1924, the stabilization crisis that brought winter unemployment to at least two million allowed industry to renegotiate with labour the terms of the social partnership that had been accepted five years earlier only under menace of revolution. The end of inflation meant the end of tacit union–industry partnership.

The Austrian inflation involved another collaboration of trade unions and entrepreneurs through a formalized index-wage scheme. In November 1919 the Social Democratic prime minister, Karl Renner, summoned employers and employees to an economic summit that accepted an indexation scheme to be worked into collective contracts and which provided bimonthly and later monthly wage adjustments. Such a compact was facilitated because Austrian industry was enjoying a surge of export demand. As elsewhere, unskilled workers kept their earnings closest to the 'peace parity'; skilled workers emerged relatively protected, while the Viennese middle classes suffered most drastically. By the end of 1921, in fact, the pace of depreciation taxed

21   Hans-Hermann Hartwich, *Arbeitsmarkt, Verbände und Staat 1918–1933* (Berlin: de Gruyter, 1967), 67, 102; Maier, *Recasting Bourgeois Europe*, 363–64, 445–50.

workers anew. As in Germany, prosperity was dissipated as the volume of money contracted and a credit crisis loomed. By October 1921, the Social Democrats declared themselves ready to cooperate with stabilization measures even at the price of ending their favoured food subsidies. Ending the subsidies, however, only briefly halted the inflation. By a round-robin of diplomatic negotiations that played on the Western powers' fear of Austria's disappearance as an independent state, Chancellor Ignaz Seipel finally extracted a stabilization loan from the League of Nations. The Geneva Protocols of October 1922 also pledged Austria to remove the government's financial measures from parliamentary scrutiny for two years. Seipel's stabilization thus cost the Austrian Social Democrats their latent coalition role, just as in Germany a year later stabilization was to be carried out at the cost of Social Democratic representation in the cabinet and the eight-hour day.[22]

Hyperinflation thus involved an implicit coalition of labour and industry at the expense of rentiers, professionals, the civil service and modest entrepreneurs. Industrialists with access to credit stood to profit greatly and industry in general could benefit by heavy demand. Labour avoided postwar lay-offs and preserved relative wage protection until the final months of the monetary collapse. The cost was intermittent lags in real income, harsh unemployment in the transition to stable currency and a sacrifice of collective political influence.[23] Inflation represented a second-best or perhaps maximin strategy of curtailing predictable losses in a situation where the preferred policy of stabilization at full employment appeared unavailable. For any social group the restraint needed to end the spiral of prices and wages seemed doomed to become just a unilateral and costly renunciation. Confidence that restraint would be fairly distributed disappeared, and

22 Charles A. Gulick, *Austria from Habsburg to Hitler*, 2 vols. (Berkeley and Los Angeles, University of California Press, 1948), I, 149–71; J. van Walré de Bordes, *The Austrian Crown: Its Depreciation and Stabilization* (London: P. S. King, 1924). Eduard März, *Austrian Banking and Financial Policy: Creditanstalt at a Turning Point, 1913–23*, Charles Kessler, trans. (London: Weidenfeld & Nicolson), 402–514.
23 Another cost hit the humbler elements of society – that of constant shopping and queueing. Sensitive observers of the Austrian inflation pointed out the sacrifice of family time together because of frenetic shopping expeditions – a task that could be assigned in upper-class households. Twenty years later Kalecki emphasized this aspect of inequality as an argument for rationing in wartime Britain. See Ilse Arlt, "Der Einzelhaushalt," in Julius Bunzel, ed., *Geldentwertung und Stabilisierung in ihren Einflüssen auf die soziale Entwicklung in Osterreich. Schriften des Vereins für Sozialpolitik*, 169 (1925); and Michael Kalecki, "Three Ways to Full Employment," in Oxford University Institute of Statistics, *Studies in War Economics* (Oxford: Basil Blackwell, 1947).

thus in a sense the true cost of inflation came to involve the very premises of civil society.

This lesson should be sobering today for those who contend that setting rigid monetary targets can make unions police their own wage demands by making unemployment the logical price of excessive claims. Most workers, of course, will evade the penalty for claiming too much but will surely pay one if they claim too little.

Latin inflation

The second class of monetary depreciation comprises severe cases of what is usually called double-digit inflation but can range easily up to 100 per cent and sometimes even to several hundred per cent per annum. For these I have chosen the designation of 'Latin inflation', for salient experiences have included France in the mid-1920s, France again and Italy in the years after World War II and over more protracted periods, Brazil, Argentina, Chile and other Latin American countries. Inflation rates in Latin America in the last few years have ranged up to 700 per cent. Britain in the 1970s and Israel also merit inclusion in terms of percentage range, even if not of ethnic designation.

It would be wrong to impose a false unity on these inflationary experiences. Nonetheless, a certain logic of social disaggregation does seem to mark them all. South American inflations are often described as the 'structural' outcome of societies afflicted with concentrated, quasi-feudal distributions of resources while undergoing rapid development. But as Hirschmann has pointed out, since inflation can be conceived of as a failure of production to respond to expectations, almost any social or economic impediment can be invoked as a cause of structural inflation.[24] Just this perspective, though, suggests a relationship to the heavy inflationary pressures in the developed European economies. The emergence of powerful group interests with divergent policy priorities characterizes all the Latin cases. Of course, this disaggregation of interests marks hyperinflation as well. What, then, distinguishes the politics of Latin inflation from hyperinflation?

First, in Latin inflation the *de facto* coalition of producers is less important. The latent collaboration of labour and industry does not coalesce, and the socio-economic cleavage tends to run horizontally between classes and not sectorally, uniting unions and management.

Second, the relationship to the international economy is also a different one in the case of Latin inflation, embodying elements of de-

---

24   Albert O. Hirschman, *Journeys Toward Progress* (New York: Twentieth Century Fund, 1963), 213–16; Denis Lambert, *Les inflations suds-américaines* (Paris, 1959), 43 ff.

pendence more than defiance. Hyperinflation can gather momentum from the widespread conviction among all classes that a stable fiscal system will primarily benefit foreign exploiters, such as Germany's victors seeking reparations after World War I, or perhaps Hungary's Soviet occupiers in 1945–6. Latin inflations are the expression less of monetary unilateralism than of relative weakness. In Germany and Austria currency depreciation against the dollar was accepted almost fatalistically as a condition for maintaining high export demand and relative social peace. In Latin America devaluation has generally accompanied conservative efforts at stabilization designed to curb wage advances and to redress the balance of payments in order to secure foreign capital. (The Brazilian resort to continual incremental devaluation is more a unilateral recourse but rests simultaneously upon thorough price indexation and in any case was a relatively late response to inflationary difficulties.) Devaluation, however, has in turn triggered new bouts of inflation led by higher import prices. Thus the susceptible economies have oscillated between phases of high employment, leading to international deficits and shortages of foreign capital, and efforts at stabilization, including currency devaluations that just renew inflation. Argentina's stop–go cycles in the 1950s were an exaggerated version of Britain's similar difficulties.[25]

The Latin cases suggest that middle-class or entrepreneurial elements wager more on foreign capital than upon a continuing high-growth, high-wage industrial economy. Their strategy often reflects economic weaknesses and domestic political strength simultaneously, whereas the German entrepreneurial strategy in the hyperinflation corresponded to underlying economic strength but post-revolutionary political weakness. Fearing a decisive rupture with labour, German

---

25 Carlos F. Diaz-Alejandro, *Essays on the Economic History of the Argentine Republic* (New Haven: Yale University Press, 1970), 351, 90; Felipe Pazos, *Chronic Inflation in Latin America* (New York: Praeger, 1972); R. C. Vogel, "The Dynamics of Inflation in Latin America," *American Economic Review*, 64 (1974); Thomas Skidmore, "The Politics of Economic Stabilization in Postwar Latin America," in James Malloy, ed., *Authoritarianism and Corporatism in Latin America* (Pittsburgh, Penn.: University of Pittsburgh Press, 1976). See also Albert Fishlow, "Some Reflections on Post-1964 Economic Policy," in Alfred Stepan, ed., *Authoritarian Brazil* (New Haven: Yale University Press, 1972); and John R. Wells, "Brazil and the Post-1973 Crisis in the International Economy," and other essays (including the editors' own "Comparative Perspective") in Rosemary Thorp and Laurence Whitehead, eds., *Inflation and Stabilization in Latin America*" (London: Macmillan, 1979); and Antonio C. Lemgruber, "Inflation in Brazil," in Lawrence B. Krause and Walter S. Salant, eds., *Worldwide Inflation: Theory and Recent Experience* (Washington, D.C.: Brookings Institution, 1977). Further citations in Albert O. Hirschman's "Reflections on the Latin American Experience," in Leon Lindberg and Charles S. Maier, eds., *The Politics of Inflation and Economic Stagnation* (Washington, D.C.: Brookings Institution, 1985), 53–77.

industry could rely upon the demand for their advantageously-priced manufactures or industrial semi-finished products. In contrast, the export capability of most countries vulnerable to Latin inflation has consisted primarily of price-inelastic minerals or commodities subject to great price oscillations and loss of revenue; or it has involved services ranging from tourism to Britain's banking. The lesser-developed of the Latin cases reveal the familiar economic dualism that tends to integrate an export-oriented élite into the investing circles of the more economically powerful nations while leaving large backwaters of poverty. The relative factor constraint for the Latin cases is capital, not labour. In fact, once capital became the major constraint in the later stages of the German hyperinflation, the tactic of monetary defiance had to be abandoned.

In a further distinction from the cases of hyperinflation, while the countries afflicted with Latin inflation embark upon stabilization efforts at lower threshholds of depreciation, their attempts seem less likely to stick. Either a political leadership friendly to labour has secured working-class acquiescence in stabilization – Peron in 1952–3; Britain 1976 – or conservatives have resorted to confrontation (army takeovers in Latin America, the Industrial Relations Act in Britain), but the upshot is often just to unleash a new cycle of inflation. Class divisiveness may spare these societies hyperinflation but it seems to condemn them to longer or recurrent periods of double-digit price increases.

The class antagonisms in the Latin cases are often part and parcel of the structural handicaps to real growth: persistent unemployment due to traditional sectors (Italy, Argentina, Brazil, even Britain), or premature expansion of the service class and large bureaucracies (Chile, Uruguay, perhaps Italy). Sometimes the inflationary process itself can help to mobilize savings and to tax incomes on behalf of real development. Brazilian growth seems to have been invigorated by heady price rises in the 1960s, and the French inflation of the mid-1920s may have accelerated reconstruction and stimulated new investment. But the inflation often lingers after growth flags and becomes counterproductive.

Springing as it does from a deeply divided society, Latin inflation can be generated by either of the opposed dichotomous class groupings. In Peronist Argentina, inflation accompanied a redistributive effort on behalf of the urban working-class migrants. But just as significantly a broad defensive reaction on the part of bourgeois holders of money and bonds often plays an important role. Thus middle-class elements end up acting less in their capacity as producers than as savers. In the face of class stalemates, the *de facto* coalition of labour and industry that acquiesces in hyperinflation does not become influential. Therefore, if hyperinflation rests upon a precarious social compact among producers, Latin inflation in Europe has often incorporated the decentralized and sometimes self-defeating choices of savers and rentiers. In seeking to protect their portfolios, middle-class interests, however, often aggravate the very levies they are seeking to avoid.

The French inflation of 1924 to 1926 revealed the capacity of a broad middle-class community to prevent stabilization under the rules of the monetary game. These precluded exchange controls and gave a politicized central bank week-to-week control over advances to the government. From 1919 to 1924 a conservative centrist parliamentary coalition sanctioned massive credits for reconstruction, which the bourgeois public largely underwrote by subscribing to government bonds. Debt charges accumulating since 1914, however, threw the budget into prolonged deficit. The National Assembly disguised rather than defrayed the deficit by establishing a 'recoverable' budget that would supposedly be covered by German reparations. The governments of the centre and right, which bequeathed an unacknowledged inflationary fiscal policy, were succeeded by those of left and centre, who moved in with inconsistent financial remedies and internal political divisions. The Socialists and left wing of the Radical Socialists around Edouard Herriot advocated a tax on capital of 10 to 12 per cent to be collected over several years. This proposal alienated the votes of the moderates in their own electoral cartel and thus fell short of a majority. The Cartel moderates were willing instead to seek the votes of the conservative opposition to impose further indirect taxes and restore 'confidence' in capital, which amounted to relaxing the controls designed to curtail tax evasion.[26]

The controversies over fiscal policy proved all the more debilitating to the left because of the trumps that monetary policy gave to conservatives. Left as well as right accepted the principle that there should be legal ceilings on the bank notes in circulation and on the advances of the Bank of France to the state. At the same time, however, the bourgeois public held directly large quantities of short-term bonds. When, alarmed by plans for a capital levy, they failed to renew these

26 See David Goldey, "The Disintegration of the Cartel des Gauches and the Politics of French Government Finance" (Diss. Oxford, 1964); also Stephen A. Schuker, *The End of French Predominance in Europe: The Financial Crisis of 1924 and the Negotiation of the Dawes Plan* (Chapel Hill: University of North Carolina Press, 1976); and Jean-Noël Jeanneney, *Francois de Wendel en République. L'argent et le pouvoir, 1914–1940* (Paris: Seuil, 1976), 178–318; and Jeanneney, *Leçon d'histoire pour une gauche au pouvoir. La faillite du Cartel (1924–1926)* (Paris: Seuil, 1977).

bills, the Treasury had to draw upon occult Bank of France advances to redeem the volatile public debt, disguising the overdrafts by covering them weekly with overnight private bank loans. The left thus became hostage both to distrustful private banks as well as to the hostile central bank, even while it was unwilling to cease frightening bondholders with talk of 'radical taxes.'

With the final exposure of the concealed overdrafts the Cartel collapsed, to be succeeded by a parade of ministries which introduced alternately left and right financial expedients. Only after dramatic political crises and flights from the franc did Raymond Poincaré form a ministry of national unity in July 1926, which achieved stabilization with no further technical innovations. By finally demonstrating the political exhaustion of the left wing of the Radical Socialists and persuading Herriot to join his cabinet, Poincaré generated the confidence that proved so crucial in the presence of the diffuse pattern of middle-class thrift, the mass of short-term bonds, and the leverage of the Bank of France.[27]

Inflation probably imposed a burden just as high as the mild capital levy suggested by Blum and Herriot would have done. Fixed-income patrimonies and deposits stood at about half their 1913 value by 1929 (allowing both for appreciation through interest and the toll taken by inflation). An alternative calculation is that a composite portfolio of money savings, bonds and shares would have been producing perhaps 30 per cent less real revenue by the time the franc was stabilized than two years earlier when the centre left government came to power. (Of course, equity returns would then have grown again.) The Blum–Herriot capital levy would actually have been collected as a twelve-year surtax on income from assets of perhaps 20 per cent per year (assuming a 5 per cent yield on capital).

Post-World War II experiences in France and Italy revealed a similar middle-class tendency to accept the indirect taxation of inflation rather than confront the direct levies needed to avoid it. In 1945 de Gaulle rejected the currency reform proposed by Mendés-France and backed away from any radical amputation of private balances.[28] The French

27 Maier, *Recasting Bourgeois Europe*, 494–507; Emile Moreau, *Souvenirs d'un gouverneur de la Banque de France* (Paris: Génin, 1954).

28 Jean Bouvier, "Sur la politique économique en 1944–1946," *La Libération de la France: Actes du Colloque . . . octobre 1974* (Paris, 1976), 835–56; Maurice Parodi, *L'Économie et la société française de 1945 à 1970* (Paris: A. Colin, 1971), 66–78; J. P. Mockers, *L'inflation en France 1945–1975* (Paris: Cujas, 1976); A. J. Brown, *The Great Inflation, 1939–1951* (Oxford: Oxford University Press, 1955); Fritz Grotius, "Die europäischen Geldreformen nach dem 2. Weltkrieg," *Weltwirtschaftliches Archiv*, 63 (1949: II): 106–52, 276–325; J. C. Gurley, "Excess Liquidity and European Monetary Reforms," *American Economic Review*, 43 (1953): 76–100; L. H. Dupriez, *Monetary Reconstruction in Belgium* (New York: King's Crown Press, 1947).

price index rose from 285 in 1944 (1938 = 100) to 1817 in 1949, stimulated by state deficits and a four-fold expansion of bank reserves through 1946–7. In Italy, the 1945 price index stood already at 16 times that of 1938 and before stabilization at the end of 1947 had climbed to 49 (retail) and 55 (wholesale) times 1938 levels. Government borrowing rose from 11 billion lire in 1938 to 152 billion for the year 1943 and 572 billion for 1944–5. At the same time the central bank made liberal credits available to the banking system as a whole, and reserves at the Bank of Italy rose from less than half a billion lire in 1938 to 1920 billion in 1945. These monetary pressures occurred, moreover, in societies whose 1945 real national income was reduced to about 50 per cent of the prewar level.[29]

Removal of the Communists from the governing coalition in 1947, the division of the labour movement, and Washington's declaration of intent to provide 'Marshall Plan' funds that would ease the constant external pressure against the lira allowed a stabilization programme to be launched by the successive governors of the Bank of Italy, Luigi Einaudi and Donato Menichella. This effort involved principally the severe restriction of central bank credits. Rome, like Paris, rejected the blocking of accounts and direct levies that other continental countries such as Belgium adopted. Nor would either emulate the tax severity imposed in Britain. Italy resorted to a contractionary monetary policy rather than a severe fiscal policy. The result included a recession that bottled up labour in the South and effectively passed much of the burden of stabilization to the popular classes.[30]

Stabilization involved a break with the Communists over wage policy. The post-Liberation governments had not been prepared to clamp down on wages. Instead the Communist labour leadership initially pledged an effort at full production and won general wage indexation (a provision they defended until it was largely dismantled in the mid-1980s). As cost-of-living adjustments dwarfed the base-pay differentials, an inflationary levelling of wages took place. This was a development Communist unions favoured and over which they separated from the non-Communists during the 1950s.

When stabilization came in France it was, similarly, under the conservative leadership of Antoine Pinay. The end of the Resistance-born

29   George H. Hildebrand, *Growth and Structure in the Economy of Modern Italy* (Cambridge, Mass.: Harvard University Press, 1965), chaps. 2, 8.
30   Marcello De Cecco, "Sulla politica di stabilizzazione del 1947," *Saggi di politica monetaria* (Milan: Giuffré, 1968); Bruno Foa, *Monetary Reconstruction in Italy* (New York: King's Crown Press, 1949); European Cooperation Administration, *Country Study (Italy)* (Washington: USGPO, 1950); Ugo Ruffolo, "La Linea Einaudi," *Storia Contemporanea*, 5 (1974); Piero Barucci, "La politica economica internazionale e le scelte di politica economica dell'Italia," *Rassegna Economica*, 37 (1973).

coalitions with the Communists was probably a prerequisite for anti-inflationary efforts. Nevertheless, even as both French and Italian governments shifted to the centre or right, they could make no drastic attempt to cut back into enlarged wage shares (especially when the Korean war and rearmament created new scarcities and inflationary pressure). The governments of the 1950s in Europe ruled out cooperation with the Communists but launched no bourgeois or business counter-revolution. Thus the political logic of the third major type of inflation we encounter: the persistent incremental price rises of the 1950s and 1960s.

Creeping inflation

The prerequisite for creeping inflation was the remarkable record of economic growth that avoided a harsh distributional conflict between classes. By the early 1950s, bottled-up demand had spent itself; capital building had brought national incomes back to and beyond 1938 levels; international terms of trade began a long-term shift in favour of commodity importers. Marshall Plan assistance eased foreign-exchange constraints; at the same time, United States enthusiasm for currency convertibility helped maintain fiscal and monetary discipline.

The related factor behind the creeping inflation was the balance of social forces. The 1944–49/51 inflation had been a unique legacy of wartime destruction. But the way in which the governments of post-war Europe had sought to allocate the losses reflected their broad political composition and the coalitions that emerged from the Liberation: wage increases for the working class, tax avoidance for the middle classes, relatively easy credit for business. Even after the Catholic–Communist–Socialist coalitions fractured, the possibilities of real growth and the felt need to prevent a renewed polarization of the working class precluded any drastic renegotiation of the postwar social bargain. Growth, pursued in an effort to reconcile all important social groups, became the objective of postwar governments.

Some differences persisted between coalitions of the centre–right and those of the centre–left. The former stressed capital formation and currency stability whereas the latter emphasized using the new wealth to pay for social insurance schemes. But these were differences of degree. Labour made no serious effort to claim a radically larger allotment of national income, and, in an implicit social contract, Conservative or Christian Democratic ministers made no effort to contest full-employment targets, even if keeping demand buoyant involved a persistent upward price trend. (Only when balance-of-payment concerns intervened did this commitment flag.)

In retrospect this era of creeping inflation may appear unique and based upon transitory advantages. The significant increase in agricultural productivity and the continuing exodus from the farms allowed a funnelling of resources to industry and services. The terms of trade favoured food and commodity importers, i.e. Europeans, at the expense of their suppliers. Old and new middle classes – employees, small entrepreneurs, bureaucrats – now pressed their own claims effectively through interest-group bargaining. They did not resort to right-radical protest to the same degree as in interwar Europe. The absence of a fascist revival on any significant scale meant in turn that no major ideological attack was levelled against the class collaboration that was occurring.

The international constellation also made its contribution. Thanks in part to the Cold War, the United States proved willing to finance Europe's deficit on current account well into the 1950s if not longer. The Cold War also led to decisions to encourage the reconstruction of Germany and Japan as productive centres for the non-Communist world in general. For many complex reasons, workers in both countries exhibited exemplary wage restraint. Success confirmed its own rewards, as persistent growth focused political dispute less upon the division of the national income than the proper uses of the expected increments. And in turn this level of bargaining did not open larger issues about what groups enjoyed basic power or real legitimacy.

The question for the contemporary observer is whether these conditions were exceptional or potentially durable. The relapse into double-digit inflation after 1973 had its proximate origins in contingent developments: the Vietnamese war with its increase in American deficit financing and its stimulus to international liquidity, and also new price rises in petroleum and food. But the pressures may be more long term. The era of rapid agricultural dividends may be closing; and as growth becomes problematic, disputes over the allocation of national income raise ugly confrontations or require increased dosages of inflation. The very structures of policy making may also heighten vulnerability. The growing role of quasi-independent planning agencies and authorities helped depoliticize distributional conflicts after 1945, but they reinforced a trend in which interests win representation not merely in the legislature, but in the executive agencies of the state. The *de facto* corporatism that eases economic bargaining also facilitates inflation.

Redistribution and coalition

We have sought hitherto to specify deductively the coalitions that help to generate inflation. This essay presupposes that there exist or are called into being relatively coherent interests which foresee (sometimes incorrectly) different outcomes for different fiscal and monetary policies. No group is likely to be an advocate of inflation absolutely; rather it is the costs of stabilization that will seem more or less acceptable.

Even this assumption, however, is problematic. The stakes of inflation are far more ambiguous than they are often presented as being. Consider some of the obvious difficulties. First, individual interests may not mesh with class interests; the worker may find his own real resources declining even while his class increases its share of national income due to higher employment of previously idle labour. Alternatively his individual wages may decline in real terms but his family income may jump as his wife seeks and finds employment. Second, inflation acts consistently only upon types of income and wealth (or economic roles), not upon real individuals. It is clearly better to be a debtor than a creditor when the value of money is eroding, but most members of the middle classes are both. If the state effectively repudiates a quota of the public debt, it likewise spares taxpayers the burden of servicing it. Third, changes in subjective welfare are hard to sort out. Each individual will certainly feel whether he is better or worse off than he was formerly. But will he also take account of the new comparative rankings of salaries across occupational lines? The formerly well-paid civil servant may feel terribly humbled in terms of his old salary but even more bitter about how close he now ranks with the skilled manual labourer. Conversely the poor charwoman may be closer to her boss but thrown from 'decent' poverty into real impoverishment. And even if the community might choose to trade a degree of wealth for an increment of equality, it may never be fully aware of the equality it purchases; for a few well-publicized cases of inflation profiteering will dominate the public consciousness. Finally, the society as a whole may be sufficiently risk-averse that even equal chances of gains or losses would not compensate for the unpleasant wager entailed.

Do these considerations mean that we must abandon efforts at a political sociology of inflation? No, but they impose great caution about imputing simple correspondence between interests and political behaviour, especially since interests are often far from clear. A further complication emerges from the fact that rational behaviour early in an inflationary surge may prove less rational later, especially if one passes to a much higher rate of inflation. (Conversely, as is to be explained below, some groups will be vulnerable both during inflation and stabilization.)

Inflation-sheltered assets are by definition more secure than monetary holdings, but such assets become rarer, more expensive and more exposed. What seems a Noah's Ark at the outset of inflation can become a millstone by the end. Rampant inflation, such as the German one, illustrates that few assets are inflation-proof. Ownership of real property, especially if it was mortgaged, seemed a windfall, unless the property was an apartment building subject to the widespread imposition of rent control. In the wake of World War I, landlords in France as well as Germany were locked into property ownership that was more costly than rewarding. On the other hand, this often helped elderly or other middle-class lodgers. Similarly many public services including transportation and higher education became subsidized. The small businessman seemed well-off at the beginning of the inflation and many middle-class investors sunk savings into enterprises. But by the later stages of hyperinflation such proprietors found themselves squeezed by the shortage of credit and working capital, especially as replenishing inventories became ever more costly. Consequently, without knowing when in the inflationary cycle an enterprise was capitalized, it was difficult to determine its value as a shelter.[31]

The effect on wages and salaries is also less simple to determine than initially appears. In Germany real wages periodically fell behind and then spurted forward when the government published new cost-of-living indices and adjustments followed. Organized workers in major industries may have seen their real wages erode as badly in late 1922, when index revisions lagged, as they did at the height of the inflation in the summer and fall of 1923.[32] In Vienna, however, real wages oscillated less but fell behind at the height of the hyperinflation.

Although trade unions may secure relative protection for their memberships (and thereby intensify inflation), there may be greater gains for unorganized workers if inflation accompanies a boom thereby creating new jobs and bidding up low wages. In Austria and Germany the fate of civil-service salaries depended upon rank; the real income of the higher grades fell perhaps 70 per cent, but minor clerks were cut much less. On the other hand, the conditions of employment seemed so secure that the bureaucracy remained a favoured occupational choice.[33] Levelling of earnings within each occupational

31 Franz Eulenburg, "Die sozialen Wirkungen der Währungverhältnisse," *Jahrbücher für Nationalökonomie und Statistik*, 122 (1924); Bresciani-Turroni, *The German Inflation*, chaps. 5, 8.
32 Bresciani-Turroni, *The German Inflation*, 308–313.
33 Karl Elster, *Von der Mark zur Reichsmark* (Jena: G. Fischer, 1928), 444–49; Eulenberg, "Die sozialen Wirkungen," 775.

group, the shrinking of differentials between the less and more qualified, seems to be universal in periods of increasing inflation. Data from different countries and periods suggest the greater proportional vulnerability of higher salaries even when conscious redistribution is unintended.[34] On the other hand, the tendency towards equalization – at least when the tempo of inflation is not too drastic – can be offset by differential relative price increases. Researchers have cited British and American experiences where the outlays for poorer families, with their greater share devoted to necessities, have risen more steeply than the consumption costs of wealthier households.[35] In wartime emergencies, when rent and food prices are controlled, however, the poor may benefit relatively on the price as well as the earnings side. Even if we assume that income-equalizing tendencies have prevailed in twentieth-century inflation, this still might not determine political (or socio-economic) outcomes in its own right. An increase in equality that accompanies a growing national product yields different results from equalization in a stumbling economy. In the former case, a vigorous demand for labour bids up the wages of the unskilled without undue penalties for the more established; while in the latter more painful case, the exposed higher-income positions are reduced more dramatically.

There are other suggestions that inflation promotes a levelling of incomes, but the political consequences are far from clear. Studies of the United States since World War II have suggested that the inflationary trends have transferred income shares to wages and salaries at the expense of unincorporated businesses, farms, rents and net corporate profits.[36] These redistributions thus reinforce the longer-term transformations that Kuznets has pulled together for the period from the late nineteenth century, reflecting the concentration of eco-

---

34 William O. Ogburn and William Jaffe, *The Economic Development of Postwar France* (New York: Columbia University Press, 1927), 164; Guy Routh, *Occupation and Pay in Great Britain, 1906–1960* (Cambridge: Cambridge University Press, 1965), 108 ff.; Hildebrand, *Growth and Structure,* 194 ff. See the agnostic conclusion by David Piachaud about redistributive effects in general, "Inflation and Income Distribution," in Fred Hirsch and John H. Goldthorpe, eds., *The Political Economy of Inflation* (London: Martin Robertson; Cambridge, Mass.: Harvard University Press, 1976) 88–116.

35 D. Seers, *Changes in the Cost-of-Living and the Distribution of Income since 1938* (Oxford: Basil Blackwell, 1949); J. A. Brittain, "Some Neglected Features of Britain's Economic Levelling, *American Economic Review,* 50 (1960); J. Muellbauer, "Prices and Inequality: The United Kingdom Experience," *Economic Journal,* 84 (1974); Jeffrey Williamson, "American Prices and Urban Inequality since 1820," *Journal of Economic History,* 36 (1976); and Williamson, "The Sources of American Inequality, 1896–1948," *Review of Economics and Statistics,* 58 (1976); also Piachaud, "Inflation and Inequality."

36 G. L. Bach and James Stephenson, "Inflation and the Redistribution of Wealth," *Review of Economics and Statistics,* 56 (1974).

nomic units and the move out of agriculture.[37] The former major regressive toll of inflation – the erosion of pensions – is now being transformed as social security pensions are increasingly inflation-proofed, while private-sector pensions lag behind. At the same time, tax schedules for nominal income strongly reinforce progressivity under double-digit inflation. Consequently, income effects in the last few years, whether in the United States or more drastically in Britain, have probably been equalitarian. The political implications, however, are far from clear-cut. Levelling has few advocates when GNP falters in its upward course or falls. And a few spectacular speculative windfalls may convey to the public a sense that inequality is rifer and more pernicious, even if aggregate income differences are actually diminishing.

Changes in wealth and assets may be even harder to sort out during the course of inflation. The debates over accounting procedures illustrate the complexity of the issue. To compare the outcomes upon families in the 1920s I have sought to measure the inheritances of the late 1920s in Germany and France against those of 1913. French patrimonies were approximately halved in real terms, and the larger the estate the greater the percentage sacrifice. German wills were apparently cut down to less than two fifths real value. The Germans virtually wrote off their entire public debt and revalued old corporate bonds, mortgages, bank accounts and life insurance policies up to only a 25 per cent maximum. The brunt of the loss may have been borne, however, by the more humble legatees, not the largest. All the more reason for a middle-class reaction.[38]

---

37 Simon Kuznets, "Quantitative Aspects of the Economic Growth of Nations, IV. Distribution of National Income by Factor Shares," *Economic Development and Cultural Change*, 7, 3, part ii (1959): 45, 86 ff.
38 Data from *Bulletin de la Statistique Générale et du Service d'Observation des Prix*, XIX, f. 2 (Jan.–Mar. 1930), pp. 206–7, and xx, f. 3 (April–June, 1931), 390–1 show the following:

Mean value of inheritance in France (pre-tax; per estate)			
	1913	1929	1929/1913
Current value	15,342	40,900	2.67
Retail-price indexed francs	15,342	7,027	0.46
Mean value of inheritances over Fr. 50,000			
Current value	Fr. 243,634	Fr. 258,706	1.06
Retail-price indexed francs	243,634	44,451	0.18

The price indices are from Alfred Sauvy, *Histoire économique de la France entre les deux guerres*, vol. 1, (Paris: Fayard, 1963), annèxe. Note the greater compression of the wealthier estates.

The role of the corporation adds to the difficulty of calculating redistribution. It has been estimated for the United States that perhaps $500,000 million had been transferred from creditors to debtors in the twenty-five years after World War II, largely at the expense of households and to the benefit of business and government.[39] These long-term transfers reflected the lowering of corporate and national indebtedness in real terms. The incidence in terms of individuals and families, however, is hard to ascertain. Individuals might lose on corporate bonds, but their stock portfolios should have risen as corporate indebtedness was reduced, and their tax bills should have been relatively lighter as government debt service became cheaper.

It is just as hard to ascertain the direct effect of inflation on share prices. While investors may initially bid up equity prices, they learned both in Britain and the United States in 1973–5 that shares could not easily keep up with double-digit inflation. Developments in the German hyperinflation might have provided a forewarning. Share prices in Germany tended to follow the dollar exchange until late 1921 largely as a hedge against inflation. Corporate profits seem to have dropped to about 30 per cent of 1913, although this was disguised by inadequate valuation of depreciation. Nonetheless, firms could cut back dividends and add to their reserves as well as seek their own inflation-proof assets through mergers, acquisition and the general process of vertical integration. By 1922, however, share prices could no longer keep up with depreciation, and in October they represented less than 3 per cent of the 1913 values. The assets of the Daimler works, according to the bourse, were worth only 327 of their own automobiles. By late 1922 the growing liquidity shortage precluded investment in the mar-

---

For Germany we have comparisons only of the legacies cousins of more distant relatives inherited in 1928 v. those of 1908–13. The number of registered inheritances in 1928 was 16.4 per cent of 1908–13; the amount of bequeathed property involved was 22.9 per cent of the earlier period. The number of inheritances below RM 10,000 was only 15.5 per cent of the equivalent in the ealier period, although the individual legacies were of almost 50 per cent higher value. The number of inheritances above RM 10,000 remained between 21 and 26 per cent of the earlier period (save for the inheritances to distant relatives of over RM 1,000,000 – down to 17 per cent). Humbler legacies, however, may have escaped registration because they were concentrated in immediate family members, so the results are indeterminate. See *Statistik des deutschen Reichs*, Bd. 276 (Berlin, 1930); *Die deutsche Erbschaftsbesteuerung vor und nach dem Krieg*. Remember, what these figures measure is the cost of war and reconstruction. Inflation represented a way of allocating that cost, not the cost *per se*.

39 Bach and Stephenson, "Inflation and the Redistribution of Wealth," 12; cf. J. J. Carré, P. Dubois, and E. Malinvaud, *La croissance francaise* (Paris: Seuil, 1972), 362–70.

ket. Foreigners were dissuaded from takeover bids by the fact that new shares carried no voting rights. However, with the collapse of the 'support action' of February to April 1923 and Berlin's ever more massive recourse to the printing press, investors returned to the bourse. The parity of shares against gold marks (1913 = 100) rose from 5.24 in January to 16 in July, and as gold-mark accounting was instituted more broadly from July share prices rose even faster to reach 40 (even 120 when the mark was held artificially high for a few weeks) and to end the year, after stabilization, at 27.[40]

Although Wall Street tended to ignore the lesson during the palmy 1960s, it learned again with a vengeance during the inflation of the mid-1970s that share prices cannot easily provide shelter against persistent inflation. The capital base of companies becomes eroded through inventory profits and inadequate depreciation. Of course, share prices become a reflection in part of the cost of holding alternative assets: relative shelter should matter more than intrinsic value. Corporation prosperity, on the other hand, may become divorced from share value and depend upon credit availability. In Germany, in Italy and France after World War II, in the United States until late 1975, access to credit was not seriously limited. The extent to which even high nominal interest rates will inhibit corporate borrowing will depend on how far the market anticipates inflation and on how the monetary authorities respond to it. Fearing a liquidity crisis, guardians of the central bank will often see the continued supply of business needs as vital; for each Einaudi there is a Havenstein – the director of the Reichsbank during the German inflation – who can argue that since advances to the state are so large, further credit to business hardly adds to inflationary pressures.

The cost, if 1975 America was an indication, may well have been at the expense of private housing and of credit availability for mortgages and smaller businesses that did not enjoy privileged relations with their banks. In this sense, inflation taxes households for the sake of corporate expansion. This transfer may help prevent a quick lapse into recession, for the deficiency of private consumption is compensated by vigorous business spending and investment. Office buildings may go up after housing starts to slow down. Ultimately, diminished household resources will dampen industrial expansion.

So long as the economy remains vigorous, however, a trade-off can be expected. If households subsidize corporations, those wage and salary earners tied in to the corporations are generally protected. The corporation may no longer reward its shareholders concomitantly, but

40 Bresciani-Turroni, *The Economics of Inflation,* 253–85.

it protects the strong unions and management. Hence there emerges an analogue to the effects of a wage price spiral at the expense of the rentier or small entrepreneur: credit availability and the delayed tightening of money differentially benefit those organized sectors – labour and management – affiliated with large-scale economic units.[41]

These results, however, do not necessarily produce clear-cut political alignments. As noted, inflation taxes economic roles in a society and not necessarily real people. If any major division emerges, it should, of course, separate those who enjoy relative inflation leverage and those who do not. Corporations, their executives, and strong unions (if not necessarily shareholders) should square off against the congeries of vulnerable middle-class proprietors, pensioners and savers. (Since pensioners are increasingly granted indexed benefits their vulnerability has recently been reduced.) One can envisage a coalition of filling-station owners, stenographers and insurance salesmen against the executives of Exxon and the United Auto Workers.

But if this latent coalition emerges under inflation, it rarely corresponds to available political alternatives. To use the jargon of the economists, there is a high search cost for alternative political organizations. Traditional occupational and class identification continues to play a major role in political outcomes.

The consequence of this political lag is often parliamentary incoherence. Any possible coalition, whether of the left or right, includes social groups with disparate interests. The left – whether in the 1924 Cartel des Gauches or the Democratic Party in the United States – includes strong unions and weaker white-collar workers as well as small businessmen. A conservative or Christian Democratic coalition includes entrepreneurs who enjoy relative inflation leverage and vulnerable petty bourgeois of the same social strata as those whom sentiment or anticlericalism or regional tradition places in the opposing camp.

The internal inconsistencies emerge most clearly during the politics of monetary stabilization, the fourth (negative) inflationary case to be considered here. Stabilization is not always welcomed, even by those groups hurt by inflation. The civil servant may find himself furloughed, as occurred in the German *Beamtenabbau* of the mid-1920s. The small proprietor may find himself deprived of credit and operating capital during the period of stringency; likewise the peasant may find that prices for his output have dropped drastically. If his mortgage has been lightened, new short-term operating credit has become cost-

41   Cf. Paolo Sylos-Labini, *Trade Unions, Inflation, and Productivity* (Lexington, Mass.: Saxon House, 1974).

ly. What is more, during hyperinflation or even Latin inflation, the aggrieved consumer/saver usually expects stabilization to bring about a recovery of the assets that inflation has eroded. Unless his society is willing to risk a grave depression and heavy tax burden, this expectation must be frustrated (as it was in both France and Germany during the mid-1920s). During the course of inflation it is the levies on real income that appear most preoccupying; the tax on savings is often concealed or believed less definitive. But after stabilization the levy on capital can be totted up. Moreover, any progressive income redistribution that might have taken place now ceases. Thus a direct government reduction or blocking of monetary assets, as carried out in Germany, Austria and Belgium after World War II, produces less resentment than the levy of inflation. Even if it is not a progressive tax, it is a more universal one.

Despite the difficulties, therefore, of accurately foreseeing gains and losses, there does seem to be a natural evolution to the political constellations that superintend inflation and stabilization: (i) workers concerned with high employment, (ii) that segment of entrepreneurs lured by export opportunities or speculative gains or able to exploit increased leverage, and (iii) middle-class constituents originally anxious to avoid heavier taxes, form a natural inflation-prone coalition. If the inflation originates in war finance, this coalition does not preclude conservative sponsorship. Since 1945, however, it has been more often characterized by the participation of the moderate left.

The third group above is especially volatile. When the levy of inflation itself becomes onerous and preoccupying, middle-class constituents revert to a more conservative coalition alongside less 'go-go' businessmen. Moderate and conservative leaders stress the protection of savings and the need for capital formation to compensate for the running down of assets that has characterized inflation. In 1974, as in the societies of the 1920s, business leaders could predict a necessary recession or crisis, what Caillaux termed the 'great penance' that must follow monetary debauch. The penance, however, has often been that of the working classes, which must suffer unemployment even if the real wages of those with jobs may actually increase.

While middle-class constituents may only slowly come to give priority to their stakes as savers and consumers (rather than producers), industry leaders previously acquiescent in inflation can join a stabilization coalition late but with more alacrity. They finally foresee a liquidity crisis being as likely to emerge on the inflationary path as on that of monetary contraction. Although it is difficult in an era of sticky wages, their costs can often be passed along to other sectors of the economy, sometimes by direct government credits. If real growth soon resumes, such a new coalition of (i) reunited business leaders and (ii) inflation-weary middle-class elements can successfully assemble around a programme of capital formation and the restraint of collective consumption.

But if prolonged recession results, or small proprietors get caught by a combination of credit stringency and tax increases, bewildered middle-class elements may turn again: now either to the left anew, or toward the radical right. Not inflation alone, but a harsh ending of inflation has provided the socio-economic ground for radical right-wing movements from the 1920s on. The first electoral success of the Nazis, and of other right-wingers, in 1924 drew in part upon the re-sentments of those who felt that their paper assets had been insuf-ficiently revalued after the inflation. And the subsequent mass vote for the party depended a great deal upon farmers who had gained relatively in the inflation (by the wiping out of mortgages) but who were hurt by credit and price squeezes after stabilization. More recently the Poujade movement rose to prominence in the wake of the first major post World War II stabilization program carried out in France.[42]

Inflation, growth and distribution

The emphasis on capital formation and the reduction of col-lective consumption has characterized conservative advocacy for a half-century or more. How many times have we heard the Delphic phrase that a country 'is living beyond its means'! What this lament amounts to is that a society is changing the ratio of capital formation to current consumption. The most noticeable way of proceeding is by refusing to curtail imports until compelled to by exchange-rate readjustment. Internally, this often signifies to conservatives that the wages and transfer bill of a modern society is growing faster than a normally glacial rate of change would warrant. Again, this is a question of per-spective. From one point of view, labour in Western Europe and North America has shown remarkable restraint in view of the enormous dif-ferentials of income that persist despite taxes and transfers.

Conservative proposals for indexation (in the 1970s) have arisen in part, I believe, from a sense that older arguments on behalf of capital formation and stable money have lost their force.[43] Why should con-servatives become more receptive to indexing? In Austria of the 1920s

---

42 Maier, *Recasting Bourgeois Europe*, 483–515; Parodi, *L'économie et la société francaise*, 77.

43 For specimens, Milton Friedman, *Monetary Correction* (London: Institute of Economic Affairs, 1974), and Friedman, "Using Escalators to Help Fight Inflation," *Fortune*, 80 (1974).

and Italy of the 1940s cost-of-living escalators reinforced the inflationary process. Supposed success in Brazil has been far from clear.[44]
Obviously, to index government bond returns or income tax calculations must be appealing. But wage indexation has also been proposed, perhaps because it seems to offer a way to restore the labour
restraint that many feel has disappeared. Indexation appeals when
'guidelines' or social compacts fail. Indexation can work, however,
only when labour (or corporations) accept their given share of the
national income as satisfactory. It will sufficiently persuade workers
to moderate claims only if they accept the productivity-linked concept
of wages. The assumption is that labour may accept this concept if
reassured that it need not constantly anticipate the next round of price
increases. The matter is more complicated when national income is
reduced by external forces, such as a deterioration in the terms of
trade. The basis of indexation then becomes crucial.[45] This complication
aside, indexation offers a chance once again to win a consensus on
growth as a surrogate for redistribution.

The concept of growth as a surrogate for redistribution appears, in
retrospect, as the great conservative idea of the last generation. By
conservative I do not mean militantly right-wing, for indeed wide
circles of social democracy and the left have implicitly embraced the
covenant it implies. Nonetheless, in the confrontation with Marxism
and socialism, conservatives had only three choices: an outworn insistence on the value of traditional élites and privileges, which had
little prospect for success under conditions of universal suffrage; or
a fascism requiring that all class rivalry must be submerged in the
search to aggrandize national authority and territory (which emerged
discredited by the war); or the non-zero-sum pursuit of economic
growth in the hope that this might make the older doctrines of class
conflict irrelevant. Inflation has played an important role in preserving
a broad consensus around the third concept; for when growth could
not keep up with expectations, inflation helped disguise the lag. But
beyond a certain rate, inflation cannot play this role as social lubricant
and instead aggravates the very distributional conflicts it helped as-
suage.

---

44 Albert Fishlow, "Indexing Brazilian Style: Inflation without Tears?" *Brookings Papers
on Economic Activity*, I, 1974; Lemgruber, "Inflation in Brazil"; and for more general
evaluations see Morris Goldstein, "Wage Indexation, Inflation, and the Labor Market," *IMF Staff Papers*, 22 (1975); Anne Romanis Braun, "Indexation of Wages and
Salaries in Developed Economies," *IMF Staff Papers*, 23 (1976).
45 See J. S. Flemming, "The Economic Explanation of Inflation," in Hirsch and Goldthorpe, eds., *The Political Economy of Inflation*, 13–36, for the effects of varying monetary adjustment schemes.

Thus inflation is integrally linked with the stability conditions of twentieth-century capitalism. Ultimately the society may have to resort to indexation; but at that point the left may well insist that income shares be not frozen, but made an issue of political determination. This will require explicit decisions on equality instead of *ad hoc* and covert ones. Will the result be a gain? Perhaps from the viewpoint of a rational social allocation of income and wealth. But whether it will assure political harmony or even civil peace is far from certain.

6

"Fictitious bonds . . . of wealth and law": on the theory and practice of interest representation

This essay was written for the first research project of the Joint Committee on Western Europe of the Social Sciences Research Council and the American Council of Learned Societies. It was published in Suzanne Berger, ed., *Organizing Interests in Western Europe* (Cambridge University Press, 1981), pp. 27–61. The objective was to survey the changing ways in which modern societies mediated among collective interests. The essay cited the ideological arguments that initially allowed particular "interests" to be seen as legitimate, and not just an expression of cabal or conspiracy. Then it traced the pressures under which parliamentary aggregation of interests in an era of mass suffrage, international economic rivalry, and an emerging labor movement might have to be supplemented by direct mediation among producer groups – the forerunner of what has become known as corporatism or neocorporatism. At the time the essay was drafted in the late 1970s, neocorporatist tendencies appeared to be advancing steadily throughout Western capitalist societies. In retrospect this trend can be partially understood as a response to the pervasive inflation that led policy makers and interest group representatives alike to search for ways of controlling the allocation of national income and political influence. Many of the social compacts then negotiated under government auspices proved ephemeral; and neocorporatism increasingly seems to have been one recourse among others for coping with the politics of distributive conflict. Thus the essay was correct, I believe, to hint that the balance between parliamentary and interest group representation might not follow a continuing trend, but could shift again. For a complementary discussion, not included here, which considered the origins of neocorporatist wage determination in particular, see Charles S. Maier, "Preconditions for Corporatism," in John H. Goldthorpe, ed., *Order and Conflict in Contemporary Capitalism* (Oxford: Clarendon Press, 1984), pp. 39–59.

In an important and suggestive essay written a decade and a half ago, Philippe Schmitter asked whether the twentieth century was still to be, as a European writer had proposed, the century of corporatism ("Still the Century of Corporatism?" *Review of Politics* 36 [1974]: 85–131). The answer through the 1970s, at least, was yes – but not only of corporatism. It has been a century of collective interest mediation; and corporatist recourses have served interest groups directly, authoritarian leaders, bureaucratic administrators, and democratic political parties. (Schmitter himself was later to differentiate more statist from more societal variants of corporatism. See "Modes of Interest Intermediation and Models of Societal Change in Western Europe," *Comparative Political Studies* 10 [1977]: 7–38.) The balance among these organizational forms has varied by country and epoch; this essay seeks to account for some of the major shifts. For democratic regimes I like to picture corporatist arrangements as the flying buttresses of a Gothic cathedral, of which the parliament and parties form choir and nave. The buttresses relieve the stress on the central pillars; without them the choir and nave might collapse. But the buttresses would never be conceived or built without the central structure. The major role of corporatist arrangements has been to settle competing claims among classes and interests that tended to overburden traditional institutions. Over a century these interests have included farmers and landlords facing long-term structural change; representatives of organized labor undergoing a long cycle of conflict, ascent, and decline; and business associations seeking to consolidate a periodically contested ascendancy. To what degree, however, corporatist forms of interest mediation will remain important in the last years of the century as the nature of collective interests evolves is an open question that I have already raised in the Introduction.

Introduction: The stages of representation

"The first requisite of a representative system is, that the representative body should represent the real public opinion of the nation," wrote Walter Bagehot one hundred and twenty years ago. "Nor is this so easy a matter as some imagine. There are nations which *have* no public opinion."[1] The statement was written to sound self-evident, but, in fact, representing "opinion" had not been considered the task of Parliament a century before Bagehot and it seems an antique aspiration a century after. In different ways, the eighteenth-century and the twentieth-century representative systems have assigned equal or

1   Walter Bagehot, "The History of the Unreformed Parliament and Its Lessons (1860)," in *Essays on Parliamentary Reform* (London: K. Paul, Trench, 1883), p. 125.

higher priority to speaking for interests, although in the eighteenth century the interests were rarely organized in a formal sense, whereas in the contemporary world they are highly structured.

Likewise for Bagehot, Parliament was the uncontested representative organ:

The accordance of the opinion of Parliament with that of the country is the principal condition for the performance by Parliament of its great function of ɹuling the country. This can only be secured by the continuance in Parliament of many members representing no special interest, bound down to state the ideas of no particular class, themselves not markedly exhibiting the characteristics of any particular *status*, but able to form a judgment of what is good for the country as freely and impartially as other educated men.[2]

The focus on Parliament, with its alleged function of aggregating the nation's best judgments on the public welfare, also has an outmoded ring. Not merely has Parliament always been an arena for the interests that Bagehot felt encroaching, but it has become reduced to only one such arena, if still the preeminent one. Parapolitical bargaining networks link trade-union confederations, associations of industrialists and farmers, physicians and public service employees with each other and with agencies of the state designed to control and encourage their activities. This chapter attempts to understand under what conditions the present system of political and economic transactions arose and functioned, hence, too, what circumstances might well limit its effectiveness.

The transactions of the "state" with the organized interests of "civil society" are not construed here as a complete alternative to parliamentary or territorially based representation, but as a functional supplement. In some circumstances this supplement plays an extensive, even dominant role, in other situations only a secondary one. These circumstances need to be specified. Analysis is further complicated because the representation of organized interests has sometimes involved the growth of new institutions, such as joint labor–management forums, or has deputized spokesmen for private associations with quasi-public functions and status (recall Blue Cross, the National Recovery Administration, continental Chambers of Commerce, or the East India Company). In other cases, representation of emerging in-

2   Walter Bagehot, "Parliamentary Reform (1859)," in *Essays on Parliamentary Reform*, p. 104. The corollary of the Bagehot view was that "opinion" was a lofty and stable discernment of community needs. For Burke, in contrast, "opinion" had signified the volatile electoral preference that a true representative often had to override. See Hanna Fenichel Pitkin, *The Concept of Representation* (Berkeley and Los Angeles: University of California Press, 1967), pp. 176, 205–6.

terests has proceeded by subtle transformation of older parliamentary parties or executive agencies so that they carry out new forms of brokerage (witness interwar ministries of commerce or labor, or late nineteenth-century conservative parties). Because this chapter considers the functions and tasks of interest representation and not merely the forms, both types of development require attention.

Institutions evolve in response to crisis or opportunity; hence the history of interest representation can be usefully organized in terms of successive challenges to parliamentary and parapolitical structures of representation (which, following increasingly common usage we will term "corporatist" here).[3] Hintze interpreted the rise of parliamentary representation as an outgrowth of the European system of estates.[4] It is just as revealing, however, to view the development as a response to the difficulties, in particular, which overtook the estatist system and not just as a general extension. In turn, the new interest groups and linkages between the state and economic life emerging in the late nineteenth century reflected an impatience with liberalism. They arose, that is, in response to the hesitation on the part of parliamentary notables or state bureaucrats to restricting the market's role in setting prices. The various European societies allowed far different scope for laissez-faire, but whatever the respective role allotted, it came under attack. If parliaments resisted infringing on the market,

3 The term increasingly used to summarize the linkage of public institutions and organized interests is "corporatism." For a recent clarifying discussion see Gerhard Lehmbruch, "Einige Entwicklungslinien und Probleme in der Korporatismus-Diskussion," unpublished paper prepared for the Arbeitskreis "Parteien-Parlamente-Wahlen" (Neuss: February 23–4, 1979); also Philippe Schmitter, "Modes of Interest Intermediation and Models of Societal Change in Western Europe," *Comparative Political Studies* 10(1) (1977):7–38. Schmitter's typology stresses the sources of corporatism; my own prior use of "corporatism" attempted to describe emerging tendencies (and not final structures) as of the 1920s. See Charles Maier, *Recasting Bourgeois Europe: Stabilization in France, Germany, and Italy in the Decade After World War I* (Princeton, N.J., Princeton University Press, 1975), pp. 9–15, 580–94. When I used the term "corporative pluralism" for the liberal states – cf. "Strukturen kapitalistischer Stabilität in den zwanziger Jahren," in *Organisierter Kapitalismus*, ed. Heinrich A. Winkler (Göttingen: Vandenhoeck und Ruprecht, 1974), pp. 195–213 – I was unaware of Stein Rokkan's prior usage in the chapter on Norway in *Political Oppositions in Western Democracies*, ed. Robert Dahl (New Haven: Yale University Press, 1966), pp. 105 ff.

4 Otto Hintze, "The Preconditions of Representative Government in the Context of World History" [1931], in *The Historical Essays of Otto Hintze*, ed. Felix Gilbert (New York: Oxford University Press, 1975), p. 353. On representative bodies see also Emile Lousse, "Assemblées d'états," in *L'Organisation corporative du Moyen Age à la fin de l'Ancien Régime: Etudes présentées à la Commission Internationale pour l'Histoire des Assemblées d'Etats*, Vol. 7 (Louvain: Bibliothèque de l'Université, 1943), pp. 231–66; and A. R. Myers, *Parliaments and Estates in Europe to 1789* (London: Thames and Hudson, 1975).

interest group mobilization could serve hard-pressed farmers and in-dustrialists, or ambitious political leaders seizing their causes. Yet be-tween an earlier age of estatist interests that waned during the course of the late eighteenth century and an era of "collective"[5] or interest group rivalry that arose toward the end of the nineteenth century lay an interval of relative parliamentary insulation from the needs and pleas of the marketplace. This era was the zenith of Bagehot's par-liament and of his informed public opinion; to borrow a suggestive, if overdrawn image: the liberal parenthesis.[6]

Of course the schema is too rigid and must do injustice to the variety of European historical experiences. Nor is one stage of representation really eliminated; instead, it is overlaid by the newer development. Parliaments have thrived while adapting to organized interest rep-resentation; the intensity of market capitalism has probably increased, even if the market is far more structured by organized interests and state agencies; the liberal parenthesis has not really been closed – nonetheless, there is transformation enough to make the typology a useful starting point. Thus the historical portion of this chapter will attempt to outline the transitions that first widened and then began to close the scope of both parliamentary liberalism and the liberal market. From the historical material it will seek to isolate some general propositions about the conditions under which different forms of in-terest representation function. It can fittingly conclude with scrutiny of the contemporary situation: a moment when parliamentary and corporatist institutions appear in difficulty simultaneously.

From interest to party: the legitimation of the partial good

The legitimacy of any political system requires that citizens feel ad-equately represented. In turn, the test of adequacy involves both out-comes and procedures. It is not surprising that systems of represen-tation should begin to lose legitimacy when results are chronically disappointing, when they fail to distribute the rewards of power or

---

5 The term "collective" was employed first by Albert V. Dicey, *Lectures upon the Relation Between Law and Public Opinion in England During the Nineteenth Century* (London: Macmillan, 1905) to describe the infringements of laissez-faire. In the corporatist sense used here the concept was taken up by Samuel Beer, *British Politics in the Collectivist Age*, rev. ed. (New York: Knopf, 1969).

6 I have borrowed the term "liberal parenthesis" from Alessandro Pizzorno. See also the description of an "era of parties" between an age of corporations and an age of professionally based groups (c. 1789–1889) in François Olivier-Martin, "Le déclin et la suppression des corps en France au XVIII siècle," in *L'Organisation corporative du Moyen Age à la fin de l'Ancien Régime*, Vol. 3 (Louvain: Bibliothèque de l'Université, 1937), p.163.

income anticipated in advance. But procedural criteria remain equally difficult to satisfy over the long run because of the lurking conflict between the representation of particular interests and any regime's commitment to pursue the general welfare. Interest groups, "private government," or "corporatist" trends have all been regarded with suspicion even when they have functioned effectively in allocating public benefits. This uneasiness is hardly novel. Viewed in historical perspective, all forms of corporate representation and party delegation have awakened distrust in their formative stages. Interest group representation just inherited the stigma attached to parties a century earlier. Parties had to overcome the suspicions raised by cabals and factions. The line between conspiracy and the legitimate representation of a partial interest remains a sensitive one. For most writers on politics the justification of any single group's claim to power or public resources remained pragmatic. Pluralist competition was sanctioned only as the price one paid for liberty. Liberalism, construed as a doctrine that stressed the emancipation of individual personality, may have a high ethical core; liberalism, construed as an accommodation of group rivalry, has been conceded (especially to labor) only piecemeal. (Between the Declaration of the Rights of Man and the 1884 French Law of Associations lay almost a century.) Much of today's uneasiness about "corporatism" just continues this longer term legacy of ambiguous acceptance.

The history of parties and interests is a complex one, intimately connected with the beginnings of a mercantile, "bourgeois" society in the late seventeenth and eighteenth centuries. As both J. A. W. Gunn and Albert Hirschman suggest, the idea of interest was refocused in the early modern era. From a concept referring to the utility of princes and states *(raison d'état)* it evolved into one evoking the advantages of subjects. This new "private sector" connotation originally awakened few concerns, for the alignment of particular interests with the public good was deemed theoretically and practically possible. The statesman, moreover, could exploit the interests of individuals and groups as a counterweight to invidious ambitions, vainglory, and other anticivic passions: Following interests meant acting rationally and predictably. Indeed the great distinction of nineteenth-century sociology between military societies dominated by warriors and priests and industrial societies, divested of aggressiveness and superstitious creeds, was adumbrated early on in the theory of interests.[7]

The ascendant concept of interest played a dual role in the political thinking of the eighteenth century. It promised a natural, even organic

7 J. A. W. Gunn, *Politics and the Public Interest in the Seventeenth Century* (London: Routledge and Kegan Paul, 1969); Albert O. Hirschman, *The Passions and the Interests* (Princeton, N.J.: Princeton University Press, 1977), pp. 32–42.

basis for governing wealthy modern societies; however, it also threatened corruption and factional manipulation. Like the classical types of government (rule by one man, by a few, or by the many), the new impulses of commerce and interest could bring about either beneficial or degenerate outcomes: humming trade or the South Sea Bubble, *doux commerce* or John Law.[8] Early eighteenth-century British writers such as Defoe and Davenant explained that the growth of commerce and the development of England's unique ability to muster public credit (hence to wage wars without the standing armies that elsewhere buttressed despotism) rested on sophisticated social covenants. Emphasis on the contractual bases for generating wealth undermined the earlier identification of civic virtue with yeoman landed property. Money itself, so Locke had argued, allowed wealth to be stored without decay and could thus justify unequal accumulation; in turn, government was erected to protect the holdings money allowed.[9] "Money has a younger sister," wrote Defoe. "Her Name in our Language is call'd CREDIT. . . . This is a coy Lass and wonderful chary of her self; yet a most necessary, useful, industrious Creature. . . ." Credit, he continued, depended not on a particular ministry, "but upon the Honour of the Publick Administration in *General*," and thus required and further nurtured social cohesion.[10]

On the other hand, outside Whig circles, money and credit remained problematic and subject to abuse ("See Britain sunk in lucre's sordid charms," Pope inveighed after the Bubble) – as they did for Montesquieu across the channel.[11] Nor were critics of a paper economy likely

8 For the ambiguities see J. G. A. Pocock, *The Machiavellian Moment: Florentine Political Thought and the Atlantic Republican Tradition* (Princeton, N.J.: Princeton University Press, 1975), pp. 426–7, 436–61; on *doux commerce*, cf. Hirschman, *Passions and Interests*, pp. 59–63; and compare Montesquieu *The Spirit of the Laws*, 1748, Chap. 20, trans. Thomas Nugent (New York: Hafner Publishing, 1949), with the *Persian Letters*, 1721, cxlii. For early United States: Ralph Lerner, "Commerce and Character: The Anglo-American as New-Model Man," *William and Mary Quarterly*, 3rd ser. 36(1) (1979):3–26.

9 John Locke, *The Second Treatise of Government* (New York: The Liberal Arts Press, 1952), Chap. 5, paragraphs 47–50, and 124, 134, where Locke argued inequality was "practicable without compact, only by putting a value on gold and silver"; however, "preservation" of property required institution of government. Cf. C. B. Macpherson, *The Political Theory of Possessive Individualism: Hobbes to Locke* (London: Oxford University Press, 1964), pp. 203–21; and on Locke's stand against legislative adjustment of monetary values (because bullion supposedly registered prior natural rights) see Joyce Oldham Appleby, "Locke, Liberalism, and the Natural Law of Money," *Past and Present* 71(May 1976):43–69.

10 Defoe's *Review* [1706] cited in Pocock, *Machiavellian Moment*, p. 452.

11 Alexander Pope, *Moral Essays*, Epistle III, line 143; cited in Isaac Kramnick, *Bolingbroke and His Circle: The Politics of Nostalgia in the Age of Walpole* (Cambridge, Mass.: Harvard University Press, 1968). For Montesquieu, see note 8.

to be reassured by the Machiavellian cynicism of Bernard Mandeville in which self-interest, deceit, and vanity combined to produce a thriving hive economy: "Thus every part was full of Vice/Yet the whole Mass a Paradise."[12] As Tory spokesmen found themselves excluded from power for a generation, they fulminated in opposition against faction, patronage, and commerce's disintegrating influences alike, as did Goldsmith (whose later hostile summary provides this paper's title):

> As nature's ties decay,
> As duty, love, and honour fail to sway,
> Fictitious bonds, the bonds of wealth and law,
> Still gather strength, and force unwilling awe.[13]

As a homeless opposition in Walpole's new England of supposed stockjobbing and clientelism, the Tories rediscovered the general interest. It was to be championed by Bolingbroke's patriot king and based on the virtuous cooperation of "the rich and great families." For the Tory critics Walpole's regime meant the same process of centralization that dismayed Boulainvilliers or Montesquieu in France, or later Justus Möser in Germany. It seemed only a petty difference that the British executive relied less on browbeating the aristocracy than on suborning them with patronage, placemen, and a general mercantile disintegration of the agrarian order.[14]

With the passing of Whig domination and George III's effort to free himself of the Newcastle network of parliamentary patronage, partisan positions were reversed. As a Whig opponent, Burke resumed many of Bolingbroke's indictments in 1770: If prerogative had declined, "influence" had replaced it. The ministry's effort to purchase its own majority (in contrast to the earlier Whig commerce in seats, which

12   Bernard Mandeville, *The Fable of the Bees*, 1705, and with supporting text, 1714; cf. Thomas A. Horne, *The Social Thought of Bernard Mandeville* (New York: Columbia University Press, 1978). For specimens of modern Mandevillism see Edward Banfield, *Political Influence* (Glencoe: Free Press, 1961), pp. 324–41; and Ralf Dahrendorf, "In Praise of Thrasymachus," *Essays in the Theory of Society* (Stanford, Calif.: Stanford University Press, 1968).

13   Oliver Goldsmith, *The Traveler*, 1764, cited in Kramnick, *Bolingbroke*, p. 80.

14   Besides Kramnick see Bernard Bailyn, *The Origins of American Politics* (New York: Knopf, 1968), pp. 37 ff.; Caroline Robbins, *The Eighteenth-Century Commonwealthman* (Cambridge, Mass.: Harvard University Press, 1961), pp. 271 ff.; J. H. Plumb, *The Origins of Political Stability: England 1675–1725* (Boston: Houghton Mifflin, 1967), for the emergence of the Walpole regime; Franklin L. Ford, *Robe and Sword: The Regrouping of the French Aristocracy After Louis XIV* (Cambridge, Mass.: Harvard University Press, 1953), Chap. 12, on the *thèse nobiliaire*; and Klaus Epstein, *The Genesis of German Conservatism* (Princeton, N.J.: Princeton University Press, 1966), pp. 297–338 on Möser.

Burke naturally did not belabor) aimed at "sowing jealousies among the different orders of the state and of disjointing the natural strength of the kingdom." Burke, however, suggested not a patriot king, but reanimation of the defunct principle of party: party as "connection" among great families (a remedy that also echoed Bolingbroke) and party "as a body of men united for promoting by their joint endeavors the national interest upon some particular principle in which they are all agreed." Party was intended to reinvigorate parliament as a control on the king by the people; at the same time parliament was to represent the nation's diverse interests. A good monarch could construct a government that would give tolerable satisfaction by choosing men with a following: "Here it is that the natural strength of the kingdom, the great peers, the leading landed gentlemen, the opulent merchants and manufacturers, the substantial yeomanry, must interpose."[15]

Burke's 1770 tract counterposed the interests of English society against the pretensions of the court; but it was equally plausible to plead the representation of interests against those who would democratize the Commons. By the 1790s, Whig as well as Tory conservatives were defending the oligarchical composition of Parliament in language similar to Montesquieu's earlier justification of the venality of offices. As William Paley argued, no matter how restricted the franchise, the House of Commons still contained "the greatest landlords and merchants, the heads of the army, the navy, and the law, the occupiers of the great offices of state. If the country is not safe in these hands in whose hands would it be?" From this view it was a logical step to the defense of "virtual representation." Since Parliament represented interests and not individuals, every man would find his stake defended, even if he himself enjoyed no suffrage. For Paley and Burke, England was governed by the crown and the estates, and the modern term for estates in a postfeudal society such as Britain's was interests.[16]

Interest representation was not merely practical representation and thus far different from the utopian notions that would soon agitate the continent; it also remained supposedly nondivisive. Unless taxes were to be vastly increased, interests would not become mutually conflicting. Moreover, they were not yet formally organized: They

---

15 Edmund Burke, "Thoughts on the Causes of the Present Discontents," 1770, excerpted in *Burke's Politics*, eds. Ross. J. S. Hoffman and Paul Levack (New York: Knopf, 1959), p. 23. The British radicals understood the oligarchic nature of Burke's critique. See Ian R. Christie, *Wilkes, Wyvill and Reform* (London: Macmillan, 1962), pp. 42–3.

16 J. R. Pole, *Political Representation in England and the Origins of the American Republic* (Berkeley and Los Angeles: University of California Press, 1971), pp. 442–57, 526–31 (citation on p. 454). On Burke's abstract construction of interests, divorced from particular real groups, see Pitkin, *The Concept of Representation*, p. 174.

were not yet interest groups. Together the interests formed the constitution in its original sense; their respective strivings augmented national prosperity and did not undermine it. What were the guarantees of harmony? Mandeville's earlier tough-minded pluralism might appear too amoral. But Adam Smith reconciled the driving force of private aspirations with the common good through the more providential invisible hand; or as Montesquieu said, "Happy it is for men that they are in a situation in which though their passions prompt them to be wicked, it is, nevertheless, to their interest to be humane and virtuous."[17] For Burke, not the logic of economic competition but the historically molded national community ensured a similar regulating principle. Interests emerged as a natural exfoliation of an organic society, compatible with the general welfare as branches might be with a tree.

Such reassurances that private goals meshed with the public welfare came easily enough during a period of trade expansion and relative harmony at home. Despite Burke's overheated rhetoric, the issue before Britain in 1770 was which segment of a national oligarchy would rule, not of parliamentary legitimacy in general. Given the restricted limits of the political community and of public debate; given, too, the buoyancy of eighteenth-century empire, and the desire to co-opt the mercantile elite into the ruling coalition, the limited competition of factions after 1760 remained compatible with an overarching consensus. The older Tory condemnation of faction and party (and the Tory temptation to reject any political role save that of the landlords) was hardly necessary: Political managers had no need for such reactionary programs, at least not before the "subversive" democratic threats of the 1790s.

In the British context, interest and parties based on interest might be viewed as compatible with the general welfare of the governing classes. But as David Hume pointed out, new principles of division were emerging. "Parties from *principle,* especially abstract speculative principle are known only to modern times and are, perhaps, the most extraordinary and unaccountable phenomenon that has yet appeared in human affairs."[18] Representation was to be justified increasingly on the basis of intrinsic individual rights, less on the basis of collective needs.

This change was part of the crisis of political mobilization that shook the Atlantic world from the 1760s through the 1790s. If the elites of

---

17   Montesquieu, *Spirit of the Laws,* XXI, Section 20; cited by Hirschman, *Passions and Interests,* p. 73.
18   David Hume, "Of Parties in General," in *David Hume's Political Essays,* ed. Charles W. Hendel (New York: The Liberal Arts Press, 1953), p. 81.

the British Empire had successfully domesticated the appeal to interests so that it was compatible with their oligarchic political regime, this regime now faced renewed assaults. Its critics sometimes proposed new, more subversive ideas of interest. Sometimes they tended to abandon the language of interest altogether as they sought more fundamental categories of representation. In the small urban arenas of American revolutionary politics, for example, the new claimants for representation merged the language of profession and interest with newer notions of majority rule. The "Mechanics" of Charleston and New York called for "the virtuous part of a free Republic . . . to Associate and Coalesce into one fraternal band," and even to impose binding instructions on legislative delegates. They conceded that political division was natural in a republic "while there exists a difference in the minds, interests, and sentiments of mankind."[19] American democrats, in short, adapted the inherited vocabulary of interest to convey a newer political division between majority and minority.

In differing degrees the oligarchic political systems of the late eighteenth century aroused criticism everywhere. Notions of interest – as expressed in terms of "estates" or "corporations" – came under attack in prerevolutionary France. Rousseauian discontent with the invidious distinctions of "civilization," with private opulence and *amour propre*, suggested that interests were identified with corruption. The French revolutionaries were more reluctant than Americans to accept the possibility that good citizens in a republic might remain permanently divided. Political virtue, the patriotic commitment of the participating citizen, replaced interest as the principle that supposedly aligned individual fulfillment with the needs of the whole. Nonetheless, by the period of the Directory, the hard-pressed Jacobins themselves argued for the naturalness of party divisions, differentiating party from "faction," which they condemned as subversive. Outside France, in the German or Italian states, or in Spain, it was often impatient royal reformers who assailed privilege; in Britain, radical critics condemned the hypocrisy of a "free Constitution" under which Pitt silenced their applause of France.[20]

19 Pauline Maier, "The Charleston Mob and the Evolution of Popular Politics in Revolutionary South Carolina, 1765–1784," *Perspectives in American History* 4 (197): 192–4.

20 For the Jacobin willingness to accept parties (once, of course, they had lost control), see Lynn Hunt, David Lansky, and Paul Hanson, "The Failure of the Liberal Republic in France, 1795–1799: The Road to Brumaire," *Journal of Modern History* 51 (4) (1979):734–59. On British opposition to Pitt see John Thelwall's *Tribune*, April 25 and May 23, 1795, cited in E. P. Thompson, *The Making of the English Working Class* (New York: Vintage Books, 1966), p. 159.

Insofar as individuals or majorities demanded representation by virtue of principle or inherent rights, political association had to change its nature accordingly. "Interest" lost its utility as a criterion for representation for both conservatives and democrats. It no longer retained legitimacy enough to serve the conservatives as a political defense. And whereas democrats might cling to the language of interest as a transitional claim, they really were calling for a broader inclusion of citizens in general. Ironically, no sooner had diverse interests been accepted as safe for the polity, than political divisions surged over the frail channels they provided. For those seeking to manage a society without revolution, as in Britain, or to channel radical change into stable, representative forms, as in the United States, the ideological task became one of redomesticating the new, potentially inflammatory associations of "party" – in Madison's concept, "curing the mischiefs of faction."

In an age of emerging liberal individualism how could political managers substitute for the earlier ballast provided by the Burkean concept of interest so as to dampen civil strife or democratic "excesses"? How did one represent majorities without endangering minorities? Memories of religious intolerance and the example of Robespierre's republic remained vivid inducements to work out mechanisms for containing conflict. In the United States, federalism and the very geographical extent of the Republic, so Madison suggested, could dilute dangerous and even majoritarian factions. In other societies deference and property might reinforce stability. Deference presupposed a "natural aristocracy" equipped by wealth, leisure, and intellect to rule and gamble on an electorate capable of judging political talent.[21] Property became the critical testimony of this independent judgment. "Property is indeed a very imperfect test of intelligence; but it is one test," as Bagehot, one of its rearguard but perceptive defenders, summarized. "If it has been inherited it guarantees education; if acquired, it guarantees ability. Either way it assures of something."[22] In France the spokesmen for parliamentary liberalism also

21 For Madison's view, *The Federalist Papers*, No. 10. On deference see J. G. A. Pocock, "The Classical Theory of Deference," and Richard W. Davis, "Deference and Aristocracy in the Time of the Great Reform Act," *American Historical Review*, 81 (3) (1976):516–23, 532–9; also David Cresap Moore, *The Politics of Deference: A Study of the Mid-Nineteenth Century English Political System* (Hassocks, Eng.: Harvester Press, 1976).
22 Walter Bagehot, "Parliamentary Reform" [1859] in *Essays on Parliamentary Reform*, p. 40.

sought a middle-class ballast. The universality of interests that Burke had found in the House of Commons as a whole, the French Doctrinaires, such as Guizot and Royer-Collard, located in the middling strata, indeed in each middle-class man. The bourgeois voter incorporated the generality of nonaristocratic interests; and because he could not favor any one of his own multiple interests excessively without injuring the aggregate, political moderation would be assured. Whereas Bagehot would rely on different parliamentary constituencies to ensure representation of diverse interests,[23] the French "whigs" sought not to incorporate diversity but to average it out. "It is in the middle class that all interests can find their natural representation: those higher up have a need to dominate that has to be opposed; underneath there is ignorance, habit, dependence, and thus a complete lack of what is needed."[24]

In effect, though, turning to the middle class and to property for political defense meant turning toward party itself as a principle of stability. By the mid-nineteenth century the European parties generally were serving to keep rival leaders and dissenters within the governing elites from stirring up the explosive elements of urban society. They routinized conflict among the middle and upper classes, and they also offered a framework for future integration of the working classes. "The great fault of the present time is that men hate each other so damnably," Melbourne had complained after the great political battles of the early 1830s; but by the late 1840s, party competition had channeled these animosities. When Aberdeen explained to the queen, "The only permanent bond of Party, according to my notions, was the possession of office or the pursuit of it," he was obviously referring to a competition within safe limits.[25] "The distinguishing influence of free institutions consists in their giving birth to popular parties," an American commentator suggested,[26] while even in the post-1848 reaction a German commentator emphasized how important parties had become. "If opinion counts for more than interest for the man of today, the times do not deem it a reproach. . . . The party today has more

23 Bagehot, "Parliamentary Reform," pp. 101–2.
24 Royer-Collard cited in Dominique Bagge, *Le conflit des idées politiques en France sous la Restauration* (Paris: Presses Universitaires de France, 1952), pp. 110–13.
25 Melbourne and Aberdeen cited in Norman Gash, *Reaction and Reconstruction in English Politics, 1832–1852* (Oxford: Clarendon Press, 1965), pp. 126, 128.
26 Frederick Grimke, *The Nature and Tendency of Free Institutions* [1848], cited by Richard Hofstadter, *The Idea of a Party System* (Berkeley and Los Angeles: University of California Press, 1970), p. 265.

political reality than the estates whose interests are definitely subordinate to party interest."[27]

Party, therefore, had become acceptable, and even convenient. What had originally threatened as an instrument for imposing ideological fanaticism had become by the mid-nineteenth century a conservative tool for managing political society. In effect, parties of opinion had come to represent interests; but living more familiarly with classes and parties, men could let the older language of interest lapse.

And yet no sooner was party, as the organizer of opinion, finally accepted as a device for order, than it began to alter under a new and urgent reintrusion of interest politics. Now with a difference, however. Interests were to be organized not just on the level of parliament as British Whig theory suggested, nor within the *juste milieu* of the bourgeois electorate, as French liberalism prescribed. Instead, interests would take form as associations on the level of civil society between Parliament and the middle-class voter. Burke and Bagehot believed that a parliament insulated from pressures from above and below could adequately aggregate society's implicit interests, without those interests organizing themselves; Guizot and Royer-Collard entrusted the 200,000 electors of the *monarchie censitaire* to give adequate vent to concrete interests. But by the last third of the nineteenth century those speaking for interests found neither solution sufficient. Instead, they appropriated the intermediate level of political "space" to ensure collective force and parliamentary leverage. They organized to exert permanent pressure.

The formal organization of interests, however, meant that no sooner had party become legitimate than it had to be itself transformed. Either the assemblies of notables that comprised the mid-nineteenth century parties had to undergo a major evolution into permanent mass electoral organizations, or they were fated to lose their impetus. Parties allegedly of ideas had to become parties of interests in a world of organizing interests. The whig zenith quickly became the whig sunset.

This is not to argue that mid-century parties had not spoken for interests, just that for a brief interval they had transmuted the lan-

27 Ludwig August von Rochau, *Grundsätze der Realpolitik,* ed. Hans-Ulrich Wehler (Frankfurt/M.: Ullstein, 1972), pp. 94–5. For another testimony of German interest in parties in the wake of 1848, see Wilhelm Wachsmuth, *Geschichte der politischen Parteien alter und neuer Zeit,* 3 vols. (Braunschweig: Schwetscke und Sohn, 1853–6). And for the rich fabric of associations in pre-1848 Germany, which, if not strictly speaking political, still helped articulate middle-class opinion, see Otto Dann, "Die Anfänge politischer Vereinsbildung in Deutschland," in *Soziale Bewegung und politische Verfassung. Beiträge zur Geschichte der modernen Welt,* eds. U. Engelhardt, V. Sellin, H. Stücke (Stuttgart: Klett Verlag, 1976), pp. 197–232.

guage. Indeed, the very stress on public opinion had expressed a deep class interest. Only an ascendant bourgeoisie, which really wrote off the stake in society of the urban and rural working classes, could have claimed the reading public as the source of legitimacy. As Treitschke, unattractive *Realpolitiker* that he might be, wrote about Germany: "Political theory . . . can seldom actually cause a party to be formed unless it corresponds to the interest of a social force. The interests of the social classes, for instance, have much more a say in party doctrine than the parties themselves admit."[28]

Nonetheless, that did not mean that there was no real institutional basis for the liberal concept of a politics of "opinion." It is important to understand the factors that even briefly allowed for the triumph of parties of opinion before examining the new world of interest groups. In a Europe of restricted suffrage, regimes briefly rested on a peculiar interstitial class basis. As John Vincent has suggested, the Victorian equipoise did not really result from the fact that a cohesive middle class had become dominant and was yet unchallenged by labor. Rather, it reflected an interim situation in which the aristocracy had relinquished its former political monopoly even if it still filled leading offices. The balance of social forces varied enormously from country to country, but in each case a relative postaristocratic hiatus of power seemed to validate liberal theory.[29]

Consider first, the factors mitigating mid-century antagonisms among elites. The major conflicts between representatives of manufacturing and champions of agriculture either lay behind (as in Britain after repeal of the corn laws) or they had not yet become so virulent as they would later, elsewhere (as in Germany between 1890 and 1900). In the countries that were undergoing less rapid industrialization, the economic conflicts between landlords and bourgeois never became so salient. Gentry and even grandees often championed the causes of liberalism and economic development, for example, Cavour in Piedmont or Szechenyi in Hungary. Antebellum plantation owners, Magyar magnates, and Orleanist notables, such as Tocqueville, comprised an international reformist aristocracy, convinced that political community must be based on the literate classes. Their bourgeois allies felt that within this coalition they could chalk up enough of their own solid achievements, so that even when middle-class influence was set

---

28 Heinrich von Treitschke, *Parteien und Fraktionen [1871]*, cited in Theodor Schieder, "The Theory of the Political Party in Early German Liberalism," in *The State and Society in Our Times*, trans. C. A. M Syme (London: Nelson, 1962), p. 96.

29 John Vincent, *The Formation of the British Liberal Party, 1857–68* (Harmondsworth: Penguin Books, 1972), pp. 12–13.

back they did not feel totally thwarted. Despite the frustrations of 1848, subsequent progress made toward bureaucratic rationalization and national unification was to reconcile important sectors of bourgeois opinion in central Europe. Progress toward breaking down caste barriers seemed assured. In Britain the advent of the public schools and the opening of the Conservative party to business interests meant the gentrification of the commercial elite. In France, the Orleanist monarchy and later the Second Empire diligently created their own notables and titled retainers. In general, all the great institutional reform movements of the 1860s involved an effort to strengthen national power by broad co-optation of bourgeois leadership. Post-Ausgleich Austria and Hungary, the Bismarckian North German Confederation and Empire (at least from 1867 to 1878), searched for *le pays réel*. These "real" forces could be little else but the interests who had spokesmen or might be available for organization. In its cultivation of Catholics, its manipulation of bureaucrats, and its initial rewards for business the Second Empire worked toward the rudiments of a plebiscitarian corporatism. In the twofold search for support – the continuing dialogue with potential collective interests, and the periodic acclamation by the general mass of voters – lay much of the innovative character of Napoleon III's government. Bonapartism prefigured the end of the liberal parenthesis.

The advent of the "great depression" after 1873 tended even more specifically to undermine the prerequisites for parliamentary liberalism. This long phase of declining prices began with a severe trade recession, and then continued with a quarter-century compression of agricultural revenues. Monetary contraction in respect to real growth may have been one cause (triggered in turn by the absence of new gold sources and by deflationary public policies), but new wheat from the prairies, the pampas, and the steppe also played a major role. The response was a turn toward organization. French iron makers had formed the Comité des Forges as early as 1864 in the face of the Bonapartist move toward free trade. Le Travail National followed in 1870, while French agrarians also organized: large landowners in the Société des Agriculteurs (3,500 members in 1878 and 11,000 by 1894) – the conservative Rue d'Athènes – and "republican" peasants in Gambetta's Société Nationale de l'Encouragement de l'Agriculture (the Boulevard Saint-Germain).[30]

---

30 See Pierre Barral, *Les agrariens français de Méline à Pisani* (Paris: Colin, 1968), pp. 105–28; also Michel Augé-Laribé, *La politique agricole de la France de 1880 à 1940* (Paris: Presses Universitaires de France, 1950), pp. 72–80, 219–20, 237–40.

Tariff protection became the major inducement to organization, as tariffs provided a public subsidy that could overcome inertia and the disincentives to group formation. In 1876 hard-pressed German manufacturers constituted the Centralverband Deutscher Industrieller to seek tariff relief, while the major agrarian pressure group, the Junker dominated Bund der Landwirte, formed in 1893 as a demagogically effective response to Chancellor Caprivi's moderate policy of negotiating reciprocal trade treaties. Only Britain resisted – and barely – the wave of tariffs in Europe and America between 1879 and 1902. Following tariffs, the new groups often wrested other legislative concessions, as in France, where the agriculturalists won public organization of their *caisses de credit* and *mutuelles d'assurance.*[31]

Tariffs comprised only one expression of a broader competitive nationalism. Late nineteenth-century imperialism, with its search for military security and naval expansion, represented just one aspect of a major transition in Western bourgeois society. Government officials, spokesmen for middle-of-the-road parties, beleaguered liberals concerned about rivals on their left, industrialists enthused by a world

---

31 In addition to those mentioned see on tariffs, Peter A. Gourevitch, "International Trade, Domestic Coalitions, and Liberty: The Crisis of 1873–1896," *Journal of Interdisciplinary History* 8 (2) (1977):281–313; Eugene O. Golob, *The Méline Tariff: French Agriculture and Nationalist Economic Policy* (New York: Columbia University Press, 1944); Alexander Gerschenkron, *Bread and Democracy in Germany* (Berkeley and Los Angeles: University of California Press, 1943), Part I; Hans Rosenberg, *Grosse Depression und Bismarckszeit* (Berlin: De Gruyter, 1967); Benjamin H. Brown, *The Tariff Reform Movement in Britain, 1884–1895* (New York: Columbia University Press, 1943); Ivo Lambi, *Free Trade and Protection in Germany, 1868–1879* (Wiesbaden: Steiner, 1963). For the emergence and manipulation of interest groups in this period, including the exploitation of the tariff issue, see also Sanford Elwitt, *The Making of the Third Republic: Class and Politics in France, 1868–1884* (Baton Rouge: Louisiana State University Press, 1975), pp. 230–72; Giampiero Carocci, *Agostino Depretis e la politica interna italiana dal 1876 al 1887* (Turin: Einaudi, 1956), especially pp. 408–9; Helmut Böhme, "Big Business Pressure Groups and Bismarck's Turn to Protectionism, 1873–79," *The Historical Journal* 10(1973):218–36; Hartmut Kaelble, *Industrielle Interessenpolitik in der wilhelminischen Gesellschaft* (Berlin: De Gruyter, 1967); Dirk Stegman, *Die Erben Bismarcks. Parteien und Verbände in der Spätphase des Wilhelminischen Deutschlands* (Cologne and Berlin: Kiepenheuer und Witsch, 1970); Hans-Jürgen Puhle, "Parlament, Parteien und Interessenverbände 1890–1914," in *Das kaiserliche Deutschland*, ed. Michael Stürmer (Düsseldorf: Droste, 1970), 340–77, and the same author's two volumes: *Agrarische Interessenpolitik und preussischer Konservatismus im Wilhelminischen Reich (1893–1914)* (Hanover: Verlag für Literatur und Zeitgeschehen, 1967), and *Politische Agrarbewegungen in kapitalistischen Industriegesellschaften: Deutschland, USA und Frankreich im 20. Jahrhundert* (Göttingen: Vandenhoeck und Ruprecht, 1975); also the essays included in *Interessenverbände in Deutschland*, ed. Heinz Josef Varain (Cologne: Kiepenheuer und Witsch, 1973), pp. 139–61.

of iron ships, organized a host of associations to lobby for military spending and planting the flag abroad. Some of this involved manipulation from above; however, veterans' leagues, nationalist student movements, provincial businessmen in search of participation and a meaningful cause, all involved a direct incursion of the middle-class public into political life. The new articulation of public opinion meant the supplementing or bypassing of parliaments; in turn it allowed neo-Bonapartist ("Caesarist") efforts by officials to deal directly with interests while it encouraged spokesmen for interest groups to secure direct access and voice. The middle-class public thus emerged with possibilities for more immediate influence, but was simultaneously fragmented into single-purpose constituencies. The unified Victorian vision (idealized to be sure) of public opinion gave way to a more fragmented politics of partial interests – and patriotic passions.[32]

The proliferation of interest groups and the new politicking deeply affected contemporary observers, who sensed that a profound change in the forms and substance of representation was underway. From one viewpoint the new groupings were just extensions of the liberal impulse toward free association. This was the case for labor unions, which had been freed from common law restrictions on "combination" in Britain in 1824–5, granted the right to organize as private associations in the German states during the 1860s, and accorded similar liberty in France by the 1884 Law of Associations (and its further liberalization of 1901). But many of the new trade associations in Germany, France, and other countries with a tradition of public law were less manifestations of liberalism than delegations of state authority. France, Germany, Italy, and Spain each possessed regional chambers of commerce, established on the base of earlier guilds by Napoleonic decree, then exported to French-occupied Europe, and thereafter preserved by the Restoration regimes. These associations were augmented by national delegations in some cases (e.g., the Deutscher Handelstag). The national or regional organs in turn came to overlap with the trade associations recognized as public law bodies which different industries

---

32 The issue of the social causes of imperialism goes back at least to John Hobson, *Imperialism: A Study* (London: John Nisbet, 1902), but the major historiographical statements have centered on Germany. See Eckart Kehr, *Schlachtflottenbau und Parteipolitik* (Berlin: Ebering, 1930); Hans-Ulrich Wehler, *Bismarck und der Imperialismus* (Cologne: Kiepenheuer und Witsch, 1969); and for a partial counterstatement, see Geoff Eley, who may overstate their analysis of manipulation from above, "Die 'Kehrites' und das Kaiserreich: Bemerkungen zu einer aktuellen Kontroverse," *Geschichte und Gesellschaft* 4(1)(1978):91–107; also Eley, "Reshaping the Right: Radical Nationalism and the German Navy League, 1898–1908," *The Historical Journal* 21 (2)(1978):327–54.

were generating.[33] By the end of the 1870s, state and private-sponsored marketing and lobbying organizations were thickly interwoven in a quasi-official legal space. Many moderate liberals felt that sanctioning these new groups was the means to effective representation. Waldeck-Rousseau, the *Progressiste* premier of the government of "republican defense" at the turn of the century viewed the 1901 Law of Associations as the true expression of French liberalism.[34] It promised a fabric of public participation more like England's and far more promising than rhetorical declarations of parliamentary sovereignty. Furthermore, Rudolf von Gneist had earlier praised German associational activity as his country's approach to *Selbstverwaltung:* the healthy, autonomous self-government that the English also enjoyed thanks to their medieval constitution. Otto von Gierke similarly saw the long tradition of *Genossenschaften* as the functional equivalent of the Western liberal tradition. Yet these theorists were simultaneously disturbed as well as reassured by the new interest groups. They interpreted the *Verbände* less as spontaneous expressions of autonomy than as disguised efforts at state organization, and Gneist himself warned in 1894 of the "dissolving of our parliaments into splintered occupation and property groups."[35]

Sociologists and political analysts commented on the emerging trend, not in isolation but as part of a new stress on group organization in general. The years of the great depression (1873–96) were simultaneously an era of post-liberal disillusion with parliamentary representation. The heroic work of national unification lay behind in Italy and Germany. In those countries, and in the America of James G. Blaine, the France of the Panama scandal, or the Spain of the *turno politico* and *caciquismo*, corruption and clientelism seemed to be the essence of popular government. As part of this jaundiced estimate, the notion came naturally that partial group interests, and not individual civic participation, formed the basis of public life. Such cynicism was hard on liberalism but creative for conservative political sociology. It fit in with a growing belief in irrationalism and an emphasis on the primitive, communal drives toward collective organization (Fustel de

---

33   Cf. Dieter Schäfer, "Der deutsche Handelstag auf dem Weg zum wirtschaftlichen Verband," in *Interessenverbände*, ed. Varain, pp. 120–38; also Heinrich A. Winkler, *Pluralismus oder Protektionismus? Verfassungspolitische Probleme des Verbandswesens im deutschen Kaiserreich* (Wiesbaden: Steiner, 1972), pp. 5 ff.

34   See Pierre Sorlin, *Waldeck-Rousseau* (Paris: Colin, 1966). pp. 208 fn., 236–64.

35   Gneist and Gierke cited in Winkler, *Pluralismus oder Protektionismus?* p. 28–9. For Gneist and Gierke see also Heinrich Heffter, *Die deutsche Selbsiverwaltung im 19. Jahrhundert* (Stuttgart: Koehler, 1950) pp. 372–403, 525–30; and, in general, Otto von Gierke, *Das deutsche Genossenschaftsrecht*, 4 vols. (Berlin: Weidman, 1868–1913).

Coulanges, Taine, Barrès), with skepticism about democracy and a search for underlying drives for power by the manipulation of ideology on the part of elites (Mosca, Pareto).[36] Arthur Bentley's analysis of 1908, *The Process of Government*, may have initiated formal American reflection on interest groups, but it logically belonged to a pattern of analysis a generation old in Europe.[37]

Revival of the Left after the 1890s, the growth of state intervention in the economy, and the wave of massive strikes that punctuated the first decade of the new century further stimulated group theories. Political and legal theorists now seized on the newer interest organizations to support antidemocratic impulses and lament what might be called "overloaded liberalism." Leon Duguit's political implications may have remained ambiguous even as he sought to deny the reality of the state as an abstract Roman law entity and substitute in its stead a web of reciprocal duties based on natural associations and groups.[38] Working along some of the same lines, the Italian jurist Santi Romano offered a sociological view of the state that emphasized "the increasing division of our society into classes and corporations." In contrast to the formalist equality guaranteed by the state under the *Code Civil*, the real relationships of society, such as those between employer and worker, "still require and probably shall always require inequality among individuals, the supremacy of some and the subordination of others."[39]

The thickening of interest groups thus seemed to suggest that the associations and conflicts of economic and social life were overflowing the juridical categories of the nineteenth-century state. Nor were pressure groups the only sign of this "lag" on the part of public and parliamentary institutions. The inner transformation of political parties

---

36 Cf. Claude Digeon, *La crise allemande de la société française (1870–1914)* (Paris: Presses Universitaires de France, 1959), pp. 215–52, 403–49; Gaetano Mosca, *Elementi di scienza politica* [1896, 1923], published in English as *The Ruling Class*, trans. H. D. Kahn and ed. A. Livingstone (New York and London: McGraw-Hill Book Co., 1939); Vilfredo Pareto, *Les systèmes socialistes* [1902] (Geneva: Droz, 1965).

37 Arthur Bentley, *The Process of Government*, ed. Peter H. Odegard (Cambridge, Mass.: Harvard University Press, 1967): "All phenomena of government are phenomena of groups pressing one another, forming one another, and pushing out new groups and group representatives (the organs or agencies of government) to mediate the adjustments. . . . The interest is nothing other than the group activity itself." (pp. 269, 271.)

38 Leon Duguit, *Le droit social, le droit individual et les transformations de l'état* (Paris: Alcan, 1908).

39 Santi Romano, "Lo Stato moderno e la sua crisi," in *Scritti minori*, Vol. 1 (Milan: Giuffrè, 1950), pp. 311–25; the passage here cited by Paolo Ungari, *Alfredo Rocco e l'ideologia giuridica del fascismo* (Brescia: Morcelliana, 1963), p. 37.

also reflected the twofold thrust of the new development: on the one hand, the fragmentation of the citizenry into a welter of conflicting roles and partial interests; on the other, a more direct and democratic political mobilization. The electoral successes of the Gladstone liberals and Joseph Chamberlain's Birmingham caucus in the 1880s, the reorganization of the German Social Democrats after 1890, the formation of the French Radical Socialist party in 1901, meant that the major European factions were evolving from whiggish clubs into permanent electoral and patronage organizations with full-time staffs, affiliated newspapers, annual congresses, and continuing communication between local and national leadership.[40] At the same time, however, some of the new parties were being virtually captured by such homogeneous social classes that they were becoming largely interest groups in their own right, although designed to struggle in the parliamentary arena rather than in the marketplace. The European social democratic parties might be viewed in this light, even though they remained committed in theory to a total transformation of society, which transcended normal interest group aspirations. A clearer case was the identification of the German Conservative party with the militant rye-growing estate owners of East Elbia, who organized their own Agrarian League in 1893 as well as coming to dominate the older Prussian-based party. Furthermore, the Italian Nationalist Association of 1910 (and thereafter party) fell under the control of Ligurian iron and steel manufacturers, who depended on government contracts and found it useful to bankroll a press that trumpeted military preparedness and expansion.[41]

Both on the Left and the Right the distinction between parties and interest associations thus tended to erode step by step with the increasing activity of European governments in raising tariffs, increasing armaments, initiating early welfare measures, and generally inter-

40 For the comment this aroused see M. Ostrogorsky, *La démocratie et l'organisation des partis politiques*, 2 vols. (Paris: Calmann-Lévy, 1903); Max Weber, *Wirtschaft und Gesellschaft*, 5th ed. (Tübingen: 1972), pp. 837–51; "Politics as a Vocation," in Hans Gerth and C. Wright Mills, *From Max Weber* (New York: Oxford University Press, 1958), pp. 99–112; and Robert Michels, *Political Parties*, trans. E. and C. Paul [1915] (New York: Dover, 1959).
41 On the Nationalists: Richard Webster, *Industrial Imperialism in Italy, 1908–1915* (Berkeley and Los Angeles: University of California Press, 1975); Franco Gaeta, *Nazionalismo italiano* (Naples: Edizioni Scientifiche Italiane, 1965); and Ungari, *Alfredo Rocco*, especially Chap. 5. On the agrarians see the Puhle citations in note 31. A contemporary judgment on the capture of the parties, although overstressed, in Emil Lederer, "Die ökonomische Element und die politischen Ideen im modernen Parteiwesen," *Zeitschrift für Politik*, 5(4)(1912).

vening in the capitalist marketplace. Liberals who remembered and sometimes idealized the mid-century parties of notables contrasted the crassness and demogogy of populist imperialism with the earlier gentlemanly game of politics. Indeed the elegiac regrets started as early as the 1860s, and by the end of the century had deepened into a major sense of disorientation and lost mission.[42]

The ramifications of the great depression after 1873, the development of an "organized capitalism," the harsher international competition provided major impulses to the direct mediation of interests. But so too did the rise of working-class organizations. Despite major uprisings as late as 1898 in Milan, 1909 in Barcelona, and 1914 in various Italian Adriatic cities, by the end of the nineteenth century the specter of violent revolutionary upheaval was passing. Reformist Socialists recognized the difficulties of armed revolution; urban insurrection seemed an obsolete romanticism. And why place in jeopardy a Socialist organization that promised to become a majority party as the working class grew? In sum, the growth of social democracy, the related expansion of trade unions (and in the German and British cases the reciprocal permeation of labor's party and labor's interest groups), the encroachments of revisionism and reformism – all opened up the Left to the same new patterns of brokerage as were emerging on the Right.

This did not mean that the forces of the Right were uniformly willing to bargain with trade unionists and social democrats. Some moderates were, many entrepreneurs resisted, and conservative politicians often oscillated between efforts at confrontation and cooperation. At the least, however, organization on the Left produced employer counterorganization on the Right. National and regional employer federations in Germany, Italy, France, Britain, and the United States were constituted early in the twentieth century to counter new union pressure. Membership overlapped, of course, with the earlier business interest groups organized to control market competition.[43]

---

42 Revealing in this regard were the Liberals' efforts to define the middle classes they allegedly represented. On this, and on the relationship to interest groups, see James J. Sheehan, *German Liberalism in the Nineteenth Century* (Chicago and London: University of Chicago Press, 1978), pp. 169–77, 248–57; and cf. Dan S. White's chapter on "National Liberalism in the Context of European Politics," in *The Splintered Party* (Cambridge, Mass.: Harvard University Press, 1976), pp. 199–222.

43 Etienne Villey, *L'Organisation professionnelle des employeurs dans l'industrie française* (Paris: Alcan, 1923); Mario Abrate, *La lotta sindacale nella industrializzazione in Italia* (Milan: Angeli, 1967); Anthony L. Cardoza, "Agrarian Elites and the Origins of Italian Fascism: The Province of Bologna, 1901–1922," dissertation, Princeton University, 1975; and the German sources cited in note 31 and Fritz Tanzler, *Die deutschen Arbeitgeberverbände, 1904–1929* (Berlin, 1929).

Just as political parties slowly won acceptance and then legitimacy, so, too, interest group brokerage gradually changed from a suspicious innovation to a convenient channel of representation. Parties had become acceptable when it was demonstrated that rather than serving as instruments for radicals and zealots, they actually contributed to channeling political passions, to facilitating political management. Parties might temper the winds of doctrine. Likewise the web of interest groups offered to dampen the distributive conflicts of industrial society; to pay off sullen and fractious farmers, to even out the business cycle for industry, to encourage working-class leaders to reap short-term benefits for their followers within capitalism, to allow religious communities (especially Catholics) to preserve their cultural identity in secular society.

World War I and the Great Depression illustrated how deep an inroad interest group representation had actually made. Economic mobilization in World War I created new ties between government and producer groups and lent business associations enhanced regulatory power. In France, for instance, the Comité des Forges took over the procurement of metals abroad. In Germany, private corporations and the armed forces jointly organized war companies for purchasing and allocation of raw materials. In Britain, the railroads were combined and controlled; cotton, jute, and insurance largely taken over. In the United States, a War Industries Board was finally established to regulate prices, allocate materials and war orders, and overcome the chaos of earlier procurement attempts. To avoid strikes, labor unions everywhere won new grievance procedures – the counterpart in the economy to the participation of Socialist party leaders in French and British cabinet coalitions. The role of the state in overseeing the new partnership between unions and industrial leaders similarly became more massive, especially when munitions ministries wrote clauses specifying labor relations into all their contracts with industrial suppliers.[44]

"State socialism" during the war prompted both business spokesmen and political reformers to envisage prolonging the system. Mait-

44 See William Oualid and Charles Picquenard, *Salaires et tariffes, conventions collectives et grèves: la politique du ministère de l'armament* (Paris: Presses Universitaires de France, and New Haven: Yale University Press, 1928); Henri Flu, *Les comptoirs metallurgiques d'après-guerre (1919–1922)* (Lyon: Thèse, 1924) with background on the war; E. M. H. Lloyd, *Experiments in State Control at the War Office and the Ministry of Food* (Oxford: Clarendon Press, 1924); W. F. Bruck, "Die Kriegsunternehmung. Versuch einer Systematik," *Archiv für Sozialwissenschaft und Sozialpolitik* 48(3)(1921):547–95; the material in Gerald Feldman, *Army, Industry, and Labor in Germany, 1914–1918* (Princeton, N.J.: Princeton University Press, 1966); Paul A. C. Koistinen, "The 'Industrial-Military Complex' in Historical Perspective: World War I," *Business History Review*, 41(4)(1967):378–403.

land familiarized English readers with the work of Gierke; Duguit's ideas crossed the channel; Mary Parker Follett waxed enthusiastic over "The New State" in America; Laski (along with Lippmann and Beard) discovered that U.S. wartime agencies were encouraging a new pluralism. On the Left, a syndicalist impulse could motivate the projects for guild socialism of G. D. H. Cole and others, whereas in Central Europe and Italy the "councils" that were observed carrying out the revolution in Russia might also serve to socialize the economy. Industrial leaders also celebrated the virtues of an industrial order that would overcome the earlier "wasteful" competition of laissez-faire capitalism. Walther Rathenau and Wichard Möllendorff in Germany and Etienne Clémentel in France outlined industrywide and regional economic councils that would continue the wartime work of allocating scarce raw materials, setting prices, and establishing output targets. With the regulation of the marketplace turned over to joint industry and labor boards, the tasks of political representation would supposedly become minimal. As the Haldane Committee on the Machinery of Government reported in 1918, effective administration required departments "to avail themselves of the advice and assistance of advisory boards so constituted as to make available the knowledge and experience of all sections of the community affected . . ."[45] Wartime institutions such as the Wool Control Board, with its representation of workers, manufacturers, and the state, suggested promising models. "For the first time in history," wrote the British historian of economic control in wartime, "the world began to have a vision of what human association, raised to its highest degree, might accomplish."[46]

What prevailed after the Armistice, however, was the far more widespread businessmen's desire to shake off bureaucratic controls, raise their prices, buy and sell where they wished. The collective vision did not readily survive in the marketplace; and the schemes for planned economies in Britain, France, and Germany were never in-

45 Cited in A. H. Birch, *Representation* (London: Pall Mall Press, 1971), p. 103. For the plans cited see G. D. H. Cole, *Workshop Organization* (Oxford: Clarendon Press, 1923); Arthur Gleason, *What the Workers Want* (New York: Harcourt, Brace and Howe, 1920), pp. 169 ff., 185 ff.; Walther Rathenau, *Von kommenden Dingen* (Berlin: Fischer, 1917) and *Die neue Wirtschaft* (Berlin: Fischer, 1918); Wichard von Moellendorff, *Der Aufbau der Gemeinwirtschaft* (Jena: Diderichs, 1919); Etienne Clémentel articles in *Journée Industrielle* (April 1919), cited by Maier, *Recasting Bourgeois Europe*, pp. 74–6.

46 Lloyd, *Experiments in State Control*, p. 1. For the general problems of wartime controls see pp. 259 ff. For a useful discussion of emerging pluralist theory among British and American writers before, during, and after World War I, which traces the filiation from Gierke and Duguit to Maitland, Figgis, Laski, Lippmann, Beard et al., see Paul F. Bourke, "The Pluralist Reading of James Madison's Tenth *Federalist*," *Perspectives in American History* 9 (1975):271–95.

stituted despite countless hours of discussion. Nonetheless, the balance of power between capital and labor could not be restored to the *status quo ante*. Individual entrepreneurs found it harder to rely on their own market power to set the terms of labor contracts. In France, Britain, and the United States, employers did recover ascendancy after major unsuccessful strikes in the postwar period. In Germany and Austria, where discredited regimes collapsed with defeat, only quasi-corporatist bargaining could achieve a *modus vivendi*. When right-wing forces tired of this compromise and recovered their strength, they resorted to dictatorship.

Still, even when dictatorship was attempted in the 1920s it had to be instituted in a careful relationship to given social and economic interests. Mussolini, for example, had to reinforce the organization of industry to secure effective control, as he defined it. Mussolini, moreover, and Primo De Rivera in Spain both made significant attempts to deal with labor and to go beyond simply bludgeoning it into submission. Because the Italian Fascist rise to power had required several years of brutality against working-class activists, Mussolini could not easily negotiate with Social Democrats and trade unions, as could Primo, who took power by virtue of a royal *pronunciamento*. Nonetheless, for the decade of the twenties at least, Mussolini's partial encouragement of Fascist syndicalism represented a notable effort on the part of his regime. It amounted to an authoritarian version of the more general attempt under Western capitalism to transform the representatives of interests into bureaucratic partners. In the nineteenth century, liberals had sought to discipline ascendant middle-class or working-class citizens by endowing them with parliamentary representation and responsibility. After 1918 anyone seeking to control the politicized marketplace, as well as the parliament, needed to co-opt the leadership of the collective economic forces into corporatist roles, simultaneously private and public.[47]

47 On Mussolini's labor policy see Adrian Lyttelton, *The Seizure of Power: Fascism in Italy 1919–1929* (London: Weidenfeld and Nicolson, 1973), pp. 217ff. and 315ff.; Renzo De Felice, *Mussolini il fascista, L'organizzazione dello stato fascista 1925–1929*, Vol. 2 (Turin: Einaudi, 1968); Gaetano Salvemini, *Under the Axe of Fascism* (New York: Viking Press, 1936); and other sources cited in Maier, *Recasting Bourgeois Europe*, pp. 556–78. National Socialist policies in Germany involved far less of an effort to establish a corporativist façade; syndicalist spokesmen met defeat within the circles of the regime far earlier (witness the slaying of Gregor Strasser on June 30, 1934); and the Labor Front represented a more naked and centralized search for control and domination. See Gerhard Schulz, *Die Anfänge des totalitaren Massnahmenstaates* (Frankfurt/Main: Ullstein, 1974), Chaps. I.3 and V (originally published as Part II of K. D. Bracher, G. Schulz, and W. Sauer, *Die nationalsozialistische Machtergreifung* (Cologne: Westdeutscher Verlag, 1960); and T. W. Mason, *Arbeiterklasse und Volksgemeinschaft. Dokumente und Materielen zur deutschen Arbeiterpolitik 1936–1939* (Opladen: Westdeutscher Verlag, 1975).

In the liberal states this process could take the form of institution-alizing social compacts directly. To be sure, some form of pressure from working-class forces was usually a prerequisite. The revolution-ary outbreaks in central Europe in 1918–19, the weakening of capitalist legitimacy due to the world economic crisis, and the subsequent left-wing electoral victories in some countries all helped redress the balance of social forces and stimulated new collective social contracts. The Stinnes–Legien agreement establishing union–industry collaboration during the German Revolution of 1918, the Matignon Accords that ended the sitdown strikes immediately following the Popular Front victory in France, and the 1938 Saltsjöbaden agreement between Swedish unions and employers (LO and SAF) were salient examples of these economic constitutions. The provisions for collective bar-gaining provided first by the National Recovery Act of 1933, and then the Wagner Act of 1935, allowed American labor to seek decentralized functional equivalents.

Thus two major variants of interest representation emerged between the wars. In the democratic states, economic elites did not feel they could use the state to enforce their predominance in the marketplace. In the authoritarian regimes, elites were not prepared to desist from coercive remedies. Either they felt themselves insufficiently organized at the level of civil society to hold their own in the economic arena, or else they were after an earlier sort of socioeconomic domination that postwar conditions no longer allowed (short of repression). Still, even when these frightened or imperious elites supported authori-tarian regimes, they had to accept some state recognition of labor's potential collective strength.

A discussion of the emergence of interest groups that opened by citing the search for agricultural and industrial protection thus must close with the issue of how European capitalism was to come to terms with organized labor. Certainly farmers, handicraft artisans, bankers, textile producers, chemical industries, insurance executives, wood producers, homeowners and taxpayers, retail shopkeepers, and so forth did not let any of their multifarious and active pressure groups lapse. The difficulties of agriculture remained to envenom much of interwar politics. Still, the treatment of organized labor became the salient issue of the interwar political economy. Industry and labor dominated public disputes because their respective claims seemed to subsume so many others. The unemployment that plagued Great Britain throughout the 1920s, that repeatedly afflicted Weimar Ger-many, that ravaged most economies in the early 1930s, called attention to labor in general more than industry branch by branch. It made the overall level of employment, not its composition, politically crucial.

The framework of interest group conflict thus underwent a simplification. Even when they meant cruel repression, the experiences of World War II, moreover, brought at least a juridical recognition of labor as a corporate group, as in Vichy France or the occupied Netherlands. Thereafter, the initiatives of the Resistance coalitions confirmed the central role of labor in postwar political and social institutions. The neo-Keynesian political leaders of the years after 1945, convinced that the state must pursue high employment and growth, were responding to an agenda set by labor and naturally looked to unions as their major political interlocutors.[48]

This dialogue with labor completed, in a sense, the legitimization of interest group representation. For with the post-1945 era and the emergence of welfare states, organized labor did not appear as just another interest group. In the post-Fascist climate, the working class and its representatives had apparently earned a broader mandate. Class representatives though they might be, they still spoke in their own right for the public interest. The identification was attested to by an implicit change in underlying economic objectives. Deep into the depression the priority of national economic policies had remained maintenance of foreign-exchange stability, even when it entailed high unemployment. After the war, a full-employment "standard" silently replaced the earlier international discipline of the gold or gold-exchange standard. Accepting the primacy of full employment meant that a major priority of the working class had become that of society in general.

On the other hand, the spokesmen for capital learned that this compromise largely guaranteed the ownership and control they deemed essential. If labor and social democracy became more than a mere interest group, business had always been and remained more than a mere interest as well. Given the decentralized signals that a capitalist economy transmitted by falling exchange rates, inflationary price rises, and changes in discount rates, propertied interests did not need to organize explicitly to reap many of the benefits of collective action. Workers required unions to compete on equal terms in a capitalist marketplace; industrialists, financiers, investors could respond without association given the signals of the price system. Each side,

---

48 See Jacques Julliard, "La Charte du Travail," in *Le Gouvernement de Vichy 1940–1942*, eds. René Rémond and Janine Bourdin. Colloque de la Fondation Nationale des Sciences Politiques (Paris: A. Colin, 1972); also John P. Windmuller, *Labor Relations in the Netherlands* (Ithaca, N.Y.: Cornell University Press, 1969), pp. 83–120; and in general, Leo Panitch, "The Development of Corporatism in Liberal Democracies," *Comparative Political Studies* 10(1)(1977):61–90.

252   *Collective preferences and public outcomes*

therefore, retained a different trump after 1945. Labor was accepted as an organized interest with a claim to speak for the general welfare in light of the earlier catastrophes of mass unemployment, fascism, and war, and the force it had displayed in the Resistance. Business was an interest that needed less organization than labor under the ground rules of the capitalist marketplace which even labor accepted. Given that trade-off, social democracy – as has been mordantly suggested – became the highest stage of capitalism.[49] Significantly, too, the ideological affirmations of the 1950s and after centered less on liberalism than on pluralism – a concept that suggested collective social actors more than individuals. With the redefinition of welfare states as pluralist, the persisting conundrum of reconciling partial interests and the common good seemed to have found a satisfactory resolution. "Fictitious bonds of wealth and law" had evolved again into a happy Burkean consensus of great interests.

Strategies and dilemmas of interest representation

The historical development previously sketched suggests that interest group organization responded to the international rivalry, economic strains, and working-class political challenges that have accumulated since the end of the nineteenth century. But important questions remain both for systematic comparative history and contemporary analysis. First, why have some societies encouraged a denser and richer proliferation of interest groups than others? Second, how have interests operated within different political systems, and how are they likely to function during the present period of economic slowdown now that the euphoric pluralism of the postwar era has dissipated?

To crossbreed the ancient animal metaphors of politics and philosophy we can define two polar strategies – that of the hedgehog and the lion. The hedgehog's strategy aims at insulation or exemption for a constituency from unfavorable trends by making outsiders' intervention appear very costly. The leonine strategy is the more ambitious one of seeking hegemonic control over a wider political system or market arena. Today's National Rifle Association is a hedgehog; the AFL-CIO growls like a lion; the Swedish labor confederation, the LO,

49 Cf. Alan Wolfe, "Has Social Democracy a Future?" *Comparative Politics* (October 1978):100–125; and on the systemic political–economy advantages for business, see Claus Offe, "The Attribution of Public Status to Interest Groups: Observations on the West German Case," in Suzanne Berger, ed., *Organizing Interests in Western Europe* (Cambridge: Cambridge University Press, 1981), pp. 123–158; and Charles Lindblom, *Politics and Markets* (New York: Basic Books, 1977).

was until recently an even more convincing lion; national medical associations are somewhere in between. Some groups begin as hedge-hogs but find themselves impelled to adopt ever more active interventions and end up behaving as lions.

Successful strategy depends in turn on the conditions set by the broader political organization of society. To measure these factors it helps to introduce the concept of corporatism, defined here as a partial devolution of public policymaking and enforcement on organized private interests. This process can be initiated by public officials to augment their own control over social and economic life. Alternatively, the process can be generated by interest group representatives themselves. In either case, the development of corporatist bargaining probably encourages an interest group to strive for the role of the lion rather than that of the hedgehog – unless it merely wishes to defend a nonzero-sum claim that does not require contesting scarce resources with other groups.

The emergence of interest groups does not make a corporatist outcome inevitable. The United States, for example, has always generated many pressure groups, in part because the committee system of the Congress and relative governmental decentralization offer multiple points of contact for vocal interests. On the other hand, the very diffusion of authority that encourages interests to present their claims has made experiments in corporatism brief and fragile. Philippe Schmitter has suggested that, in general, early growth of associations from the humus of civil society "upward" may forestall a later, more cohesive corporatism and disciplined governance.[50] The search for corporatist institutions in Italy in the early twentieth century, before and during the Fascist era, was more intense than that in France because Italian society had found it harder to generate effective bourgeois interest associations. Those that had emerged remained fragmented and unable to defend what the elites felt were their vital interests during a period of democratic mobilization and radical challenges.

Obviously, not all societies entered the era of interest group formation with the same capacity for organization. Nor was this capacity itself the result of any single line of development. Liberal or democratic regimes may nurture associations more than authoritarian ones. Nonetheless, if democratic vigor requires associations (de Tocqueville's judgment), association does not depend solely on democracy. The independence of city states and fragmented territories, the ubiquity

---

50 Philippe Schmitter, "Modes of Interest Intermediation and Models of Societal Change in Western Europe," *Comparative Political Studies* 10(1)(1977):7–38.

and vigor of guilds, persisted long enough in Germany so that the
transition from a pre-liberal to post-liberal proliferation of interest
groups was easy. As Jürgen Kocka and others, following Max Weber,
have emphasized, the prestige of officialdom remained strong because
of the bureaucracy's role in state building and its recruitment from
the nobility. Hence occupational groups recreated bureaucratic organization and sought their own official relationship with the state.[51]
Although this behavior may have handicapped German liberalism, it
helped make Wilhelmian and Weimar society peculiarly "modern" in
the major role that interest groups easily assumed. Elsewhere, traditions of religious or ethnic pluralism could encourage the formation
of interest associations, as in the Netherlands with its accommodation
of confessional differences by "pillarization" or *Verzuiling*.[52] In terms
of the outcome for liberal and tolerant governance during the first
half of the twentieth century, German and Dutch legacies seem to
have had opposed results. Both backgrounds, however, could produce
high associational levels.

Beyond diverse national traditions, the structure of regimes sets
important parameters for interest group activity and corporatist trends.
Granted that the reconciliation of group demands must be a basic task
for any political system (Bentley's old postulate), modern interest
group bargaining is still only one of several possible alternatives. An
older parliamentary politics sufficed as long as the voting elites could
preserve an overriding gentlemen's consensus. Depretis's and Giolitti's
trasformismo, Canovas's *turno politico*, the ritualistic debates between
Disraeli and Gladstone, served that need. Two developments, however, threatened the coziness of parliamentary representation. The
powerful ruler had to satisfy the economic and status requirements
of his national elites, but he could do so by intervention from above,
by bureaucratic negotiation with industrialists or agricultural associations. Strong executive authority might inhibit political parties but
it often encouraged the formal constitution of groups out of latent
interests. In fact, as executive regimes tended to lose their initial pleb-
iscitory authority they had to cast about all the more widely to secure
interest group support. Napoleon III after the Cobden Trade Treaty
of 1860, Bismarck after 1876, de Gaulle after the explosion of 1968

51 See Kocka, in Berger, ed., *Organizing Interests*, pp. 63–81; also his influential *Un-
     ternehmensverwaltung und Angestelltenschaft am Beispiel Siemens 1847–1914* (Stuttgart:
     Klett, 1969). Cf. Winkler, *Pluralismus oder Protektionismus?* p. 32.
52 See Arend Lijphart, *The Politics of Accommodation: Pluralism and Democracy in the
     Netherlands* (Berkeley, Calif.: University of California Press, 1968).

(and his successors) all resorted to increasing logrolling tactics to minimize parliamentary gains.

If declining Caesarism encouraged interest representation outside of Parliament, so, too, did ascendant mass democracy. The weakening of old liberal or conservative elites meant the rise of new parties and the appearance, so frequently noted at the turn of the century, of a new political class. "Class" was a misleading term, for what united its members was less a station in life than a professional commitment to mobilize voting blocs either by crusades, chauvinism, or patronage. The new political leadership arose in parliaments that the *Honoratioren* were being forced to relinquish. No more than Caesarist executives did the new leaders have reason to turn back toward the old elites: Their task was to pulverize and then reassemble on the basis of interest, ideology, or ethnicity the constituencies earlier organized by deference. Thus the growth of interest representation was also a likely accompaniment where political assemblies underwent the transition to mass democracy. Where political elites remained cohesive enough to slow down this transition – in Italy until the period, 1900–15; in Spain until, 1898–1917 – interest group intervention lagged. At best interests remained organized on the basis of older regional "chambers," such as the Lliga in Catalonia or the Unione Industriale of Turin. Interest group intervention also lagged where the older elites might themselves patronize the transition to mass democracy, as in Great Britain.

To summarize, then, oligarchy and interest group representation should correlate negatively. Bonapartism, or at least Bonapartism under stress, and mass democracy alike provide a stimulus for the organization of interests.

How these interests will behave within the larger political system is a further question. Hedgehogs or lions? The choice, as noted, depends in good part on the strategy rewarded by the larger system of brokerage. Consider, for example, the case of France. If declining executive regimes encourage interest group organization, then interests should have been stronger during the 1860s and after 1968 in comparison to the respective earlier decades. If ascendant mass democracy also mobilizes interests, there should likewise have been organization during the period from 1877 to 1906 as the forces of democratic republicanism waged successive battles against older elites. On the other hand, the strategy and styles of interest representation should have been significantly different. The executive regimes sought nonparliamentary mediators for broad social forces; they encouraged an implicit corporatism. The Third Republic in its formative period, however, encouraged interests but hardly corporatism. Its parliamentary class depended on local voters and regionally based *notables* in departmental councils. As problems came to require national solutions and central allocations – starting with the tariffs, then encompassing wartime regulation and post-1914 fiscal dilemmas – the hedgehog disposition of interest groups was slowly modified. Nonetheless, in pre-1914 France, as in the United States before the New Deal, a national legislature with important committees responsive to differing interests, encouraged vigorous pressure groups but allowed a minimal encroachment of corporatist trends.

This brings us to a final set of questions. What logic carries a system of interest groups, or latent interests hitherto loosely organized, into a structure of corporatist bargaining? And thereafter, what forces will limit the corporatist trajectory and perhaps even reassert parliamentary authority? Is there an equilibrium mix of parliamentary and corporatist representation? It may be that corporatist organization must increase apace with the increased functions of government. Every centralization of an allocative task prompts a new search for consultation and codecision making. The crises involved in wartime provide just the clearest and most dramatic example of calling in delegations from industry and labor. At these points the organizations credentialed or sometimes actually called into being can no longer content themselves with a hedgehog posture; they must protect their interests by negotiating over a broad range of issues and cannot just pursue a search for enclaves. Once begun the process is contagious: Member organizations discover the advantages that quasi-public participation provides in securing internal discipline and broadening recruitment. Potential rival organizations seek equal privileges. The corporatist tendency would appear to be ineluctable.

In fact, the trend may not be monotonic or stable. No matter how efficient a system, the legitimacy of corporatism can still be questioned. For every celebration of "pluralism" there are reproaches of vested interests, *féodalités financières,* and other abuses of the popular will.[53] Moreover, recent developments suggest that several sorts of difficulty will arise to beset the corporatist system. Corporatist tendencies can either augment or confuse the cleavages within a polity. Since World War II corporatist trends have generally centered on industry–labor organizations that parallel the political party divisions between social democracy and Christian democracy (or other conservative parties).

53 On the continuing lesser legitimacy of corporatist arrangements see Hans Daalder and Galen A. Irwin, "Interests and Institutions in the Netherlands: An Assessment by the People and by Parliament," in *Interest Groups in International Perspective,* ed. Robert Presthus, *The Annals,* 413(1974):58–71.

The centrality of incomes policy has encouraged this development; indeed Schmitter has correlated the progress of corporatism with the strength of social democracy. Lehmbruch, too, finds corporatist alignments reinforcing political coalitions and cleavages.[54] Nonetheless, this reinforcement is not the only possibility. Persisting religious and ethnic divisions can cut across class lines. Differences on nuclear policy can fracture the labor movement. Issues concerning inflation have in the past separated those concerned with protecting assets (lower middle-class savers) from those concerned with protecting income (higher income managers with "leverage," and sometimes wage earners concerned about a deflationary crunch on jobs).

These and other strains make it likely that the tendencies toward corporatism also have limits: There will probably be no corporatist euthanasia of the European constitutions. In contemporary Europe, corporatism may be most advanced where the working class is best organized; but as Peter Lange has recently pointed out, the corporatist temptation for working-class parties in the political wilderness of opposition is lower than for those long in power. Swedish social democracy can allow its affiliated unions to be deputized by the state because the Social Democrats themselves are virtually part of the Swedish constitutional order; but Italian Communists are more likely to use the market power of their affiliated workers to wrest a coalition role for the party than quasi-official "concerted action" on incomes policy.[55]

Yet assuming that the mix of parliamentary and corporatist representation is not likely to be radically shifted, is the representational system stable as a whole? From a pluralist perspective, interest group formation and brokerage should function well with no immanent tendencies toward breakdown. From a Marxist viewpoint, corporatist tendencies represent an adaptive response of capitalism, but one that is ultimately liable to succumb to underlying contradictions. Without subscribing to theories of inevitable breakdown, but recognizing that no institutional patchwork is immortal, we can at least discern the fault lines. These considerations suggest that the corporatism that divides economic groups along the same lines as parties may well magnify polarization and ideological conflict. The negotiations between

54 Gerhard Lehmbruch, "Liberal Corporatism and Party Government," *Comparative Political Studies* 10(1)(1977):91–126; also Philippe C. Schmitter, "Interest Intermediation and Regime Governability in Contemporary Western Europe and North America," in Berger, ed., *Organizing Interests in Western Europe*, pp. 287–327.
55 Peter Lange, "Sindacati, partiti, stato e liberal-corporativismo," *Il Mulino*, (266) (November–December 1979):943–72.

labor and capital may indeed originate as a means of taking allocative disputes out of the parliamentary arena; however, the distributive conflicts may become acute enough to reintensify ideological confrontation and again strain all institutions. (The crisis of 1930 in Germany offers a classic example. The dispute between labor and industry negotiators over the costs of unemployment insurance grew into a conflict that destroyed the last democratic parliamentary coalition.)

On the other hand, the formation of corporatist alignments across party lines, whether around inflation, ethnic issues, or energy, is conducive to policy paralysis. It reflects not so much a disagreement between parties or classes but within them. It tends to yield ad hoc politics as one group after another wins an accommodation that cancels out the previous concession. Tendencies toward clientelism between particular bureaucratic agencies and diverse interests may well be intensified. The upshot may be a paralysis on socioeconomic issues reminiscent of ethnolinguistic fragmentation; pillarization becomes Balkanization.

In both cases the strains on political party or parliamentary representation resurface in corporatist bargaining systems. Interest group formation and mediation may temporarily shift the locus of brokerage, may cool down an overheated clash of forces. But if social groups are claiming more income than an economy generates, more "positional" goods than are logically available, conflict results in any case. Interest group mediation thus provides a political analog of price and wage indexation. If the social "partners" press for gains only from insecurity and out of fear they may be victimized, then corporatist bargaining, like indexation, can clarify the gains and losses at stake and reduce conflicts that arise from uncertainty. If, however, the given interests are asking for more than others are willing to cede, harsh struggle must attend any system of representation, parliamentary or corporatist.

Finally, there are two further difficulties in corporatist representation: the widening issues that must be brought in and the alienation of those who must be left out. On the morrow of World War II, labor strove for the social reforms loosely described as the welfare state. But the welfare state implied a dualist concept of the capitalist economy. Working-class representatives sought a guarantee that those left out of prosperity – the victims of unemployment, age, or disability – would be given support. In return, the organization of production itself would be left to management and capital. This division of function, however, seems less feasible in an age of rapid technological change and obsolescence, especially as Third World nations emerge as major industrial competitors. Aging of populations through the remainder of the twentieth century will make the earlier compartmentalization of welfare policy and production policy even less viable. Just to support redundant labor prevents reallocation of resources and limits industrial investment. No intelligent architecture of welfare seems really feasible without some degree of social investment control as well. Hence the splitting of functions accepted after 1945 may no longer make sense; at the least, it may not appear to make sense to a new generation of the European Left. The great social *Ausgleich* on which corporatist equilibrium has been constructed during the past generation – rendering welfare and high employment unto labor, rendering control of investment to management (and sometimes the state) – may be nearing its term. Renegotiation of the compromise may not be impossible, but it probably will not be easy.

The list of difficulties finally includes those left out. Every move toward the organization of corporate interests is simultaneously a step toward exclusion of those not subsumed in a state-supervised structure of bargaining. To credential unions is to consign nonunion labor to a marginal status of passive citizenship. These outsiders may benefit from welfare rights but do not participate in making allocative decisions. Whether this exclusion must lead to crisis is also impossible to predict. Marginalization of social groups is hard on those emarginated but not always fatal to those within the charmed circle: The handloom weavers suffered, rebelled . . . but lost.

Ultimately, the difficulties afflicting interest representation and conciliation do not seem to depend on the format or the locus of group bargaining. From the viewpoint of those with an interest in social stability, the "century of corporatism" has helped take Western society through two major transitions that might have been far more revolutionary than they actually became. As an issue of political party conflict, the reduction of the European peasantry contributed decisively to the weakening of interwar parliamentary liberalism. As an issue of interest group bargaining, the transition could be completed with far less damage. Likewise, the "integration" of much of the industrial working class into welfare states required the conversion of ideological confrontation into the lesser disputes resolved by interest group bargaining. The one-time farmers work in the city; the workers vacation in the country: The transformation testifies to the achievements of a postwar society that was increasingly "corporatized." Nevertheless, it is far from clear whether the forms of political and economic mediation produced this outcome or themselves emerged from other, deeper trends. It is impossible to assess postwar "success" or contemporary institutional vulnerability without knowing whether the decades after World War II represented an exceptional period of economic growth and collective social discipline or a more enduring transformation. That issue is crucial to historical evaluation and contemporary analysis, and it is still open.

Conclusion:
Why stability?

Any student of twentieth-century Europe must ponder issues of social and political stability. Why did it break down in the first decades of the century? How was it reconstituted in the second half? Does it mean anything more than order? Metternich certainly thought in terms of European stability, though most often he used the eighteenth-century term *équilibre*. But through the nineteenth century, as social conflict became more preoccupying, the contrast between order and disorder became more prevalent. "Order" was originally a concept linked to the ancien régime: a quasi-legal status ascription related to "estate." By midcentury it was reinfused with the authority of a dubiously scientific sociology: order, for Comte, rested on primal social groups. The Party of Order was Marx's scathing catchall description of the French bourgeois conservatives who rallied after the June Days of 1848 and engineered the Bonapartist reaction; *L'Ordre* appeared as a rightist newspaper title throughout the Third Republic and "l'Ordre Moral" provided a watchword for the conservative coalition of 1876–7. "Disorder," in contrast, implied purposeless and frightening insurrection; it evoked the lurid flames of the burning Tuilleries and the hostages shot by the Communards of 1870–1. The term "disorder," of course, did not give any credit to the often coherent schemes for workshops and welfare, nationalized banks, cooperatives, and manhood suffrage that protesters advanced.[1] "Count on us," Thiers had told Bismarck in May 1871, "and the social order will be revenged in the course of the week."[2] Conservatives were in a position to impose the lexicon.

1 For a good example of how dedicated to a functioning social order (admittedly postcapitalist) the adherents of the European far Left might be, see Temma Kaplan, *Anarchists of Andalusia, 1868–1912* (Princeton, N.J.: Princeton University Press, 1978).
2 Cited in Allan Mitchell, *The German Influence in France after 1870: The Formation of the French Republic* (Chapel Hill: University of North Carolina Press, 1979), 20.

The essays in this collection have treated diverse strategies for averting social conflict or overcoming disorder. But I have preferred to think of the objective in terms of "stability" rather than "order." In part this merely reflects the fact that "stability" tended to supplant "order" in postwar social science terminology. I have also wanted to avoid describing the protagonists of these essays as unalloyedly conservative. That would be inaccurate, whether for Frederick Taylor, Walther Rathenau, Edmondo Rossoni, or Paul Hoffman. Stability can accommodate a more dynamic state than order: a balance of countervailing social and political movements rather than mere quiescence. Stability, as Henry Kissinger wrote in his study of Metternich and the Vienna system, rests on an equilibrium of forces that is deemed legitimate.[3] Achieving stability implies a less reactionary enterprise than restoring order. It can make more allowance for gradual change; it incorporates a democratic vector as well as a conservative thrust. This does not mean that the reader or the writer has to endorse any given project for stability (more on that below). Rather, by using the term "stability" the historian can avoid labeling the advocates of interest-group power or scientific management or economic growth or even authoritarian labor relations as spokespersons for restoration. It need not prejudge their politics.

Not only does the concept of stability accommodate more democratic potential than does the slogan of order; it has also come to suggest an extra feature, not entirely absent in the nineteenth-century sociology of order, but less explicit. Stability implies a cybernetic capacity for self-correction, a homeostatic tendency to return to equilibrium. Stability means that the social order, to recall Thiers, should never have to wreak revenge, because it no longer loses its grip. The strategies for stability all sought some underlying automatic authority that would impose itself. Showing how this was supposed to function, finding the common homeostatic denominator, is the first task for the conclusion to this volume.

The rhetorical tone of postwar sociology often suggested to critical readers that the self-corrective capacity of the social system was a happy situation, that Western stability was a good thing.[4] However, one need not share the congratulatory mode to exploit the analytic possibilities. Nonetheless, once the historian has uncovered the common denominator of stabilization strategies, a moral issue does remain.

3 *A World Restored* (New York: Grosset & Dunlap, 1964), 1.
4 Critics of Talcott Parsons and of structural functionalism complained, first, that his approach tended to celebrate homeostasis; second, that it analytically undervalued the centrifugal forces of disruption within a society. The systemic focus allegedly presupposed that every feature must contribute to the stability of the whole. The first critique is irrelevant here. Whether Parsons did or did not like stability or a

It concerns the costs and benefits of stability, as the historian perceives them. Of course, that sort of normative question must entail historical judgments, just as historical assessments often rest on moral evaluations. But that is precisely why it must be taken up.

Strategies of stabilization

"Stability" describes a political condition, "stabilization" a process. In one sense *political* stabilization is a contradiction in terms. Since the nineteenth century, stabilization has in fact entailed *de*politicization. If politics is seen as a competition for the legal power[5] to influence such basic collective outcomes as the distribution of wealth or "life chances" or the enforcement of community values, stabilization has often meant removing these divisive issues from political determination. Stabilization therefore suggests an enterprise more conservative than merely attaining stability. It often imposes limits on democracy. Political struggles can be waged by violence and intrigue; but what has characterized the modern era, as commentators pointed out throughout the nineteenth century, has been the decisive potential of "the masses," that is, of mere numbers, whether mobilized through electoral politics or collective action. Recent critics of "overloaded democracy" have been only the latest to worry about this allegedly demagogic potential.

Efforts at stabilization have naturally followed periods in which the issues subject to politics and the forces participating have tempestuously expanded. Stabilization means closing an agenda, deciding in effect that the community will accept no further *cahiers des doléances* or peoples' charters or other demands. It amounts to telling the eco-

---

given form of it, those who do not can still usefully learn from Parsons that they face an uphill battle. Understanding the resilience of a social order is useful for the Left as well as consoling for the Right. Gramsci, after all, taught the same lesson when, after bitter experience, he wrote about the power of "civil society" to resist change. The second complaint is of more weight for the historian. No matter whether an ideal-type, atemporal society has nonfunctional structures, real societies in history certainly incorporate features inherited from different epochs. They are layered or palimpsestic, not all of a piece. There is no reason to think that the persisting social elements play a homeostatic role: Peasants are as conducive to disruption as to stability; so are peers. But observed with skill, these discontinuities allow the historian the same possibilities for deconstruction that inconsistencies allow the critic of a text. Indeed, early modern historians have had a field day with them. Historians of the twentieth century need to catch up.

5 The fact that public norms and legitimate force are at stake separates political power from, say, the private violence of the Mafia or even the prerogative of a corporation to close a plant and lay off workers. These actions can, of course, occasion political interventions from outside. And there can also be a political struggle within a private organization if its own resources of power and internal norms are up for grabs.

nomically aggrieved that they must go back to the market. Stabilization therefore entails the political exclusion of groups as well as the dismissal of claims.

Political life follows rhythms of opening and closing, gathering in and turning away. These phases are integrally related. Democratic movements have repeatedly opened civic participation (and greater economic power) to new social forces. The extension of the suffrage in the nineteenth and early twentieth centuries to middle classes, to workers, and later to women was one dimension of change. Granting legal sanction to collective bargaining and bringing representatives of organized labor into governing coalitions was another. The process of inclusion is not a smooth and continuous one. Formerly inchoate social groups have discovered shared grievances, created a collective identity, then pressed against the walls of the political community and forced those within to admit some or all of the claimants. But this very process of enlarging the political community, redrawing a new, if wider perimeter, must ultimately create new classes of outsiders. Admitting reformist socialists to cabinet coalitions may reinforce the radical commitment and organizational strength of communists outside. If economic prosperity and the welfare state apparently absorb the native working class as such, migrants, students, women, and other groups discover a new collective persona. Hence, there can never be any final act of universal entitlement. Granting voice to some groups means excluding others. Even granting voice to all in terms of a given political role, say as voters, still leads many to conclude that the rights they gained are less important to their aspirations than the attributes they still lack. No political settlement can be all-inclusive. Institutions repeatedly generate aggrieved outsiders.

But regimes also decide that enough is enough: Inclusion can proceed only so far. Every revolution imposes Thermidor or Kronstadt. Less radical upheavals also reach a point of political inflection. Once begun, stabilization takes on its own momentum. In part it may derive from a mere flagging of public energy, but it often involves a conscious transition from what can be called transformative to normal politics. This means dismantling a highly charged ideological conflict in which participants have been convinced that public power can restructure society and hammer out stubborn inequalities. Transformative politics is marked by utopian and reformist projects; in periods of normal politics alternative regimes are literally unimaginable. Normal politics comprises administration and peaceful party rotation in office, what Otto Kirchheimer uneasily greeted as "the waning of opposition."[6]

6 Otto Kirchheimer, "The Waning of Opposition in Parliamentary Regimes" [1957]. Included in Otto Kirchheimer, *Politics, Law, and Social Change,* Frederic S. Burin and Kurt L. Shell, eds. (New York: Columbia University Press, 1969), 292–318.

Transformative moments have included the great revolutions since 1789, the 1930s in Spain and France, the liberations of 1944–5, the late 1960s throughout much of the United States and Europe, and the year of Solidarity in Poland. Stabilization efforts have marked the post-revolutionary decades of the nineteenth century, the 1920s, the 1950s, and the late 1970s to the present. Some seek to equilibrate the new and more democratic order that emerged in the preceding era; others seek repression or rollback. Some work; others fail. Ultimately, as noted above, each effort creates the bases for a new wave of trans-formation, even if the principles of a future challenge are not to be divined.

Advocates of stabilization propose decision rules for public issues that are based on nonpolitical criteria. The alternative sources of authority have included religion, society, the market, and science. In the postrevolutionary periods of the nineteenth century, once appeals to religion became too divisive, society itself beckoned as a source of authority. The social realm was construed as being prior to the political. Associations below the political level would supposedly provide a cohesion that would obviate collective struggles over the distribution of wealth or abstract principles. As Pierre Rosanvallon has argued, French liberals of the early nineteenth century posited society as an active force in its own right. Representation meant less a mechanism for aggregating individual wills than a device that drew on collective abilities. Guizot envisaged a "social power." "Authority," he maintained, "is never based on thin air; it can't live from its own substance. If it is isolated, authority appears in vain to control public revenue, the administration, the army, and all the means for action. In fact, they halt, dissolve, and evade authority if the latter merely instills in these mechanisms external principles that do not derive from within." Real authority required "the deliberating and active organization of society."[7] In practice this meant relying on citizens with special capacities, that is, the elites of learning and industry, rather than on universal suffrage.

After 1848, the appeal to the social realm became more intense. Redefining or restricting representation no longer sufficed; society itself had to be restructured. This meant legalizing interest groups, including craft unions and cooperatives, establishing *caisses* to administer social insurance, and in general encouraging a proto–welfare system of mutual aid, not to strengthen government, but to develop a rich associational life between the individual and the state. The same enthusiasm also stimulated a major restatement of legal theory by such "juridical syndicalists" as Leon Duguit, who stressed that legal forms

---

7   Pierre Rosanvallon, *Le moment Guizot* (Paris: Gallimard, 1985), 43, 58–59.

must correspond to the realities of group life, not the abstraction fiction of the state. The new discipline of sociology provided a theoretical grounding – whether deeply conservative as in the case of Taine's work at midcentury or reformist by the time of Durkheim. The wave of turn-of-the-century social reform throughout Europe and the United States can be understood as part of this "invention of the social."[8] Settlement houses, social Catholicism encouraged by Leo XIII, the influence of the Protestant social gospel, the widespread interest abroad in Bismarck's national old-age and sickness insurance incorporated reformist impulses but simultaneously amounted to an effort to unburden politics of highly charged ideological conflict. By the end of the century, society itself – whether organized by elites according to a conservative vision of "service" or articulated into a web of solidaristic and mutualist networks in the reformist alternative – was supposed to recapture the mission of distributive justice from the state or the market.

Yet at the same time that social reformists sought to modify market outcomes, economic science could also appeal as an alternative to politics. Hume had suggested that politics might be reduced to economics. As Hirschman has pointed out, for eighteenth- and early-nineteenth-century philosophers the pursuit of economic interest would discipline the passion for glory that had motivated so much political ambition. Commerce would knit individuals together and establish networks that reduced the need for the state.[9] As classical economics evolved into a body of theory, could not the laws governing the distribution of product worked out by Smith, Ricardo, Say, and Mill, later by Marshall and the marginalists, remove the whole issue of allocation from political debate? Capital, labor, and land would be rewarded according to their marginal product: by the end of the nineteenth century Walras and Pareto had refined the matrices of partial derivatives that settled the most efficient rewards among classes. Did this distribution by marginal product not provide a higher return for society as a whole than any politically legislated alternative? Here was a source of authority and an appeal that would continue to motivate champions of supply-side economics and more orthodox believers as well, way into the 1980s.

Economic science confirmed its claims after the Second World War because the processes it described ensured continuing growth. The return to capital was not merely a rent to those who held a scarce resource. It was the basis for future expansion of the national product.

8   See Jacques Donzelot, *L'invention du social* (Paris: Fayard, 1986).
9   Albert Hirschman, *The Passions and the Interests* (Princeton, N.J.: Princeton University Press, 1978); Rosanvallon, *Le moment Guizot*, 24.

To be sure, the interaction between politics and economics was reciprocal. On the one hand, growth economies provided the conditions for transcending ideologically charged distributive issues. On the other hand, it took a political operation to install the right economic policies.[10] But in Britain and the United States, at least, the war experience seemed to have carried out that political operation behind the scenes, confirming that policies for growth would painlessly create their own consensus by delivering the economic goods they promised. The economic dividends were highly visible, the political premises often forgotten.

As Chapter 3 has indicated, doctrines of productivity and of growth based on productivity became central to postwar American stabilization concepts. A generation later (after the mid-1970s, as during the mid-1920s) the anti-inflationary strategies described in Chapter 5 also seemed to rest on new and convincing rules for economic growth. The power that had capital, whether a bourgeois coalition at home or the United States or IMF abroad, intervened to make growth seem dependent on adjourning the inflationary battle over income distribution. If the political battle over shares could be transmuted into a consensus built on optimal growth, ideological and social divisions would naturally become outmoded.

Science and technology provided the other source of nonpolitical authority. As demonstrated in Chapter 1, the engineer emerged as a social arbiter. The engineer's vision of production conflated factory and society. Just as economic laws might provide apolitical principles for distributing wealth, so scientific management would impartially dictate how best to allocate labor. Productivity, in effect, linked the two sources of authority – its methods worked out by technologists of production, its rewards guaranteeing growth.

Although scientific management, market allocation, and what Donzelot has called "the invention of the social" have all served as stabilization strategies, it would be misleading to label all their exponents conservative. To be sure they represented efforts to depoliticize some

10 Keynesianism exerted an ambiguous influence on these ideas. Keynes himself argued in *The General Theory* of 1936 that Western economies had overstressed savings (Smith's "parsimony"). He felt capital did benefit from a scarcity value much as Ricardo's landlords had effortlessly benefited from the limited supply of good land. He envisaged an era in which apparently innovation slowed down, capital became less scarce, and society could enjoy more affluent consumption. These ideas in their own right were unlikely sources for the politics of productivity. But more generally Keynes suggested to the generation of younger postwar economic advisers that government could structure the conditions for economic growth, in effect could intervene to establish a growth economy as a normative framework.

of the great divisive issues of industrial (as well as preindustrial) civilization: Who controlled the work place? Who determined economic rewards? Who determined access to the cultural resources that conferred social status? Nonetheless, proponents of these apolitical visions could deploy their doctrines on behalf of hitherto disadvantaged groups. Reformist economists, left-wing Taylorite engineers, pressed programs that would give subordinate groups more collective power or more rewards.

Nonetheless, it must be asked whether such strategies represent a healthy approach to politics even when they are more reformist than conservative. For one thing, the vision of apolitical decision rules remains misleading. None of the supposedly nonpolitical sources of authority – not religious dispensation, not the social order, not the market or technology – can be established as legitimate without a prior political operation. Its advocates must control the resources of politics, including influence over the media and the capacity to shape public discourse. Once stability has been achieved, the political premises may indeed disappear from discussion. Indeed, the objective for any strategy of stability must be to make people forget politics. It must reimpose what Burke called "the decent drapery of life." This is not without wisdom. The Weimar Republic, to take a negative example, was a system in which the political implications of every distributive or cultural decision were always visible. The length of the working day, the percentage of contributions to the social insurance pool, the permissiveness of art and mores were all issues that implicated the regime itself. If one wants to avoid civil war, or simply the attrition of the private self, there is an argument against too much politics.

The history of efforts at stabilization during the past hundred years is the history of coming to terms, or trying to avoid coming to terms, with modern politics. What is modern politics about? In terms of procedure it is politics in which numbers are decisive. In terms of substance it involves demands for corporate recognition and reward on the part of emerging collective identities (the proletariat, national or racial minorities, increasingly women). Modern politics is also still about conflicts over community values, which have long been political. These include the role of religion and the church in the public order, the scope for private activity not directly harnessed to a public purpose (e.g., sex, drink, and drugs). Finally, it is about the appropriate frontiers and security for national communities or identities. These are all hard and divisive issues. They are not fun to settle through politics. How much easier to discover an underlying principle of natural or social science, allegedly to resolve them by optimalization. When "the social'' is elevated, however, "the civic" may atrophy. To adjourn public discussion of collective choices and their consequences must undermine citizenship and democracy. If and when a society seeks respite from invidious struggles for the sake of a common effort, the resolution should follow from a conscious political compromise, extensively discussed, not by virtue of historical amnesia. Divergent wills should be tolerated, not aligned. Too often the visionaries of stability have forgotten their original political victories, the blood in the machine.

Judging stability

After devoting so much concern in preceding chapters to strategies for overcoming conflict – conflict among nations, parties, classes, interests – the historian might well be summoned to reflect on his own preoccupations concerning stability and conflict. How do private agendas and historical issues interact? How is historical judgment influenced? Has his stress on productivity and growth underplayed the coerciveness involved in stabilizing twentieth-century capitalism? That is, has he felt uncomfortable with the latent conflict inherent in the social order and painted too harmonious a picture and depicted too unanimous a consensus? Has he glossed over the repression of alternatives – not the obvious repression by fascism, but the foreclosure of political options involved, say, in imposing the ideals of productivity or controlling communist unions or ending periods of inflation? Or, conversely, has he made his own perception of inequality and stabilization into a supposedly historical problem, when it really did not bother most citizens? Has he ascribed an agenda of control and domination to business or political leaders that did not really describe their efforts? Has he – like Thersites, an earlier critic of elites, "disorderly, vain, and without decency" – projected his private rancor onto the wider society?

Of course, the reader is also hostage to subjectivity on the same issues, so there can be no final resolution of these uncertainties. Still, the historian owes it to the reader to take cognizance of ways in which ideological preferences and psychological makeup might well have influenced judgment. Thereafter, *caveat lector.* One way may be to wrestle with a frankly nonhistorical question: Is stability a good thing? That question incorporates many others. Should stability – as a form of civil peace, or like liberty – be welcomed in its own right? Does it accommodate aspirations for participation in a political community? Or can it become tiresome? Since stability often firms up old social hierarchies or establishes new ones, does it allow enough improvement in the lot of those less advantaged to compensate for the privileges it confers on those with more resources?[11]

Obviously there are different forms of stability. Reject at the outset those built upon continuing repression. And grant, as was argued in Chapter 4, that stability does not mean stasis. It does not imply merely the preservation of the status quo. It does not exclude change and development. Stability can indeed be conservative – one thinks of Tokugawa Japan or Brezhnev's Russia – but it can also be reformist. It allows the possibility of evolutionary trends that alter, even if they do not rupture, institutions. Looking back over four decades of postwar stability in Western European and the United States, the historian must record momentous social transformations. The ethnic mix of European and North American cities, the structure of occupations, attitudes toward religion, sexual relationships have changed in significant, often startling ways. Affluence has become more widespread; television and travel have attenuated regional differences and altered mass culture; higher education has become more accessible; women have achieved more control over their reproductive lives and have entered the professional work place in greater numbers.

Nonetheless, these important changes have been accommodated for the most part without violence or authoritarian reactions. We can talk of an underlying stability, because Western society has not laden these great transformations with risks of imprisonment or death. This tolerance may be diminishing once again. But so far political coercion has not been found a desirable (or perhaps just not an effective) means of slowing down economic and social transformation. We can say, therefore, that a society enjoys stability if, even as it undergoes rapid

11 What constitutes "enough" improvement, of course, varies according to commentator. The criterion of utilitarianism would require only that the less-well-off do not lose more than the better-off gain: Utility should not be diminished. The more stringent Rawlsian principles would not allow any improvement for the well-off without compensation for the least advantaged. In both cases the distribution of goods can become more skewed. Albert O. Hirschman has argued in *Essays in Trespassing: Economics to Politics and Beyond* (Cambridge University Press, 1981), chap. 3) that a temporary increase in inequality need not make the poor unhappier. They may sense that their absolute position, if not their relative one, will soon improve – a psychological dividend he calls the "tunnel effect." Let us call the opposed phenomenon "the gridlock mentality": no toleration of advantage for the other driver even if it is the only way to get things moving (i.e., no compromise with aspirations for equality even at the cost of overall economic performance or political harmony). Then, no matter what one's philosophical commitments, it is clear at least that the historical process of stabilization requires a major change in collective commitment from the gridlock mentality to the tunnel effect. Conversely, a revolutionary situation is characterized by dissipation of the tunnel effect and reversion to the gridlock mentality.

change in some dimensions (e.g., ethnic migrations, family and sexual relations, or economic growth), it preserves familiar, noncoercive institutional arrangements in other dimensions (say, party competition, judicial procedures, or national frontiers).

Still, stability can seem stultifying. Before 1848, Lamartine claimed that France was bored: *La France s'ennuie*. But the negative side of stability involves more than the ennuie of the intellectuals. Over time representative mechanisms wither into mere routine. Payoffs replace participation. Dissent is coopted and the public sphere becomes the preserve of hacks and time servers. Citizens feel trapped by bureaucracy, and institutional change seems beyond the imagination of those who aspire to leadership. What stability often inhibits is precisely the sodality of collective action, the feeling that each participant can help shape history. These are important, if fugitive, experiences. They are decisive both for endowing individual lives with meaning and for replenishing the stock of collective memory, hence for forging collective identity. Stability may perhaps allow or even nurture Wordsworth's "emotion recalled in tranquility" but not the rush of political eroticism he originally drew from revolution: "Bliss was it in that dawn to be alive, / But to be young was very heaven!"

For most people, of course, the revolutionary alternative to stability hardly remains fun for long. Revolutions may briefly restore the sense of participation and charge public events with personal meaning. But they also make opponents of change appear to be conspirators who must be dealt with by summary justice. They bring forward the most ruthless and ideologically obsessive leaders who merge private animus with public grievance: those, again in Wordsworth's lines, "Who doubted not that Providence had times / Of vengeful retribution." When stability collapses, politics can become the *kto-kovo* envisaged by Lenin or the extension of physical warfare that Carl Schmitt saw as its defining characteristic.

Are we doomed, then, to ceaseless alternation between the dessication of public life and excesses of radical mobilization?[12] To think about this question, it helps to distinguish *two* components or "moments" of intense political mobilization, whether that of France in 1789 or 1944, or Milan in 1945, Budapest in 1956, Chile in 1970, or Gdansk in 1980. The first (but not necessarily first chronologically) amounts to a change in collective mentality. It involves the discovery that what seemed virtually a natural (or at least imposed) order of

---

12 This question is similar to that posed by Hirschman in his essay on the oscillation between private and public commitments: *Shifting Involvements: Private Interest and Public Action* (Princeton, N.J.: Princeton University Press, 1982), 132.

subordination and hierarchy has no justification beyond its mere persistence. Accompanying this awareness is the burst of conviction that institutions need not be cages, that people acting together can break out of them and "make history."

This first "moment" of radical mobilization often has an anarchistic or utopian thrust, an impatience with institutions (seen now as suffocating bureaucracies), and the yearning to forge a face-to-face community: the elusive "fraternity" of the French Revolution. The anthropologist Victor Turner has provided a typology of "liminal" moments, his examples drawn largely from religious rites, that allow participants a transcendence of structures, an excursion beyond the everyday, that is needed to reinfuse institutions with the bond of community.[13] Or as Emma Goldmann recognized, a revolution needs dancing.

This anarchistic moment is vital, but if collective life is to be reformed for the long run, trashing existing institutions does not suffice. The second radical component or "moment" is precisely the one that should have been but was not confronted long before stability decomposed, that is, the renewal of institutions. This, too, can be a heady and invigorating task – as it was in Philadelphia in 1787 or Madrid in 1977. Nonetheless, the problem is that radical movements can dissipate themselves merely in the search for "communitas." *Sous le pavé la plage*, "Underneath the paving stones lies the beach," was one of the more charming slogans of 1968. But some sort of institutions will congeal again, and more ruthless leaders will seize them if alternatives remain in the realm of Turner's "antistructure." It would be wrong to reduce the revolutionary moment to merely an instance of expressive acting out, "psychodrama," as Raymond Aron slightingly (and too superficially) called the student revolts of 1968. Still, if an upheaval involves no more than a *fête de la fraternité*, it may ultimately reinforce the status quo, not transform it. It allows a holiday from domination, but does not transform the hierarchies of everyday.

Thus the question – Is stability a good thing? – can serve only as a preliminary inquiry. The binding question is stability at what cost? Or given what alternative? After periods of upheaval, stability, like peace, may seem good in itself: Citizens need time to recapture their

13   Victor Turner, "Social Dramas and Ritual Metaphors," "Passages, Margins and Poverty: Religious Symbols of Communitas," and "Metaphors of Anti-Structure in Religious Culture," in *Dramas, Fields and Metaphors: Symbolic Action in Human Society* (Ithaca, N.Y.: Cornell University Press, 1974), 23–59, 231–299, presents some of the terms he relies on, such as "liminality," "communitas," and "anti-structure." See also Turner, *The Forest of Symbols: Aspects of Ndembu Ritual* (Ithaca, N.Y.: Cornell University Press, 1967); and Turner, *The Ritual Process* (Chicago: Aldine, 1969).

private selves after intense political mobilization (and sometimes violence). But the stability that intensifies inequality and atrophies civic commitment, not even to cite the stability that undermines free association and civil liberty, is a bad bargain in the long run. (Admittedly, political bargains are usually intended for the short run – but they have a way of being prolonged.) Hence a focus on stability alone – interesting analytic problem as it is for the historian – offers little guidance for making political judgments. It is the nature of institutions, not stability per se, that must be judged. As Machiavelli wrote about an earlier republic, "Those who blame the quarrels of the Senate and the people of Rome condemn that which was the very origins of liberty, and they were probably more impressed by the cries and noise which these disturbances occasioned in the public places than by the good effect which they produced."[14]

I have tried in these essays not to make a fetish of stability for its own sake, whether monetary, political, even social or international. But if stability is risked or cast aside, both moments of radical change described above should remain in view. The final objective must be the pursuit of a new institutional framework that allows more liberty, delivers more equality, and gives promise of a continuing, not merely a spasmodic opening, of civic life. In the same spirit, when stability is renegotiated, its structure must be scrutinized to see if it, too, will nurture these elements. I think that despite the aspects of political exclusion in Western Europe and the United States in the generation after 1947 – the ghettoization of much of the European working class, the celebratory consensus around managerial hierarchies, the narrowing of American political discourse – enough liberal and democratic components, enough possibilities for continuing democratization still prevailed to justify the bargain. The postwar order allowed decolonization, expanded the welfare state, enhanced equality of opportunity, and except for a brief period in America did not persecute dissent. But it would be too celebratory a reading of postwar history not to recognize that political alternatives had to be ruled out. Whether they might have been realized without bringing the coercion of East European regimes to the West or – what seems more likely given the difficulties from 1945 to 1948 – whether they would not have incurred economic stagnation and continuing political demoralization, I still cannot answer. Historians are no better than poets at evaluating roads not taken. But like the poet, the historian should always remember the turning.

---

14 *The Discourses*, chap. 4 in *The Prince and the Discourses* (New York: Modern Library ed., 1950), 119.

Index